TypoGraphic Writing

Published in 2001 by the ISTD.
The ISTD Secretary's address is: Helen Cornish, Chapelfield Cottage,
Randwick, Stroud, Gloucestershire, GL6 6HS, United Kingdom.

ISBN: 0 9540127 0 4

Editor and designer: David Jury
Text output in *Foundry Form Sans* and *Foundry Form Serif*
Proofreaders: Clive Chizlett and Clive Abbott

Printed by Drukkerij Rosbeek, Nuth, The Netherlands
Bound by Handboekbinderij M Geertsen, The Netherlands

TypoGraphic Writing edited by David Jury

This publication is dedicated to all the writers, designers and
previous editors of *TypoGraphic* in recognition of their dedication
to the preservation and promotion of typographic knowledge
and standards of practice.

Foreword David Jury

TypoGraphic is the journal of the International Society of Typographic Designers. It was first published in 1971 and although its publication has, on occasions, been erratic, it remains, by any standards (and particularly by those of journals specialising in typography) in remarkably good health. It is currently published three times a year.

Until recently, the journal had no pretensions to reach a wider audience than the ISTD membership, its content directly reflecting the genuine, practical concerns of typographers, principally working in the UK, during the last thirty years. Nowhere else have the changes in working practise resulting from technological reform been more comprehensively recorded than in *TypoGraphic*.

Many of the authors included here would not consider themselves to be professional writers, but rather, designers and educationalists who felt inclined – or allowed themselves to be persuaded – to share their thoughts and experiences with fellow members.

The articles contained in this book have been arranged into four specific areas: working practice, technology, education, and history. On the whole these categories served their purpose well, although there are a number of articles which could comfortably appear within two, three, or even all four sections.

The articles have been arranged in date order of their original publication. This works particularly well for the 'working practice' and 'technology' sections. The order of the articles within 'education' was adjusted slightly to place the subject matter in the appropriate chronological order. The 'history' articles, deal predominantly with events of the twentieth century and chronologically overlap each other. For this reason, there seemed little point in altering the order from that of original publication.

Some words have evolved somewhat during the period covered here, notably fount to font and programme to program. With fount and font, the original usage has been kept (Beatrice Warde, even though American, can not be quoted saying 'font') whilst program is used in connection with computers and programme in all other cases.

Almost all of the images reproduced here had to be scanned from the journal in which they appeared. Their quality, therefore, reflects that of the original printers (and the artwork they had to work with) and not the printers of this book.

On the rare occasions when I have chosen to clarify the text, my comments are presented within square brackets.

List of contents

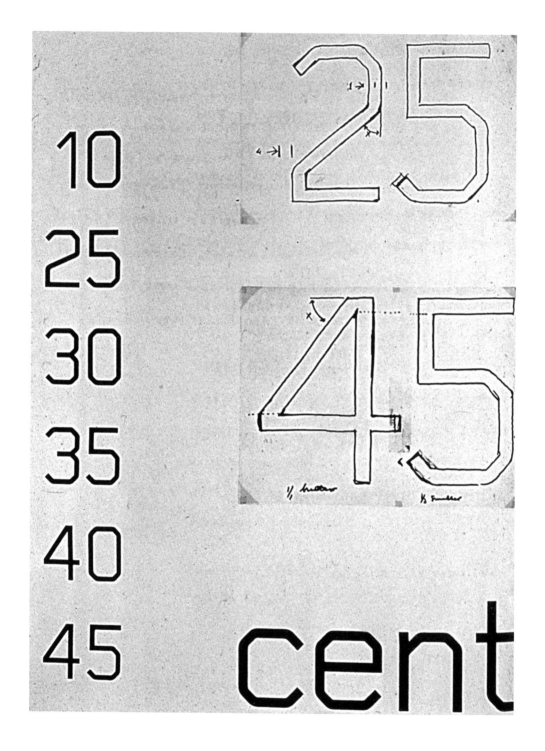

Introduction Wim Crouwel

Since the first issue of *TypoGraphic* was published, graphic design and typography have gone through a period of fundamental change, exploring new directions and causing more confusion than ever before!

Emphasis upon change has influenced a large part of the twentieth century. This urge for modernisation was also strongly present in the visual expression of our culture. Modernism with its idealism and its utopian dreams drove important artists to adopt progressive attitudes: the principal idea being that society had to be improved.

Undoubtedly, the editorial team of the first issue of *TypoGraphic*, in 1971, were not aware of being at the beginning of the turbulent years that marked the end of this inspired century; years that were to be dominated by criticism of, and revolt against, the ideas of modernism. Disbelief, disappointment, cynicism, pragmatism: just a few of the terms that were at the root of this changing mentality. The rebellion showed many facets, from purely revisionist and eclectic, to utmost experimental or highly superficial. Typography saw a revival of interest in the same classical forms that the modernists had rejected and, simultaneously, the acceleration of movements that took their influence from the issues of the day as their principal theme. We were haunted by rapidly changing fashion which reflected the fast-changing times in which we thought we were living.

Of course, the advent of the computer had a great impact: it's electronic invasion of our discipline putting the whole process of design under considerable pressure. At first, there were the rumours concerning 'experimental' computers, influencing those eager for change. Some of the early experiments were shown in London, at the ICA Gallery in 1968 at the exhibition *Cybernetic Serendipity*, which displayed computer technology and processes in relation to creativity and inventiveness. Already in the early sixties the first letterforms for telecommunication appeared: boldly simplified typefaces reduced to a system or grid of dots. Shortly after, this development reflected itself in typography, and the first electronic typesetting devices appeared.

Simultaneously, there was the influence of television, which, by then, had reached maturity, encouraging the introduction of the third dimension to what had previously been the flat surface of print. As the computer was slow in being introduced to design studios, a lot of effort went into trying to achieve, by traditional means, the integrated

(facing page) One of the sketches by Wim Crouwel for a typeface originally developed for a typewriter company but never used. However, the numerals were used by the Dutch Post Office (PPT) for their low denomination postage stamps. David Quay and Freda Sack at The Foundry recently recreated the typeface and developed a complete font family of four weights named *Foundry Gridnik*, with full approval of Wim Crouwel.

image to which we had grown accustomed to seeing on the TV screen. Next, the first 'graphic' computers stunned us with their potential: for instance, the 'Aesthedes' featuring a table surface covered in clusters of keys and three monitors. The artwork studio was made redundant in one blow. The machine was capable of working in more layers than designers could ever have imagined at the time.

During those early years one could see from the results that there was a lot of experimentation, of exploring all the potential of this new technology. The screen was expressively replaced by paper, which became an evil we could not avoid as we rushed to express our excitement about the new electronic medium. We had thought the use of paper was about to end!

When, eventually, the Macintosh computer dedicated itself to our discipline and the 'new experience' became routine, it was clear that the 'miracle' machine was, indeed, a blessing. Everything had become possible within a mere fraction of the time previously required. Unfortunately, 'creativity' was not a built-in component of this new technology.

In conjunction with this period of revolutionary technological inventions, an entirely new visual language developed. One of the first to postulate this new language was Wolfgang Weingart, who had the initial courage and inspiration to tackle the constraining aesthetics of Swiss design. Based on the lectures of Emil Ruder, who had inspired an entire generation of Swiss to follow the concept of clear functionalism, Weingart challenged the dogmas that accompanied this approach. So-called logic was moulded to his will, legibility was replaced by poignant images, and the traditional harmony between image and typography was rebelliously violated.

As Robert Venturi pushed architecture over the threshold of post-modernism with his 1966 publication 'Complexity and Contradiction in Architecture', Weingart, teaching at the Basle art school from 1968, showed graphic designers a new typographic language. Because of his tutorships in the United States, his ideas, there, were immediately embraced and formed a 'New Wave' throughout the country. In Europe, however, we saw a more individualistic interpretation. Here the realignment of graphic design and visual arts was of major influence. In some art schools, the division between the different disciplines was made progressively more transparent as students specialised only towards the end of their education. Graphic design, typography and visual arts were having a strong influence on each other. Characteristic in this context is the work of the artist Joseph Kosuth whose 'walltexts', made invisible by thick strokes, can be traced back to Weingart's typographic experiments. Kosuth stated the following: '...it is language reduced to words, making the texture of reading itself an arrival at language, an arrival which constructs other orders, ones that blind as they make themselves visible...' This statement sums up much of the spirit of graphic and typographic work being produced in the eighties and nineties as a reaction to the utopian-modernistic range of thought.

Apparently, in some of the most beautiful and advanced expressions of new design, image and atmosphere prevail over legibility. Conveying a contemporary sense of life and its corresponding milieu appears to have priority.

Certainly, legibility of the printed word is hardly an issue any more; designers seem to have lost interest in the discourse on this subject. Far into the sixties there was not one conference or symposium on typography and graphic design that did not have introductions on this subject programmed. Research results on, for instance, the difference in legibility between serif and sans serif typefaces were endlessly elaborated upon. Supporters and opponents were at each other's throats, arguing whether or not such differences were significant. Besides, someone would always step into the breach for the metric system in typography. Which designer nowadays knows the names of researchers such as Zachrisson, Ovink, Tinker, Evans, Vartabedian or Wendt?

One of the reasons for the loss of interest in this subject is possibly the passing of its apparent relevance. If similar research were carried out today, the odds are that no differences would appear in the perception of legibility any more, as our reading habits have changed dramatically. While former research was based, primarily, on printed typographic material, we are now used to triple-overlaid texts being sent by fax, and reading low-resolution texts from a screen. If research in this field were undertaken today, its findings would not reach most designers'. In 1970 and 1971 the publishers Lund Humphries issued *two* publications with legibility research abstracts, and from 1971 to 1976 the Royal College of Art published several volumes with the results of research into legibility under the direction of Herbert Spencer and Linda Reynolds. But since then, there has been silence in the design community concerning this subject.

On the other hand, graphic design, typography and type design are enjoying a renewed and vigorous interest. More and more is printed and published on the subject. Internet typography is developing strongly and, increasingly, new means of communication demand our full attention. We can look forward with both anxiety and excitement to what is to come.

Regardless of what does come next, it is of the greatest importance to learn from the experiences of the past. What is written about our discipline today is research material tomorrow. Thus, everything in this compilation of typographic writing is secured as essential luggage for those who follow us.

This introduction was translated from the Dutch by Jan van Son.

Working practice

1971/72 **Whatever happened to Bob Gill?** Interviewed by Peter Proto

Bob Gill was born in 1931 in New York. Studied design at the Philadelphia Museum
School of Art, painting at the Pennsylvania Academy of Fine Art and not too much at
the College of the City of New York. Was drafted into US Army from 1952 – 54. Worked
independently as a designer/illustrator from 1954 – 60. Also taught at the School of
Visual Arts. Was awarded a Gold Medal by The New York Art Directors' Club in 1957.
Came to London on the spur of the moment to be the art director of an advertising
agency in 1960, resigned in 1962 to form the design group Fletcher Forbes Gill with Alan
Fletcher and Colin Forbes – the Group, later joined by Theo Crosby, an architect, became
the most important new design office in Britain. Resigned in 1966 to work independently
as a designer/illustrator again. Has written and illustrated many books for children of
indeterminate age, is author of 'Graphic Design' with Fletcher and Forbes, and 'Illustration'
with John Lewis. Had one-man shows in New York, London, Frankfurt, Stuttgart and at
the Stedilik Museum in Amsterdam.
He is represented in all major international collections and books of graphic design,
including those of the Museum of Modern Art, New York. Was one of the founders of
the Designers & Art Directors Association, London, and is the winner of two of their
Silver Awards.

Did you start as a freelance designer originally? As soon as I left art school,
I freelanced out of my bed-sitting room in New York. Later, even when I could afford
a studio, I still preferred to work where I slept. In 1960, I was brought over to London
as the art director of Charles Hobson Advertising. That was the first full-time job I ever
had. It was a mistake. The advertising agency, that is, not London. The following year,
Alan Fletcher, Colin Forbes and I started Fletcher Forbes Gill and in 1965 we invited
Theo Crosby to join us.
What was it like working at Fletcher Forbes Gill and who were your clients?
We had a beautiful collaboration because we respected each others' work and above
all, we liked each other. When we first moved into Durweston Mews, the office con-
sisted of the three of us, three assistants, a secretary and an overdraft at Barclays Bank.
Although each of us was individually responsible for a particular job, no design ever
left the office unless all three of us approved it. In that way, I hope, we evolved a

standard which was higher than any one of us had originally. We did a lot of work
for Pirelli including their first few calendars. We did posters for the Evening Standard,
Penguin book-jackets, house-styles, booklets, ads, etc. We also helped to start DADA,
and our book, *Visual Comparisons* sold almost 50,000 copies.

Why did you leave CFFG? The decision was made very quickly. I suddenly realized
that the more successful we became, the larger and the more complicated were the jobs
that came in and the more staff we needed to get the jobs out. I also appreciated that
from the point of view of Theo, Alan and Colin, this was a desirable thing, but I started
to lose interest. So the only thing to do was to leave.

What did you do when you left? I began freelancing from my house, and taught
one day a week at the Royal College of Art. Perhaps it was inevitable that I should
revert to working where I slept.

How did clients treat you – leaving an organization and starting up for yourself?
As I had never planned on leaving CFFG, I didn't really have any sources of work. It
was quite exciting knocking on doors trying to find new clients. Obviously, I had
some advantages over the average freelancer. I had capital. I had something of a reputation. And I knew quite a few people.

Did you find the pressure greater, being alone? I missed the companionship of my
partners at first, but I guess, the challenge of the situation stimulated me. I also wasn't
alone. I had just married my fiercest critic, Bobby.

What did you try to teach the students at the RCA? Was it professionalism? It
certainly wasn't professionalism. I simply tried to point out what I think is the real
difficulty for the designer who wants to be more than just a hack…who wants to produce work of quality. You see, the designer has an 'art' training and his client has not,
this means that there is a difference of taste between them. The client does not, necessarily, like the designer's colour schemes, his layouts, his style of illustration etc. And as
the client is paying for it, he's continually frustrating the designer's attempt to produce
beautiful art. I suggest that the designer should be concerned with solutions to the
client's problems, and that all of the visual niceties should come as a direct result of
the solution, not merely reflect the designer's taste. In a sense, if a designer has a good

(above) Illustration for a booklet
(facing page) poster

solution, he should be able explain it over the telephone.

Yes, but surely only a successful designer like yourself can say that... I think that any designer, whether successful or not, must have his priorities right. Time spent doing crap, regardless of how much money it brings in, is wasted time. Time spent doing the very best that one is capable of, regardless of how little money it brings in, in the short run, is the only real measure of success. And incidentally, in the long run, it brings in more money.

But I think you would admit Bob, that when you started, surely, you were taking on any problems that came along? Not only did I take on any problem that came along when I first started, I still take on any problem. What I am trying to say, is that it's not the problem that determines the potential of a job, it's what you do with the problem. You're probably trying to say that in the beginning I had to do things as a designer that would embarrass me today. The truth is that the only difference between my first jobs and my latest work, is that I'm obviously more experienced, more capable and more aware of possibilities today, but my attitudes haven't changed. And I still do most jobs the night before.

Even a client who supplies you with 4 pages of copy and a photograph? This surely can't be discused on the telephone? As far as I'm concerned, if he only wants you to lay-out his photograph and his copy, then you are not functioning as a designer. You can be sure that I'd tell him that over the telephone.

Why did you stop teaching at the Royal College? After five years, it seemed that it was time for a change. I went to the Central School of Art where I now teach one day a week.

When did you first get interested in doing films? About three years ago, Joe Losey, the director asked me to go to Spain with him as a visual consultant. It was a film with Robert Shaw and Malcomb McDowell called *Figures in a Landscape*. The job came at a time when I was getting bored with graphics. After all, I had been working continuously as a designer for almost twenty years. When I returned from Spain, the only thing I could think of was to make films of my own. I found myself knocking on doors again. This time for documentaries.

What films have you done since? I've been more or less continuously writing, producing and directing documentaries for the past three years. They've been commissioned by a variety of clients: VFW, an aircraft manufacturer in Germany, Fabergé, who launched a new perfume, Pirelli, Olivetti, ORT, a charity in Switzerland, Cheshire Homes, British Leyland, Hertz, Singapore Airlines, etc.

Have you done any television commercials? During the past six months I have directed sixteen for The Sunday Times, Family Circle Magazine, the COI, etc. Although it was an interesting experience, I've decided not to do any more unless I can write the script as well.

Do you think you will stay in films, or don't you know? Don't know.

Do you still handle graphic design? Not really. I'm only interested in making films. Occasionally, I do a job for a friend or a cause in which I'm interested. You might say that graphics is now just a hobby.

Can I mention your age, Bob? Sure, why not? I'm four months older than Fletcher and years younger than Forbes.

Do you intend to stay in England? Not England, Notting Hill Gate.

Pentagram has been criticized for being made up of too many slightly old designers. Do you feel this matters? CFF, later Pentagram, has always been criticized for the wrong reasons. The critics fall into three groups:

Criticism one: they laugh too much. They're not serious enough. This group of critics produce work which is not taken very seriously by designers out of England. These critics compensate for this by taking their own work too seriously.

Criticism two: they charge too much. These critics can't cope with the world of commerce. They make a virtue of their inadequacies by revelling in garrets. They think that this makes them more of an 'artist'.

Criticism three: ten years ago, they were too young, too small an organization. Clients, happy to give them a tiny trade ad to do, were terrified to give them a more important problem. Instead they went to large advertising agencies, who, in turn, came back to CFF for a solution. And now they are supposed to be too old, too big an organization.

May I suggest three alternative criteria by which one might criticize a designer or design office: the quality of work produced, the way they treat their staff and whether the solutions that are arrived at are socially useful, or not. And in all three respects, I think that Pentagram has done much of which they can be very proud.

(left) Logotype for George Hoy 1964

(middle) Poster 1963

(right) Announcement card

Letraset International Typeface Competition results 1973 Peter Proto

A total of 2,590 entries from designers and typographers from more than 43 countries were submitted to a special International Typeface Competition organised by Letraset International Ltd.

The object of the competition was to find 25 new typefaces. All winning entries will receive royalty agreements from Letraset for the sale of their typefaces on Letraset Instant Lettering sheets, which will also carry their names. In addition, the winners' names will appear in all relevant publicity literature. Prizes of £1,000, £750 and £500 are being awarded to the first three winning designs. In addition, the outright winner will be invited to London – all expenses paid – to participate in a Letragraphica type-face selection meeting (a range of typefaces marketed internationally by Letraset). This competition has offered the opportunity for a number of talented designers and typographers to get their work put to commercial use. It will enhance their reputations as well as being of some positive financial benefit. In return, Letraset will have an array of typefaces to choose from which to meet the ever growing demands for new and original typefaces. The standard of the winning entries is defined by the individual reputations of the international panel of judges:

Derek Birdsall, Omnific, London. Roger Excoffon, Excoffon Conseil, Paris. Colin Forbes, Pentagram Design Partnership Ltd, London. Armin Hofmann, School of Arts & Crafts (AGS) Basle. Herb Lubalin, Lubalin Smith, Carnase, Inc. New York. Marcello Minale, Minale, Tattersfield, Provinciali, London & Milan. The judging took place at the Design Centre, London, 15th January 1973.

Carla Bombere Ward, Art Director of Duffy & Associates of Washington DC heard on the night of Monday the 15th January that her entry to the competition was placed first out of the 2,590 entries submitted. 20 typefaces were selected by the judges as winners.

Carla Ward wins £1,000 plus royalties on the sales by Letraset of 'Bombere' the name she has chosen for her design. She also wins a trip to London to participate in the next Letragraphica selection meeting. Twice a year, eminent graphic designers meet in London to select typefaces for addition to Letragraphica, a range of contemporary typefaces marketed by Letraset International, through their distribution network represented in 92 countries.

Nine of the final choice of 25 new typefaces chosen for Letraset's Letragraphica series.

(top) *Bombere*, designed by Carla Bombere Ward (USA).

(second down) *Magnificat*, designed by F Friedrich Peter (Canada).

(third down) *Stilla*, designed by Francois Boltana (France).

[editors note: The other six examples illustrated here were not credited in the original publication].

Carla Ward, 22, attended the Corcoran School of Art, Washington DC and the Richmond Professional Institute in Virginia. Her past experience has been as a designer, artist, art director and freelance for a number of advertising agencies and design studios. Her design, selected for its graphic appeal and originality, is an outstanding three dimensional alphabet formed by a geometric extension to a san serif typeface. Carla Ward and her husband jointly plan to build upon the opportunity of going to London by travelling and working together in graphic design throughout Europe for at least the next 6 months.

The second prize, £750 was awarded to F Friedrich Peter, a graphic designer and art lecturer in Vancouver, BC. His design *Magnificat* is a marvellously intricate and stylish piece of calligraphy. *Magnificat* has a quality and style reminiscent of the old masters of the art of writing.

Stilla, an outstanding italic alphabet of an ultra bold weight, designed by Francois Boltana, a student at the Ecole des Beaux Arts, Toulouse, was awarded the third prize of £500. The swash nature of *Stilla* lends vitality and flair whilst maintaining legibility and sound basic type.

The other 22 typefaces selected were also display typefaces. The winners will be awarded royalty agreements in return for exclusive rights granted to Letraset International Ltd. The international aspect of the competition is illustrated by entries received from 43 countries. The winners selected were from Australia, Canada, Colombia, France, Germany, Spain, Sweden, United Kingdom and the United States. The competition was launched in May 1972 and was promoted throughout the world with an advertising campaign. Posters and leaflets were also printed in five languages. Letraset dealers and art colleges were natural focal points for displaying the posters. The winning typefaces will be available on three separate series on Letragraphica throughout

The Letragraphica panel, who were, in fact, also the judges for the competition (left to right) are: Derek Birdsall, Omnific Ltd, London. Armin Hofmann, School of Arts & Crafts (AGS) Basle. Marcello Minale, Minale Tattersfield, Provinciali Ltd, (London & Milan) Roger Excoffon, Excoffon Conseil, Paris. Colin Forbes, Pentagram Design Partnership Ltd, London and Herb Lubalin, Lubalin, Smith, Carnase Inc, New York.

1973, through the chain of over 3,000 retailers Letraset companies supply.

Commenting on the competition, Herb Lubalin felt the standard of entries was much higher than a similar competition he judged several years ago, though Marcello Minale expressed the view that many of the designs were retrospective, being modifications, some good, of existing typefaces.'*Bombere*' was, however, selected for its originality. Asked whether any specific national design characteristics had been apparent during the judging, Marcello Minale replied that this had not been noticeable. Indeed, the judges were convinced that two particular typefaces had been executed by the same designer. In fact, one was from Canada, the other from Sweden. He felt there was evidence of wide knowledge of new trends in typeface design throughout the world. It was a major contribution to design by Letraset that the student in Yugoslavia and the student in Canada had available the best and latest in typeface design through the medium of Letraset Instant Lettering.

Expressing the regrets of the judges on the absence of any traditional typefaces suitable for text as display setting, Derek Birdsall commented that this was disappointing. The judges tried very hard to find such typefaces, but the standard of those submitted was not sufficiently high and added nothing new to existing typefaces in this category. Marcello Minale mentioned that display typefaces were in evidence primarily because they come most naturally to designers, who like exploring the graphic expression of their imagination. During the judging, Armin Hofmann commented that a consequence of this free expression in display typefaces was that many of them broke the cardinal rule of typeface design, namely legibility. An interesting development provided by dry transfer, Colin Forbes said, is the facility given to the designer, with many of the typefaces selected, to amend the basic letterform in an individual, creative way. Commenting on the prevalence of geometric designs, the cause of which he felt was due to the new methods of setting type, Herb Lubalin stated that the constraints previously imposed on the type designer by metal type have now disappeared.

The importance of the event is clearly demonstrated by the fact it drew 432 entries from the USA, 487 from Germany, 598 from the UK and 116 from France. It even attracted one entry from Russia!

The full breakdown of entries from individual countries is as follows:
United Kingdom 598, Germany 487, USA 432, Canada 117, France 116, Austria 66, Yugoslavia 64, Italy 62, Netherlands 60, Spain 52, Argentine 51, New Zealand 48, Australia 48, Denmark 45, Switzerland 38, Sweden 36, Norway 28, South Africa 26, Mexico 25, Israel 19, Finland 16, Czechoslovakia 15, Poland 12, Ireland 11, Japan 8, Brazil 7, Colombia 3, Lebanon 3, Russia 1, and the rest of the world 96.

1972/73 **Do we need more or fewer typefaces?** Alan Jones

It is perhaps the oldest commercial truism of all that a supplier should aim to provide his customer with what he wants – and not simply to offer him a standardised product which represents the lowest common denominator of market research analyses.

In typesetting, more than in any other branch of the graphic arts industry, this requirement is particularly significant. It is true that over 70 per cent of the jobs that come into a general printing office (in an English-speaking country) can be labelled 'straight text'. Even so, in most of these jobs there are usually one or two problems which call for special typographical treatment.

And the 20 – 30 per cent of 'complex matter' is hardly a contracting market. In a world where the 'information explosion' has to deal with increasing technical sophistication, and where the 'literary explosion' has to cope with the widening range of languages, it is bound to grow.

In the desire for greater speed and productivity, are we to overlook these problems and lower our standards with regard to what is typographically acceptable? Are we to reverse the rôles of printer and print-buyer – and those of machinery supplier and printer – and allow the former to dictate to the latter what he can have?

Perhaps in some spheres of work, where immediacy of publication or lack of finance may make a poor-looking piece of print preferable to no print at all, our typographical standards have to be readjusted. However, The Monotype Corporation find little in their dealings with customers to show that such a trend is more than very exceptional. If anything, the evidence proves that printers and print-buyers are more insistent on maintaining standards than ever before.

For example, there has been no let-up in the demand for 'special' matrices (non-standard letters, figures, symbols, etc). Each week, Monotype manufacture about 400 new 'specials' at their factory at Salfords. To appreciate this in proper perspective, one must take into account the fact that a complete seven-alphabet fount of a 'Monotype' face contains 633 standard matrices. The non-standard 'specials' are over and above this figure.

The annual output of 20,000 'specials' is a significant factor in Monotype's thinking, especially in relation to typesetting machine design, where interchangeability of matrices has always been a fundamental principle. A packaged deal of fixed matrix arrangements

would greatly simplify manufacturing problems; but in their 70-years-long experience, Monotype have found it is no good asking the printer to tell his customer to make do with what already exists.

Of course it is desirable to standardise, but only when this can be achieved to the satisfaction of all the parties concerned. Monotype's two mathematical formulae systems exemplify this: by encouraging authors, publishers and printers to accept one typeface (*Times New Roman*), it has been possible to produce two series – one for metal with over 8,000 matrices and for film with nearly 6,000 matrices – which are adequate to meet most mathematical requirements. If other spheres of knowledge could be handled in a similar way, there would be less need for 'specials'. That of phonetics, for instance, is particularly problematic, since no two phoneticians seem to agree about desirable standards. This is one reason why Monotype's repertory of special letters is so extensive. It contains, for example, over 2,700 different forms of the letter E.

If all these different forms were to be made in all sizes of all the Latin faces available, the number of matrices required would amount to several million.

Another field in which attempts have been made to standardise is that of non-Latin scripts. This has been due largely to the problem of containing languages with a large range of characters within the matrix configurations of typesetting machines.

So far as metal composition is concerned, Monotype have split characters into two, and even three, parts and have developed special duplex and triplex moulds for casting. It has been a process of rationalisation rather than standardisation.

Filmsetting offers considerable advantages in this field. Not only is the machine matrix capacity greater (597 positions on a 'Monophoto' 600 filmsetter), but the facility of double exposure and the use of floating accents has helped to simplify the setting of languages such as Vietnamese with its great preponderance of accented characters.

Monotype's non-Latin repertory now totals over 120 metal series covering 24 different scripts, and half of these series are also available as film matrices. To a great extent, choice of typeface design is limited. There are, for example, different faces to suit Arabic-speaking people in North Africa, in the Middle East and in Asian countries, but a typographer in Teheran must envy his opposite number in London or New York. He is restricted to a choice between two or three faces and can hardly comprehend the possibility of having 320 metal series and over 120 film series at his disposal.

This raises the question: How far will it be practicable to offer a better typographical deal for non-Latin languages? Obviously, supply must be conditioned by demand, and it is perhaps significant that Monotype are now working on more new non-Latin text faces than Latin ones. Two important Devanagari designs (for Hindi and related languages) have recently been released, and other non-Latin designs are in various stages of manufacture.

Fashion must be both led and followed. So far as Monotype are concerned, *Univers* (made in collaboration with Deberny & Peignot) represents the former and *Helvetica* (made under licence from Linotype GmbH) the latter. But are both these not dissimilar faces really necessary? And should we really allow ourselves to be dictated to by typographic fashion?

As in every aspect of design – be it clothes, furniture or buildings – there is a pleasure, even if it is a subconscious one, to be derived from changes in typographic style and structure. It is possible to imagine a world of print based upon only two typefaces – *Times New Roman* and *Univers*. But what a dull world it would be. In Monotype's repertory, for example, there are over 80 sanserif faces. A typographer may exercise his preference for *Gill Sans, Grotesque, Univers, Helvetica* or *20th Century*. At a time when standardisation is tending to put blinkers on our typographic eyes, let him savour the increasingly wide variety of sanserifs at his disposal and not rest content with a single brand. For it is the typographer, as the double agent of the print-buyer and author, who counts. He is the professional who determines how a piece of printed matter will look. There may be bad typographers who abuse this position of responsibility – there are bad members of other professions – but there are plenty of good typographers who care enough about the printed word to ensure its typographical 'fitness for purpose'.

That is the goal to which everyone concerned with the printed word, in whatever language, must work. If high standards of typographical appearance are to be maintained for the sake of legibility, of comprehension, of persuasion, of pleasure, there is a con-tinuing need for a wide and versatile repertory of typefaces and for a range of specials which extends far beyond the 633 standard characters of a typeface fount. Although standardisation can and will, play its part in certain complex spheres of work, the vast majority of printed jobs defy rationalisation to a strictly utilitarian level. So long as typographical needs are infinitely flexible – and so long as the printer and his customer want to accept their challenge – the typesetting machinery supplier must cater for them. Another question is how far the wealth of material available to the typographer working in the Latin script is justifiable. Henry Ford might have said 'You can have any typeface you like, so long as it's *Times New Roman*.' But is this desirable? Surely, typographers must be allowed maximum freedom in the choice of typefaces, unless factors of economy and efficiency make such freedom impracticable.

There are two design justifications for this: function and aesthetics. So far as function is concerned, the case is clear. A typeface that is suitable for a magazine printed by gravure may not be satisfactory for an encyclopædia printed by letterpress, and a type-face designed for the special requirements of newspaper production may not lend itself to the printing of a glossy art catalogue.

The conditions are infinitely variable. They concern, on the one hand, such technical factors as the printing process, paper surfaces, typesetting equipment specifications: and on the other hand such typographical factors as the nature of the work, its language, legibility requirements, and consumer marketing considerations. Even in Monotype's extensive repertory, there are functional typeface gaps which still remain to be filled.

The aesthetic case is more debatable. Consumer needs have been mentioned in relation to function, but does the man-in-the-street really care about typefaces? The statistical psychologists have shown that he likes best what he knows best: but if that were entirely the case, we should never have progressed beyond Gutenberg's black letter. There must be some sort of development in typeface design if only to meet the changing technical conditions.

Monotype have recognised the need for development but not to the exclusion of providing their customer with what they want. It took 12 years after the first 'Monotype' machine installation in 1900 for an original typeface – *Imprint* – to be designed specifically for mechanical composition: so long as printers wanted their Moderns and Old Styles, these faces were the order of the day. One can see the same pattern emerge with the introduction of phototypesetting over 50 years later. So long as people were happy with their *Bembo* and *Baskerville*, which Monotype had themselves pioneered in the 1920s, there was no apparent need for a 'Monophoto', *Apollo* or a 'Monophoto' *Photina*.

1973/74 **The rules of the game** F H K Henrion
The text of the concluding talk to the 16th International Congress on Education in Letter-forms, in Copenhagen, 1973.

I should like to come back on three things which Adrian Frutiger brought out very clearly at the beginning of his talk. The first was that letters of the alphabet are images well anchored in our memory: through constant repetition in one size or another they are clearly engraved and when a similar letter comes up again we recognise it at once because there is a hole, or I would rather call it a matrice, in our memory which retains not only letters but whole pictures of words which have gone through our consciousness deep down into our sub-conscious, and are recognised at once when they re-occur. Thus we have in our brain certain Platonic ideas of each letter, and any letter A is a solution which aims at and goes towards this original abstract ideal A, the Matrice A; which all literate people carry in their mind. This is one fact I readily endorse and I will make it one of the bases of my talk.

The other point I would like to make is that there are two kinds of lettering, one is the text for pure information, clearly conveyed and received, and the other is what Mr Frutiger calls display lettering: the kind of lettering which can be shown in all imaginable type variations and imaginative evolutions and deformations, in German: verfremdung (alienation), to a point where they become almost illegible without, however, impairing the process of reading. It is this kind of lettering I would like to talk about today because my own experience is based very much in this area. Not only display lettering but titling, for messages, for posters and illuminated signs, the kind of lettering which is referred to as logotype: the kind of words, like 'Coca Cola', or 'Mobil' or 'Shell', which have become ways of writing the particular word in a peculiar way, which makes it instantly recognisable in all countries and in all contexts. Nicolette Gray distinguishes between private and public reading matter and identifies the physical difference in both.

I should like to go a little further, assuming that private reading is what we choose to read, and public reading matter is what we are expected to read, but who expects us to read it? I think this public reading has to be subdivided again into:

1 the reading of relevant information we need to survive, like a traffic sign, or an aid we need in order to find something for which we are looking such as a direction sign, etc, or

information which we do not look for but which imposes itself on our consciousness because somebody wants us to buy something, etc and this information we some times call visual noise because it interferes with our perception of the essential information we need.

Display lettering occurs in both these areas but because of the different function of this area, its appearance varies considerably, if it is appropriately designed for each.

The third concept I would like to borrow from Mr Frutiger is what he calls 'the rules of the game'. In his own context, he says it is essential to understand them because these rules are made by reconciling a number of different requirements: the design of the alphabet, the kind of quality to be achieved within clear economic parameters and the speed of setting, as well as the selling and maintenance price of the setting machine. If all these factors can be satisfied, we are likely to come up with the right solution. I should like to develop the idea of the 'rules of the game' a little further because I think they are the basis of all consistent solutions of all design problems.

It has become axiomatic of late to refer to design as a problem-solving activity, no matter whether it is industrial design, communication design or any other kind of design with-in which we play. These rules apply of course equally in the areas of designing display letters and alphabets. If we do equate design with problem-solving the proper sequence of action is:

1 state the objective to be achieved

2 analyse the situation

3 make a list of requirements and the criteria

4 put the list of these requirements into a priority order and you define the rules of the game.

These rules of the game can only be ascertained in each case through analysis of the problem and, once established, they provide criteria for judging whether something is right, wrong, appropriate and optimal. Nicolette Gray has listed a number of criteria by which lettering should be judged and I entirely agree with her list. Rules of the game however determine the varying emphases of these criteria in any particular case, the priority of each over the other and, therefore, by establishing them we are one step further towards understanding particular problems.

If we play football the objective is to kick the ball into the goal; the requirements are not to touch the ball with hand or arm, to keep the ball inside the playing field and not to indulge in foul play. Furthermore, there are eleven players on both sides and the game lasts twice forty-five minutes. All these criteria could also be called parameters and the objective should be achieved within these parameters. Other examples would perhaps be the following, borrowed from the writer, Edward de Bono, who has written about 'lateral thinking' and 'the mechanism of mind'. These illustrations, however, come from a book entitled 'The Dog Exercising Machine' where a number of children were asked to design a machine for exercising dogs. 'This may seem an odd choice for a subject but it does have many advantages:

1 such machines do not actually exist so the child has to invent something instead of just reproducing an existing machine.

2 in a dog exercising machine the child is not only dealing with a mechanical device – he has to deal with the dog as well, and the dog is a living thing. In addition, to understanding wheels and engines, the child has to contribute some dog psychology as well.

3 the dog is part of a child's world.

4 both machine and exercise are subtle abstract ideas which even an adult might have difficulty in handling. How do children handle them?'

Now the objective in inventing this machine is that the dog should be exercised without anyone being obliged to walk with it in the normal way. The requirements are:

1 to understand dog psychology

2 not to be unkind to the dog

3 to achieve maximum exercise for the dog and minimal effort by the controller.

This list of requirements also establishes the criteria but taken together they are the rules of the game. Now in spite of the requirements and limitations there are many different solutions possible:

Illustration 1. This shows a robot and you will see that the robot, to save him the trouble of having to adjust his head has a face on each aspect of the cube head. The arms are jointed but end abruptly without the need for hands. There is a place for four batteries and, unlike most other robots which stand woodenly, this one is running along – he even appears to have spiked running shoes and he leads the dog by the lead that goes round the dog's ears.

Illustration 2. This is just one idea. The author explains the dog has an artificial hand clipped on to the end of its lead with an aerial sticking out of the top. The girl can control it with a board with buttons on it. It can go backwards, forwards, fast, slow, left, right, and it can turn round. This is a quite different and very clever device using most modern electronic technology.

Illustration 3. Another attempted solution is the maze – on the top end you put the dog in and at the very end of the maze is a plateful of meat and the dog smelling the meat has to find his way through the maze. The maze is quite well conceived although there are some areas which are inaccessible and therefore useless, but the idea is again very good because the dog must be exercised in order to get to the meat.

Illustration 4. This one shows a floor on top and the dog follows the bone thinking 'I am going to get that bone' and the bone is on the end of an engine on a long metal pole. The engine is under the floor and the author has also thought of an electric plug to make the engine work.

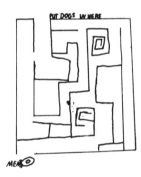

These are all examples of typical design problems where the aim to be achieved is very clearly stated, certain limitations imposed, but the ways and means to achieve these aims within these limitations are left completely free so that they can be, as we have shown here, greatly varied.

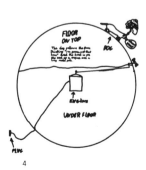

What has this to do with the design of alphabets? In fact everything. Any design problem can be solved and the result measured by comparing a number of solutions as to its appropriateness. Nicolete Gray made the difference between private reading and public reading, between type design and display design and lettering. Now in the

following I will only deal with display lettering design because this is my field engine of work. At the beginning I accepted Adrian Frutiger's thesis that all letters are established as matrices on the memory of literate people, a kind of Platonic alphabet as a matrice for all A s, B s, etc. Every A is somewhere on the way towards this A matrice, the moment it is recognised as an A. It can come very near towards this triangular A with a crossbar, it can be of equal thickness like some sans lettering, it can have a thin upstroke with a very bold down-stroke like Bodoni, or it can be ornate like Baroque lettering, or it can look like an organic growth like the A in Art Nouveau; or it can be ambiguous to the point where one is not sure whether it is an A at all by alienating it from the original A.

That the rule-of-the-game theory does apply to the design of letters and alphabet can be demonstrated.

I would like to think of an alphabet as a sign system consisting of twenty-six signs where each sign can be put next to any other of the twenty-five signs so that it can form words. In order to do so the letters must have certain common denominators to show that they belong to the same family and certain differences which show their meaning. They must have a measure of being alike and a measure of being different and they must be designed in such a way that every letter (or sign) fits comfortably to any other letter or any other sign. This is the rule of the alphabet game which has to be accepted if the letters are to form words which are easily read and which have a certain unity and rhythm so that the words form lines – again sufficiently alike and suffciently different for legibility. The rule of the alphabet game is that twenty-six signs must all relate to each other in any combination.

As the system itself is stronger than its component parts, the serif alphabet makes the O part of its system, although it is really a sans character. By surrounding this O with serif typefaces within a word the O becomes, in the context of its other twenty-five component signs, a serif O. It plays by the rules of the game.

If we look at fifteenth century, or nineteenth century or twentieth century alphabets, like the ones which are specially designed for photosetting or dry transfer processes, the rules of the game vary considerably in each typeface but they always apply to the whole twenty-six sign system. (For example, photosetting, Letraset, Hollenstein, Schrofer, etc.) A street paving detail shows three systems, each true to itself although the component parts vary in size and shape considerably. Three different rules of the game are side by side, look quite different from each other, but true to themselves.

If we now come to the design of a logotype, consisting of three or four letters, these rules are changed as there are only three or four signs which have to relate to each other and no longer twenty-six. Through this change of the rules we can arrive at a different letter-form – in fact a letter-form which does not only belong to an existing alphabet as in the case of Mobil but a sequence of five letters, in this case of a known typeface; but through the very simple device of having blue letters with a red O or black letters with an outline O becomes a familiar and legally registerable word feature, ie logotype.

In corporate design, in packaging, in initials for a well-known international company,

Illustrations on page 27 by kind permission of Edward de Bono and Jonathan Cape, Olivetti Ltd, and HDA International.

the designs of logo-types has become very important. In fact in many ways it has become more important than the design of symbols, because every symbol must have a word reference. This is one reason why Olivetti two years ago abandoned their well-known and world-wide established symbol or ideogram in favour of a very carefully developed logotype. It might be worth showing the evolution of this typeface (left) designed by Olivetti's chief graphic designer, Walter Ballmer.

Conclusion

These are just indications how letter design in logo-types and display lettering can enrich our environment on the lines indicated and advocated by Nicolette Gray. I can only very warmly endorse what she has said: that the challenge is enormous and our environment capable of great improvements with the contributions of professional designers who can apply themselves to whatever problems they find; be it one of pure information or advertising, or of illuminated signs. Whatever we do, we either impoverish or enrich our environment, and we can only do a proper job if we are aware of the rules of the game, what the criteria are. If we set the appropriate criteria to establish the particular rules of the game, we can achieve our objectives in the most imaginative and the most appropriate manner.

1975 **Data for stationery design** Brian Grimbly

Business stationery is used by every organisation or individual that needs written communication and/or needs to record transactional information, whether internally within the organisation, or externally. The variety of formats, information requirements and usages is enormous. While this article attempts to be definitive, it cannot be exhaustive because every organisation has its own different requirements based on its own internal procedures and the needs of its transactions.

The number and diversity of forms in use today suggests that generic groups should be used as the basis of definition. That this normally happens is clear from the fact that the words 'invoice' and 'statement' are generally understood even though the information on an 'invoice' will vary greatly between one form asking for payment for telephone calls, and another asking for payment for the construction of an oil refinery.

Sequence of usership

The archetype of printed communications is generally considered to be the book, which is written by an author, handed to a publisher, produced by a printer, and sold probably through a bookseller to a reader.

The business form is, however, a much more complex matter. A business letter, for example, must be written on the organisation's official letterhead. This is originated by the organisation's designer, to reflect the nature and image of the organisation and to communicate the basic information which is common to all the letters from that organisation. The letterhead is then printed and delivered to the client who, before sending it to the recipient, adds further information to make the communication meaningful. Thus the normal sequence of use for a letterhead would be:

Originator of stationery requires that the visual image of the form should reflect the attitude and requirements of his organisation.

The **author** of the communication on the business form needs that form as a proper vehicle to carry his message effectively.

The **typist** needs to be able to type the message of the author accurately and efficiently. That means that not only must the form work for the information the typist has been given to communicate, but it must also be related to an efficient use of the type-writer. Therefore the mechanics, ergonomics and cybernetics of the typewriter

become major factors in the design of stationery.

The **author** must then approve, normally by signature, that his communication has been accurately transcribed on the appropriate form.

The author's checklist might be as follows:

1 Ensure that the right form has been used for the communication.

2 Ensure the accuracy of the information of the communication.

3 The grammar of the communication the typing style of the communication.

4 Approve the document by signature (this adds another graphic element).

The **filing clerk** in the author's organisation needs to be able to file copies of the document correctly, and therefore he needs to be able to identify easily the relevant data which enable the copies to be properly positioned in the overall filing system.

The **despatcher** must be able in terms of the system to ensure that the container or envelope is properly addressed and that proper instructions are given for the method of delivery.

The **recipient** must be able to identify the name of the organisation from which the communication comes, the author, any reference or code relating to either the author's or the recipient's organisation, the date and the information content of the document.

The **recipient's filing clerk** must be able to identify the data in the document accurately and be able to file it easily, generally or equivalently with similar communications from a number of other organisations. Consequently, the document must be physically compatible with a standard filing system.

Description of normal business forms

The range of forms used in commercial activities has over a period become common to all companies involved in commercial transactions. The basic classi fications are:

Letterhead: The basic business form, the letterhead is used for all written communications where the standard transaction forms, such as order, invoice, etc. do not apply.

Compliments slip: A note that is normally used to accompany an enclosure, and can quite properly carry a short manuscript message.

Business card: A card for use as a personal introduction, it is intended to be used as a record of the person's name, company, function or position in the company, address and telephone number.

Envelope: An outer wrapper to contain the business communication. It normally carries the name and address of the recipient, or allows this to be seen through an aperture. It may also be printed with the name and address of the sending organisation.

Quotation, estimate or **tender** states the price, availability and discount offered against an inquiry from a customer. The document would normally set out, probably on the reverse of the sheet, the company's normal terms of business to include delivery, guarantee, payment, etc.

Order: This is an official and legally binding document asking for goods or services to be supplied. An order normally specifies delivery arrangements and the agreed price for such goods or services.

Acknowledgement of order informs the customer that the order, together with its

terms and conditions, been accepted.

Advice or **Despatch note** informs the person who is to receive the goods that they have been despatched. The intention is to enable the customer to make arrangements to receive delivery and to check against non-delivery or delayed delivery. The term 'advice note' is often used for a combined order-acknowledgement and despatch-note.

Delivery or packing note: A delivery note normally accompanies the goods at delivery to enable the customer to check that the goods are in accordance with the order and the supplier's interpretation of the order. It may well require a signature for the receipt of goods.

Invoice or bill states the amount of money outstanding against a particular order and normally gives full details of all the items delivered together with prices, discount, VAT charges and any delivery charges.

Statement of account shows the amount of money due to a supplier from a customer. A statement is normally an account listing the invoice numbers of transactions and the amount of money due against each transaction, together with a total of the debt over a given period.

Credit note: A credit note is a contra-invoice to correct any overcharging invoiced or to negate any charges invoiced when goods have been returned.

Debit note is sometimes used to increase the value of an invoice when a customer has been undercharged.

Internal forms: Every organisation or business of any size will use internal forms to cater for activities which need to be recorded within the organisation. These can be bought from manufacturing stationers, or printed for the organisation or by the organisation internally. The printing of internal forms should be a cost-conscious exercise as these forms have no sales or marketing validity.

Because so many different types of internal forms are needed by different types of organisation it is impossible to draw up a fully comprehensive check list. However, a basic list would include:

Petty cash voucher to record a small transaction paid in cash.

Time sheet on which an employee records the amount of time he has worked, sometimes detailing the work with which he has been involved.

Pay slip shows the amount of pay, overtime, bonuses, etc set against the amounts for tax, national insurance, pension contributions and any other deductions to give a final amount to be paid.

Internal memorandum enables a typewritten or manuscript message to be communicated and recorded between one department or individual and another.

Requisition is used when a company needs to keep an accurate account of its materials and supplies for accountancy, tax or reordering purposes. The object of a requisition is to provide an exact account of the transference of materials from stock to a department and to show authorisation.

Pre-printed information that appears on business forms
All business stationery has information pre-printed on it. Indeed, it would hardly be

defined as business stationery without pre-printing. The information [displayed on pages 34 and 35] has two main functions. First, it identifies the organisation concerned, together with its nature, image and description (this includes name, address and telephone number). Second, it indicates where special information should be entered to make the pre-printed form an effective communication.

Pre-printed information is conditioned by several factors, some of which are dictated by common sense, some by statutory and Post Office requirements, while other factors relate to business practice and convention.

Variants and options as to the information to be shown obviously depend on the nature of the business activity and the administrative attitudes of the particular organisation. Nevertheless, it is reasonable to work within accepted norms to ensure not only that essential information is communicated but also that the manner of its communication is accepted without ambiguity or misunderstanding.

Over a long period of time a 'case law' situation has developed whereby conventions have been established among a large number of disparate entities and organisations, and these conventions are today generally recognised and accepted. This case law is common to commercial and organisational transactions throughout the world.

The pre-printed information requirement for any form falls into four basic groups:

1.0 Name, description and address

1.1 Name (individual or corporate)

1.2 Description of organisation

1.3 Address and postcode

1.4 Telephone number, telex and cable address

The interaction matrix below shows the information that should be included on a business form with 1 at the point of interaction. Information required by the EEC Act 1972 and the Registration of Business names Act is shown with 2. Information required to be shown by the Inland Revenue for VAT purposes is shown as 3.

	Name	Description of Organisation	Address and Postcode	Telephone number	Date	Own reference	Clients reference	Other reference (Form number)	Company registration number	Place of registration	Registered office	Directors names	Directors nationality	VAT Registration number	VAT Amount	Name of form	Quantities	Description of goods or services	Date required by	Delivery address	Price	Discounts	Conditions of contract	Method of delivery	Receipt of goods acknowledged	Limited liability	Tax point	Type of supply	Reason for credit
Letterhead	1	1	1	1	1	1	1		2	2	2	2	2													2			
Business card	1	1	1	1																									
Compliments slip	1	1	1	1																									
Quotation	1	1	1	1	1	1	1	1	2	2	2	2	2			1	1	1	1	1	1		1			2			
Order	1	1	1	1	1	1		1	2	2	2	2	2			1	1	1	1	1	1		1			2			
Acknowledgement of Order	1		1	1	1	1	1	1								1	1	1	1	1	1								
Advice or Despatch note	1		1	1	1	1	1	1								1	1	1	1	1				1					
Delivery note	1		1	1	1	1	1	1								1	1	1	1	1				1	1				
Invoice	1		1	1	1	1	1	1						3	3	1	1	3			1	3	3				3	3	3
Statement	1		1	1	1	1	1	1						3	3	1						3	3				3	3	3
Credit note	1		1	1	1	1	1	1						3	3	1	1					3	3				3	3	3
Debit note	1		1	1	1	1	1	1						3	3	1	1					3	3				3	3	3

2.0 Internal and mutual referents
2.1 Date
2.2 Your reference
2.3 Our reference
2.4 Other referents, such as subject or an order number

3.0 Legal requirements
3.1 Company registration number
3.2 Registered office
3.3 Place of registration
3.4 Names of directors
3.5 Country of origin of directors
3.6 VAT (value added tax) registration number
3.7 VAT percentage
3.8 VAT amount
3.9 Tax point
3.10 Type of supply

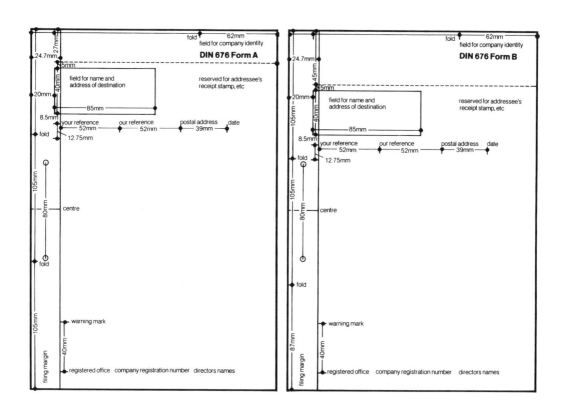

4.0 Communication

4.1 Name of form (invoice, statement, etc)

4.2 Quantities

4.3 Description of goods or services

4.4 Date required by

4.5 Where required (delivery address)

4.6 Price

4.7 Discounts

4.8 Conditions of contract

The interaction chart (preceeding page) shows which elements apply to each business form. It is suggested that this form of analysis should be the first step in the planning and designing of any stationery range.

EEC information requirements

Chapter 68 of the European Communities Act 1972, section 9, paragraph 7, requires that 'Every company shall have the following particulars mentioned in legible characters in all business letters and order forms of the company, that is to say,

(a) place of registration of the company and the number with which it is registered;

(b) address of its registered office; and

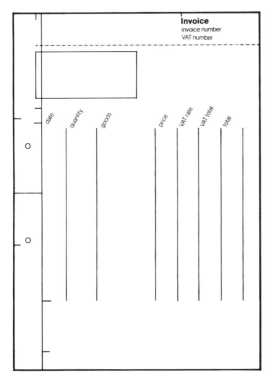

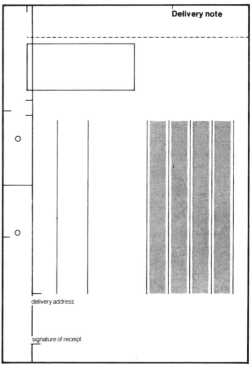

(c) in the case of a limited company exempt from the obligation to use the word 'limited' as part of its name, the fact that it is a limited company; and, if in the case of a company having a share capital there is on the stationery used for any such letters or on the order forms a reference to the amount of share capital, the reference shall be to paid-up share capital.

If a company fails to comply with this subsection, the company shall be liable to a fine not exceeding £50, and if an officer of a company or any person on its behalf issues or authorises the issue of any business letter or order form not complying with this subsection, he shall be liable to a fine not exceeding £50'.

Companies Act 1948 requirements

Section 201 requires that business letters which show the company's name should also show the present fore-name or initials and the present surname of each of the directors. Any former fore-names and surnames of the directors nationality of any directors who are not British.

The Registration of Business Names Act 1916

This act also requires the information necessary to comply with the Companies Act to be shown.

VAT requirements

The Value Added Tax (General) Regulations 1972 require that a company or individual registered for VAT who supplies or trades with a similarly registered company or individual must supply them with a tax invoice. The tax invoice must show: an identifying invoice number and the date on which it was issued. The tax point (date of supply); the name, address and VAT registration number of the supplier; the name and address of the company to whom the goods or services are supplied; the type of supply, which would normally fulfil one of the following definitions:

Sale

Cash sale

Hire purchase

Credit sale

Conditional sale

Loan

Exchange

Hire

Lease

Rental

Process (labour or process only, materials supplied)

Sale on commission

Sale or return

The quantity of goods and/or a description of services with the amount payable for each exclusive of tax

Rate of any discount offered

The rate of tax chargeable for each item

The amount of tax for each quantity or service

The total amount of tax

For amounts lower than £10 excluding tax, it is required to show only the name, address and VAT registration number, tax point (date of supply) description of goods or services supplied, amount payable, including VAT, and the rate of tax payable.

Layout of stationery and forms

The layout of any letterheading or form will depend entirely upon the attitude and information which the originating organisation wishes to communicate. Nevertheless, clear functional requirements indicate that some areas of a form are best used for certain sorts of information.

The British Standard 1808 : 1963 gives a very general recommendation as to layout. The Deutsche Industrie Normen 680 : 1967 (properly for window envelopes but nevertheless indicative of form layout) and the Sciveizerische Normen 010130 : 1970 are more explicit, and suggest particular areas for general functions.

The DIN 676 suggestions are more in accord with British practice than SNV 010130. Nevertheless, it is best to work from the premise that when material has been filed the best location for the position of reference material to assist retrieval is in the top right hand corner, and that a filing margin is required on the left hand side so that information is not obscured. If this premise is accepted, other components will be conditioned by these two factors. The dominant component is the communication of the necessary message, and all other information must be regarded as supportive.

The 'fields' for components of a form can be described as:

The **Head** which contains the name of the company, address, telephone number, etc and the title of the form, invoice or statement, etc.

Filing margin is required at a minimum of 25 mm (25.4 mm BS 1808). This requirement is often taken too literally, as a wider margin often helps the form to function more effectively and also allows a more readable line-length to be used in letters.

References will vary from document to document and, while it is not possible to give an absolute protocol, it is advisable that they appear in a sequence starting with that of dominant use, that is: customer's reference, supplier's reference, date and subject.

Instructions: This area will only be used in certain documents, such as orders or despatch notes, but it is nevertheless preferable to leave a field available wherever a systemised form design is carried out. The material used in this field would normally relate to delivery dates and addresses and the method of transit.

Foot of form is often used in complex form design to take required information which would otherwise encumber the head. Directors' names, company registration details and similar items may well occupy this position.

Communication area is the body of the form that will contain the message particular to that form.

It is common for transactional forms (invoice, acknowledgement of order, despatch note, etc) to be designed as a set, which will be typed simultaneously. Consequently,

the fields shown in 2 should be regarded as having to work for a complete set, although when the typist uses the complete set of forms, not all the information she types will necessarily appear on all the forms. (It will be omitted by varying the carbon areas, or obscured by other means.) Obscuration is commonly achieved by a close pattern of solid dots, and non-printing on the typewriter by having forms precarbonised so that only required areas print. It must be emphasised that the fields indicated are conditioned by the assumed logical use of a window envelope and, except where conditioned by standards, they are general in area rather than specific in size.

Columns and rules will be used on many forms and it is essential that their positioning should relate to the means of entering information, whether by manuscript or typewriter, and that a realistic assessment is made of the words or numbers that are to be entered. It is for example pointless to allow for six digits to be entered when only four would ever be used.

Paper sizes

Even though information on paper sizes is freely available elsewhere, it seems worthwhile including it here as many of the references in this article rely heavily on the use of ISO paper sizes.

For stationery uses it is almost inevitable that the designer will use International Paper Sizes, simply because they are used by the majority of organisations and will therefore fit into the filing systems of recipient organisations.

The ISO paper sizes are recommended by both the International Standards Organisation and the British Standards Institution.

The International Paper Sizes are based on the A series. The base size A0 is one square metre, conformed in the proportion of 1: square root of 2, giving the numerical proportions 1:1.414. This proportion has, uniquely, the practical advantage that it produces exactly the same proportion when it is halved on its longest side.

The subsidiary sheet series B is derived by taking the dimension (rather than the square) of a metre for the shortest side and conforming the longest side to 1: square root of 2.

The sheet series C takes the 1000 mm of the short side of B0 multiplied by the long side of A0 (1189 mm) to be the area of C0. This is then conformed by the proportions 1: square root of 2 to become 917 x 1297 mm.

Just as the metre is based on an inaccurate measurement so the A, B and C series are only approximations to the principle used. This is due to the insistence on using the millimetre as the smallest unit.

This approximation occurs as:

Series and size	actual area	theoretical area
A0 1189 x 841 mm	999,949 sq mm	1,000,000 sq mm
B0 1414 x 1000 mm	1,414,000 sq mm	1,414,213 sq mm
C0 1297 x 917 mm	1,189,349 sq mm	1,189,000 sq mm

The intended uses for the International Paper Sizes are:

The A sizes should be used for all items of stationery, publicity and reference literature, catalogues, magazines, books and other items of print. (However, the suggestion that these sizes should be used ad hoc for magazines and books is a matter for debate)

The B sizes should provide 'special' envelope sizes to accommodate C envelope sizes (for 'reply' envelopes, etc) sizes for large charts, maps, folders, posters and other display material.

The C series should give a range of sizes for envelopes to enclose the normally used A size.

For the history of the International Paper Sizes it seems best to quote the note from *Typographic Norms* by Anthony Froshaug:

'In 1796 Georg Christoph Lichtenberg, the German satirical writer and physicist, proposed standard paper formats based on the golden section. Two years later the French government, the Directory prescribed standardisation of official sizes of paper (Law of 13 Brumaire, year vii/4 November 1798). The proposal was based on the proportion of 1:1.41, the largest size to measure one square metre. Wilhelm Ostwald proposed a 'world-format' for printed matter in 1911 based on the same proportion, but generated from a size measuring 10 x 14.1 mm (Borsenblatt f.d.dt. Buchbandel, 1911, 243, p.12330 et seq). In 1917 the German Standards organisation set up a working party, which mainly through the efforts of Dr W Porstmann, proposed the A, B and C series of sizes, similar to the 120 year old French proposal. These were codified in din 476 in 1922. The German Standard was accepted by the International Standards Organisation in 1958.

The iso recommendations were incorporated into British Standard 4000 in 1968 subsequent to bs 3176 in 1959'.

International paper sizes (trimmed)

	A series	B series	C series
0	1189 x 841	1414 x 1000	1296 x 917
1	841 x 594	1000 x 707	917 x 648
2	594 x 420	707 x 500	648 x 458
3	420 x 297	500 x 353	458 x 324
4	297 x 210	353 x 250	324 x 229
5	210 x 148	250 x 176	229 x 162
6	148 x 105	176 x 125	162 x 114
7	105 x 74	125 x 88	114 x 81
8	74 x 52	88 x 62	81 x 57
9	52 x 37	62 x 44	
10	37 x 26	44 x 31	

Traditional English paper sizes for writing and ledger papers are still used by some of the more recondite professions such as medicine and the law, but most designers would, nevertheless, discourage their use.

Envelopes

An envelope serves to protect a communication and maintain its confidentiality.

It is usually best to obtain envelopes from stock as the minimum order for special makings is 10,000 and delivery period about twelve weeks.

British practice in giving measurements has normally been to give the vertical dimension first and the horizontal dimension second, and in envelopes the practice has been (and generally still is) to give the longest dimension first, whereas the ISO standard is to give the shortest dimension first. It is probably advisable to follow the English procedure for the time being, but to be aware of the International procedure.

Basic styles for envelopes are:

Banker: Opening and flap are formed on the longest dimension of the envelope.

Wallet: Flap is of the same depth throughout the greater part of its length, and the opening and flap are formed on the longest side of the envelope.

Pocket: Opening and flap are formed on the shortest side of the envelope.

Window or **Aperture Banker:** Wallet and pocket envelopes are all available in window or aperture versions. There are, however, problems with aperture envelopes in that they are not within the Post Office Preferred range and may at a later date attract a heavier rate of postage. The methods of gumming are listed as:

Edge or **shape** gumming: In this style the gum follows the contour of the flap.

Gummed across flap: The adhesive is spread across the flap, parallel to the opening.

Latex gumming: One or two bars of adhesive are placed on the flap and on the body of the envelope so that the envelope flap adheres by pressure.

Window envelopes: Regarded by many designers and organisation and methods officers as the optimum envelope form, because the extra cost of the window is greatly outweighed by the cost of a typist finding a plain envelope, inserting it into a typewriter, and typing the address. There is the further advantage that the address is typed once only, on the letter, and this is the address that the postman sees. Consequently there is no danger of the letter being put in the wrong envelope and sent to the wrong person.

British Standard recommendations for window envelopes seem to be rather inadequate, giving a window size of 39 x 93 mm for DL and 37 x 90 mm for C6. It is therefore suggested that designers should follow the Deutsche Industrie Normen 680 as far as possible. Most English manufacturers of envelopes approximate surprisingly close to the dimensions given in DIN 680.

Post Office regulations and recommendations for envelopes

The Post Office requirements fall into two distinct categories, prohibitions and preferences. Prohibitions are:

Colour Cards or envelopes should be white. However, there is no objection to 'colours (other than red) provided the shades are not glaring, vivid, dazzling in effect, or too dark; and provided that the dyes used do not contain phosphorescent substances. The ink used for the address must be sharp in contrast to the colour of the paper and

the background to the address should be of one colour only.'

A **window envelope** must have the panel parallel to the envelope edge. The panel located minimally 44 mm from the top edge of the envelope and 15 mm from the left, right and base edges of the envelope. 'The panel must not be bordered by a coloured panel or frame'. 'No writing or printing other than the address may be displayed through the panel and the address must appear... so as to be read easily'. 'The enclosures must be folded in such a way as to ensure that they do not move about in the envelope and thus cause the address to be hidden'.

Aperture envelopes must not have a cut out panel larger than 32 mm by 95 mm and must also accord with the requirements for window envelopes.

Transparent envelopes are prohibited.

Trap packets: To avoid entrapping smaller postal packets during delivery, envelopes should not be more than 114 mm deep and the unsealed opening no longer than 165 mm. Where trap packets are over 114 mm in depth the opening should not exceed 120 mm.

The Post Office Guide gives exceptions to these prohibitions when over 2000 identical packages are posted in bulk.

'POP' Post Office Preferred range

The Post Office has had the right to charge an increased rate for postal packets or cards which fall outside the POP range. The Post Office has not yet enforced this right, but it is generally felt that most business stationery should fall within this range.

Typewriting and style

The majority of business stationery is written on with a typewriter, consequently the base measurement unit on any form will be that of one space, digit or numeral of the typewriter which is to be used to enter the required information on the form. When a variable pitch machine, such as the IBM Selectric, is used the base measurement will be the tabulation interval, and tabs must be set and used (rather than relying on space bar intervals) to position the impression point at the correct information point on the form.

However, the most common space increments are either one tenth or one twelfth of an imperial inch.

The equipment to be used for entering information should always be thoroughly checked before the design of a stationery range is begun, to determine size and suitability. Typewriting style should be as much the 'style of the house' as the typographic conventions used in the pre-printed information on forms, reports and publicity of the organisation concerned. Unfortunately many typists are still trained in an archaic style which used a plethora of punctuation, differential spacing after commas, colons and full points together with huge indents and complex indentation systems.

It is necessary for the designer to produce a style that not only takes into account the capabilities and limitations of the typewriter but also is capable of being introduced into the organisation with full acceptance. Over complicated styles normally meet with strong operator resistance and consequently become gradually bastardised and eventually ignored altogether.

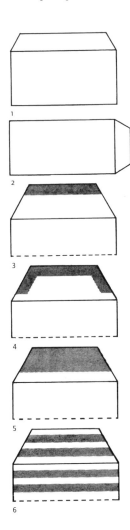

1 Banker envelope

2 Pocket envelope

3 Edge gumming

4 Shape gumming

5 Gummed across flap

6 Latex gumming

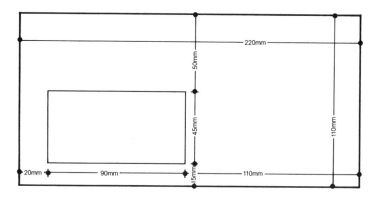

The best standard for window envelopes would seem to be that shown above, which accords with DIN 680.

An asymmetric layout works effectively with a typewriter and this immediately suggests that the norms of modern typographical detailing should be used. A minimum of punctuation in styles, titles and abbreviations should be used. It is preferable to use a ranged-left setting (since the typewriter is automatically non-justifying) and line spacing rather than paragraph indention.

Continuous stationery

Continuous stationery is normally purpose-made by a particular supplier to suit the needs and the systems of particular clients. Therefore any work involving the use of these forms requires close liaison with the client and the stationery manufacturer. The following definitions and diagrams have been adapted from BS 1808, Part 2, 1967, to give a background as to the types of continuous stationery available. The types of stationery shown relate to those that would be used on normal business machines. It must generally have specific requirements as to limits, tolerances and paper weights, and should be dealt with by the designer quite separately.

Continuous stationery is used where sets of forms are to be typed with the same impression. There are four basic ways of providing copies:

Carbon paper fixed to the continuous form feed mechanism allows the forms to travel continuously while the carbons, being anchored, are used and re-used.

Continuous carbon paper is a lightweight, one-time-only paper, generally of a much lighter paper weight than traditional carbon paper, and therefore giving better reproduction. This is interleaved continuously through the stationery and disposed of after use.

Carbon backed: The carbon is printed on the reverse of one form to allow the information required to be printed on the following form. This method is especially useful where it is desirable that some of the information appearing on one form of the set should not appear on another form.

No carbon required (NCR): Here the paper of the form is itself impregnated with a carbon preparation so that the form itself acts as the carbon for the subsequent copy. The most popular forms of continuous stationery are 'interleaved' and 'fanfold'.

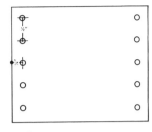

1

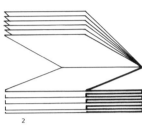

2

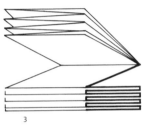

3

Interfold stationery: Continuous lengths of forms interleaved in sets are folded concertina fashion to a common depth. They are perforated at the base of each form to enable the typist or billing operator to remove each set as it is completed.

Fanfold stationery: The sheet is folded both horizontally and vertically in a concertina fashion. Each fold is perforated to enable separation of copies as each form is completed by the typist.

Both the foregoing types of stationery are available with or without sprocket holes. The sprocket holes for accounting machine systems are required to be 12.7 mm from centre to centre of adjacent holes and 6.3 mm from the vertical edge of the paper, and the sprocket hole itself should be 4 mm in diameter.

Post Office requirements (other than those appearing in the section on envelopes). The Post Office Guide is an essential reference for every office that uses the postal system. It contains full information on all Post Office services, prohibitions and charges and consequently in this section only information of particular importance to designer is given.

Sizes and weights for posting: The maximum sizes for letters are 610 mm long, 460 mm wide, 460 mm deep. In a roll, the length plus twice the diameter must not be greater than 1,040 mm, and the greatest dimension must not exceed 900 mm. The minimum size is 100 mm long, 70 mm wide. There is a weight limit of 750 g for second class letters but no weight limit for first class letters.

Preferred method of addressing: The Post Office now requires that the post town, that is the area postal description, be written in capitals and that the postcode be given on a separate line. Shown below left, are two examples from the Post Office Guide.

1 Sprocket holes for continuous stationery should be as the above dimensions.

2 Interfold stationery

3 Fanfold stationery

(below) Preferred method of addressing.

```
Universal Compendiums Limited
123 Great Central Street
LONDON
W1N 9UZ
```

```
Universal Compendiums Limited
Middle Trading Estate
Middle
NORWICH
Norfolk
NO19 2SZ
```

1977 **A house-style for the seventies** Shona Burns
The guidelines described here were used for *TypoGraphic* number 10 and for a number of following issues.

What is the purpose of a house-style? One of its functions is to achieve unity of purpose among a publisher's editorial and design staff, so that copy published by that house is uniform in spelling, punctuation and typographic style. It might be thought that this is the sole purpose of a house-style, but a glance at the illustration below left will disprove this idea.

Nobody would be very happy with that sort of thing today: the twentieth century eye has (as far as the printed page is concerned) quite different expectations from the mid-nineteenth century one.

So a house-style will not only aim to achieve editorial consistency, but will also impose its own particular visual style on the printed page. That style might be (or incline towards being) either florid (heavily capitalised, hyphenated and punctuated) or simplified (the minimum of capitalisation, hyphenation and punctuation consistent with good sense). To achieve the latter: copy that is literate, uniform, and with the fewest possible distractions for the reader involves being alert to what is best and most acceptable to the eye in current practice. Way-out avant-gardism is as distracting as archaism. A good house-style is anonymous,– and, above all, consistent.

A page from the *Diary of Lady Willoughby*, set in Caslon and printed by Charles Whittingham at the Chiswick Press in 1844.

For this reason, a good house-style must move with the times, and must be constantly revised and updated as current fashion changes. Many publishers rely on one of the several published guides to style (notably Hart's *Rules for Compositors and Readers at the University Press Oxford*) but these published guides can be revised only infrequently. Hart's *Rules,* for instance, was last revised in 1967 and in any case, being the style of a scholarly publishing house, it tends to be more conservative than current journalistic practice. Many magazine publishers, and those concerned with ephemeral material such as catalogues and publicity matter, prefer a style that is more of the moment than that embodied in Hart's *Rules.*

There is another disadvantage inherent in the published guides to style. Apart from Hart's *Rules,* which does say definitively 'Do this, not that', published guides have an unhelpful tendency to present the options and allow the reader to make his own decision. This leaves the poor copy-editor exactly where he was – confused. He does not need options (there are far too many of them already). He needs rulings. It is the

Use the following spellings:
inquire
judgment
acknowledgment
medieval
encyclopedia
centred
connection
dispatch
reflection
premiss (proposition)
all right
already

Distinguish between:
dependent (adj.)
dependant (noun)
forbear (abstain from)
forebear (ancestor)
stationary (immobile)
stationery (writing paper)
forgo (go without)
forego (go before)
affect (verb: have an influence on)
effect (verb: have as a result)

No full point in sets of initials:
STD
HMSO
ie
eg
mph
am
pm
mm
cm

No full point after contractions:
Mr
Mrs
Dr
St
Ltd
ft
yd
edn

No full point for:
lb
oz
But use full point for:
etc.
vis.
Co.
in. (inches)
no. (number)
ed.

1 Hesketh Pearson, *The Smith of Smiths*, Hamish Hamilton, 1934.

job of a house-style to provide those rulings.

Because drawing up a house-style is such an enormous task, however, it is as well to use one of the published styles as a base. Then all that is necessary is to codify the areas of disagreement with it, and make definitive rules where necessary. The following checklist defines the main areas which need to be examined, and the decisions that have been made to arrive at the *TypoGraphic* house-style. By substituting his own decisions, any publisher could arrive at an outline of his own house-style. This simple guide, backed by one of the published guides, would greatly reduce the areas of uncertainty and inconsistency.

Spelling

Use a dictionary. I can not recommend the use of a good dictionary too highly, but to judge by current standards of spelling in published material, dictionaries appear to be going out of fashion.

Unfortunately, using a dictionary is only the beginning of the matter, since the English language offers many alternative spellings, all equally correct. To avoid pages littered with variant spellings it is necessary to decide which forms are going to be used. One way out is to use *Collins' Authors' and Printers' Dictionary*, which offers one definitive spelling in place of alternatives, but if you decide to rely solely on *Collins*, you need to be sure that you will like what you get. For instance, *Collins* offers -ize endings (for words such as organize, realize, etc, which can equally well be spelt -ise). *TypoGraphic* prefers -ise endings, and this choice also rids one of the problem of remembering which words must in any case be spelt -ise (televise, advertise, supervise and plenty more must be spelt -ise for etymological reasons explained in Hart's *Rules*).

Preferred spellings of the most frequently occurring words likely to give rise to inconsistencies need to be listed separately on the style sheet.

It is also worth setting out on the style sheet common words with different spellings having different applications – another fertile field of confusion.

Punctuation

Few things irritate the sensitive eye more than full points peppered all over the page, producing a spotted dick effect. The full point is unecessarily used in between sets of initials (S.T.D.), after contractions (Mr., Mrs., Dr., Ltd.) and among lower case initials (i.e., e.g., m.p.h., a.m, p.m), not to mention other abbreviations (mm., cm., ft, yd.) These are at the end of a sentence and after most abbreviations. (Abbreviations do not include the last letter of the whole word – contractions do.)

Quotation marks should be used consistently. Either single quotes can be used, reserving double quotes for 'quotes within quotes':

Someone asked (Sydney Smith) whether a certain bishop was going to get married. 'Perhaps he may,' was the answer; 'yet how can a bishop marry? How can he flirt? The most he can say is, "I will see you in the vestry after service."' [1]

or double quotes can be used for the primary quotation throughout, and single quotes for the secondary one.

Commas need to be used sparingly, and in pairs where they mark out a phrase in parenthesis: 'I behaved through most of the war with gallantry tinged, I suspect, by a strong urge to show off.' (Noel Coward) [2]

For anyone who can face reading seven pages on the use of the comma, Herbert Rees has some excellent things to say on its essential and inessential uses in his *Rules of Printed English*; and in *Mind the Stop* G V Carey devotes twenty-five pages to the comma – but this is probably purely for punctuation addicts.

Capitalisation

Amateur copy, particularly that originating from committee secretaries, tends to come lavishly decorated with initial caps. Honorary Chairmen, Presidents, Secretaries and Treasurers, and even Committee Members, dearly love to be dignified by upper case, possibly to compensate for the lack of financial reward. But in the interests of uncluttered copy their ranks must be decimated. Every initial cap should be asked 'Are you really necessary?' If the prime minister can do without this sort of meretricious ego boosting, so can lesser men.

Even Collins seems somewhat overdisposed towards initial caps. He advocates, for instance, Government, Prime Minister, the Press, Parliament, the State. For this reason, it is as well to define rather carefully what capitalisation you are going to go in for, as relying on Collins may produce more capitalisation than you want.

Apart from pandering to the self-importance of the incumbent of an office (what is to be done about the Vicar, the Minister, the Queen?), initial capitalisation can serve a valid purpose in differentiating fine shades of meaning.

Names of offices can be capitalised when used before the incumbent's name.

Names of political parties can be a problem. It is probably safest to stick to initial caps if only because this will serve to distinguish them, one hopes, from toddlers' tea parties.

Proprietors insist on trade names being capitalised.

Hyphenation

Hyphenation has caused me more headaches than any other editorial detail. Even Fowler, in his *Modern English Usage*, says 'No attempt will be made here to describe modern English usage in the matter of hyphens; its infinite variety defies description.'

The uncertainty engendered by this 'infinite variety' is compounded by the liberal-mindedness of some publishers who, rather than make definitive rulings on commonly used forms, generously leave the copy-editor to make his own decisions for each text. I quote from a leading publisher's *'Notes to Proof-readers'*:

When there are a number of possible forms of a word (for example, halfway, half-way and half way are all used commonly), change them only where different forms are used in the same book…

In this one instance alone the lack of a clear ruling has, over the years, driven me halfway round the bend.

It is advisable to make a list, once and for all, of the forms to be used for half-way, good-bye, goodnight, etc., and any other hyphenated or unhyphenated words that are

2 Quoted in Sheridan Morley,
A Talent to Amuse,
William Heinemann, 1969

Differentiate between:
the church (building)
the Church (institution)
the press (wine or printing)
the Press (Fleet Street)
the house (residence)
the House (of Commons)

Prime Minister James Callaghan
but
James Callaghan, the prime minister
Queen Elizabeth
but Elizabeth, the queen
Liberal Party
Labour Party
Communist Party
and the Party

Monotype
Smash

likely to crop up time and again in your own field.

On the whole one can, in the words of Sir Winston Churchill, 'regard the hyphen as a blemish to be avoided wherever possible'. It can be eliminated either by allowing the two words to stand separately (motor car) or, as is more usual in current practice, by running them together (motorcar).

Prefixes can frequently dispense with the hyphen.

But care must be taken to avoid ambiguous conjunctions. Cooperation may be fine, but take the hyphen out of co-op and you finish up with a hen-run.

Omitting the hyphen from words such as re-adjust and re-educate may lead the unwary reader to grapple with some unfamiliar words pronounced 'reed-just' and 'reed-ucate'. Words that give rise to this kind of confusion need to retain the hyphen.

It is worth noting, too, that the hyphen (or contiguity) can be used to distinguish a composite adjective from a noun plus adjective.

Italics

In the eighteenth century it was a fairly common practice to italicise all proper names. This is exhausting for the twentieth century eye, and in the same way the over use of italics for emphasis (itself a sign of bad writing) rapidly becomes counter-productive as the eye, and reader, wearies.

Italics are still commonly used for the names of books, journals, films, plays, paintings and ships.

If this list is adopted, it is also as well to get clear what will not be italicised. Names of articles in journals, pubs and restaurants are more usually set roman in quotes.

What is to be done about radio and television programmes? As one has not yet been mentioned in *TypoGraphic,* a decision has not yet had to be made.

Italics are normally used for foreign words and phrases not yet assimilated into the English language. Hart's *Rules* gives a long list of these but *TypoGraphic* feels that many of these are now so familiar that they should be promoted to roman.

Numerals

Numerals are nasty. They are a disruptive element, breaking up the unity of the page and introducing another code which is utterly different from the roman alphabet code. As far as possible, numerals should be suppressed. The same goes for other disturbing elements such as the ampersand, the % sign and other primitive marks which are unfit companions for the dignified characters of the roman alphabet.

Numbers above 1000 do not need a comma. Above 10 000 a space can be used instead of a comma.

Other decisions intended to make numerals as painless as possible are listed left. Ugly conjunctions such as 4th, 22nd are to be avoided (although in references and bibliographies the forms 2nd edn, 18th edn, etc., are inescapable). In dates, the numeral can stand alone, and in other instances the word can be spelt out in full.

No hyphen in:
halfway
goodbye
goodnight
typesetting
filmsetting
intercharacter
underdeveloped
subsection
interrelate
predispose

cooperation *but* co-op

Keep the hyphen in:
re-adjust
re-educate
re-enter

Distinguish between:
commonsense (adjective)
common sense (adjective plus noun)

Use italics for names of:
books
journals
book-length poems
films
plays
paintings
ships

Set roman in quotes names of:
articles in journals
chapter titles
short poems
pubs
restaurants
hotels

Set in roman:
ad hoc
a priori
coup d'etat
en route
fait accompli
in situ
laissez-faire
nom de plume
pro forma
raison d'être
status quo
vis-à-vis

Numbers: spell out all numbers
between one and ninety-nine.
except for:
weights
measurements
percentages

Set:
2000
20 000

Set:
18 per cent
£24 millon
28 June 1977
fourth not 4th
twenty-second not 22nd
eighteenth century

Conclusion

This article has not set out to be a comprehensive guide to editorial house-style. Rather it has aimed to alert readers to the multitude of editorial and typographical decisions that must be made to arrive at a style that is both literate and consistent, and at the same time produces on the page a visual style that reflects the character of the relevant journal or publishing house. This is an area in which typographers can well bring their influence to bear on editorial staff, who often have little or no understanding of how their editorial decisions will affect the look of the printed page.

References:
Hart, Horace, *Rules for Compositors*
and Readers at the University Press
Oxford, 37th edn,
Oxford University Press,1967.

The Concise Oxford Dictionary
of Current English, 6th edn,
Oxford University Press, 1976.

Collins, F H, *Authors' and Printers'*
Dictionary, 11th edn,
Oxford University Press, 1973.

Rees, H, *Rules of Printed English*,
Darton Longman and Todd, 1970.

Carey, G V, *Mind the Stop*, revised edn,
Cambridge University Press, 1958.

Fowler, H W, *Modern English Usage*,
2nd edn, Oxford University Press, 1965.

Further reading:
Butcher, J, *Copy-editing:*
The Cambridge Handbook,
Cambridge University Press, 1975.

BS5261 *Copy preparation and proof*
correction (Part 1: 1975: *Preparation*
of typescript copy for printing),
British Standards Institution, 1975.

1978 **Is the quality of typeface design deteriorating?** Günter Lange

It is often said that phototypesetting has brought about a decline in typographic standards compared with hot metal setting. This widespread opinion apparently needs sorting out.

Gutenberg, and likewise all the other early printers, naturally followed the written example of the calligraphers and tried to copy them as closely as possible. Which means to say they copied them using their own technique. For the printed book, they not only adapted the type-design for casting metal type but also the layout of complete pages with initials and borders. At first, only the text was printed, the sheets then being passed on to the illustrator for adding initials and illustrations.

Objective appraisal of technical conditions and the interaction between printing surfaces and type shows that early printing never got anywhere near the sharpness and quality of written letters. Casting the characters, inking, pressure when printing on rough paper were bound to result in optical deformation of the cut image. The rectangular limitations of the body brought about restrictions of letter-shapes. That alone made it impossible to compare it with handwritten books.

It is remarkable that typefaces from the 15th century were set much closer, than those cut after 1500. Looking at early printed works of the 15th century it becomes obvious that the design of the typefaces closely followed the rhythm and appearance of calligraphic handwriting. The writer, when writing fast, will always begin and end the pen strokes with a thin hairline thus combining one letter with the following one to form logotypes, ligatures, in short – word images. This is what makes up the attraction of written as opposed to typeset letters. The former combines characters with less space between them while the latter isolates them like building bricks with, of course, wider gaps between them.

The appearance of handwritten type varies from character to character. Not one letter is strictly congruent with another, just like leaves on a tree. The shapes are heavily influenced by the personality of the writer. Each script has its own psychology and physiognomy of expression and this also varies within the different periods of work. There were only a few different designs and sizes.

The construction of the series of typefaces in the present sense was unknown in the early days of letterpress printing. One was confined to a few different typefaces which

Gutenberg's characters had variants to more closely resemble manuscript. Compare the different widths of alternative characters and logotypes.

were only cut in the most common sizes. It wasn't until the beginning of the 19th century that typefaces became available in carefully graded cuts and weights and numerous sizes, the small to medium sizes in metal and the large sizes in wood.

For ornaments, one used borders, flowers, and initials made of the same material. For the harder wear and tear by bookbinders, this was later complemented by casting brass type, brass rule, and brass ornaments. The printer's material was three dimensional and complete formes were virtually put together with single elements.

Compared to this, phototypesetting shows the following main differences: all typefaces are available on founts in all sizes; all have the same baseline and are thus compatible with others. The construction of elements for the printing forme is two-dimensional. The early scribes worked under the same basic conditions. In this context it is of no importance to us whether the image is created from a negative or whether the letter-shapes are formed by linear scanning using cathode ray tubes or lasers.

As to the setting width – that is, the distance of one letter from another – and the possibility of using initials and swash characters, phototypesetting today offers almost the same supply of different shapes available to the scribe of books. Now executed with prefabricated photographic elements, then individually written by hand.

The limitations in adapting old hand-cut typefaces to hot metal line composition machines are widely known. The design compromises, in accommodating regular, italic and medium characters onto the same widths, happened at the expense of quality, especially as far as the italic weights were concerned. The character shapes of separate sizes in founders' type are quite different as each size is individually cut. Compare recent designs such as *Palatino* or *Sabon* in the text sizes on line-casting machines and the same typefaces in the larger sizes of founders' type. Printers have learned to live with these limitations which limit quality for the sensitive expert.

Bodoni cut exactly 42,148 matrices, he designed and printed more than one thousand titles in his workshop in Parma. In his own words he worked like a 'galley slave' to realise his ideals. It seems only right to call him the king of printers and die-cutters.

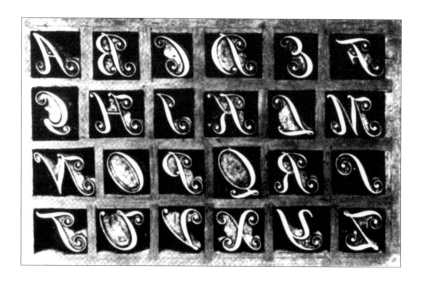

A notable exception deserving a special mention is Monotype which unfortunately never achieved the same importance in Germany as it did in the rest of the world over. There were only a few large companies using this system whereas in Britain, the USA and the English-speaking world, in Scandinavia, Holland, Switzerland, and even in Czechoslovakia firms with less than fifty employees successfully use mono-casting.

One can not praise enough the leading rôle played by English type design from the first third of the nineteenth century until the beginning of the twentieth century. Whatever was of value in Western typography was reflected in the ranges of English and American typefoundries. This does not, however, mean that one ought to forget the great part played by German typefounders during the last one hundred years. Apart from a few adaptations of Anglo-American styles the biggest part of their range was dominated by the influence of the individual 'lettering artist' and reflected in numerous artistic and private press typefaces. But these, too, were initiated by the examples of Englishmen like Morris, Cobden-Sanderson, Edward Johnston and Stanley Morison.

(below left) Bodoni title page using the italic shown in the preceding illustration.

(middle) Bodoni's sketch for a title page giving exact setting instructions. Note the classic proportions of the type area and margins.

(right) There are more than a dozen versions of *Bodoni* in founders' and machine-setting typefaces. Every manufacturer chose what seemed to him the best size from a printed specimen. The version shown here is almost unknown, but shows the close setting which corresponds to today's usage in photosetting.

With varying priorities, these efforts were based on the written letter. Its typical shape experienced significant changes only through the work of the engravers, much more through the commercial lithographers and, in more recent times, through painters and architects.

The styling element in Art Nouveau was the brush, in Expressionism it was the woodcut, and the Constructivists used set square and compass.

The standards set in the States are accepted in all Western countries, even copied in detail, as the language of advertising is English, verbally and visually. It seems almost inevitable that ITC (International Typeface Corporation) established itself in New York; an enterprise which sees its main function in creating a steady flow of alphabets for phototypesetting. This principle has proved to be right since ITC started in 1970. Every

important typeface manufacturer has an ITC licence.

The application of these new, typically American characters, however, needs getting used to, and needs a fresh typographic thinking. It seems consistent for ITC to popularise their typefaces worldwide by displaying a variety of well designed examples in their magazine U&LC.

It is remarkable how this proves the point made by international experts that tradition's highest values can be integrated after careful study. The conditions are there. Technology has to leave enough room for aesthetics and the sensitive type designer will have to adjust to technical requirements in order to achieve the finest results in type design and typesetting. The gaps in the level of setting standards are enormous between different manufacturers and need to be examined carefully.

It would therefore be wrong to simply blame phototypesetting for reducing the quality of setting. In the past few years, even months, far reaching changes and

When adapting a metal face, every manufacturer starts with a proof on baryta paper. Here are 10 and 24 point Monotype *Plantin*. The vertical lines show the edge of the body.

Barytabzug 10p und 24p

ABCDEFGHIJKLMNOPQR
STUVWXYZÆŒ
abcdefghijklmnopqrstuvwxyzæœ
1234567890 ffifflfiffl () !? ;&£''.,:-

berthold
ototype

refinements have been brought about by new software. Apart from that, however, there are not enough good machine operators and the way things look, there will be even fewer in future. For that reason we need to systematically improve typographic knowledge in order to once again get first-class setting. Much of this can be programmed and is being programmed.

Good typography always takes subtle expertise in the choice of typefaces and in production. Considerable progress has been made. In the USA at present, still only on a small scale, but increasingly, the standards of expert typesetting are set by Europe's best typographers in Switzerland, Sweden and last, but not least, Britain. The demand for higher standards in setting is growing within advertising agencies and publishers in Germany.

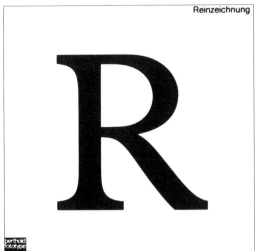

(above) The enlargement of the 24 and 10 point size to 120 mm as the basis for the finished artwork. The text size is bolder and wider, the large size much narrower and lighter.

(above right) The testword 'Hamburg'. Top line is ten point metal. Middle line is twenty-four point metal. Bottom line is the new type design. The weight, angles and the serifs of the new design are between the two above.

(right) The daggers and exaggerated points are not used now. In 1973, however, when this face was developed, film material and emulsions were'nt as sensitive as they are today.

1978 **Extracts from talks with Derek Birdsall on the subject of book design** Peter Rea

There (putting down this year's *Monty Python Book of Scripts*) is a book that's absolutely not designed. I think it has only one piece of typography in the conventional sense at all.

It had to be 'Pythonesque'. The Python characteristics in this book come from the fact that there are several scenes in there that they could not shoot – they ran out of money!

Really, it is an edited facsimile of the actual shooting script. The size is, in fact, a quarter-inch smaller. This book is seven and three-quarter inches by nine and three-quarter inches. It was the nearest we could get, economically, to the script's original size. It was printed on a big Mann Perfector and I just went to the press, and said what is the fattest book we can have for the money, given that we want this sort of thing in it, and what is the most economic page size. The Pythons agreed that it was better to have a smaller thick book than a bigger thin one. So the typewriting is slightly reduced from the original.

Almost all of my books are, in fact, square: where I've got a choice and where the books are illustrated, which almost all my books are, I've found it almost impossible to beat the square format. For illustrated books, and particularly catalogues with horizontal, vertical and perhaps circular illustrations, it seems to me the square is the most logical format, because you can have a horizontal illustration as equivalently large as you can have a vertical illustration. Any landscape format that suits mostly horizontal objects doesn't suit vertical ones and it doesn't help square or round ones.

There's another thing too… the impact of a double spread which is a double square is more dramatic than any other shape. You see, a landscape format when you open it out to get a double landscape shape, is still landscape. A portrait book which you open out to become landscape, whilst being dramatic (becoming landscape from portrait) is not as dramatically different as the square becoming, horizontal double its size.

In the A series, by definition, a double spread of an A4 book is precisely the same shape as the closed book.

The whole point of using square books is for dramatic effects. You're giving the biggest amount of impact, the biggest difference from the original format. A double square is totally different from a square. You don't expect it from a square book. You don't expect to get landscape and it's very dramatic. There have been times when, for

economic reasons, or preconceptions about the undesirability of square books, I have been dissuaded from using the square format. But there's no real rhyme or reason for that convention.

The square shape, I think, is good for books. To go to A size would create enormous problems. When you bind the back edge it really is uncomfortable, unless you have a narrow measure and a generous back margin.

A5 is not altogether uncommon, but A4 certainly isn't very common, though I think regrettably common in certain other kinds of books. But in general publishing, it never occurs to anybody to go between A5 and A4 because they don't use the A series anyway. An eleven and three-quarter inch high book is rather difficult to hold; it is not big enough to be an epic book, and not small enough to be comfortable in the hand to read. For poetry, on the other hand, there are conventional formats. The A5 size I find particularly suitable for poetry. [1]

In the early sixties, designers thought that A sizes were the answer to all the madnesses inherent in modern society. One of the plausible arguments was that it would be more economic for paper stockists to stock only these sizes, supplying them straight off the shelf.

If you required an odd size you had to pay a premium. I think I am right in saying that nowadays there is no difference. By bartering and taking discounts it will often work out cheaper to have a special making than to buy straight off the shelf. People do not realise that today the vast majority of paper is specially made. Since the paper boom of the seventies, paper manufacturers have virtually stopped stocking paper.

For any reasonably sized job, paper is specially ordered and it does not matter whether it is ordered to a standard or non-standard format, as it is paid for by the overall weight.

1 In poetry there are pentameters or rhythm which create short lines. This allows you space for the back margin, which you would normally lose with longer lines of text. There is room for the thumb automatically, and because poetry is generally short in depth it gives you space between the lines and room for a pause.

(below) *Art of the Arab World*, 248 mm x 248 mm. Catalogue of the exhibition of the same name. The large detail is a full size section of the base of the bucket. The bucket itself measured greater than the catalogue. This double-page spread also show the use of the four-column text-grid.

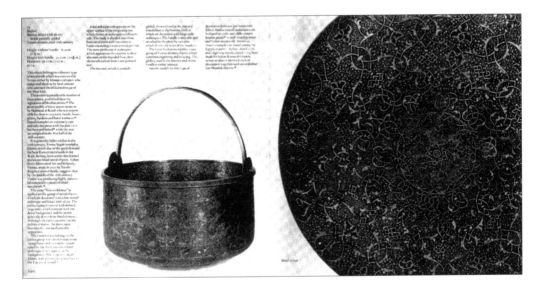

There are, of course, other parameters. It is extremely difficult to get a book bound if the fore-edge to back-edge is greater than 21 and a bit inches. There are only a very few case-binding machines which can cope. A couple of binderies in England and two or three on the Continent are capable of binding a larger size.

If you want to make a square book, it can not be larger than this fore to back capacity of the binder (ie, the overall double-spread width of the pages plus spine).

There has always been a monopoly on certain special bindings such as spiral binding. The spiral binding schedule was one of the parameters in producing calendars. (Derek Birdsall designed many of the early Pirelli calendars.) The critical path for the production of the calendar was always the bindery. Everyone has their calendar spiral bound and there are only one or two places where this can be done in England.

One thing I have become very vividly aware of recently is that designers cannot, and must not, work separately from the production team. It is, however, going to be a long time before it is possible to achieve this, particularly in publishing. Publishers are surrounded by huge production departments, and most books are handled by a designer who is almost invariably an outsider, and so hardly ever speaks to the printer.

(below) Art of the Arab World,
248mm x 248mm. Catalogue of
the exhibition of the same name.

(facing page) The Cambridge
Encyclopædia of Astronomy.
A same-size detail and the full page
including the 'abbreviations' from
which it is taken.

You cannot produce the best work other than by working first-hand. A common mis-conception is that you must give a complete and unambiguous job specification. Well, that's all very well in theory, but suppose the printer has a better idea than you. He has no way of getting in touch with you, and he may sense that you have designed that job to suit a set of circumstances which simply do not pertain in his plant. If he is very bright, he may guess that there is something you would rather have done, but thought he would be unable to do it, when he could. Again, what, in theory, could be done may be completely out of the question. So in practice, it is better to sit down (at an early stage of course), scribble down your ideas without any preconception about whether

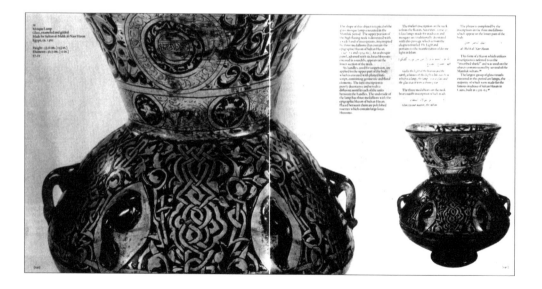

chemical elements

H	hydrogen
He	helium
Li	lithium
Be	beryllium
B	boron
C	carbon
N	nitrogen
O	oxygen
Ne	neon
Mg	magnesium
Si	silicon
S	sulphur
A	argon
Fe	iron

symbols

a	semi-major axis of ellipse
b	galactic longitude
c	speed of light
e	eccentricity of ellipse
G	gravitational constant
g	acceleration due to gravity
h	Planck's constant
i	angle of inclination
l	galactic latitude
m	mass
m_e	electron mass
m_p	proton mass
n	neutron
p	proton
PSR	pulsar
QSO	quasar
r	radius
t	time
v	velocity
γ	photon
ν	neutrino
☉	Sun
⊕	Earth
☾	Moon
☿	Mercury
♀	Venus
♆	Neptune
♅	Uranus
♂	Mars
♄	Saturn
♃	Jupiter
♇	Pluto
♈	First point of Aries
♎	Longitude of ascending node
☋	Longitude of descending node

you can or can not do it, and go to the printer with it.

Of course, in one sense I am preaching heresy, because I do also respect a healthy separation where you respect each other for your own function. Then you may well design something and give lengthy instructions to the printer for it to be carried out.

To give you an example of the way I work, I almost never write on colour proofs. I insist on speaking to the man and give him my general view on what might be put right or altered, but I never suggest what they should do to put it right; because (a) they might take it literally, and (b) if it is worse, I should be totally to blame.

Another thing I have learnt is never to specify paper. I say, all these sorts of paper are OK by me but *you* pick the one that is right for the job. I say I would like a shiny paper, or a medium matt paper, or a very matt paper. I never say I would like a blade-coated cartridge. I use common-sense terms.

Although the appearance of the paper, its opacity, colour and printability are important, they are not more important than whether the whole book is too heavy to hold in the hand, or too heavy for its binding or size.

I'd like to make a kind of summary – it's a paradox really.

It is that while one must have preconceptions about the design, the feel of things, and how things should look, and predilections for certain kinds of typeface and colour of printing, the biggest problem of all is to get one's priorities right in planning a job, and the rest should, given that one's got good text, good judgement and a good printer, take care of itself.

You can create the most enormous rod for your back by creating a grid, or even a paste-up, or even a sample spread, before you've started to think about how big the book is going to be, how thick it's going to be, and what price it's going to be in the end; or how easy or difficult it's going to be working with a given author, how flexible

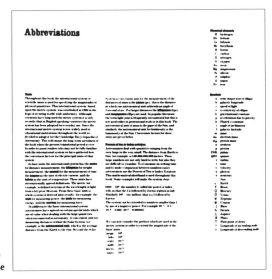

he is going to be, and whether you should adhere entirely to his text and choice of illustrations.

The author is usually quite willing to listen if there is sufficiently good reason. Listen for the possibility of his changing his mind. Any amount of difficulties can be created by a chapter that runs too long, yet you may have other difficulties within, such as tail ends hanging over the end of a section which is going to turn the corner. The best solution you can think of objectively is that the copy should be cut, rather than making all the other changes that would be necessary to make it fit. It is a big decision to even ask of the author.

The whole satisfaction with designing is to get better at pleasing yourself – to get better at developing your own taste so that your own taste is more demanding. I just don't agree with the philosophy that the solution has got to be self-evident. That would make it meaningless – a cliché.

What really matters is how *you* think it should be, and how good *you* are at getting it right and convincing others by your conviction and professionalism that it is right.

One of the most original things today is to produce work beautifully. Most people seem to have forgotten how to do it.

1978 **The typography of Wolfgang Weingart** Bernd Zürker

Weingart's typography can be called lively, free and unorthodox. He acknowledges Swiss typography as his starting point, and considers that his work is a logical continuation of it although he does not subscribe to any design dogma.

The key to Weingart's typography is the wide variety of syntax he uses. Typography for him is the successful combination of the creative idea, the typographic elements and the practical techniques employed. The range of typographic elements constitutes the syntax.

His aim is to enhance the semantic and persuasive effectiveness of the message. His typography may be relatively difficult to read, but this is counterbalanced by the fact that it is very enticing. His typography is not intended to be used for consumer advertising but for applications aimed at 'thinking people' and used for exhibition catalogues and so on.

Weingart defines the aims of typography as: 'enhancing the communication process;

Eight examples of possible treatments for a book jacket. The more elementary the brief, the more difficult it becomes to carry it out. Simple typographic exercises are necessary preparation for solving more complex problems.

adapting to changes in message and culture; and also expressing subjective patterns of thinking and designing based on artistic and personal qualities'.

This last point, which he himself acknowledges is subjective and provocative, seems to me to be a significant factor in his typography. As far as designing information material for 'thinking people' is concerned, this idea represents an innovation. The conscious use of subjective responses results in the wide variety of Weingart's syntax.

Is this kind of typography appropriate for our time? Typography needs to reflect the spirit of the times; the zeitgeist. Most people think they are in touch with the feeling of the times, but in fact no one individual can fully reflect the feeling of his time. Only the sum of all men's activities at one time would be a full representation of the zeitgeist. Since Weingart's typography is being created right now in order to discover new possibilities, I find it modern and relevant.

When designers try to make their work acceptable as objectively correct to as many people as possible, their work tends to look sterile. Some designs, labelled 'Swiss typography', certainly give that impression. This sort of objectivity could be called quantitative, since it aims at fast and easy consumption. Weingart's typography is the opposite. Conflicts and problems are evident in the design, and involvement is asked of the reader. This kind of typography, which makes the reader think, could be called 'open typography', meaning that it does not patronise the reader, but emancipates him. It is typical that open typography puts more emphasis on pictures than traditional typography does.

Creating characters: limiting factors include the availability of typefaces in the workshop and the student's own creative talent.

Weingart's typography explicitly asks the reader to take issue with it, although it would be wrong to see that as a purpose in itself; it serves the message and does not consider itself as more important than the message. But by not presenting the text as

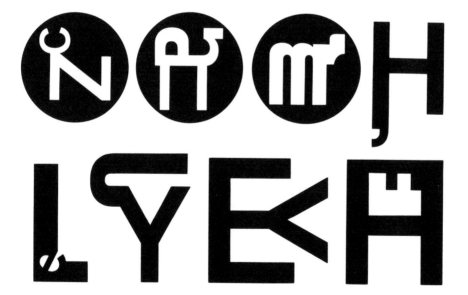

absolutely and objectively readable, it invites intensive discussion, which, in the long run, might make people more sensitive to typography.

On the other hand, incorporating subjective ideas runs the danger of isolating typography and turning it into a formal exercise. That is why Weingart stresses that typography also expresses subjective patterns of thinking and designing. Experiment is the base for his work, and this experimentation will certainly enrich all areas of typographic design.

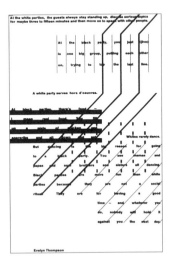

(right) Two interpretations of the same copy.

(below) Collage.

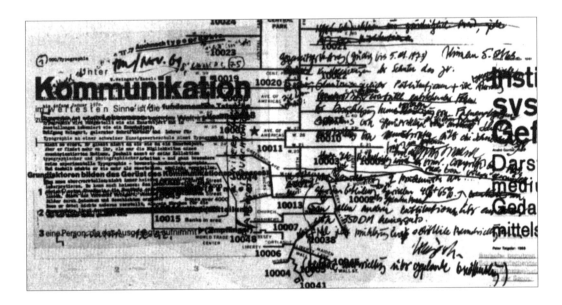

1978 **A process in typography** Daniel Friedman

Process is a system of operations or a series of changes or actions in the production of a result. It is an operation which really only begins with the recognition of a specific need. That need becomes the goal which must be fulfilled and each result in the sequence of events therefore becomes an expression of each part of the process which occurred beforehand.

The design process has three levels of significance. First, we are simply interested in the way things get done. In fact, we are often more fascinated by the steps taken toward some result than by the result itself.

Our second level of interest in process is in terms of the visual or formal methods which designers have in their repertoire to express process in the works they do. This is the essential basis for the exercises shown here. An expression of a process becomes the significant content of each visual message. It is really through these means that we come to the third level of interest: the way we digest the information in an image or message, ie, the process of receiving a communication. As designers we evaluate and organise information to facilitate, control and encourage the process by which it is

Making the process part of the message. A construction barricade has been made into a symbol of process. It is an interface between urban traffic and a New York City block undergoing a transformation. *Designed by Dan Friedman for Anspach Grossman Portugal Inc.*

Expressing process. Design is the study of fundamentals. It is a means of analysing the methods by which process can be expressed in the images we create. There are three visual structures available to express process: repetition, progression and opposition. *Student work by Randi Korn (State University of New York) and Peter Laundy and Tom Lennon (Yale University).*

consumed. The typographer, for example, manipulates positions, sizes, weights, spacing, etc and, if lucky, even the writing. Through this process of structuring, emphasising and de-emphasising, the way and sequence in which our audience receives a message is significantly influenced.

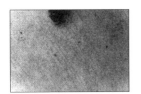

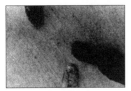

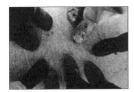

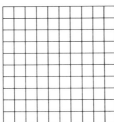

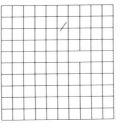

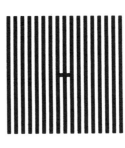

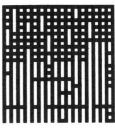

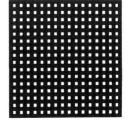

(left) **Observing process**. By documenting process as it occurs in nature and in our environment, we find a basis for all observation and abstraction. Cities are a particular fascination. They are essentially the crossroads of all forms of communication. The processes of destruction, repair, change, evolution, fitting, misfitting, transformation, permutation and combination are all generic to both basic design exercises and to city renewal, planning and organisation. *Photographs by Dan Friedman.*

(above and right) **Processing information.** Investigating various typographic permutations. They are not meant to be results, ready to be applied, but an expression of a process of perceptual learning. The purpose of these exercises is to play out, in sequence, a number of different design operations upon a given message. Changes in position, weight, size, spacing, grouping, etc, result in showing states of simplicity and complexity, the normal and the distorted, the static and the dynamic, and their subsequent effects on legibility and on originality. *Student work by Nancy Fleischer Hoffman (Kent State University).*

(below) **Visual metaphor.** A linear abstraction becomes a visual metaphor for the route of a bus. The letter D symbolises the D bus and its process of moving through a city. *Student design by Joe Moore (Yale University).*

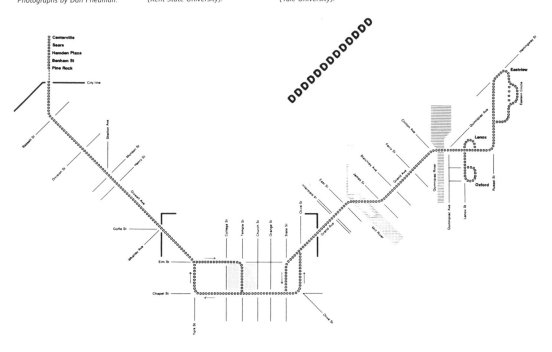

1983 **Where you are, where you've been and where you're going** Richard Dragun

At DRU we are familiar with the problems of transport design. In the 60s and 70s, much of our reputation was thanks to the work we did for British Rail and London Transport, cases which we are now hardly willing to show to clients, they are so over-exposed.

The British Rail corporate identity, launched in 1965, was fêted at the Design Council, and received perhaps more publicity than the nationalisation of the railway system had had 15 years earlier. This wouldn't happen today. Corporate identities, however good, are regrettably no longer national news, and the application of smart, co-ordinated design schemes to transport systems is commonplace.

Sir Misha Black used to like to say that the aesthetics of transport should be 'robust, assertive and vigorous'. With the exception perhaps of London Transport, which has a graphic style still very much based on the polite typography of Edward Johnston, and Washington DC (where discreet signing by Massimo Vignelli forms almost a counter-reaction to the conventions of transport graphics), most modern systems have followed Black's bold recommendations.

The whole approach to transport signing has in fact become so systematised that it has achieved an almost international look. A look, I must add, which most of our transport design clients seem to want.

Having concentrated our attention for so many years on UK transport, DRU's work in this field is now almost exclusively for foreign clients. We were design and architectural consultants for the Hong Kong Metro (first line completed in 1980) and we are currently working on two major transport projects in Baghdad and Taipei.

All three have involved corporate identity programmes and signing systems, and it is fair to say that having gone straight into the Hong Kong job, nursing our own preconceptions on how transport signing should work, we have learned more than a few things in the process.

There are certain basic requirements which a good transport signing system must meet. Primarily, it must convey information. It must express complex information simply and legibly. Signs must be visible at a distance, through crowds and sometimes at speed. Passengers must be able to find and understand information when they are rushing, and sometimes panicking. They need to be told where they are, where they have been, and where they are going. In addition, they need secondary information such as access for ticket holders, where the toilets are, which exit to take to emerge on the right side of the street, and where to pay excess fares.

With metro systems which are completely underground, signing soothes. It acts as the one reassurance that you have alighted at the right stop, are going in the right direction or have taken the right escalator. It is the only visual reference available, the unaccustomed passenger's only hope of finding his way back to daylight.

With bi-lingual systems, the difficulties in producing the perfect signing system are naturally increased. In Hong Kong and Baghdad, English is applied as a second language, for foreigners, and in both instances the primary language is in a non-Roman alphabet,

(facing page above) The symbol for British Rail, designed 20 years ago and still often cited as the best railway symbol in the world.

(facing page below) Concourse signing employing suspended canvas banners, giving a traditional local flavour to what could otherwise have been a sterile environment.

(below left) traditional style design incorporating 'Baghdad Metro' in a kufic script, running below the date palms of Baghdad.

(below middle) Calligraphic design using the word 'Metro'.

(below right) Design based upon traditional calligraphic shapes, incorporating the idea of a round walled city with four gateways.

creating graphic problems of emphasis, balance and space.

In Arabic, for example, several factors are helpful. A line of Arabic text can be relatively easily lengthened to fit a given measure. In addition, because Arabic reads from right to left, when placed alongside English it always appears first to the Arab reader, even though the English (reading left to right) appears first to us.

From a purely visual point of view, however, Arabic can be a headache, for when a word written in Arabic sits side by side with its English equivalent written in the same size Roman alphabet, the latter is far more powerful. And the only strong Arab face is a stylised Kufic script which even the average Arab, has difficulty reading.

With Chinese, difficulty is encountered when expressing abstract ideas. An idea expressed by a single word in English could take several Chinese characters to explain. With the names of locations, however, the reverse is often true. A place may be written with only one or two characters while its English counterpart is extremely lengthy.

In order to cope with Chinese, a vocabulary of about 3000 characters is needed. The complexity of the written language creates technical problems. For instance, dot-matrix Signs need about 3 times the number of dots required for Roman characters and could end up being so large that in the limited height of the average underground station, their use is effectually ruled out.

The use of the dot-matrix in Arabic presents a separate problem, for in the Arabic alphabet, the addition or subtraction of a dot can change not only the pronunciation but the meaning of a word.

Even the fundamental issue of assigning a generic name to the transport system itself is complex in both the Middle and the Far East. 'Metro' is an alien word to both the Arabic and Chinese languages and in neither case do other words exist which readily fit the bill. In Chinese, a number of characters are required to explain the concept, and in Arabic the word has to be created phonetically.

In non-Western cultures, symbols which we might accept as international are simply not understood. For example, the white slash across a red ground meaning 'no entry'. Directional arrows in Taiwan are not always drawn as in the West and in some parts of the Middle East are not understood at all. 'Man' and 'woman' symbols which in the West denote toilet, in other parts of the world simply denote a 'man' and 'woman'.

In the West, red means 'danger' – to the Chinese, however, it means 'good luck'. Common railway terms such as 'down line' and 'up line' mean nothing to passengers, so much so that the actual working terminology must be reinvented. Illiteracy, which can be all but disregarded in Western signing systems, because its incidence is comparatively low, must be taken into account in other parts of the world. In Mexico City, every underground station has its own colour and visual symbol, such as a town hall, to alert passengers as to where they are. In Hong Kong, strong station colours were used for another reason – some stations are so close together, the platforms are so long and trains are so fiercely packed with people that it is sometimes difficult to tell when you've left one station and arrived at another!

Even pictograms, which might seem to be the answer to conveying information clearly and simply, have limited applications in cities such as Baghdad and Taipei. Apart from

(top) Two initial proposals for the Taipei Metro.

(above) Hong Kong Metro; a 'happy sign' representing the linking of Hong Kong island and mainland Kowloon.

the fact that the confined space of the average Metro station does not allow the scale and high levels of positioning which pictograms demand (as in the case of airport terminals, for instance), the meanings of the symbols are quite often obscure to Chinese and Arab passengers. Very few pictograms are immediately obvious, even to conditioned Westerners. Even in the case of the most common symbols, we have usually been taught the meaning rather than left to figure it out.

All this, I suppose leads to the obvious conclusion that Far Eastern and Middle Eastern passengers will have to learn to use their systems in the same way that Westerners have. In designing identities for British Rail and also for the non-Western systems in Hong Kong, Baghdad and Taipei, we have tried to capture distinctive characteristics of movement and speed or to encapsulate local meaning – such as the four gates of the circular city of Baghdad. At the end of the day, however, the success of the graphic scheme symbols used will rest on their overall suitability and consistent application. Once learned they will be recognised. Western designers can make it easier for the passenger to understand his way around but in the case of strong cultural barriers, we can only, if you will forgive the pun, carry them most of the way home.

Many of the ideas we take for granted in the West can not be automatically transferred. The international 'lost and found' symbol would be quite meaningless to someone for whom an umbrella and gloves are not a part of his wardrobe even if he understood what the question mark meant. Our Western stylised symbolism is often confusing in the Middle and Far East.

1987 **Record sleeve design, the graphic trend-setter** Catherine McDermott

The day of the long-playing record as we know it faces impending obsolescence. In ten years' time, records will become merely archaic reminders of times past, and for generations of teenagers born after 1980, the 33 rpm will be relegated to the status of the curious collector's commodity. Only fast diminishing numbers of the faithful will guard the vinyl heritage and refuse, on point of principle, to buy the new laser beam technology and electronic sound systems. But this reality does nothing to alter the seminal impact the record-sleeve has had on British graphic design over the last ten years. In fact many consider that the record-sleeve has provided the single most important influence on new directions in contemporary typography, and during the 80s this mood of experimentation became mainstream. Widely imitated abroad and at home, sleeve design affected such diverse areas as supermarket packaging, High Street retailing, and bank advertising.

Recently, three exhibitions have taken the theme of the record-sleeve and explored its contribution to British design and culture. *Pop! British Music in the Eighties* will tour 35 countries over five years, using cheerful canary-yellow high-tech stands, built to stand the strain, from the Eva Jiricna-Kerr Partnership. The exhibition, designed by The Partners, was commissioned by the British Council to show off a rich and creative home-grown industry that last year earned Britain nearly £70 million in exports. Travelling to Iraq, Turkey, Zambia and further, it's a powerful statement of a new kind of British cultural imperialism in the form of music and its products.

The emergence of these ideas, and talent developed in the 60s when the pop culture boom created a more acute level of market awareness for the sleeve, with high points like the celebrated Peter Blake cover for the *Sgt Pepper album*. Last November, a show called *Interaction Art-Music-Art* at the Camden Arts Centre took up this theme of the record-sleeve and its relationship with traditional fine art methods.

Its underlying premise was the idea that the record-sleeve had provided one commercial area which allows a creative crossover of talent. In the music business, graphic designers can work with photographers, painters, sculptors and musicians on an equal footing. While *Disc Cover/The Art of the Record Sleeve*, which ran until January at the Edinburgh Arts Centre, celebrated the contemporary sleeve design as a vehicle for superb photography, graphic effects and typography. Lesley Woodbridge, who organised

the Edinburgh exhibition used the work of the seminal Jamie Reid as a starting point.

Reid masterminded all the design work for the Sex Pistols, not an immediately obvious qualification in typographic terms but the style he engineered is here to stay. Ten years on its influence appears in the shape of commercial greetings cards, baked bean ads and even the unlikely context of cut-out letters for the British Gas *Tell Sid* campaign. In the early 70s, Reid had experimented with cheap and dramatic graphic effects for his political activities, and perfected the art of DIY methods, the power of the slogan and the ability to work with limited budgets. He applied those lessons to Punk and approached typography through the use of cut-out letters, found images, torn paper, minimal technology and the use of fluorescent colours borrowed from soap powder packaging. These devices became an expression of anarchy and discontent and suggested a complete reappraisal of precisely what impact record-sleeve graphics could achieve. It all made a deep impression on the younger generation of designers. Punk's power to inspire included the deeply revered talent of the late Barney Bubbles, who introduced a further element of experimentation into record sleeve design – the rediscovery of Russian Constructivist typography. As an aspect of history was waiting to be explored and Bubbles' covers for groups like *Generation X* coincided with major exhibitions such as *Paris-Moscow* in Paris and *Dada* at the Hayward Gallery.

These different strands of research came together in the work of three of the most important young sleeve designers, Malcolm Garrett who works with Assorted Images, Peter Saville and Neville Brody. Garrett started his training at Reading University's influential Department of Typography but switched to Manchester Polytechnic to join his friend Saville. He took with him, however, a feel for research and an eye for historical

Jamie Reid: original artwork for the *Pretty Vacant* single and poster.

detail, such as for the pages of a set text a book that has since become legendary amongst graphic designers, Herbert Spencer's *The Pioneers of Modem Typography*.

Peter Saville remembered their student experience as a period when virtually no-one was interested in typography. 'It was all ideas-based and somehow the British tradition of typography was lost'. For talented young designers like Saville and Garrett, record companies, and in particular the rise of the independents, seemed the obvious place to extend their creative ideas. Even so it was often hard going to realise the effects they wanted. Saville described the situation, 'Printers just couldn't set type, for example, no-one could do *Gill* setting properly. The kind of everyday jobbing language of type was lost. Printers didn't keep original cuts of faces and if they did then they didn't know what to do with them. It was almost impossible to have serifs printed without them touching and in the end you had to take books along and say, please set it like this'.

Determined to change the approach to type, Brody, Garrett and Saville experimented with the mixing and placement of faces in an entirely unconventional way, using classical references, technical and information graphic devices, and in Brody's case even designing a new face, *Brody Bold*. Their work in record sleeves created a tremendous interest in the possibilities of typography. Certainly Saville thinks so: 'I don't have a serious view of myself as a straight typographer I have the fashion designers approach to graphics and I'm settling down to a sense of style rather than a sense of fashion. But I think our achievement has been to interest design students in the discipline of typography and design history. It's given them a real need to go back to source'.

Creative energy like this has inevitably filtered through to retailing and advertising and sleeve design has remained the area in which to identify strong, individual approaches to typography. The work of Vaughan Oliver and his partner the photographer and filmaker Nigel Grierson is a case in point. They work as 23 Envelope for the record company 4AD and trained at Newcastle Polytechnic under the printmaker Terry Dowling, a teacher they unashamedly admire and regard as their mentor. At Newcastle, Oliver studied illustration and remained blissfully ignorant of typography, 'In fact, I thought of it as an element that actually spoilt the illustration'. A job with Michael Peters

(left) Malcolm Garrett
sleeve design for Simple Minds.

(far left) Neville Brody
sleeve design for Cabaret Voltaire.

(facing page) Peter Saville
sleeve design for Peter Gabriel.

provided a chance to experiment with packaging and labelling. It was the beginning of the obsessive research into drink-labels, titles-pages, sweet-wrappers, European shop fronts that mark one of the signs of the natural typographer.

23 Envelope have now made their name specialising in the kind of detailed textural approach to covers for bands like The Cocteau Twins, and the result integrates typography with the movement and colour of the photograph. Type becomes part of the image in an illustrative rather than an informative manner: 'We desperately wanted to avoid the banality of a photo and logo approach. We believe that type should reflect and complement the atmosphere and texture in the music'. Their work combines a sense of the ironic with the intense, a combination not unknown in their native North-East and may explain why they list their influences as Guinness (the drink not the posters) with Samuel Beckett and the filmaker Tarkovsky. The effects are achieved by mixing typefaces, redrawing decorative faces from old encyclopædias, tampering with the percentage tint of photographs and exploiting the old idea of the found object.

Vaughan Oliver has also no doubt that sleeve design is still the area for creative graphics. 'In general the mainstream gets its ideas from existing images and not from any real use of imagination. On the other hand sleeve designers try and innovate and experiment, and if they are not fully appreciated it is because of unconvincing finish or a smaller audience'. He suggests that if you want to find out what's really happening in British graphics you should get down to your nearest record store.

1987 **Rhetoric and design** Hanno Ehses

2,500 years ago the Greeks were already concerned with proficiency in communication. Having studied the practice of successful orators, and firmly believing that some of the skills involved in making a speech could be taught, they brought together a set of precepts to aid other people in acquiring those skills. They called this holistic approach to communication, rhetoric. Aristotle defined rhetoric as the 'faculty of observing in any given case the available means of persuasion,' and he pointed out that all people have a share in rhetoric because they all attempt to persuade one another of various ideas and beliefs. To find the reasons behind successful efforts of communication is to discover the art behind persuasion.

For rhetoric, language is never simply a form of expression: it is a functional tool that is manipulated to achieve desired ends. A common prejudice and misunderstanding associates rhetoric with the bombastic and hollow, with fraud and seduction, with deceit and sheer ornamentation. The long history of this art, in contrast to popular assumptions, tells us that rhetoric has been concerned with imagination, with form-giving, and with the appropriate use of language to facilitate human affairs.[1]

1 See Walter Ong, Ramus: *Method and the decay dialogue*, Cambridge, MA: Harvard University Press, 1958.

The prejudice against rhetoric is as old as Western philosophy; Plato condemned language as the mere outward form of an essential inner thought, while other thinkers held it to be a necessary instrument of social expression. The Renaissance humanists revitalised rhetoric after centuries of distrust by scholastic logicians, and applied it to painting, architecture, and music, as well as to oral and written discourse. The rhetorical tradition fell into decline, however, by the eighteenth century, because of the restricted identification of rhetoric with elocution (style, novel effects, ornamentation), and the increasing prestige of a formally and semantically strict language of science.

The international signs for 'man' and 'woman' aim, in their style, for the status of pure information stripped of persuasion. The image is ultimately culturally determined, however: 'man' is naked; 'woman' is signified by the addition of a customery feminine garment.

In the mid-1500s, the French scholar Peter Ramus divided the holistic art of rhetoric into separate disciplines: rhetoric and logic. Discovery and arrangement of material he assigned to the province of logic; elocution and the other parts, however, were subsumed under rhetoric. Whereas logic was assigned to the intellect, rhetoric was assigned to the imagination. Logic was scientific and exact; rhetoric was peripheral and decorative.

At about the same time, the English scientist and philosopher Francis Bacon fostered this view by claiming that imagination and reason were two distinct faculties. Because he considered imagination and emotion subservient to reason, he advocated the

precedence of *res* (what is said) over *verba* (how it is said). Consequently, elocution for Bacon and his followers is to logic what clothing is to the body. Style becomes the 'garb of thought', or the rhetorical wrapping. This kind of judgment was expressed in statements like 'Truth loves the light, and is most beautiful when naked.' [2]

The seventeenth century was concerned with the development of a simple, utilitarian, scientific style, advocated particularly by a committee formed by the 'Royal Society' to improve the English language. The aim was to determine linguistic symbols that would have univocal and constant meanings not unlike mathematical ones.

The contemporary distinction in design between 'information' and 'persuasion' reflects historical discussions about plain and ornamental style, stemming from the ancient distinctions between content and form, logic and style. Many designers believe that information can be presented without ever referring to modes of persuasion. Yet all communication, no matter how spare and simple, has meaningful, stylistic qualities which exceed the stated 'content' of a message. Consequently, the question that designers must face relates not to persuasion or the lack of it, but rather to the *intentions* behind it. In other words: designers cannot avoid discussing the moral issue; they must question the ends of design, to ensure that the work disseminated does not persuade its public for undesirable ends. There have been some fruitful endeavours over the last thirty years to make rhetoric respectable again, to free it from the prejudice that regards it as a cunning and morally questionable technique. According to the Italian scholar and semiotician Umberto Eco, speaking for the 'New Rhetoric': 'Almost all human reasoning about facts, decisions, opinions, beliefs, and values is no longer considered to be based on the authority of absolute Reason, but instead is seen to be intertwined with emotional elements, historical evaluations and pragmatic motivations. In this sense, the new rhetoric considers the persuasive discourse not as a subtle, fraudulent procedure, but as a technique of 'reasonable' human interaction, controlled by doubt and explicitly subject to extra-logical conditions.' [3]

2   Randolph, *The Rise of Modern Prose Style,* Cambridge, MA: MIT Press, 1969, p 209.

3   U Eco, *A Theory of Semiotics,* Bloomington: Indiana University Press, 1976, p 227-288.

(below left) Diagram from a 15th century rhetorical primer for school boys. The table of logical terminology is coded with more or less arbitrary images. The pictures are a memory device: abstract verbal terms are recalled by means of a familiar image. They form a pictorial signage system distributed through-out the text.

(below right) This emblem is based on Cesaro Ripa's 1603 *Iconology*, a catalogue of allegorical symbols for use by painters and writers. The translation of the allegory reads: 'The compass indicated that design is based on measure, and that it holds to single proportions; the mirror indicated that design reproduces not the external world, but the internal organ of the soul...' (Schone).

Since all human communication is, in one way or another, infiltrated rhetorically, design for visual/verbal communication can not be exempt. The potential value of the rhetorical system within a semiotic framework was discussed by Gui Bonsiepe who published the article *Visual/Verbal Rhetoric* in 1965, probably inspired by Roland Barthes's essay, *Rhetoric of the Image,* which appeared the previous year.[4] Bonsiepe demonstrated that visual rhetoric can be studied by focusing on the relationship between image and text in contemporary advertisements. A similar interplay was central to the *emblem book,* a genre which proliferated during the sixteenth and seventeenth centuries. The typical emblem is composed of three parts the image (*pictura*), and two text elements, the motto/title (*inscriptio*) and the narrative text (*subscriptio*). The combination of image and narrative usually results in a riddle, the solution of which comes about through an explanatory, third part, the narrative text. An emblematic image is not simply a mute representation but refers to didactic and moral meanings.[5] Many modern advertisements have a similar three-part structure: a picture and a motto explained by a discursive text.[6]

The relationship between the image and text in a Baroque emblem book tends to be highly abstract: objects are linked to concepts by almost arbitrary associations, similar to the relationship between a word and the object to which it refers. The effectiveness of a rhetorical design methodology depends on the use of symbols and patterns which are familiar and alive for a given audience. When an image is able to communicate a message without the aid of a lengthy verbal key, its meaning is, nonetheless, socially determined. Thus, meaning is not an innate quality of visual forms: it is a matter of relationships. A legible message is one that succeeds in connecting with the habits and expectations of a particular culture. In so far as design has wit or emotional impact, it surprises those expectations.

Shaping the appearance of any visual object involves rhetoric. To propose a rhetorical paradigm for graphic design is to suggest a new attitude of thinking about design, the way we see it, and consequently, the way it should be taught: it implies a shift away from a formalistic, aesthetic/stylistic imperative towards a functional, aesthetic/ethical imperative. The former tends to offer perfect models only to be imitated and technically refined: imitation instead of invention. The latter accepts that all design has social, moral and political dimensions, that there is no sphere of pure information, and accepts the challenge to make designs that are conceptually, visually, and functionally appropriate for particular clients and audiences in particular environments. And this, in my opinion, requires designers who show more respect for visual symbolism than for aesthetic doctrines.

4 G Bonsiepe, *Visual/Verbal Rhetoric*, Ulm 14-16, 1965: 23-40 R Barthes, The Rhetoric of the Image, in Barthes, *Image/Music/ Text*, New York: Hill and Wang, 1977.

5 A Schone, *Emblematik und Drama im Zeitalter cles Barock*, Munich, 1964.

6 P J Vinken, *The Modern Advertisement as an Emblem*, Gazette 5, Number 2, 1959.

1990 **British design: image & identity** Frederique Huygen

The identity of British design is no easy thing to pin down. The more one looks at British design, the more difficult it becomes to put it under one heading. Fashionable tendencies intermingle with a tradition, visual styles from elsewhere are quickly absorbed, and most design areas testify to a great diversity. Influences come from the street, from tradition, from both modernism and classicism. Seen as a whole, British design is a many-faceted affair. There is little question of a single British identity, in visual terms, that holds true for all design sectors. Any such *leitmotiv* is elusive indeed.

Take the craft ideal, for instance, a tradition that in the United Kingdom is still very much in evidence. This can be attributed largely to the British predilection for nature, a weakness for the amateur, and a taste for individualism. But we should not forget a love of materials, the narrative, literary side of British culture, and the age-old importance attached to skilled workmanship. The craft mentality has long been the decisive force behind British design giving it its practicality, its 'doing-as-designing'. British arts and crafts proved itself capable of self-renewal, just because of this very continuity and its isolated, introverted position. The continuity and a strong ideological basis have given British Arts and Crafts its identity. The narrative aspect, the decorative, linear elements, and a love of materials have been ever present in British craft movements. Its aloof position and scepticism towards industry emerged as a weakness at those times when faith in industry dominated culture, and as a strength at moments when industrial values were faced with a crisis, as in the nineteenth century or today. Now in particular, British craft-based perspectives seem able to offer new inroads for industry. Up until now, these qualities have been tapped mainly by non-British manufacturers.

As for British graphic design, its characteristics include classicism, symmetry, and structure. It is well balanced, explicit, and uncomplicated in its approach; pragmatic, even. The British typographical tradition of books and love of the letter is at the root of this. In British graphic design, a modernistic, more dynamic approach to typography, such as that of Germany or the Netherlands, is nowhere to be found. So, although Neville Brody did create new typefaces for the magazine *The Face*, he used them in a wholly decorative way; they bear no relation to the treatment of the text in general. Words and images in British graphic design are often two separate entitites. This is because, besides typography, graphic design also has roots in illustration, a tradition that tends more towards

the narrative and anecdotal than to structure or abstraction. A noteworthy aspect is the openness to foreign influences, which British graphics assimilates effortlessly. And nor is this a phenomenon of the twenties and thirties either, for today its feelers are, once again, going out to countries like the Netherlands and America, and to historical styles too. Periods of foreign influence seem to alternate with years when 'neo' styles set the trend, as in the fifties. In addition, the technological changes of recent years have sparked off a great deal of experimentation. And of course graphic design is less limited than other branches in terms of execution. Expensive research or product development are unnecessary, and the commercial risks much smaller. British graphic design comes across as a ragbag of styles and influences: Constructivism; the ad hoc juxtaposition of components; tasteful, classical packaging; sweeping American-style statements; and a subtle mildness of manner. It is both eclectic and synthetising.

Adjectives emerging from these observations and common to the above branches of design include narrative, decorative, anecdotal, eclectic, and not tending to abstraction; classical, well-balanced, pragmatic, and synthetising.

Structure

Many of the above-mentioned characteristics can, I feel, be traced back to a lack of structure. The romantic individualism of the Arts and Crafts practitioners stood in the way of integration with industry. Mass production was slow in catching on amongst British designers. There have always been few clients willing to encourage new, and thus more risky, undertakings. Firms imbued with a sense of culture, such as Olivetti, Braun, and IBM, are few and far between. Designers trying to gain entrance to the manufacturing industries generally have a hard time doing so. After all, it was the makers of consumer goods (tableware, furniture, domestic appliances) who suffered greatly from the economic crises. And the few who remain feel no real need to take risks. Hence deferential and respectable, with an exception now and again, is about as far as it gets. It is not for nothing that so many British designers are throwing in their lot with foreign manufacturers, or starting production themselves. An enterprising industrial culture has long been conspicuous by its absence. Scientific discoveries and inventions make little headway in terms of commercial application followed by effective marketing. Industry reacts defensively instead of taking pre-emptive steps, and often lacks a long-term outlook. Amongst the authorities and governmental institutions, design has yet to become institutionalised. In graphics, too, British clients give designers little room to move. Innovations and fresh impulses in British design come almost invariably from the fringe areas, like graphic design and designer-makers, or from outsiders. Inventors generally are engineers or self-taught individuals with a sense of form, or people outside the design establishment in some other way.

Status quo

The second major underlying factor is in my opinion the hierarchy of Britain's class society. Refusing to accept, or steering clear of, extremes and conforming to the established order of things (the pragmatic approach); being respectable and not breaking

the rules: these are attitudes very much at home in a culture in which maintaining the status quo is the highest good. By and large, British design is not given to powerful statements and shooting straight from the shoulder. Equally, engineers are still having to struggle to shake off their traditionally low status. A multi-disciplinary approach – though developed early on amongst designers – has barely filtered through to the industries. And government institutions seem only open to 'design' as an image-builder. A matter-of-fact, practical approach and taking things in stages have always appealed to British designers more than extremes, whether these be home-grown or from abroad.

Nor do British designers cling to principles or theories. Unlike British architects, who can claim a long tradition of questioning their profession, designers seem less stricken by self-doubt. This could be explained as the consequence of designers having spent too many years trying to get their profession recognised. Nor have they found an industrial structure capable of serving as a basis. As long as one of these two needs remains unsatisfied there could well be no room to stand back and take an objective look at the profession. And if they finally do succeed in putting design on the cultural and economic map, euphoria would probably prevail to begin with. The general British aversion both to intellectuals and abstract thinking comes in here too. Possibly it is these factors which have made it difficult for designers to take a detached look at themselves and their task, trade in the homely for the worldly, and question their commission. As for those who succeeded in this, such as Christopher Dresser and Charles Rennie Mackintosh, it was probably due to their outstanding individual capacities. But the lack of dogma or structure makes for a greater toleration and freedom as well.

Therefore, one cannot say there are no extremes in British design. The outsiders, to be found in fashion and amongst the designer makers and inventors, time and again add a spice to British design. The class structure, status quo, and an avoidance of emotions give rise to a veritable cauldron of extreme reactions, brimful with energy and boiling over on occasions. But these extremes are, for this reason, short-lived. Punk could never have arisen in a more moderate, levelled down, welfare state like Sweden or the Netherlands. But, if it were to do so, it would not be so apolitical and superficial (ie it would not leave the existing order undisturbed). Because this protest was chiefly visual and symbolic, it could easily be appropriated by commercialism. Furthermore, we may well ask just how extreme such counter currents really are, and how heavily they lean on the developments elsewhere, as is the case with graphic design. Moreover, breaking the rules and elevating individual originality was something that occupied young designers in other countries as well.

Design ideologies, until recently providing certainty, broke down and set a new zero level in the eighties. It is striking also that extremes occur chiefly where they are meant to occur, such as in fashion, music, and the media. Transience and rapid obsolescence are second nature to these areas.

At all events such extremes always seek a means of expression beyond existing channels. Tradition, with all its deep-seated structures and prejudices, or rather the lack of tradition, is the cause of the acceptance of this creative aggression. For it is chiefly the non-traditional sectors, unencumbered by a past, which assimilate them. Tradition

and innovation, hierarchy and anarchy – in British design each enables the other to exist.

Whenever the burden of the past is absent, or has been jettisoned, there suddenly seems much more room for all manner of new utterances. Design can flourish providing it comes across as commercial and fashionable. When dependent on research and industry, or related to social values, its acceptance is a far more laborious affair. Consequently, ephemeral products, packaging, posters, interiors, and style constitute the groundwork for the professionalising of design in Great Britain. Advertising and PR consciousness have played a major rôle here. In this respect I consider the British advertisement to be most representative of the qualities I praise in British design: ironic, humourous, understated, subversive, provocative, visual, ephemeral, adult, and powerful.

The capacities in the fields of advertising, corporate identity, image, and commerce are being strengthened further by Prime Minister Thatcher's 'enterprise culture'. Packaging and selling products are better suited to British designers than are the technological and structural aspects. This ability ties in with the current British industrial *elan* borne aloft largely by the younger businesses and by a no nonsense commercial approach. The openness of British society is another vitally important aspect. It is often foreigners who introduce change to the ranks of British design. But British culture itself has become much more international in recent years too.

Having become more professional and more international, coupled with a receptiveness to ideas, British design is given a tremendous advantage over that of other countries, and makes it well-equipped for 1992. I can only hope that there is still room for subversion and critical alternatives; that the basis broadens and becomes stronger, that 'design' as hype does not mean the end of design proper – and perhaps, above all, that all the hedonism and the emphasis on money will be balanced by the British propensity for putting things into perspective.

1990 **The new British telephone directory** Colin Banks

We were interested in the idea of having a go at the telephone book a long time ago.
When we did the total Post Office identity in 1972, the Post Office ran the telecommunications business and so it was part of our visual identity to mark Post Office Telecommunications as part of the Post Office. At that time we could see that the telephone
directory got into nearly everybody's home and it was the biggest vehicle for announcing in print the Post Office presence. We made proposals for full colour covers and
a new format, but the time was not thought to be right to develop them.

My interest in the inside typography of telephone books got sharpened through
the work we did on the railway time-tables twelve or thirteen years ago. At that time
British Rail was changing over their method of production from hot metal to offset,
together with computer-driven data-retrieval systems linked to typesetting. We were
invited in as designers to see what contribution we could make; but we were asked in
when the project was half-cooked and British Rail management thought a designer's
rôle was to decorate the product afterwards. Programs had been written for the computer typesetting and the brief to the program writers had been to do it exactly as it
had been before, and that is what they did. When we tried to alter anything, whether
it was a comma or whatever, we were told that all had been programmed and would
cost tens of thousands of pounds to change: we couldn't alter anything. I sat in
timetable development meetings once a month for two years, with over twenty people
there; people in charge of signals in the West Country and that sort of thing. Few of
them seemed to know what it was all about, and it was a very wasteful exercise. Against
these odds, we were able to make a few significant changes and the timetable as you
see it now is essentially what we designed, but I regret not being able to dig much
deeper into the typography. The most important of my innovations was to reduce the
size from A4 to A5. It was then that I became aware of huge cost savings possible with
these big productions. We also saw the opportunity to draw off from the same data
bank, timetable information in different formats, so it was possible to have pocket
timetables and station platform timetables straight from the data bank by varying
the computer coding. I used to go down to the railway terminus and watch the people
using the timetables up on boards and found them clustered six deep at rush hour
peering over one another's shoulders trying to see what time the next train was going

and this happened because the timetables were arranged chronologically. We redesigned them so that they could be destination specific and spread out down a concourse.

The essential thing is getting the designer in early, but with the phone book, again the programming people were there before us. When we were commissioned to design the new British Telecom corporate identity in 1980, we again designed new four-colour covers; which was a complete break with tradition. We didn't get what we wanted. Nevertheless, we have always been aware that the real thing is the meat inside the wrapping and if we can improve the business, as against the way we wrap it up, then we are making a solid contribution as designers. We have always been uneasy about what we do as visual identity specialists for companies in that we might be over-stating their case. There could be a rare opportunity for us to have a hand in British Telecom's *performance*.

I was interested in the insides a long time ago when Stuart Rose and Dick Stevens were respectively heads of Post Office Mail and Post Office Telecommunications and we talked then about redesigning the directory. At that time there was a very confused situation: the directories were produced and to some extent designed by HMSO who had two printing plants, which were in a period of flux. Eventually they closed one of the printing plants and moved everything to Gateshead. At that time, Matthew Carter was HMSO's Typographic Adviser (a job which was subsequently taken over by John Miles). It seemed that if anyone was going to do anything about it, Carter would; but he had commitments to Linotype in the United States where he was asked to redesign the Bell telephone typeface. He then left permanently for the States. When we were commissioned to look at the British Telecom visual identity as a separate 'go it alone' organisation, we again earmarked the phone book as being a high public profile vehicle for getting our identity across. The business itself was in

(below) Two earlier examples of the information, tried out in bold by Colin Banks.

(facing page) The final version at [approximate] actual size.

Fox J, 343 Bury St Wst N9	01–360 2408
Fox Jasper, 15 Hillier Ho,Camden Sq NW1	01–485 6681
Fox J, 69 Clark St E1	01–790 3371
Fox J, 148 Crowborough Rd SW17	01–672 9750
Fox J,Rags & Mtl, 39 Douro St E3	01–980 1649
Fox J, 109 Michael Cliffe Ho,Finsbury Est EC1	01–278 4541
Fox J, 41 Forest Rd N9	01–805 4481
Fox J, 1 Forest St E7	01–534 2950
Fox J, 4 Gibson Clo E1	01–790 7402
Fox Jack, 120 Glenarm Rd E5	01–986 2391
Fox J, 15 Harewood Rd SW19	01–542 4685
Fox J, 28 Homecroft Rd N22	01–889 6016
Fox J, 2 Jago Clo SE18	01–316 1493
Fox J, 79 Kingsley Wy N2	01–458 5908
Fox J, 16f Linden Gdns W2	01–243 0854
Fox J, 3 Manor Hall Av NW4	01–203 1692
Fox Jeffrey, 34 Manor Hall Av NW4	01–203 1528
Fox J, 49 Maplin Clo N21	01–360 9383
Fox J, 36 Matlock Rd E10	01–539 2829
Fox J, 48 Midmoor Rd SW12	01–673 3593
Fox J, 34f Milner Sq N1	01–609 4430
Fox J, 66 Mottisfont Rd SE2	01–310 5893
Fox Jack, 5 Highstone Ct,New Wanstead E11	01–989 0316
Fox J, 68 Pattison Rd NW2	01–435 0475
Fox J, 17 Pier Pde E16	01–474 4394
Fox J, 81 Portobello Rd W11	01–229 8130
Fox J, 118 Powys La N13	01–886 0150
Fox J, 291 Prince Regent La E16	01–476 3879

Barfield E.M, 28 Wall Pk Clo	Brixhm 51930
Barfield J.W, Kerscott Fm	Swimbdge 830269
Barfield S.C, 5 Orchard Clo,Newton Poppleford	Colatn Raleigh 68107
Barfoot Construction,Bldg Contrs,Developers, Torbay Trading Est,New Rd	Brixhm 55971
Barfoot C.W, Purvyese,Old Barnstaple Rd	Bidefrd 75425
Barfoot G.E, High Vw,Derriton Rd,Pyworthy	Holswthy 253530
Barford J.C, Leigh Ho,Holy St.	Chagfrd 3383
Bargain Beds, Unit 16 The Old Ice Fcty Rolle St	Barnstple 46985
Bargain Box,The, 81 Winner St	Paigntn 558829
Bargain Centre, 8 Greenswood Rd	Brixhm 6663
Bargain Footwear, Unit 8 Broadmeadow Indust Est	Teignmth 6525
Bargain Footwear,Shoe Shop, 22 Exeter Rd	Exmth 277525
Bargain Footwear, 16 Fore St	Seatn 23688
Bargains Of Torquay Ltd,Walk Around Store, 7 The Strand	Torquay 23409
Barge E, Briar Ho,Crickerfield Rd	Torquay 37441
Barge G.A, 33 Prospect Pk	Exeter 77074
Barge J.D, 98 Hele Rd.	Torquay 37905
Barge M, 491 Babbacombe Rd	Torquay 212549
Barge R, 35 Corfe Cres	Torquay 34493
Barge R, 173 Ellacombe Church Rd	Torquay 24693
Barge R.H, 17 Fourth Av.	Teignmth 4323
Bargery Dr A,M.A DRcog MRCGP – Res, 2 The Mill,Landkey	Swimbdge 830277
Surgery, Health Centre,Vicarage St	Barnstple 75221
Bargery M.C.J, 17 Joslin Rd.	Honitn 2114
Bargery N.M, Clare Cott,Burnt Oak	Sidbry 495

considerable upheaval and changing the directories was not high on their priorities. There were also changes taking place at the Gateshead printing plant: this was bought by Ben Johnson, now the sole printer of telephone listing directories in the UK. Then Ben Johnson was in turn bought by Donnelley in Chicago, one of the biggest printers in the world, and they were busy introducing new technology (and Carter's type-faces) into American phone-books.

There was so much improvement being made to phone-books in the States that we were tempted to follow what they do exactly. But the situation in America is different. Although Donnelleys are massive, they do not print all the directories in the States. Carter's typefaces are used in other printing plants in the States, which don't all have the as high standards as Donnelley, so there is some variation in the quality of printing.

One thing we identified for the British directory was that all the printing was totally controllable. They were changing over from hot metal to printing offset, to generating all the type digitally and using Monotype Lasercomps. British Telecom were centralising their data-base, so massive computers were bringing all the information together in one place to be directly fed into the printers, so there were real opportunities at last. Eventually, the Design Department of British Telecom said 'all right, we'll give you some money to do some experimental work to see what can be achieved'. We had put forward the case that we could make some material saving and Eichi Kono worked with me on this research project. We got an enormous amount of support from British Telecom designer, Chris Bourne; it was really he who made the thing possible. Results were convincing, in that by adjusting the minute detail of the typography, we could make a small percentage saving overall on the existing three-column format, which would save turnover lines. Turnover lines in three-column books account for 8% of the total book and have big scale implications for the over all costs, but at the end of that

ALLSOP A.C, 33 Harvard Ct,
          Honeybourne Rd NW6 1HL...435 2097
  A.G, 55 Montagu Rd N18 2LX.................... 884 0737
  C, 22 Park Hl Ct,Beeches Rd SW17 7LX 767 3013
  C, 18 Greet Ho,Frazier St SE1 7BB............. 928 6467
  C.A, 45 Hartington Rd E17 8AS................. 521 6034
  C.S, 9/25 Cheyne Pl SW3 4HJ................... 352 3581
  C.S, 19 Wolseley Gdns W4 3LY................. 995 9390
  D, 68 Chandos Av N20 9DZ 445 7067
  D, 96 Disraeli Rd SW15 2DX 789 7476
  D, 24 Thornaby Gdns N18 2AX.................. 807 7155
  D.C, 22 Crabtree La SW6 6LN 385 4036
  David J, 64 Mysore Rd SW11 5SB............. 223 9003
  D.S, 91 Waverley Rd N17 0PA................... 801 0389
  E, 48 Elmdale Rd N13 4UL........................ 888 6700
  G.F, 50 Athelney St SE6 3LB 697 3499
  G.W, 2 Woodlands Av E11 3QZ 530 4629
  H, 19 North Birkbeck Rd E11 4JF 556 0392
  H.B, 9 St. Elmo Rd W12 9EA 749 0814
  J, 42 St. Georges Rd E10 5RH 556 5081
  J.A, 24 Warwick Rd E17 5NP 531 4920

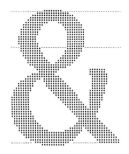

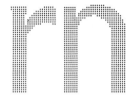

(top) The ampersand with clear loops and firm terminals.

(middle) A clear difference in the typeface design of the letterforms r and n, where if the loops were not clearly different the r might bridge and look like an m.

(bottom) The numerals 3 and 8, with fairly open terminals on the 3 to avoid confusion with the 8.

exercise we proposed that we could go onto a four-column layout.

One of the means to this was by dropping repeat surnames. As Ladislaw Mandal says, 'there are different national characteristics in telephone books'. Designing American directories is a simpler task, because addresses tend to be very much shorter, like '132 Lexicon' and that's it. They don't have 'The Old Grange, Chipping Sodbury, Cirencester' as part of the address. The other advantage was the wide American page, which makes it very much easier for them to get four columns on a page without radical surgery. We had a harder task, there was no possibility of increasing the page width, partly because of the way the brief came to us and machining capabilities, so we had to work quite hard to shoehorn four columns into an A4 book. The clue to achieving that was not only editorial decisions, like supporting our proposal to drop repeat surnames; that alone would not have worked if we had not been able to reduce the width of the entries over-all. That meant re-designing the typefaces and here two important factors came into play. Previously the old Linotype metal typesetting determined that the light address and name entries were on the same set width (the same duplex matrix) as the bold; but with digital setting we were freed from duplex matrices and we were able to totally change the scale of the parts of the message. Since we argued that the address was just a confirmation of the most important thing; the name of the subscriber and his or her phone number, the address could be smaller. There was a lot of sympathy for this argument at that time in British Telecom, partly because they did not have the same obligation for supplying postal addresses as when they were linked to the postal service; and this reasoning allowed them to concentrate on the telephone numbers. British Telecom were also prepared to listen to anything that would relieve directory enquiries, which is a horrendously expensive service.

We experimented with lots of different typefaces; *Franklin Gothic, Bell Centennial, Bell Gothic*, to see what sort of result we were getting. Out of this came the need for a new typeface, but this did not emerge until after we had completed our original pro-posal. What we concentrated on in the original proposal were the changes to the format, using the best typeface off-the-shelf, reducing the inter-letterspacing, and other typo-graphical aspects. The idea of a new typeface did not arise until we were put in touch with a unit called Phone-book Development in British Telecom who had started to work in parallel with the Design Unit on looking at the new technology that was to be intro-duced. It was a 'just in time' exercise. The programmers had been brought in and asked to produce a phone book much as it had been produced before, and it seemed a lot of possibilities were going to escape us, again because we were not in at the beginning. It ran to the same form as the railway timetables, with regular fortnightly meetings; but this time the whole team were very supportive. The team, headed by Kevin Kearnan from Phone Book Developments, were joined by people from Ben Johnson; and we as designers were there to make a typographical case and everybody listened. We were working on this stage of it for a year or more.

Having identified the name and the telephone number as the most important thing, they had to be made as legible as we could make them. We could then reduce the scale of the address entries, without altering the line feed which was kept at 5.75.

The Monotype Lasercomp system was using bitmap generation rather than contour generation, which was fine for us because we were designing dedicated typefaces for one size only. That meant we could have total control over every pixel that formed the letter. The final letter design was very much in the editing of pixels, so I as designer had a direct hand in every aspect of the letterform. There must, of course, be a very clear distinction between the numerals. With bad inking, 6, 9, 8, 3, 5, get confused, so we kept the terminals within them fairly open where there was a break in the loop.

People search phone books vertically: this is the radical difference from other kinds of reading. What we are looking for is not a change in a word, but a change in a letter, therefore changes in letters must have every chance of leaping out. I was trained to make letterforms that make a harmonious word and pattern, but the directory letters had different criteria. Although we want to achieve some sort of balance in telephone directories, we shouldn't do anything to blur the change from one letter to the other. This was reflected in the typeface we designed. If you put an r next to an n, the r and the n loops are often not clearly different and the r might bridge and look like an m. Whereas in a typeface, normally one looks for commonalities of letterform, here we were trying to make clear differences in form whilst keeping the weights harmonious.

By the time we had completed our experiments, Gerard Unger had started work on his numerals for the Dutch directory, Mandal in France had completed some typefaces, and Carter had implemented his designs for the States. We were very grateful that Carter had set a marker on the road, to which we could refer, and thought of using his typeface as it stood, transferring it to Lasercomp. But the fact that all the printing was centralised in Ben Johnson's Gateshead plant meant that we had control over it, and we were sure that they could achieve a very high standard of printing, which could not be guaranteed from one side of the States to the other. This made us feel that we could make changes to the letterforms which allowed us to set them closer together. We wanted to do this for two reasons. US setting, because of the shortness of lines,

The comparison of sample entry page-settings for space-saving done by Colin Banks in 1983. Reproduced from the London L–R directory section 103, June 1983.

reads very vertically, whereas English lines need some help in connecting one letter and the next because the lines are longer. We therefore put more horizontal stress into the letterforms than Carter had. The space had to come from somewhere, so we reduced the inter letter spacing throughout the whole design, which was risky, but we were reckoning on a high standard of machining. This was a new springboard of departure. Another thing was that Carter could not supply us with original drawings, so there would have been a matter of interpretation to switch from one system to another, and at 5.75 size, every pixel you change is significant. We were, at this point, already looking for a new typeface, but building on the advantages that Carter had pinpointed. We designed seven type variants (there were only three in Carter's), so we had different uses and weights to look after, trying to work all these together, was a different mix. Some of the display advertising faces were in different sizes. 10pt does not sound very big, but it is almost twice as big as 5.75!

We did not really have a proof, which was an extraordinary thing. Monotype were taking our drawings and turning them into rough bit-maps, then each time we were editing the bit-maps through three or four progressive stages. Monotype would print them out as a PMT and that was all we had to go on by way of a proof. We were very aware that we wouldn't know what a printed page would actually look like until we had a complete book in our hands, no way in which we could test type characteristics. We tried to degrade PMT's by running them twenty times through a photostat machine to see the worst that could happen, but we couldn't do anything else until the first phone book was printed. It was a cliff-hanger, but when we got the first one from Plymouth, we were absolutely delighted and nothing has been altered since.

There are small details that I would change now, but they are small details. There is an errant ampersand in one of the typefaces which I feel could do with some doctoring. By and large, what you see is what we designed.

Something that worried me was the public reaction and British Telecom monitor everything with public opinion surveys. In the first year, they did this extensively, with questionnaires and they got an 80% acceptance, which was comforting. As a final point, there is the paper question. On my first visit to Ben Johnson, there were one hundred rolls of newsprint going into that factory every day, and I imagined those hundred rolls thundering up some motorway every day. If we could save a few of those it would make a difference to the quality of life as well as a saving in cash. It was not just paper; the total energy that was consumed was huge. The amount of ink (800 tonnes) and every sort of resource that goes into production of a phone book is big stuff. It seems we have contributed to reducing all this.

(facing page) Comparison of different sizes of type in *Bell Gothic*. Done 1984 to show relative saving of paper space in different sizes. (Reduced in size from original.)

dth: 61mm (3 columns/A4 page)

McDonald F, 51 Acton Ho,Horn La W3..............01-993 5722
McDonald F, 41b Naylor Rd SE15....................01-639 6620
MacDonald F, 31 Pulteney Clo E3....................01-981 4178
McDonald F, 67 Rancliffe Gdns SE9.................01-859 4645
Macdonald F, 60a Turners Rd E3......................01-515 7469
① Macdonald F, 37 Leylands,Viewfield Rd SW18 ......01-870 0591
McDonald F,
44 Livingstone Ho,Wyndham Rd SE5...01-703 5256
MacDonald F.A, 60 Alwyn Av W4.......................01-994 2194
McDonald F.A, 141 Buchanan Gdns NW10..........01-969 7862
McDonald F.A, 8/146 Craven Pk Rd N15............01-802 7016
MacDonald F.A.A, 21 Warwick Sq SW1..............01-834 7713
McDonald F.B,
6 Cornerways,Daylesford Av SW15...01-876 5420
McDonald F.E, 7/3 Hanway Pl W1 ....01-580 2911
McDonald F.F, 3 Harting Rd SE9.......................01-851 3387
MacDonald F.G, 34 Ascot Ct,Grove End Rd NW8 ...01-286 6315
McDonald F.H.R,
49 Chippendale Ho,Churchill Gdns SW1...01-834 8743
MacDonald F.J, 21 Ambleside,Augustus St NW1 ....01-388 0083
MacDonald F.J, Basil Mans,Basil St SW3 ....01-589 1857
Macdonald F.J, 1/37 Clapham Com N Side SW4 ...01-627 0187
McDonald F.J, 72 St. Thomas Rd N4.................01-354 0443
Macdonald F.J,
4 Polesworth Ho,Warwick Est W2...01-286 8359
MacDonald F.J, 51 Wells Ho,Well Wlk NW3 ....01-435 8264
McDonald F.L, 104a Braemar Av NW10 ....01-450 6025
McDonald F.M,
11 Aynhoe Mans,Aynhoe Rd W14...01-603 0709
McDonald F.M, 15 Cottingham Rd SW8.............01-735 5530
McDonald F.M, 392 Greenford Av W7 ....01-578 7826
McDonald Frederick M, 23 Murchison Rd E10 ......01-556 7255
McDonald F.O, 140 Norbury Cres SW16 ....01-764 5396
McDonald F.W, 35a Sangley Rd SE25................01-653 0645
McDonald G, 12 Marlbury,Abbey Rd NW8...........01-328 3910
MacDonald Gary, D/19 Barcombe Av SW2 ....01-674 3200
Macdonald Gregory,
4 Catherine Vill,Copse Hl SW20...01-946 4486
Macdonald G, 111 Corringham Rd NW11.............01-455 8602
MacDonald G,
1 Birchington Ct,Crouch Hall Rd N8...01-348 3381
MacDonald G, 34 Hyndewood,Dacres Rd SE23 ......01-699 2635
Macdonald G, 25 Ivinghoe Ho,Dalmeny Av N7 ....01-607 9045
McDonald G, 43 Disraeli Rd W5 ....01-567 0765
MacDonald G,
9q Peabody Est Fulham Pal Rd W6...01-748 2809
McDonald G, 7 Macdonald Rd E17.....................01-523 0866
Macdonald Gordon, 6 Malvern Ter N1.................01-607 2509
MacDonald G, 41 Sherington Rd SE7 ....01-858 5714
McDonald G, 67 Shirley Rd E15........................01-534 8925

61mm (3 cols/A4)

McDonald F, 51 Acton Ho,Horn La W3 .... 01 993 5722
McDonald F, 41b Naylor Rd SE15 .... 01 639 6620
MacDonald F, 31 Pulteney Clo E3 .... 01 981 4178
McDonald F, 67 Rancliffe Gdns SE9 .... 01 859 4645
Macdonald F, 60a Turners Rd E3 .... 01 515 7469
Macdonald F, 37 Leylands,Viewfield Rd SW18 .... 01 870 0591
② McDonald F, 44 Livingstone Ho,Wyndham Rd SE5 .... 01 703 5256
MacDonald F.A, 60 Alwyn Av W4 .... 01 994 2194
McDonald F.A, 141 Buchanan Gdns NW10 .... 01 969 7862
McDonald F.A, 8/146 Craven Pk Rd N15 .... 01 802 7016
MacDonald F.A.A, 21 Warwick Sq SW1 .... 01 834 7713
McDonald F.B, 6 Cornerways,Daylesford Av SW15 .... 01 876 5420
McDonald F.E, 7/3 Hanway Pl W1 .... 01 580 2911
McDonald F.F, 3 Harting Rd SE9 .... 01 851 3387
MacDonald F.G, 34 Ascot Ct,Grove End Rd NW8 .... 01 286 6315
McDonald F.H.R, 49 Chippendale Ho,Churchill Gdns SW1 . 01 834 8743
MacDonald F.J, 21 Ambleside,Augustus St NW1 .... 01 388 0083
MacDonald F.J, Basil Mans,Basil St SW3 .... 01 589 1857
Macdonald F.J, 1/37 Clapham Com N Side SW4 .... 01 627 0187
McDonald F.J, 72 St. Thomas Rd N4 .... 01 354 0443
Macdonald F.J, 4 Polesworth Ho,Warwick Est W2 .... 01 286 8359
MacDonald F.J, 51 Wells Ho,Well Wlk NW3 .... 01 435 8264
McDonald F.L, 104a Braemar Av NW10 .... 01 450 6025
McDonald F.M, 11 Aynhoe Mans,Aynhoe Rd W14 .... 01 603 0709
McDonald F.M, 15 Cottingham Rd SW8 .... 01 735 5530
McDonald F.M, 392 Greenford Av W7 .... 01 578 7826
McDonald Frederick M, 23 Murchison Rd E10 .... 01 556 7255
McDonald F.O, 140 Norbury Cres SW16 .... 01 764 5396
McDonald F.W, 35a Sangley Rd SE25 .... 01 653 0645
McDonald G, 12 Marlbury,Abbey Rd NW8 .... 01 328 3910
MacDonald Gary, D/19 Barcombe Av SW2 .... 01 674 3200
Macdonald Gregory, 4 Catherine Vill,Copse Hl SW20 .... 01 946 4486
Macdonald G, 111 Corringham Rd NW11 .... 01 455 8602
MacDonald G, 1 Birchington Ct,Crouch Hall Rd N8 .... 01 348 3381
MacDonald G, 34 Hyndewood,Dacres Rd SE23 .... 01 699 2635
Macdonald G, 25 Ivinghoe Ho,Dalmeny Av N7 .... 01 607 9045
McDonald G, 43 Disraeli Rd W5 .... 01 567 0765
MacDonald G, 9q Peabody Est Fulham Pal Rd W6 .... 01 748 2809
McDonald G, 7 Macdonald Rd E17 .... 01 523 0866
Macdonald Gordon, 6 Malvern Ter N1 .... 01 607 2509
MacDonald G, 41 Sherington Rd SE7 .... 01 858 5714
McDonald G, 67 Shirley Rd E15 .... 01 534 8925

} 4 % saving by reduction of line space
} 6 % saving by reduction of turn-over lines

Total 10 % saving by HL-2 setting.

61mm (3 cols/A4)

McDonald F, 51 Acton Ho,Horn La W3 .... 01 993 5722
McDonald F, 41b Naylor Rd SE15 .... 01 639 6620
MacDonald F, 31 Pulteney Clo E3 .... 01 981 4178
McDonald F, 67 Rancliffe Gdns SE9 .... 01 859 4645
Macdonald F, 60a Turners Rd E3 .... 01 515 7469
③ Macdonald F, 37 Leylands,Viewfield Rd SW18 .... 01 870 0591
McDonald F, 44 Livingstone Ho,Wyndham Rd SE5 .... 01 703 5256
MacDonald F.A, 60 Alwyn Av W4 .... 01 994 2194
McDonald F.A, 141 Buchanan Gdns NW10 .... 01 969 7862
McDonald F.A, 8/146 Craven Pk Rd N15 .... 01 802 7016
MacDonald F.A.A, 21 Warwick Sq SW1 .... 01 834 7713
McDonald F.B, 6 Cornerways,Daylesford Av SW15 .... 01 876 5420
McDonald F.E, 7/3 Hanway Pl W1 .... 01 580 2911
McDonald F.F, 3 Harting Rd SE9 .... 01 851 3387
MacDonald F.G, 34 Ascot Ct,Grove End Rd NW8 .... 01 286 6315
McDonald F.H.R, 49 Chippendale Ho,Churchill Gdns SW1 .... 01 834 8743
MacDonald F.J, 21 Ambleside,Augustus St NW1 .... 01 388 0083
MacDonald F.J, Basil Mans,Basil St SW3 .... 01 589 1857
Macdonald F.J, 1/37 Clapham Com N Side SW4 .... 01 627 0187
McDonald F.J, 72 St. Thomas Rd N4 .... 01 354 0443
Macdonald F.J, 4 Polesworth Ho,Warwick Est W2 .... 01 286 8359
MacDonald F.J, 51 Wells Ho,Well Wlk NW3 .... 01 435 8264
McDonald F.L, 104a Braemar Av NW10 .... 01 450 6025
McDonald F.M, 11 Aynhoe Mans,Aynhoe Rd W14 .... 01 603 0709
McDonald F.M, 15 Cottingham Rd SW8 .... 01 735 5530
McDonald F.M, 392 Greenford Av W7 .... 01 578 7826
McDonald Frederick M, 23 Murchison Rd E10 .... 01 556 7255
McDonald F.O, 140 Norbury Cres SW16 .... 01 764 5396
McDonald F.W, 35a Sangley Rd SE25 .... 01 653 0645
McDonald G, 12 Marlbury,Abbey Rd NW8 .... 01 328 3910
MacDonald Gary, D/19 Barcombe Av SW2 .... 01 674 3200
Macdonald Gregory, 4 Catherine Vill,Copse Hl SW20 .... 01 946 4486
Macdonald G, 111 Corringham Rd NW11 .... 01 455 8602
MacDonald G, 1 Birchington Ct,Crouch Hall Rd N8 .... 01 348 3381
MacDonald G, 34 Hyndewood,Dacres Rd SE23 .... 01 699 2635
Macdonald G, 25 Ivinghoe Ho,Dalmeny Av N7 .... 01 607 9045
McDonald G, 43 Disraeli Rd W5 .... 01 567 0765
MacDonald G, 9q Peabody Est Fulham Pal Rd W6 .... 01 748 2809
McDonald G, 7 Macdonald Rd E17 .... 01 523 0866
Macdonald Gordon, 6 Malvern Ter N1 .... 01 607 2509
MacDonald G, 41 Sherington Rd SE7 .... 01 858 5714
McDonald G, 67 Shirley Rd E15 .... 01 534 8925

} 7 ~ 8 % Saving by reduction of typesize and line space.
} 7 ~ 8 % saving by reduction of turn-over lines.

Total 15 % saving by HL-3 setting.
Note: This indicates ultimately 40 % saving in the layout of

HC-1

MacDonald K.M,
1 Leigh Ter Malling Rd,Teston...Maidstone 812653
McDonald K.M, 10 Sussex Dv,Chatham ....Medway 62224
MacDonald K.R,
Kendor Ldg,Chequers Rd...Minster (Sheppey) 873116
Macdonald L.C, 27 Denesway ....Meopham 813409
McDonald L.C, 166 Milton Rd,Gillingham........Medway 578119
Macdonald L.D, 37 Campleshon Rd,Rainham ......Medway 35774
Macdonald L.J,
Millers Ho,Water La,Ospringe...Faversham 534912
Macdonald M, 12 Ashford Dv,Kingswood.......Maidstone 843595
McDonald M, 57 Ayelands,New Ash Gn ....Ash Green 872995
McDonald M, 33 Cedar Av ....Gravesend 332221
McDonald M, 41 Dial Rd,Gillingham ....Medway 573404
McDonald M, 107 Medhurst Cres................Gravesend 23284
Macdonald M, 10 St. Hildas Wy ....Gravesend 51752
McDonald M, 4 Sherbourne Clo................W Kingsdown 2819
McDonald M, 19 Thames Av.....................Sheerness 666020
McDonald M, 58 The Ferns,Larkfield ....W Malling 844324
McDonald M.A, 6 Mallingdene Clo,Cliffe Wds ...Medway 221729
MacDonald M.G, 36 Hill Brow,Bearsted.........Maidstone 30153
McDonald M.J, 74 North St ....Sittingbourne 76055
Macdonald M.J, 13 Worcester Clo,Strood ....Medway 722028
McDonald Malcm.J.G,
Turks Hill,Taylors La,Higham...Shorne 2209
McDonald M.L, 35 Old Road Wst ....Gravesend 60540
McDonald M.P, 66 Wayfield Rd,Chatham ....Medway 46722
MacDonald P, 19 Broom Rd,Murston ....Sittingbourne 22158
McDonald P.A, 106 Chestnut Av,Walderslade ......Medway 62218
McDonald P.J, 45 Park Av,Northfleet............Gravesend 51028
McDonald P.M,
9 Birchington Clo,Vinters Pk...Maidstone 675100
MacDonald R, 154 Luton Rd,Cnatham ....Medway 407975
McDonald R, 45 Ryde Clo,Chatham ....Medway 668461
McDonald R, 7 Terrace Rd...................Sittingbourne 78404
McDonald R.A, 102 Oak Rd ....Sittingbourne 78235
MacDonald R.F,
C chard Ho,Old Rd,Wateringbury...Maidstone 812680
MacDonald R.J,
Tolcarne,Amsbury Rd,Coxheath...Maidstone 45758
Mcdonald R.J, 78 Sidney Rd,Borstal ....Medway 49740
Macdonald R.J, 2 Stonecroft,Vigo,Meopham .....Fairseat 823463
Macdonald R.L.M, 55 Stone St ....Faversham 535355
McDonald R.P, 15 Clarence Av,Rochester ....Medway 811007
McDonald R.P, 72 Wilson Av,Rochester...........Medway 400395
McDonald Dr R.P.C,Phys—
Brook Ho,Lr Stoke..............................Medway 270345
MacDonald R.V, 63 Leicester Rd ....Maidstone 58905
McDonald S, 165 Ballens Rd,Walderslade..........Medway 63918
McDonald S.D, 31 Greenfield Clo,Eccles ....Maidstone 77032

HC-2

MacDonald K.M, 1 Leigh Ter Malling Rd,Teston .... Maidstone 812653
McDonald K.M, 10 Sussex Dv,Chatham................ Medway 62224
MacDonald K.R, Kendor Ldg,Chequers Rd . . Minster (Sheppey) 873116
Macdonald L.C, 27 Denesway....................... Meopham 813409
McDonald L.C, 166 Milton Rd,Gillingham .... Medway 578119
Macdonald L.D, 37 Campleshon Rd,Rainham .... Medway 35774
Macdonald L.J, Millers Ho,Water La,Ospringe .... Faversham 534912
Macdonald M, 12 Ashford Dv,Kingswood.......... Maidstone 843595
McDonald M, 57 Ayelands,New Ash Gn .... Ash Green 872995
McDonald M, 33 Cedar Av .... Gravesend 332221
McDonald M, 41 Dial Rd,Gillingham .... Medway 573404
McDonald M, 107 Medhurst Cres.................. Gravesend 23284
Macdonald M, 10 St.Hildas Wy .... Gravesend 51752
McDonald M, 4 Sherbourne Clo .... W Kingsdown 2819
McDonald M, 19 Thames Av .... Sheerness 666020
McDonald M, 58 The Ferns,Larkfield............. W Malling 844324
McDonald M.A, 6 Mallingdene Clo,Cliffe Wds .... Medway 221729
MacDonald M.G, 36 Hill Brow,Bearsted .... Maidstone 30153
McDonald M.J, 74 North St .... Sittingbourne 76055
Macdonald M.J, 13 Worcester Clo,Strood .... Medway 722028
McDonald Malcm.J.G, Turks Hill,Taylors La,Higham ..... Shorne 2209
McDonald M.L, 35 Old Road Wst .... Gravesend 60540
McDonald M.P, 66 Wayfield Rd,Chatham .... Medway 46722
MacDonald P, 19 Broom Rd,Murston .... Sittingbourne 22158
McDonald P.A, 106 Chestnut Av,Walderslade .... Medway 62218
McDonald P.J, 45 Park Av,Northfleet .... Gravesend 51028
McDonald P.M, 9 Birchington Clo,Vinters Pk ...... Maidstone 675100
MacDonald R, 154 Luton Rd,Chatham .... Medway 407975
McDonald R, 45 Ryde Clo,Chatham .... Medway 668461
McDonald R, 7 Terrace Rd...................... Sittingbourne 78404
McDonald R.A, 102 Oak Rd .... Sittingbourne 78235
MacDonald R.F, Orchard Ho,Old Rd,Wateringbury. Maidstone 812680
MacDonald R.J, Tolcarne,Amsbury Rd,Coxheath .... Maidstone 45758
Mcdonald R.J, 78 Sidney Rd,Borstal .... Medway 49740
Macdonald R.J, 2 Stonecroft,Vigo,Meopham .... Fairseat 823463
Macdonald R.L.M, 55 Stone St................... Faversham 535355
McDonald R.P, 15 Clarence Av,Rochester .... Medway 811007
McDonald R.P, 72 Wilson Av,Rochester.............. Medway 400395
McDonald Dr R.P.C,Phys— Brook Ho,Lr Stoke .... Medway 270345
MacDonald R.V, 63 Leicester Rd .... Maidstone 58905
McDonald S, 165 Ballens Rd,Walderslade .... Medway 63918
McDonald S.D, 31 Greenfield Clo,Eccles............ Maidstone 77032

} Total 8 ~ 11 % saving

HC-3

MacDonald K.M, 1 Leigh Ter Malling Rd,Teston....... Maidstone 812653
McDonald K.M, 10 Sussex Dv,Chatham .... Medway 62224
MacDonald K.R, Kendor Ldg,Chequers Rd .... Minster (Sheppey) 873116
Macdonald L.C, 27 Denesway .... Meopham 813409
McDonald L.C, 166 Milton Rd,Gillingham .... Medway 578119
Macdonald L.D, 37 Campleshon Rd,Rainham .... Medway 35774
Macdonald L.J, Millers Ho,Water La,Ospringe ...... Faversham 534912
Macdonald M, 12 Ashford Dv,Kingswood .... Maidstone 843595
McDonald M, 57 Ayelands,New Ash Gn................ Ash Green 872995
McDonald M, 33 Cedar Av .... Gravesend 332221
McDonald M, 41 Dial Rd,Gillingham .... Medway 573404
McDonald M, 107 Medhurst Cres .... Gravesend 23284
Macdonald M, 10 St.Hildas Wy .... Gravesend 51752
McDonald M, 4 Sherbourne Clo .... W Kingsdown 2819
McDonald M, 19 Thames Av......................... Sheerness 666020
McDonald M, 58 The Ferns,Larkfield .... W Malling 844324
McDonald M.A, 6 Mallingdene Clo,Cliffe Wds .... Medway 221729
MacDonald M.G, 36 Hill Brow,Bearsted .... Maidstone 30153
McDonald M.J, 74 North St .... Sittingbourne 76055
Macdonald M.J, 13 Worcester Clo,Strood .... Medway 722028
McDonald Malcm.J.G Turks Hill,Taylors La,Higham .... Shorne 2209
McDonald M.L, 35 Old Road Wst .... Gravesend 60540
McDonald M.P, 66 Wayfield Rd,Chatham................ Medway 46722
MacDonald P, 19 Broom Rd,Murston .... Sittingbourne 22158
McDonald P.A, 106 Chestnut Av,Walderslade .... Medway 62218
McDonald P.J, 45 Park Av,Northfleet .... Gravesend 51028
McDonald P.M, 9 Birchington Clo,Vinters Pk......... Maidstone 675100
MacDonald R, 154 Luton Rd,Chatham .... Medway 407975
McDonald R, 45 Ryde Clo,Chatham .... Medway 668461
McDonald R, 7 Terrace Rd .... Sittingbourne 78404
McDonald R.A, 102 Oak Rd .... Sittingbourne 78235
MacDonald R.F, Orchard Ho,Old Rd,Wateringbury ... Maidstone 812680
MacDonald R.J, Tolcarne,Amsbury Rd,Coxheath....... Maidstone 45758
Mcdonald R.J, 78 Sidney Rd,Borstal.................... Medway 49740
Macdonald R.J, 2 Stonecroft,Vigo,Meopham .... Fairseat 823463
Macdonald R.L.M, 55 Stone St .... Faversham 535355
McDonald R.P, 15 Clarence Av,Rochester .... Medway 811007
McDonald R.P, 72 Wilson Av,Rochester .... Medway 400395
McDonald Dr R.P.C,Phys— Brook Ho,Lr Stoke.......... Medway 270345
MacDonald R.V, 63 Leicester Rd.................... Maidstone 58905
McDonald S, 165 Ballens Rd,Walderslade................ Medway 63918
McDonald S.D, 31 Greenfield Clo,Eccles .... Maidstone 77032

} Total 12 ~ 15 % saving

1990 **Bell Centennial** George Sadek

Before 1938, telephone directories were set in whatever typeface suited the local publisher, with chaotic results. The Bell System was impressed by the work Chauncey Griffith of Mergenthaler had done to increase the legibility of newspapers, and in 1937 asked him to design a face specifically for Linotype composition of telephone directories. The result was *Bell Gothic*, which became the standard for directory composition around the world.

In the early 1970s, Bell began to compose phone directories on high speed cathode ray tube (CRT) typesetters and problems arose. *Bell Gothic* was designed to the specifications of the Linotype and did not fit the new equipment well. In addition, *Bell Gothic* retained a definite flavour of, which clashed with the new AT&T identity program designed by Saul Bass. In 1974, AT&T approached Mergenthaler to see if a new *Bell Gothic* with a contemporary look could be designed to suit the characteristics of CRT typesetters. The challenge was given to Mike Parker, Director of Typographic Development, who brought in Matthew Carter as designer. Over the next four years, they worked closely with AT&T; with Pat Desmond of New York Telephone in the early stages, and thereafter with a special task force of the Directory Managers from several of the Bell Companies meeting under the chairmanship of Ernest Buckstine.

A quality-control study of the performance of existing *Bell Gothic* fonts under the new production conditions was undertaken by Jim McElrath of Western Electric. His report served as an invaluable design brief for the development of the new typeface.

AT&T's main concern was to make the directories more legible. When set on CRT machines, *Bell Gothic's* stroke weights became too light and pinched out. When addresses were condensed on the typesetter to avoid over-runs, letters became illegibly squeezed. Another concern was for space economy: the new face had to allow at least as many entries per page as *Bell Gothic* to avoid increased paper costs. One of the advantages of the new typesetting technology lay in the ability to get away from Linotype dup-lexing (which forced Light and Bold characters to share the same widths) and to load as many fonts as necessary into the typesetter at the same time. In the new unduplexed series, the width of the *Address* font could be diminished so that the *Name and Number* font could be made more legible.

This article presents the progress of the design from initial sketches in 1976, through

final acceptance of four fonts under the name *Bell Centennial* in 1978, the centennial year of the Bell Directories.

The designer

Matthew Carter, the designer of *Bell Centennial*, is the son of the late Harry Carter, distinguished typographer and historian of type. On leaving school, Matthew spent a year studying punch-cutting at Enschede's in Holland, one of the few modern printers to maintain their own type-foundry. He worked as typographic adviser to Crosfield Electronics in London (manufacturing agents for the Photon phototypesetting machines) before joining Mergenthaler in New York in 1965. After six years he moved back to London as a freelance type designer working in continued association with the Linotype Companies. Carter is now a vice-president of Bitstream, a company located in Cambridge, Massachusetts, which designs and manufactures digital fonts.

Some of Carter's type designs have derived from historical origins: *Snell Roundhand*, a joining script based on the models of a seventeenth century writing master; and the four weight *Galliard* series inspired by the types of the French Renaissance punchcutter Robert Granjon. Other faces have been designed to meet the needs of contemporary printing: *Olympian*, a newspaper text series; *Video*, a sans serif for CRT composition; and a digital face commissioned by the National Geographic magazine for setting picture captions. Recently, non-Latin faces have formed a large part of Carter's output: *Hangul* (Korean), several Greeks, a Raschi Hebrew, and a Devanagari.

Carter's close working relationship with the Linotype Group has given him a thorough understanding of the ever-advancing technology of typesetting, a necessary qualification in undertaking a project such as *Bell Centennial* in which technical considerations must influence – but not dominate – the utilitarian and aesthetic priorities of design.

The process of development

As the first stage of the project, Mergenthaler agreed to provide 'sketches of a new typeface… preliminary in nature' in the form of drawings for an agreed number of characters in three fonts: *Name and Number*, a lighter *Address* and an all-capital *Bold Listings*. Carter drew something over two hundred characters for alternative fonts that varied in weight and degree of compression. These represented choices that came up in the course of his work and which he thought important, too important to be made by Mergenthaler alone. In March 1976, Carter and Parker showed the preliminary design to the AT&T Graphic Task Force. The following text is the presentation which Carter gave to explain the design. It summarises, in his own words, the limiting factors and the line taken to achieve maximum legibility and economy within rigid restraints.

The problem of character weight was very much at the heart of what AT&T called 'designing for printability'. The following paragraph is quoted from their study: '…we have found that the final printed image can be considerably different in contrast and readability from the software design of the image prior to the CRT output. The various steps in the processes can introduce as much as .003" variation in the thickness of the vertical line of a character with an average variation of between .001"and .002" within

Bell Centennial: Matthew Carter.

a page, between pages and, most important, between pages of daily lots. This adverse accumulation of tolerances can become extremely important, because such variation can account for a 40% – 50% variation in the thickness of a vertical line of a character. The final printed pages of four- or five-column compressed type, therefore, can range from very light to very dark in overall appearance, with characters running together and touching, resulting in an undesirable printed product which is virtually impossible to control during the press run'.

The black line is the *Bell Gothic* design on paper, vintage 1937. Superimposed on the originals are the effects of a tolerance of .003", made up of the loss of .0015" (the black image) and the gain of .0015" (the white-on-grey image), the accumulated variation caused by production processes. This, in graphic form, is what the AT&T report describes.

The black image has become very feeble – eroded completely away where the arch springs from the stem. The most common complaint of Bell's subscribers is that the directory pages are too light; if they are trying to read characters with a stem weight of .0025" (that of the black image) they are not being unreasonable. It is the effort to counteract this distressing lightness that leads to over-inking, the blurring of character image, the sacrificing of readability and frequent press stops for washdown, with the consequence of increased printing costs. It seems essential, therefore, that a new directory face should show a gain in stroke weight, a controlled gain incorporated in the design by the designer, not applied remedially in subsequent production processes.

The stem weight of the lighter Address font letter is now .007", the minimum recommended, with results that are unexceptionable. The implications for the right-hand letter (*Bell Gothic Bold*, the *Name and Number* font) are much less satisfactory: firstly in order to preserve sufficient contrast between light and bold faces, rather more weight had to be added to the heavier h than to the lighter one; and, secondly, in both letters it was necessary to add weight only on the inside of the strokes. This last measure – the preservation of ample side-bearing (the white space between adjacent letters) – is vital in countering the tendency of CRT-set characters to spread and occasionally to

(below) The lowercase h's from *Bell Gothic* (the Address font) and *Bell Gothic Bold* (the *Name and Number* font).

(below right) The same two *Bell Gothic* h's with weight added.

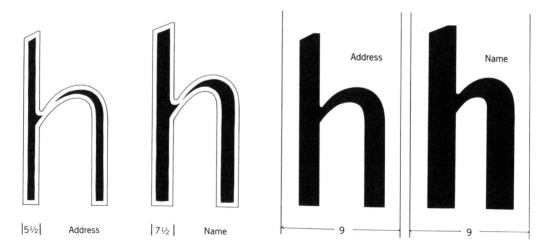

|5½|　　Address　　|7½|　　Name　　|←——— 9 ———→|　　←——— 9 ———→|

Address　　Name

bridge when electronically compressed in the typesetter. It was found that the resulting letter in the bolder *Name and Number* font was unacceptably narrow and illegible on its original width of 9 units; the combined pressures of added stem weight and maintained side-bearing forced the font onto bodies one unit wider than *Bell Gothic Bold*.

The increase in weight between *Bell Gothic* and the designs, already discussed and the increase in lower-case x-height – the most important single factor in a typeface's legibility – are very noticeable. There is a difference of two units in width between *Bell Gothic* and *Helvetica*. (A unit is one-eighteenth of the point size). There is a generic similarity between *Helvetica* and the new designs: the more symmetrical arch, characteristic of contemporary sans serifs, and the square-topped ascender. In the new designs, however, the crotch (where the arch joins the stem) has been relieved of weight to reduce the risk of trapping ink.

The difference in weight between font 1 and font 2 is the thickness of a single raster line in a CRT typesetter having an output resolution of 850 lines to the inch.

The point at which the characters come nearest together has been indicated by a grey bar, and the measurement of this distance in thousandths of an inch has been written below each combination. The lighter version actually shows a slight gain over *Bell Gothic Bold*; while in the heavier drawing the results are virtually the same as in *Bell Gothic Bold*. These clearance dimensions are critical when it comes to the electronic compression of these fonts. By going to a wider unit-width, weight has been added to the *Name and Number* font without sacrificing side-bearing.

Fonts 1, 2, 3 and 4, represented by their h's. Fonts 1 and 2 are different weights of the *Name and Number* face; fonts 3 and 4 are different widths of the lighter *Address* face.

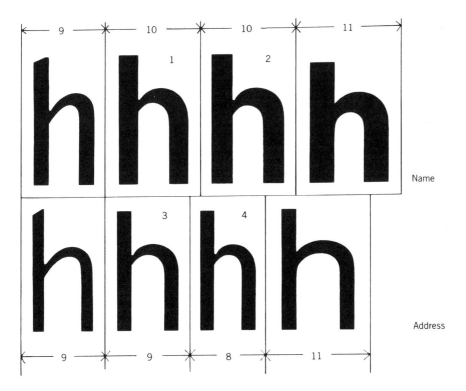

Name

Bell
Bold

(above) New design for the lower-case fonts.

(below) Trial drawings for the newly designed lower-case letterforms and figures.

acegs

acegs

356

356

During the initial discussion, AT&T expressed a desire for a design of more contemporary look (*Bell Gothic* is nearly forty years old), one typographically compatible with *Helvetica* and other modern sans serifs with which it is likely to be associated in some of its applications. Carter tried to bring these aesthetic considerations and the technical imperatives together and in many cases they combined excellently to work in his favour. But *Helvetica* was not designed to be at its functional best at 6 or 7pt (nor was any other modern sans serif – their purpose is more general). The new design was not considered simply as a miniaturization of *Helvetica*. The *Helvetica*-like characteristics were retained when they served the essential purpose of design for printability, not if they interfered with it.

In one case, style and function are somewhat at odds. Only five lower-case letterforms are involved in this problem, but all occur frequently in the language and hence are influential in the overall appearance of the printed font. The version at the top, labelled Grot (for grotesque, a term which, like gothic, is largely synonymous with sans serif), is typical of modern sans serifs, such as *Helvetica*, *Univers* and *Folio*, and has a certain amount to do with their clean-cut, elegant lines. However, by resolving the ends of the strokes in this way – cutting them off on the horizontal – the letterform is made more enclosed, the interior counters are made smaller and given a narrower outlet to the surrounding white space, causing the positive parts to approach closer together.

The alternative forms in the lower line, closer in style to those of *Bell Gothic*, *Gill Sans*, and others of the older, more humanistic sans serif designs, are manifestly more open. In small sizes and condensed faces they are probably more legible. This is a case in which adherence to the Grot form's aesthetic grounds may have undesirable technical repercussions. There is no difference in width between the two versions.

In the case of the five lower-case letters in the previous illustration (and capitals CGS) there is perhaps room for debate, but when the same design problem occurs in the figures there seems to be no argument. The *Helvetica* forms (the upper line), analogous to the Grot letterforms in their enclosure and treatment of the stroke terminals, are both much wider at 6 and more ambiguous than those in the bottom line. *Helvetica*'s figure 3 must be more easily confused with 8, its 5 with 6, 6 with 8, etc, particularly when condensed or when the similarities are compounded by imperfect printing or imperfect eyesight. In the lower line are newly-designed figures of open form, consistent, in this principle at least, with *Bell Gothic*: functional and clear.

Another factor that must be considered is the electronic condensing of typefaces on CRT typesetters. A few years ago Mergenthaler released a family of sans serif faces called *Video*. Users of Linotron CRT typesetters relished the ability to condense type by reducing set-width independently of point size, obtaining in this way typographic variety and emphasis without the loss of production time required to change font in the conventional sense. Unfortunately, the sans serif faces in the library, most popularly *Spartan* and *Helvetica*, were designed before the invention of CRT typesetting and obviously, therefore, took no account in their design of the effects of an amorphic distortion on their letterforms, effects that, in the event, were less than flattering. After analysis of the behaviour of the forms during distortion, the characters were modified

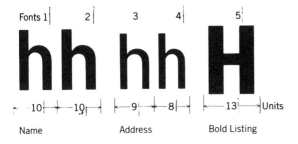

Fonts 1   2   3   4   5

hh hh H

10 · 10 · 9 · 8 · 13 Units

Name   Address   Bold Listing

jwqnskgf

4556788

(above top) The five trial fonts Carter designed, font 5 being a single version of the all-capital *Bold Listing* face.

(above middle) Drawings from the trial design of the *Name and Number* font which Matthew Carter presented to AT&T in March 1976.

(below) The trial design.

(without prejudicing the normal version) in such a way that they stood up to compression much better, both in appearance and legibility. The lessons learned from *Video* have been applied to this directory design.

The *Name and Address* fonts are on different widths. In *Bell Gothic* they are the same widths because, they were duplexed on Linotype matrices. Compressing the *Address* face onto a narrower body is appropriate to its relatively less importance in the directory. The combination of wider *Name* font and narrower *Address* font gives an aggregate

Blumberg Herman 332E14 – – – –**AL 6-8085**
Blumen Louis atty
     51 Hawthorn Hampton Bays **125-6983**
Blumenfeld Irving 254 Amity – – –**986-3042**
Blumenthal Ernest 1135 Bensn –**LO 3-8997**
Blumfarb A 1245 Avenue B – – – –**712-4850**
Blundell Thos 44 BrghtnBchAv – –**641-5751**
BOCHIETTO SELHAM SCHOOL
Borderline Educations LindenBlvd **580-0432**
Boxleyheath Opthalmics 5123 Hooper
   Employment Ofc – – – – – – – – –**986-3042**
   Immediate Treatment – – – – – – –**125-6983**
   Information – – – – – – – – – – – –**853-8002**
Brooklyn Tavern Owners Assoc Inc
     1424 BushwickAv **712-4850**
Bush E Arthur 452 Henry – – – – – –**596-9441**
Busick Timothy 513E23 – – – – – –**HE 7-6576**
Bustamante H 3 AvenueL – – – – –**924-0383**

result very close to setting in *Bell Gothic*, 'to provide an equal content on a page as presently achieved' as required in AT&T's specifications.

Carter pasted up photo-reductions of his trial drawings to simulate a few typical lines of a directory column. AT&T approved this specimen and gave the go ahead to Mergenthaler to typeset a complete directory page. It was considered that in some directories the *Address* face was too condensed to be used for also setting sub-captions (subsidiary listings indented under a main entry). A fourth member of the *Bell Centennial* family was accordingly commissioned to be of the same weight as the *Address* face but more generous in width.

Carter made working drawings (in black ink on mylar drafting film) to Mergenthaler's manufacturing scale. At this stage, complete lower-case and figure sets were drawn with a smattering of capitals and punctuation.

The digital fonts were used to compose pages on a high-speed CRT typesetter, in this

(below) Typeface image produced on a Linotron 606, high-speed CRT typesetter.

(bottom) Photographically reduced image on emulsion-coated glass plate.

mtdeulry jwqnskgf 4556788

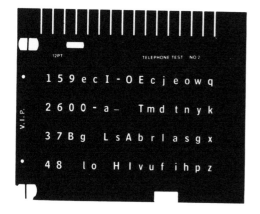

case a Linotron 606, running at approximately 3,000 characters per second.

A font for a conventional photoypesetter, a VIP, was manufactured so that typeset proofs of the new face could be studied. The drawings were photographically reduced on emulsion-coated glass plates called plaques.

The images from these plaques were further reduced to produce the film font.

Once the VIP pages had been judged as satisfactory the actual digitization began. To set directories economically, CRT typesetters must run at their highest output speed, which means at their coarsest resolution. When 6 characters are defined at coarse resolution, the total number of digital elements (bits) of which they can be built is necessarily small. Adding or subtracting a single bit, let alone a row of bits, can make a critical difference to the shape and weight of a letter and, by repetition in text, to the whole alphabet. To keep tight control over these sensitive matters of shape and weight, Carter painstakingly constructed each character bit by bit, first in sketched roughs, then as finished bit-maps. Set-widths, calibrated in discrete raster lines, are indicated below each letter (see illustrations on previous pages).

The inked bit-maps were reduced photographically to judge the shapes in miniature.

The bit-maps were manually encoded. The vertical raster scan-lines are numbered from left-hand to right-hand edge of the character in the column at left, with turn-on and turn-off points along each scan line tabulated to the right.

The encoded numbers were proofed on a Versatec hard-copy printer. These Versatec bit-maps were checked against Carter's original drawings to confirm that shape, alignment and fit were correct. At this stage Carter made revisions at a video terminal.

1990 **The books of Ken Campbell** Ken Garland

'Processional' is the word that comes to mind when I look at a book – any book – by Ken Campbell. The word is customarily applied to a book 'containing litanies, hymns, etc for use in religious processions' (*Shorter Oxford Dictionary*). There are, it is true, frequent allusions throughout his work to Hindu, Judaic, Christian and Islamic observances, and in one instance – *Martyrs* (1989) – the text is not his own but the Gaelic version of Psalm 79, arranged as for singing by a minister and congregation. Yet, as far as I know, Campbell follows no creed and certainly engages in no formal religious observances: his reference to such rituals is entirely eclectic. Even in *Broken Rules and Double Crosses* (1984), in which a sequence of disturbingly distorted shapes is eventually resolved into a Latin cross, the references that accompany the sequence are to Islamic and Judaic, as well as Christian, precept.

Processional also denotes the way in which, for the most part, the books are planned and structured. There is a measured tread about them. The ritual allusions that are apparent in so much of the text are echoed in the configuration of layout and print process. Thus, planes of colour rotate, advance and retreat, overprint progressively, mutate from one hue into the other, always with an underlying visual logic – not necessarily an obvious, pin-downable logic it is true, but accessible, given the effort – which is reassuring when you are still trying to sort out what other meanings may lie behind that structure.

But of course, in works like these, which have been so woven with text and image as warp and weft into an integrated whole, the sense of them emerges by a process of exchange, whether instantaneous or delayed, between the one and the other. Sometimes, as in *Tilt: the Black-flagged Streets* (1988), the verse poem is at first obscured, rather than revealed, by the thick overlay of colour and pattern. Each successive line appears initially on the left-hand page of each spread, facing the preceding lines of the poem on the right-hand page; this single line only being recognised as anything other than an isolated phrase when it is seen to join the accumulating whole on the right-hand page of the next spread. In some parts of the book, the verse may even seem irrelevant, dominated as it is by the figure of Siva, the Hindu god of destruction and procreation, who prances in front of it, and by the crooked shape of the cover boards that lie open behind the pages. Even when the process of the poem is grasped, it is still

difficult to follow through, because Campbell has laid such dark tones of colour over the text on certain pages that it is almost impossible to read them.

Almost, but never quite. I don't know whether Campbell is being consciously reticent, even shy, about his verse, hiding it beneath more forceful images (as in *Tilt*) 'cancelling' it with heavy horizontal bars (*Father's Garden*, 1989), angling it steeply away from the reader as though seen in sharp perspective (*A Knife Romance*, 1988) or setting it in a relatively modest typeface before and after the sequence of main images (*Broken Rules and Double Crosses*, 1984) so that the text appears in a subordinate rôle. In the end, it comes out of hiding in all these works, of course: a slender, insistent thread of meaning that (for me, at any rate) frequently demands to be read out loud, even incanted.

1

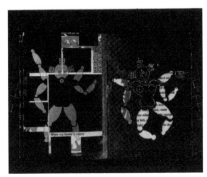

3

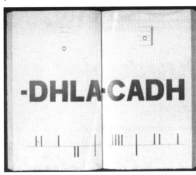

2

4

5

1 and 2 Double-page spreads from *Martyrs* (1989).

3 and 4 Double-page spreads from *Tilt: the Black-flagged Streets* (1988).

5 Double-page spreads from *Father's Garden* (1989).

Another form of incantation is suggested. I believe, by Ken Campbell's most purely typographic book to date, *AbaB* (1984). An overlapping conversation between A and B, it's arranged in two primary and two secondary lines of type, running parallel to one another and crossing the vertical folds of the concertina format. The conversation itself is fractured, unpronounceable, but you find you're attempting to proclaim it in your head – a silent incantation by means of which you can embrace both primary and both secondary lines of the piece at the same time.

This work, in particular, is a powerful reminder of Campbell's early training as a compositor and his subsequent education and continuing skill in graphic design. But it's a skill that gives all his books a special authority: he is not a 'fine' artist who has ventured, daringly, into a new activity; his is not a naive pleasure but a knowing one, as he handles familiar tools. The territory traversed, however, is new with each new book. In this respect he has moved well outside the purlieu of orthodox graphic design, where experience seeks to confirm expectations rather than to uncover surprises; where you get – or should get – exactly what you specify, no more and no less.

Because he uses his skills as a printer and graphic designer to make discoveries, Campbell surprises, first himself, then us. There is room, consequently, for serendipity, the happy chance, and nowhere is this more evident than in *A Knife Romance*, the richest, most complex and elaborately worked of his books to date. In an edition of twenty-five, combining letterpress, etching, blind embossing, metallic dusting and other mysterious manipulations, it has been arrived at through much trial and error. Many experiments must have been discarded on the way and many effects embodied that could not possibly have been foreseen. Essentially, though, the end product is no haphazard fusion of 'interesting' devices but a precise assembly.

To label Campbell's work as 'experimental', therefore, is misleading, in the same way as it was misleading to apply the same description to, say, James Joyce's *Ulysses*. These works are not, in themselves, experiments, but the fulfilment of a carefully planned and well-defined purpose.

Double-page spreads from
AbaB (1984)

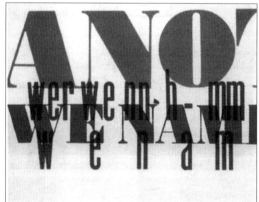

As to the meaning of the books, I have made no attempt to go into detail, for three reasons: first, because the meaning of each book, however elusive and hard to extract, is there inside it, and only there; second, because I am still, after years of familiarity with those five books that I possess, still finding new meanings in them, and third, because (and this is true most especially of *Broken Rules and Double Crosses*, which often has a place on the lectern at home for weeks at a time) they function as catalysts, evoking thoughts in the reader that the maker of the books could know nothing of. That is a most valued and secret pleasure that I have in Ken Campbell's beautiful books and one that I know would delight him.

Long may it last.

(below left) Double-page spreads from *Broken Rules and Double Crosses* (1984).

(below right) Double-page spreads from *A Knife Romance* (1988).

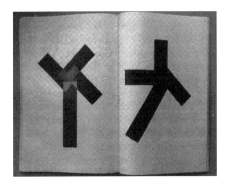

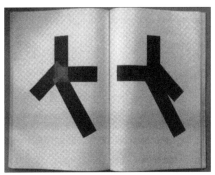

1994 Adventure on the Underground Giovanni Lussu

We often refer to the experience of Peter Behrens with Walter Rathenau's AEG. Less known by us, however famous the Underground 'bulls eye' and Henry Beck's map might be, is the history of London Transport under the direction of Frank Pick, an extra-ordinary 'humanist' manager. Architecture, furnishings, 'travelling material', signs and printing, all aspects of the design can be considered to be exemplary, in this London adventure. At the heart of the communication structure, lies the typeface that was, in 1916, specially commissioned from Edward Johnston, the great craftsman of the revival of calligraphy in our century. It was with Johnston's *Underground Railway* block letter alphabet that the first large 'corporate image' of modern design was created and the sans serif typeface acquired its dignity. *Underground Railway* is the precursor of *Erbar* (Jakob Erbar, 1922), *Kabel* (Rudolph Koch, 1927), *Futura* (Paul Renner, 1927) and *Gill Sans* (Eric Gill, 1927).

The recent redesign of Johnston's typeface by Banks and Miles, due to its precision and competence, is a design episode of rare dignity. We asked Banks to tell us about this model for design in our times.

Colin Banks trained as a calligrapher (with teachers who were taught by Johnston, such as Charles Pickering) and then went on to typography and then to graphic design in general. He is the current President of the Society of Typographic Designers. In 1958

Original drawings for
Underground Railway Sans
(Victoria and Albert Museum).

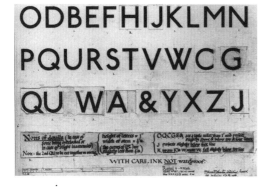

he formed a partnership with John Miles, who studied with Jan van Krimpen in Holland and who worked with Hans Schmoller at Penguin Books. Banks and Miles have been responsible for some prestigious projects, such as the visual identification scheme for the UK Post Office (with the design of a specific typeface, the *Double Line Alphabet*) and the corporate identity of Her Majesty's Stationery Office. They have continued to grow and now have offices in London and Brussels.

London Transport asked Colin Banks to report on the company's visual identity in 1981 Banks delivered his report. In substance, he said that while Pick's style was apparently being followed, the overall image of London Transport was confused. Since the time of Pick there had been two wars, followed by difficult years; new Underground lines had been built and new services introduced with the consequent increase in the complexity of the whole system; recently investment in LT has been reduced (and changes have taken place due to the government's policy of deregulation).

According to Banks, even if printed promotional materials looked decent enough, overall control of the system had been lost and with it 'the authority' of the organisation. This led to a paradoxical situation where, in the worst case, the materials actually worked against the organisation. There had been a weakening in the basic elements that represented the organisation: the way in which the words 'London Transport' were presented was not uniform; the drawing, colours and proportions of the 'bulls eye' symbol varied; the typefaces used were chosen using different criteria. The various advertising agencies employed by London Transport for the promotion of a single service used different typefaces for each campaign. In fact the agencies had paid little attention to the organisation's own typeface, that of Johnston, which had been a feature of London for more than 60 years.

Banks noted: 'there is much in an advertising agency make-up that limits its focus to the short term result, and there is even more in human nature that encourages designers to make their mark in the world however briefly that may last. The more palatable explanation was that '*Underground Railway Sans*' only existed in a limited range of wooden and metal types and in two weights and one condensed variation derived from the medium; this did not give the agency enough typographical muscle and flexibility. All this was true and when put up alongside commercial advertising posters selling wine or banking services, or washing machines, '*Underground*' often looked lightweight, too widely spaced and weak. Furthermore the technology of type reproduction was already changing rapidly and the previous way of doing things by letterpress was expensive and slow.'

The Banks report, in conclusion, emphasised the extraordinary opportunity that existed with Johnston's typeface to pull together the whole system: 'the lettering could act like a ribbon to tie up the disparate parts of the LT business into one well organised parcel.'

London Transport 'understood' and asked for a demonstration of this idea. Banks and Miles then began a twelve year programme of redesigning Johnston's typeface and putting it onto modern reproduction systems. The moment had arrived to deal with the peculiarity of Edward Johnston. Banks notes 'Johnston's simplicity, his need to nail down

facts, and the establishment of perfection came together to form a canon of dogma about the making of letter shapes that regenerated Western calligraphy, but in Britain at least, also put a brake on further advances for another fifty years'.

It seems to this observer that no one moved out of his long pale shadow: not Eric Gill, not the private presses, not Stanley Morison and his stable, and certainly not the Society of Scribes and the Johnston disciples therein. Johnston called himself a 'craftsman' not a 'designer', and was opposed to any form of reproduction of his work, he hated industry, because it was primarily linked to money, and in part hated design because it was linked to industry and the processes of reproduction. To him, a thing to be well made, had to be an end in itself, not part of a filter where the end thing is produced by some hand other than the begetter'.

It was out of these formidable contradictions between this 'craftsman' viewpoint and the inevitably 'industrial' requirements of Frank Pick that the Johnston typeface was born (and certainly not from any design theory). It was into these contradictions that Banks had to impose himself when he started his redesign work.

The declared aim was the continuity of the original typeface, but so that, in today's terms, *New Johnston* could efficiently communicate within the organisation, the problem needed to be dealt with on a much wider scale. It was certainly not just a matter of redesigning the alphabet, a whole system of communication needed to be constructed. There was a need for bolder variants, so that, when necessary, more strength could be provided, and more need for the widespread use of lower case letters.

(below) A direct comparison. On the left is Johnston's version and right, Colin Banks.

(facing page, top) Johnston and below, Colin Banks.

(facing page, bottom) Breaking Johnston's rules, the changes in x-height.

It was important, said Banks, to respect the spirit of Johnston rather than to adhere mechanically to the construction rules which would have made any further development of the design impossible. *New Johnston* breaks three of Johnston's fundamental principles, each of which corresponds to an essential aspect of the redesign:

1 the ratio between the height of a capital letter and the width of stroke could not be greater than 7 to 1 (this meant that bolder variants could not be made);

2 letters should be made of even strokes (not like nineteenth century sanserif designs where the strokes were thinned and thickened for optical appearance);

3 a ratio between the height of a capital letter and x-height of 7 to 4 (and therefore quite long ascenders).

The breaking of the first principle, with the reduction in the ratio between height and thickness, provided bolder type. On the other hand the medium weight of *New Johnston*, being bolder than the reference model, allowed inter-letter spacing to be improved. Banks says, '…for instance, in Johnston's theorising, the space within a lower case o is equal to two thickness of the circular line that defines it. This is best balanced by having the visual equivalent of one stroke thickness of space between the o and the letter on each side. In this way words become rhythmic units, ready to be assimilated in one view, no parts of the word jump out or become tangled'. The bolder the type, the smaller the space between the letters. The original type was made in metal (and therefore with spaces at the sides of the letter, called 'the shoulders') and wood (with no shoulders). For wooden type, Johnston set out complex spacing rules, showing how

ABCDEFGHIJKLMNOPQ
RSTUVWXYZ   abcdefg
hijklmnopqrstuvwxyz
1234567890   (&£.,:;'!?-*)

ABCDEFGHIJKLMNOPQ
RSTUVWXYZ   abcdefg
hijklmnopqrstuvwxyz
1234567890 (&£.,:;≤!?-*)

heightx xheight

space was to be added using small strips of lead placed between the letters.
The application of these rules was at first carefully followed by the well trained
compositors and printers who supplied London Transport. With the reduction in the
level of skills, these rules were neglected and letters became badly spaced. In the
meantime, the advertising agencies were using the boldest type they could find and
also squeezing out the space between the letters (something they tried to do with
New Johnston, going as far as to cut off the tail of the i and the l). The result of all
this was disorder and bad typography. When the variants of *New Johnston* became
computer 'fonts', Banks and Miles prepared the kerning tables (for letter spacing)
which automatically provided correct composition.

We now come to the second principle that was broken (the constant weight of the
stroke) and the second innovation. This is a direct consequence of the choice to produce
bolder type: the evenness of stroke is only possible in light to medium weights
(consider letters with a closed internal shape, such as a, e or 9) and bolder type, adds
Banks, emphasises the visual perception that the horizontal strokes appear thicker
than the vertical ones. It was therefore necessary to 'model' the stroke, and this was
done in *New Johnston*. An exception was the o; modelling this letter in the way it was
done for others (by making the top and lower curves thinner and introducing therefore several centres for the curves) would have meant straying too far from its original
characteristics. Therefore this squat looking circle has been retained, while most of the
other letters, where possible, have have had their top and lower curves slimmed. The
abandoning of the third principle (ratio between capital letter and x-height of 7 to 4)
was necessary to make greater use of lower-case letters. The first appearance of
Johnston's typeface (significantly on an Arts and Crafts exhibition poster in 1916) was
only in capital letters. It is still the capital letter that prevails today (where stations are
named, and lettering appears on the cross-bar of the 'bulls eye', they are in capitals).
However, Banks believes that the lower-case could be put to more wide-spread use,
and that the availability of *New Johnston* as a computer font would favour its application. It was therefore necessary to give more strength to the lower case, so that it
could be used in station names and to provide more compact composition. This was
achieved by reducing the ratio (from 7:4 to about 7:5). *New Johnston*, therefore, has
shorter ascenders and descenders. The design of the *New Johnston* family as a computer
font also takes into account that the vector description (the digital outline) is the
same for different sizes. Until 1921, Banks tells us, the original Johnston types were
only available in large sizes in the form of sheets of transfers that were put on a lithographic stone and blacked in. It is doubtful that Johnston approved, or even knew, the
plans that later materialised, to make it into letterpress type. This was presumably

carried out using pantographic reduction (a procedure that went completely against the craftsman ideals held by Johnston) and never at a size below 36pt. Cutting smaller sizes would have meant making the traditional optical and technical typographic adjustments, the shortening of ascenders, the thickening of strokes, to provide the same shape at different scales, and larger spaces within a letter so that they do not become clogged with ink. Until the automatic correction of shapes within electronic scaling becomes the norm then ideally it would be best to have different drawings, and digital versions for different sizes. Meanwhile, *New Johnston* has been designed to provide the best results in various composition sizes and at low resolution output on screen and printers.

Today, *New Johnston* has restored visual coherence to London Transport. Signs, posters, leaflets, the Underground map, are all progressively being redesigned using the new typeface. The organisation's computers have the new fonts installed and these are accompanied by the simple application rules laid out in the Banks and Miles guide lines.

The underground adventure continues.

1993 **Through the eyes of a child: perception and type design** Rosemary Sassoon

pin pin

for
the
men
and

(top) Written and printed letterforms side by side, from the *Adelaide First Primer*, 1987.

(above) Cursive letters, designed to show how hand-written letters join.

One of the principles of typography has always been to ensure the suitability of the typeface for a particular purpose. It is astonishing, therefore, that little thought has ever been given to designing specific typefaces for those learning to read. Typographic researchers, Ovink (1935) above all others, have stressed the atmosphere values of types and how this might affect the reader. Zachrisson (1967) pointed out that,'Good typography tries to make the message as legible and accessible as possible. Thus the relation between the reader and the image is the function whose efficiency is to be judged. Typography will consequently have to be regarded as a psychological problem'. The decision about letterforms, however, has always been taken for children by adults.

Such decisions are often made by educationists without specialist knowledge of letterforms, or by designers whose criteria for making a page attractive may not be in the children's best interest.

Watts and Nisbet (1974) noted 'No study of the legibility of typefaces which uses children as subjects has been found. The inference made by many researchers regarding the legibility of different typefaces for use in children's books has been based on:
1 legibility studies carried out with adults or older children;
2 their idea of what is involved in the process of learning to read;
3 the relation between reading and writing skills.' (This last consideration is not strictly a matter of legibility, although it may influence a teacher's opinion of what constitutes a 'legible' typeface.)

As far as can be established, nothing has been done actively with children since then. Raban (1984) used a questionnaire to ask teachers about their views on typefaces. This revealed that when asked to choose between serifed or sans serif typefaces, there was a clear indication that a sans serif typeface was preferred by two-thirds of the teachers for books through the infant stage. However, when questioned further about their priorities for typefaces under the rather widely interpreted heading of 'Styles of Print', the picture was somewhat more revealing. 54% of respondents thought that styles of print didn't matter after 7 years of age; 39% thought that it should match handwriting; 14% thought that the 'infant' a and g were important; 11% mentioned size of print; 10% advocated simple letter-shapes; 5% thought it didn't matter at all; 2% mentioned consistency of spacing; 1% thought that sans serif typefaces were good and 1% said that a good story mattered more.

The meagre 2% who considered spacing important even when coupled with the term 'consistent' illustrates how little those teachers' priorities reflected children's real needs.

Yule (1988) expressed refreshing and informed views on the subject in an aptly named paper: 'The *Design of Print for Children: Sales Appeal and User Appeal'*. She also had to report that, apart from Watts and Nisbet, it is difficult to find any research about print for learners. I particularly like her remark that, '…there has been a trend for some aspects of lettering and layout to be designed for sales appeal rather than user appeal. The goal of sales appeal is often for print that is meant to be looked at rather than read.'

She also pointed out that, '…the current fashion for very closely spaced words and letters produces blocks and line of print which have a pleasing overall pattern when glanced at. The complex pattern is not designed to be looked at closely – the effect is like an intricate all-over carpet pattern.'

My views – for what they are worth, leaving research aside and using only common-sense observations, many of the features of typefaces that are fashionable today are entirely adult-oriented, suited admirably to the fluent reader. The combination of fashion and the desire to pack as many lines as possible onto a page, has resulted in decreased ascenders and descenders. This tendency eventually codes the shape of a word as well as the actual identity of individual letters.

After a decade's work in handwriting problems, I was well aware of the injustice of the imposition of various idiosyncratic handwriting models on young children, and the harm that could be done by not considering this from the writer's point of view. When it was brought to my notice that similar attitudes in the area of typographic design and layout might affect children's reading performance, then it seemed that this deserved investigation.

The project

The project that led to the design of a family of child-oriented typefaces started in relatively low-key manner. It was initially concerned with spacing rather than with the letterforms themselves. There was no precedent for testing children on their perception either of spacing or of the different elements of letters. Almost everyone with whom I discussed this considered this task to be beyond the capabilities of young children. No funding was sought, and its success was dependent on the co-operation of hard-working teachers. The teachers involved had no particular typographic knowledge. It was, perhaps, better that they should know as little as possible in case their own views

The joined typeface in outline. From *Ginns*.

affected their judgement. It was essential, however, that they should have detailed knowledge of individual pupils' reading capacity. This project was offered to several special needs teachers in various parts of Great Britain. An exact method of testing was not specified. This was because all the work would have to be undertaken during professional working hours. It is not surprising that only one teacher was able to produce a worthwhile study, and that took her over a year to produce.

The task

The text of the original problem page was re-set in five different spacings through the generosity of the Monotype Corporation. It was then that a choice of typefaces had to be made with little guidance from previous research it could be called arbitrary. In the field of learning difficulties, however, such matters were already under discussion in an informal way. The choice was, of course, confined to existing typefaces and between serifed and sans serif letters, either upright or slanted. *Times Roman*, the establishment's usual recommendation, was an obvious choice. *Times Italic* was included as some people involved with children with reading problems were already recommending it. *Helvetica* (with simplified a and 9) was chosen because of its popularity with educational publishers, and my personal inclusion was a slanting sans serif typeface. In this way twenty variables were available.

How this information was used

It would not be true to say that the educational typefaces now called *Sassoon Primary* were based entirely on the evidence provided by this survey. Certain elements could be isolated from the survey, in particular the desirability of a slight slant. While designing the letterforms I had always to be aware that the children had only adult features to choose from. My job was to build extra legibility, and friendliness into the forms. Balancing the overall preference for sans serif with the comments about liking the 'kick-up' of *Times Italic* a new kind of letter evolved that cannot be described in typographic terms as either serifed or sans serif.

If this typeface had to be described by ATypI's 'parameters of originality' it might upset their neat categorisation. The child orientated letters have sans serif terminals for the ascending strokes to maximize clarity along the top of the line of text. However, letters that terminate on the baseline do not have anything that could be termed a serif It is more a flowing 'kick-up'. This 'exit stroke', to use a handwriting term, has two functions: to ensure clear letter-spacing while at the same time clumping the letters

(below) Some of the alternative lower-case letters.

(bottom) two examples: on the left, the most favoured typeface from the survey, originally set in 18/30 point.

k k

q q

f f

He was right out of the water and away from the waves and he lay still. He rolled on to his back, and lay very still. He lay there for a long time. He blew and puffed, and lay there on the sand. And as he lay there, the wind blew more

He was right out of the water and away from the waves and he lay still. He rolled on to his back, and lay very still. He lay there for a long time. He blew and puffed, and lay there on the sand. And as he lay there, the wind blew more

of each word together along the baseline into a more cohesive shape. The lengths of the ascenders and descenders were increased, bearing in mind the uses of such a typeface and the need to allow for moderately close line spacing. The smooth arches were designed to accentuate the movement, and particular care was taken to simplify the counters. As well as improving legibility, these features added a juvenile and friendly atmosphere to the letterforms.

Bridging the gap between reading and writing

The typeface was researched and designed to be read, but the elements that children chose, and therefore formed the basis of my design, included many of the features of handwriting. There is little historical precedent for the two sets of letters to be identical.

The teachers in Raban's survey reported that it was desirable to have identical letters for reading and writing. This comment is likely to have a different interpretation from that stated by Schonell and Goodacre (1971) that; 'The type should resemble as nearly as possible the print script that the child is acquainted with in his writing. This can be achieved by 24 point *Gill Sans* type'. By 1984 the teachers were more likely to be looking at it from the other angle. They were probably trying to justify the use of print script as a handwriting model by claiming that it was a good idea to write the same letters as those that appear in reading books under the mistaken impression that only sans serif typefaces are used in children's books.

In answer to a publisher's investigation into attitudes to the new typeface, one teacher went further than surveying it for reading purposes. She volunteered, 'I pursued a separate issue with my question "would you like to write like this?" The children replied enviously that they certainly would. They were obviously impressed with the *style of print* (my italics) and I as a teacher saw tremendous advantages in developing a typeface that could link with a handwriting scheme'. There would be advantages for a publisher too, as a handwriting-style typeface would bypass the extremely expensive business of hiring a 'scribe' to produce all the necessary copybooks. When the inevitable proposal turned up I could not have prevented it, even if I had wanted to. I am not particularly in favour of commercial handwriting schemes and have no intention of producing one myself, but by then anyone could buy the PostScript version of *Sassoon Primary* Type, install it on their computer and go straight ahead – but were these letters right for a handwriting model? They had a certain amount of movement built into them so perhaps it was only a matter of increasing the ascenders and descenders – or was it? Not only did this project become, from that moment, market-led, but the new uses meant a completely new and more flexible attitude to the set of letters.

The informality of the typefaces mean that they work well in comic-strip format.
Cambridge University Press.

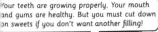

Market-led innovations

An upright typeface both for reading and writing was yet another market-led departure. This is quite a simple alteration to make using the original Ikarus data. By now the whole project was getting further and further away from its relatively researched beginnings, and more was to come. A joined version was a challenge that could not be

resisted but it brought with it considerable complications. These have not yet all been solved in a satisfactory way. More than any previous venture, the joined letters mark the point where the priorities for reading and writing differ.

The joined version for teaching handwriting needs handwriting, not typographic ligatures. It needed to show how etters joined, not only give a cursive appearance. Half a dozen joins to the letter e or to and from s were needed, for example, making the keying in of continuous text rather tedious. There was also a major ideological problem for me. I believe that the hand needs a rest as it progresses along the line, and recommend pen-lifts every few letters. This is not necessarily in any particular mathematical sequence. The need for a pen-lift is governed partly by how many complex movements have had to be made in any series of letters. The frequency of pen-lifts is also likely to vary with individual size, speed and style of writing and the handiness of the writer. My convictions put me in no mood to provide anyone with the means of printing out long lines of continuous cursive to torture the children who might have to copy them. Then there is the matter of the need for alternative letterforms for such letter as s, f, and t when they are joined. These alternative joins are easy to design but impossible to program in such a way that they would suit individual writers. So far, I have limited the use of the joined handwriting fount to pairs of joined letters. These can show how to join, and can be used for demonstrating various alternatives to encourage experimentation.

Visually these 'handwriting' joins disrupt the midline in particular and, in doing so, they interfere with the smooth scanning of text. From the typographic angle any looped ascenders and descenders that would be practical (or, in this case, dare I say, aesthetic) to write would be far too long for any reasonable line-spacing. A simplified cursive-looking typeface, perhaps for use in advertising, is now possible, but even that would be unlikely to be practical for long texts.

Now, as national and more localised bodies pursue their enquiries into uses of this family of typefaces, both in main-stream education and in special needs, we are all in the same situation: working on the edge of knowledge. We are in an ever-changing environment, and there is nothing with which to make real comparisons.

I would welcome parallel research and other child-oriented typefaces, but doubt if others are likely to be forthcoming in the present economic conditions. The original research, and the type-design, were both time-consuming and expensive.

Opportunities for usage in education

There are no precedents for such flexible usage of typefaces, if that is even the right name for these sets of letters. There are still considerable problems to overcome. The question arises: should there now be separate founts recommended for reading and for writing? How much does the way you write affect the way you are able to decipher letters, especially joined ones? Could the use of a joined-up typeface help young writers to understand the joins in their own handwriting – or to decipher adult writing?

An ever-increasing number of books for young children are now using one or other of these typefaces. This is the result of the enthusiastic response from publishers and others. As these new letters become more familiar to young children, perhaps they will

lead to progressive improvements in reading capacity.

Now individual schools, districts, counties or even countries can produce on their own computers consistent reading, spelling and writing materials for use with young children.

Implications for computers in education

The purpose of this article is not only to report on this particular project but to bring to everyone's attention the need to consider the requirements of different classes of readers, and also to highlight the implications for computer-generated letters in education in general. While earnest deliberations no doubt take place before investment is made in new hardware, from what I see, even in specialist schools, little thought seems to be given to the actual letterforms produced by the latest, most expensive, printer.

Once more, Yule (1988) had something relevant to say: 'Mechanical factors in print design can also operate against readability by children. This includes the desktop printers' spacing which produce letter-spacing where wide letters looked crammed and narrow letters isolated'.

Not long ago I visited a school for the blind, which actually had a large proportion of partially-sighted pupils, in the hope of investigating the special needs of that unusual and very variable group of children. The attitude of the establishment was that bold sans serif letters were precisely suited to all their children's needs. I accepted the verdict meekly then (I would not necessarily do so now after a few more experiments of my own) and took up an invitation to see the resource department that produced all their reading matter. The form of sans serif that was installed was appallingly spaced. The fact that the print was much larger than usual made matters worse. Even with normal vision it was often impossible to see where one word was supposed to end and the next began, letters ran into each other and 'mm' was a disaster. A few adjustments would have made all the difference, but no one wanted to listen.

Specialist teachers are now installing both upright and sloping versions of the new typefaces, normal weight and bold, into their 'laptops' and giving partially-sighted children a choice in addition to traditional sans serif. It is early days, but the results are not all negative. However, a completely new set of readers deserves a completely new survey, with a completely open mind. Any volunteers?

1993 **Serving author and reader** Wolfgang Tiessen

Since I have often been asked questions in recent years about the books I produce, I take the opportunity offered by the fiftieth Tiessen publication to explain my views on fundamental matters in order to give a better insight into my work.

When one talks about books, one usually talks about texts. When, on the other hand, one talks about private press books, we think of the presentation: typography, illustration and binding. I am not comfortable with this distinction. The main intent of every book should be the presentation of the contents.

I shall refrain from discussing specific examples or commenting on my publishing programme and the ideas, intentions and convictions behind it. I will only point out that all my books are related to each other primarily by way of the text. This should become obvious if one looks closely through my catalogue. The reader will discover certain links connecting one text with another, a weft and warp loosely woven at times, but sometimes more tightly. I will not go into details, the discovery of which should be part of the pleasure of exploring the output of the Edition Tiessen.

The remarks which follow are meant to show how deeply my small private press is committed to the principle that each and every detail of book production and design should be subservient to the needs of the reader. That is also the reason for my wanting to discuss such matters without referring to any specific texts. The wayward direction of these thoughts and the deliberate avoidance of certain more general issues reflect my intention not to add anything dramatically new to the already abundant literature on book design.

Book typography begins with the text page: the typeset line as evenly spaced as possible, with the optimal amount of leading – (a decision that hinges on a number of factors) and with margins carefully determined to harmonise with the grey surface tone of the type page. Book typography, therefore, begins with close attention to the details affecting legibility. Obviously the typographer also has to deal with proportion, arrangement and emphasis.

I never misuse a text as a pretext for showing off with strange devices which may well dazzle the observer but are bound to hinder the reader. When I arrange the typesetting as evenly and naturally as possible, I have in mind the needs of the reader. Should the careful typography succeed in persuading one to start reading the text,

to want to get into it, then I have accomplished my primary function. Only if it fulfils this main creative task does typography take the book as a medium seriously. And only if a typographer regards himself as a go-between, who must discreetly keep in the background, does he take the author seriously. Such a typographer focuses attention on the text and rejects superfluous embellishments and distractions. Whoever thinks this dull and looks for active visual effects has completely misunderstood the function of the book, which is to serve both author and reader.

I am a typesetter who, through long experience, has come to rely mainly on one typeface, a typeface – misleadingly known as *Janson* – cut three hundred years ago in Holland by Miklos Kis (1650 – 1702) a Hungarian. (More on the history and characteristics of this typeface can be found in a special publication of the Edition Tiessen, Horst Heiderhoff's *Die Original-Janson-Antiqua*. See also the English translation in the January 1984 issue of *Fine Print*.)

The decision to use only one typeface for all Tiessen publications calls for an explanation. It has never been my intention to impose any kind of uniformity. I do not want to print each text in what might be considered the ideal typeface most suited to the aim of the typographer. Such an endeavour – as anybody knows who has ever dealt with these problems – can only be realised approximately. The quest for the ideal match between a certain typeface and a certain text is all too often a reflection of the typographer's subjective viewpoint, which becomes all the more pronounced the more he succumbs to the urge to interpret.

Type and typography are not meant to emphasise the individuality of, each of my books and the differences that lie between them; their pupose is, rather, to clarify visually the books' underlying affinities. This was one of the main considerations when I set up the Edition Tiessen. Whether, and how far, it has been successful has to be decided on the basis of each individual book. The decision to use only one typeface for all publications is a valid one, especially where the publisher adheres to some distinctive image coupled with a finely circumscribed list of subjects. (Similar considerations prevailed at the famous Bremer Presse.)

Why, then, did I decide on *Janson* for all my books? Let me first quote Heiderhoff: *Janson* is 'on account of its rationality a sort of universal typeface, but at the same time – because of its unusual variety of forms – it is able, and suitable, to express the peculiarities of any language. Because today poetry and prose, more than ever before, try to make clear the incommensurable and imponderable and therefore reject smoothness and harmonic surfaces, since *Janson* on the other hand succeeds in hinting both at something special and exquisite and at a profoundness of thought, it is able to supply the modern sensibility with typographical soundness and lasting strength. It does not superficially mediate between extremes, does not gloss over differences, but allows opposites to be interpreted as entangled and intertwined. This accounts for its modernity, if modernity is understood as plurality created through stresses and strains.'

I would add that *Janson* manages to suffuse many different kinds of texts with its own clarity, delicacy and dignity without losing its character, which emphasises the affinities between texts without becoming bland and non-committal.

I admit that one or two other typefaces might have suggested themselves. But *Janson,* in addition to those qualities already mentioned, has another which among the typefaces available today makes it unique: it is the original historic letterform as cut by Miklos Kis, without even the slightest modification or realignment. Its various small irregularities are evidence of its hand-cut origin, setting *Janson* apart from all new typefaces, be they recut or redrawn from old models; by comparison they look too smooth, too well groomed. Perhaps it is due to these slight irregularities that *Janson* also shows a dash of vivacity, imperfection and nonchalance all its own. At a time when everything is pushed towards greater technical efficiency, this trait, so human, is surely appealing. At any rate, its very lack of polish or streamlining makes it especially well suited to accompany handcrafted graphics because wood-cuts, etchings and lithographs, like *Janson* do not try to conceal the natural irregularities of handcraftsmanship. Thus the formal association between original prints and my favourite typeface is based on a natural companionship. Since these remarks are concerned only with general ideas, I refrain from giving specific examples.

I have dwelt at some length on the question of typography and my chosen typeface because both are distinctive and constant features shared by all publications from the Edition Tiessen. Other features they have in common are the format, which varies only occasionally, the use of the same paper, and of just a few kinds of binding. If a particular feature has shown itself to be good, one need not fear to repeat it; though receptive to modifications, I feel there is no need to follow fad and fashion. Each book on its own should convince by the harmony of its constituent parts.

Having given some reasons why typeface and typography are the common link between my publications, I should now like to explain how the individuality of each book is brought out through the choice of various illustrators and illustrations. Considering that the first fifty titles include original prints from thirty-one artists from thirteen countries, some questions will naturally arise.

Horst Heiderhoff, *Die original-Janson-Antiqua.* Cover and colophon double page spread.

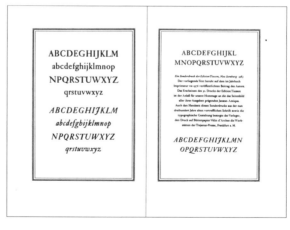

First, having myself called for reticence on the part of the typographer, how does this square with the fact that I often give to the text a counterfoil in the form of illustrations? Is there not a danger that artwork will distract from the text?

Much has been written about the reasons for, and relevance of, book illustration. I will add a few words to clarify my own position. Most important, I think it wrong to define the concept of illustration too narrowly. What should illustrations do? No general rules can be applied. One generally expects illustration to be a mirror-like transfer of something in the text into a visual image of that something. I prefer to think of it as a dialogue between author and artist. Illustration, to me, is more than the continuation of a text by other means. I regard the artist as an autonomous participant in a dialogue with the author, a dialogue which finds concrete expression in the resulting book. In the same way that a conversation means different things to each participant, the dialogue that is the book – in which the reader joins as a third participant – may answer various needs. If the image adds to the spiritual dimension of the text instead of forcing upon it a more narrow and superficial meaning; if it raises questions which might lead to a deeper understanding of what interests us about the text; if it emphasises, by whatever means, the unique underlying texture instead of obscuring or overshadowing it; then, I believe, the dialogue has come to a successful fusing.

How far can such a dialogue be controlled? The question concerns both publisher and designer. As a publisher I try to fashion certain well-chosen texts into books, texts that come from a wide variety of sources and fit in with feasible publishing projects. With this large but not unlimited literary stock on the one hand, there are, on the other, a number of artists with whom at some time I would like to work. Here I deliberately keep an open mind about different modes of expression. As a publisher my most difficult (and most enjoyable) task is to find the best matching partner for the dialogue. Until I am convinced that a certain text will challenge and bring forth the artist's deepest strengths, until I see the possibility for dialogue of substantial value, I prefer

(below left) *Als ich das Licht verlöschte*. Drypoint etchings by Jochen Geilen.

(below right) *Zen. Aussprüche der Zen-Meister*. Woodcuts by Ian Tyson.

to wait for something more convincing to present itself. The text in any case has to fit in with my publishing programme, perhaps continue a certain line. Which texts to print is, after all, the publisher's decision.

As a typographer, I must arrange the dialogue within the implied limits. These are mainly defined by the size of the book and the type area. I expect artists, whom I have usually found most co-operative in this respect, to share in the typographical spirit. Producing a text free of extraneous typographical flourishes presents the author in a restrained manner. In effect, this means that the artist has to be willing to work within a smaller format than is usual for his art. He must accept that there is a difference between art for art's sake and art for a book's sake. Books by their very nature are a 'soft-spoken' medium.

The design of the book covers, too, must adhere to the principle of a harmonic inter-play between the constituent parts. On printed wrappers, this harmony can be achieved by obvious methods: by having the graphics on the cover, for instance, evoke a certain theme or tone played out at greater length in the illustrations inside. It is also common to take one of the motifs from inside and develop it into a pattern. This points up the individuality of the book and at the same time, particularly if labels are used on the cover, reveals its relationship with other books from the same publishing house. This will help explain that the form and content of my books are complementary features which reinforce each other; they do not wander off in different directions.

Finally, I would like to answer one more frequently-asked question: in this time of great technological changes within the printing industry, what is the point of producing books which, by their insistence on traditional methods, tend more and more to move towards the outer fringes of mainstream book production?

People producing books by traditional methods are motivated by many different reasons, yet one thing unites them. To a greater or lesser extent, they all treat the book as a medium of creative expression, however competently this may be done and irre-spective of style or intention. The techniques of craftsmanship involved in letterpress production remain attractive because, obviously, here the hand is in closest possible contact with all materials. It is not for reasons of efficiency that people work as artisans but because this gives them the opportunity to express a creative urge as directly and intimately as possible through a chosen medium. From this there follow certain benefi-cial effects on commercial book production.

We have been discussing questions regarding the interconnection of form and content. Do I have to emphasise that new techniques need not necessarily be enemies of crafts-manship? Certainly not, if they encourage creativity and give it a chance and a place to express itself. Safeguarding this should remain one of our most urgent priorities. For, to quote Theodor W Adorno, 'Today, against all the other manifestations of the mind which go by the name of communication media, it is the book both as a physical and spiritual entity which has to insist on the notion that links craftsmanship and lasting qualities, a notion that would otherwise disappear from the world.'

1997 **Wim Crouwel – the 1997 remix** Alice Twemlow

In July 1997, The Foundry re-issued six typefaces which were originally conceived around thirty years ago by the Dutch designer, Wim Crouwel. For those who are familiar with the work of this graphic designer, or have already appropriated his letterforms, it will seem less like re-issuing and more a case of remixing, or a legalisation of the boot-legging process. But, for a whole new generation of designers and typographers who were not there to sample the fruits of Crouwel's *avant garde* experimentation the first time around, now is their chance, thanks to the efforts of Freda Sack and David Quay.

For about four years now, The Foundry has, under the subtitle of Architype, been salvaging and rebuilding letterforms (often from fragments which were used in poster or brochure designs but never issued as complete fonts) which are of historical signifi-cance, or of aesthetic interest. These include *Architype Tschichold, Architype Renner,* and *Architype Bayer*, among others.

In each project, the typeface is contextualised with an explanation of how and where it was originally used, and how it has since been modified or developed. In this, the most recent archaeological dig into the subsoil of typographic history, David Quay has worked closely with Crouwel to extend typefaces such as *Stedelijk* and *Fodor* which were never issued in their complete forms at the time of their use. Together, Quay and Crouwel have added, for example, a $ sign, and some punctuation marks in order to make a font, such as *Fodor*, internationally useful.

Crouwel, talking about the reissue of the *New Alphabet*, says that even though 'It is a strange idea to have the type available today…I gladly gave my permission to re-issue it, together with some other experiments carried out in the late 60s.' He had seen some of the ways in which, in recent years, it had been used in magazines, '…usually badly reproduced from copies, or hand drawn and always in a typographic context that is not mine; new wave and pop music publications for example.' Although the design of much contemporary music packaging and advertising is not really Crouwel's 'cup of tea,' he is, nevertheless, 'interested in the new directions that typography is taking today. I like the experiments in modern magazine design, even when the atmosphere seems more important than the legibility.' With characteristic self-effacement, he acknowledges 'I do feel honoured that young designers incorporate it (the *New Alphabet*) in their work.'

The typeface that Quay and Sack have renamed *Foundry Gridnik*[1] and which has been described as 'the thinking man's *Courier*', was originally developed for a typewriter company but never used. However, the numerals were used by the Dutch Post Office for use on the low-value Dutch postage stamps, and indeed it is still used today. Traditionally in The Netherlands, even though stamps for ordinary inland letters and higher values must carry the effigy of the head of State, those with lower values show the amount only, so Crouwel's numerals are displayed to full effect.

The *Stedelijk* and the *Fodor* faces have been named after the Museums that they were were designed to publicise (they were used on posters, brochures and catalogues during the 60s, 70s and 80s.)

Of all the faces being reissued, however, it is perhaps for the *New Alphabet* that Crouwel is most famous. It was in 1967, when the first electronic typesetting devices were appearing on the market, that Crouwel 'saw the horrible type coming out of that first-generation machine,' and he proposed a single alphabet typeface (in the tradition of Herbert Bayer, Kurt Schwitters and Jan Tschichold, who all explored this format) as an attempt to answer the new needs of this technology.

In order to avoid the digital break up that tends to distort rounded letter-shapes when composed upon the cathode-ray tube, it uses only horizontal and vertical lines and 45-degree sheared corners. In every size, the outline is then the same. Inspired by a rich heritage of Dutch experimental typographers, such as Sandberg, Schuitema, Werkman and Zwart, who had championed the use of lower-case type, and influenced, perhaps, by the low lying geography of the Dutch landscape, Crouwel designed the *New Alphabet* as a lower-case typeface only, with devices to specify italics, bold or light, and lines above letters to denote capitals.

At the time it was conceived, Crouwel commented that 'The proposed unconventional alphabet shown here is intended merely as an initial step in a direction which could possibly be followed for further research.' It was always provisional, therefore, and open to debate. The forays into the realm of computer-generated type design were applauded by an elite typographic circle, and Crouwel enjoyed a period of lecture-touring at the end of the 60s, but mostly his work was declared anti-human and old fashioned in a period when Bauhaus functionalism was being questioned.

With hindsight, though, it is evident that Crouwel's prescient recognition that the computer was about to revolutionise the ways in which type could be designed, repro-duced and integrated with image, was nothing less than visionary. He realised that although 'the precision of the human eye coupled with an aesthetic feeling can never be equalled by any mechanical device,' computerisation was inevitable and that type design was in danger of being left behind. He recalls that '…in the 60s nobody under-stood what I was after. There was, together with curiosity, also much misunderstanding and much criticism. May be it was wrong to think that the logic of the computer should be followed. I was intrigued by the possibilities of the new technology and dived into it.'

The limitations of the emergent technology were to play a significant part in a commission Crouwel undertook in the 1970s when he was commissioned to redesign

1 Sketch by Wim Crouwel for his orignal version of this font is illustrated on page 8.

(facing page) *New Alphabet*, originally designed by Wim Crouwel. Modified and reissued by David Quay and Freda Sack at The Foundry.

new alphabet

a b c d e f g h i j k l m n
o p q r s t u v w x y z
a b c d e f g h i j k l m n
o p q r s t u v w x y z
a b c d e f g h i j k l m n
o p q r s t u v w x y z

wim crouwel

the Dutch telephone directory. The Dutch Postal Organisation had for long been a patron of lower-case typography having used Piet Zwart, Paul Schuitema and Gerard Kiljan's work previously. Crouwel was taking the lower-case baton forward with his selection of type – a condensed 7pt *Univers* – for use in the directory. The essential design decisions were fuelled as much by pragmatism as they were by aesthetic preferences. The typography was governed by the need to save paper, and by the capacity of the computer system which he had to use (the number of signal changes in the programme which allowed him to shift between capitals, lower case, full stop or comma was limited to nine). So, given the choice between using capitals or punctuation marks, Crouwel opted for the latter, reasoning that it is more difficult to read an address without punctuation than it is without capitals.

Two of the strands of Crouwel's design practice – his type design and the ways in which he implements type – are linked by his almost religious devotion to grids. 'The digital technique is a pure grid in itself. Look how a typeface is reconstructed,' he 'says, it is in a smaller scale closely related to my way of working.' Compositional and organisational structures are fundamental to all his work, both as a solo performer and as a collaborator. In 1963, he and four colleagues established the multidisciplinary consultancy Total Design (which was modelled upon the newly inaugurated Fletcher, Forbes and Gill in London.) He explains that 'we (in Total Design) used grids for typography all the time as a means of creating visual order. We designed many types of grid for many purposes; the grid was always the result of the analysis of the given commission. We believed in a kind of objective typography.'

Although Crouwel is officially retired from his position at Total Design, from his pedagogic and curatorial rôles (he was Professor at Delft University of Technology and Director of the Boymans van Beuningen Museum in Rotterdam) it doesn't look as if he is about to stop designing in a hurry. Instead of purchasing the accessories more usually associated with retirement, Crouwel went and bought himself a Power Mac and is currently mastering this tool. He is delighted to find that he can 'even make grids on it!'

1997 **Never confuse fine words with good deeds** Michael Caine

From my run-down London suburb, Paris beckoned like a pleasure palace – full of wonderful book-shops (dealers in exactly the type of books I was producing), galleries, workshops and printmaking studios. The life-style seemed 'bon vivant' even in the midst of serious work and I had been a student at the *Beaux-Arts* at Nancy for three months in 1981, so I felt I knew what to expect.

France had always seemed 'civilised' and I hoped that something might just rub off on me. I suppose that I emigrated for a change of scenery, in order to re-define myself and widen my interests. Sales of my books were very good in France – I was publishing lots of French Surrealism and suddenly seemed to have a small network that I thought I would be able to exploit once I was 'in situ'. I sent off my cv to many art colleges in Paris (receiving an offer immediately from one), made contact with a small type studio offering me free half day access to equipment, and although a friend offered me the use of a settee, I miraculously found a very cheap flat, by chance, on the very day I arrived in Paris, 1990. I furiously set to work.

My publications, all hand-printed using letterpress, rarely exceed forty pages in length and are intended to be exuberant in spirit, yet modest in volume.

Once I have the text for my next edition, I set about deciding on an appropriate format and a paper that is suitable for both the subject and the type of prints I hope to create. My editions are usually in between octavo and quarto size in a portrait format (*à la française*). Any format smaller than A5 does very little to enhance any print, and as an illustrator I want my images to work to full effect, whilst as typographer I want the text to be as clear and legible as possible. I would compare the size of a text within a book to a voice, too small it becomes a whisper – too large, a hectoring rant. Ideally, a poem is declaimed, and sensitive souls, who attach themselves to small books, risk confusing the intimate with the unintelligible. Small books also have a habit of slipping into oblivion behind larger ones.

A large format book, perhaps A2, is hideously expensive to produce by letterpress; in terms of paper consumed, the number of printings required, and, worst of all, one inevitably has to 'set and diss' two pages at a time. All things considered, a book can be as small as a postage stamp or as big as a wardrobe, although I can't really see the point of either.

My books are invariably printed on hand-made (*à la forme*) and mould-made (*à la ronde*) papers, although as a student I did once print an edition of Mayakovsky on newsprint. I've lost count of the number of books I've 'almost' printed on some sumptuous handmade paper at £2.50 a sheet but have ended up printing on a modest, attractive mould-made paper at a third the price. Because all the real labour-time in letterpress is in setting-up the job, the running time is negligible. The more copies I can physically run off, sheet by sheet, the better. I'm also vaguely tied to a budget and so rarely pass the 200 copies mark.

Indeed, there are certain drawbacks to using beautiful yet deadly handmade papers. Firstly, it often needs dampening if you want to seat the type properly into the paper and get reasonable ink coverage. Ideally, the paper should be left overnight in a sealed plastic bag after dampening evenly the whole surface with a minimum of water. During printing, it has to be kept humid for recto and verso. Getting the moisture out afterwards is no fun, pressed in dry blotters twice, replacing the first set once they have got out the worst of the wet, and finally drying out the sheets aired flat, preferably on racks (screen-printing-style) but not stacked. The paper is still prone to cockling, and because it shrinks and expands when damp, registration is difficult; four deckles and not a right-angle anywhere! I also find that French handmade papers vary in grammage in a pack, so that you may have 200g, 280g and even 320g in a consignment of 250g paper. The tint of hand-made paper can vary in a pack, and if one suddenly needs to re-order more of the same there can be unwelcome surprises.

So the cautious and impecunious printer/publisher opts for mould-made papers which, like hand-made, also occasionally begin to stick to the type once 'stiff' inks begin to dry out on the printing rollers. Both hand-made and mould-made papers can be too

René Crevel by Ezra Pound. Original 180 x 250 mm, printed on Somerset cream paper.

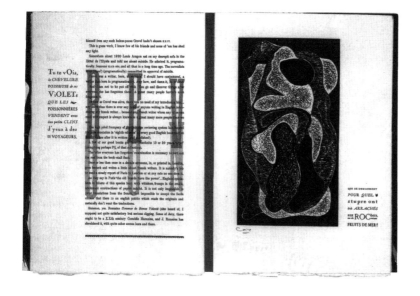

soft for bookwork and lack the body (*la main*) required for an item that will be handled many times – the dilemma being that felty papers can print superbly well because their fibres aren't oversized with ink-repulsing glues – but they consequently aren't tough enough to form pages of a book.

Because pages of poetry are sparse and rarely seem to fill out and occupy the page, the ideal choice of letter would seem to be a wide, seriffed face, with small x-height, in a semi-bold weight that isn't too black and heavy. I have seen some typefaces inter-letter-spaced to good effect for short lines of poems, notably *Centaur.* To my eye, most Monotype faces look too grey and lack presence on the page. I am very inclined to 'double-roll' them, ie ink once before printing, and use more than average packing on the cylinder to fatten out their appearance, perhaps an extra tissue-paper of 25g weight.

Personally, I like the feeling of sharpness in printing, and choose faces whose fine pointed serifs testify to the skill of the designer and punch-cutter, and whose lines recall the earliest humanist Venetian types. I love Van Krimpen's *Lutetia, Spectrum* and *Romulus,* Mardersteig's *Dante, Zeno* and *Pacioli,* Tschichold's *Sabon,* Frutiger's *Méridien,* Deberny-Peignot's *Cochin,* and Goudy's *Kennerley.*

Even though I like these very 'classical' typefaces – what the French call *caractères nobles* – I have a reputation as a publisher of essentially radical or 'left-wing' texts, which challenge the existing order and wish to be unconventional. I enjoy the irony of employing the 'neo-classical' to express the subversive and seditious. Baudelaire said that 'One should never confuse fine words with good deeds'; the same might be said of my attitude towards producing books.

As a practising typographer, I am obsessive about bringing out the best in any given typeface and will happily stop to wash up the press, clean out the type as much as

Futurist & Zaum poems
by Velimir Khlebnikov.
Original 180 mm x 300 mm and
set entirely in Nebiolo types.

I see right **through** you, **Numbers.**
I see you in the **skins of animals,** $\theta \doteq \varsigma \doteqdot$
coolly p r o p p ed *against uprooted oaks.*

YOU offer **us** a **gift** ⊂⊃ **unity** betw**e**en
th*E snakey* M*o*V*e*M*e*N*T*
of the **backbone** *of* **the universe** a N D
TH E**D**IPP**E** R**D**ANCIN G**o**v**e**rh**e** a**d.**
Y**o**u help **us** t**o s**ee *centuries as a FLASH*
of laughing **t** 0 e 2 Ⴑ. See my wisdom-**wide**
▐:▐▐▐▐▐▐▐::▐▐▐▐N E D *E Y E S.*

Recognise   W*b*AT I   wiLL *B* E
when i**t**s *divid*end i**ṣ** *O N E.* ✳✳✳

necessary, before and during impression (preferably with a hog's hair brush we call a *chien*, Essence C, or turps and a resistant rag), adjust the height of my inking rollers, modify the packing and make-ready on the cylinder (overlays) or beneath elements on the press (underlays).

One big difference, I find, is that by double-rolling the type, inking once before printing, rather than carrying more ink and laying it on thick in one fell swoop – I manage to cover the paper's surface correctly without filling in the counters of the type. This provides pages of solid type on papers that prove difficult to seat the type into. I also avoid, where possible, using sprays designed to stop the inks from drying, as I have never felt convinced that my colour was as clean on the second day as the first, even after running through lots of waste sheets 'to clean up the press'. I prefer to wash up the press and begin with fresh ink that is as stiff as possible, every day.

For the best-quality work, I buy founts of founder's type because the drawing of the letter is generally superior to that of Monotype and the composition of the metal is far more resistant than its poor relation. Founder's type is now very expensive and the choice limited in England to what remains of the old stock. The one remaining supplier, Stephenson Blake, prefers to liquidate rather than re-cast anything from their list. All these factors lead me to be very careful with the pressure on the type during printing, particularly when I know that I have bought the very last of a particular face.

'Romantics' like smears and smudges as signs of hand-printed work. This has never been my aim. I aspire to print clean, crisp type that is evenly inked across the whole sheet. I hate pages of differing colour-density and try to keep recto and verso identical. Inks do dry into the paper, taking the colour down slightly and this has to be taken into account when matching up two printings.

My most recent work has consciously echoed computer-generated design with its transpositions, over-printings, recherché choice of contrasting faces and type generally set free on the page. After all, metal type can do anything a computer can! I certainly remain hopeful that one can create layouts contemporary to 1997 even if the means may vary. I actually like some very narrow and very wide faces, especially in formats which flatter their proportions. For my own catalogue of printed books I used a particularly narrow titling face called *Iris* from the 1950's, which looks for all the world like a 'deformed' computer face. For a book exhibition in Paris, I employed an exaggeratedly expanded metal face called *Orator* (also 1950's), which is three times wider than its normal version, *Promotor*.

In terms of colour, my books are extremely vivid, probably because of my training as a print-maker, the marrying together of unusual tints is an integral part of my design work. I have a special fondness for exotic colours – such as one finds in Guatemalan textiles, on Mediterranean house-fronts, and in Schmied's 'over-the-top' art deco books. Austere texts that demand, at all costs, to be printed in black are not my domain. I also find that direct blacks are too intense on the tinted papers I use, they need taking down with another colour to soften up their harsh and synthetic feel.

For colour work, I use opaque white to bolster up often overly-thin and transparent coloured inks. This allows me to keep more detail on type and in my illustrations, and

avoids unnecessary 'filling in' of fine detail, even if the result is slightly *gouaché* in appearance. I avoid using pale colours made up of transparent white because they tend to appear 'under-inked' to my eye; I can get exactly the same washed out effect by running too little of an ink, as I do by reducing down with transparent base.

All in all, letterpress provides me with a direct and economic way of producing my own editions. If I decide to run six printings on a sheet, varying the inking according to the scale of the different masses of type and image in my form, I know it's my own time and labour I'll be consuming. By having permanent access to the finished job, I can amend, revise and tinker with any part of it right up to the last moment and beyond. There is no such thing as having to re-repro everything or make entire sets of printing plates twice, I just take out my tweezers and pluck out the offending solecism.

There is a richness about the direct colour and the sensuality of the imprint into the paper that makes letterpress a particularly attractive medium. All the idiosyncrasies and irregularities, that make certain metal typefaces so distinctive, seem to have been sacrificed on the altar of 'rationalisation'. A good page of metal type gives off an almost imperceptive feeling of movement, there is a nervousness about the synthesis of gently syncopating letter-forms; certain letters were conceived to be inclining with varying degrees of incision on the vertical strokes, serifs that curve differently from letter to letter in crazy asymmetric arcs that pass through the baseline at a variety of angles and depths. I can't help feeling that some of the modern versions of humanist types had a virtual scalpel put through them by a computer technician, apparently devoid of sensitivity or a knowledge of what makes type really work. A good page of metal type is alive, like handwriting; a bad page of computer-generated type is as dull as lined graph paper – those all too perfect regular vertical strokes and insistent right-angles can be terribly monotonous.

My main concern, above the aesthetic considerations dealt with in this article, is to publish texts of real importance and lasting value. The chosen text has to merit the long hours of hand-setting and printing. My work goes against current book-production methods, whose 'built-in obsolescence' seems so cynical. All those acidic, yellowing paged, *ersatz* cloth-paper hardbacks, whose glue ensures that they are busily rotting away on the shelves of innocent and hapless book-lovers! The aim of *my* press is to produce books that enhance texts of lasting importance, in humanist editions that should, theoretically, last for ever.

1997 **Glasgow 1999: competition to design a corporate typeface** Patrick Baglee

The typeface designed by MetaDesign for Glasgow 1999 UK City of Architecture and Design had to strike a balance between practicality of application, diversity of use, and appropriateness to the brief. Ascertaining the breadth of likely implementation is key to a typeface whose rôle will be to give personality to an events programme for its first year and, thereafter, in all its various guises.

For MetaDesign, it was critical that a typeface which would be adopted and disseminated throughout a creative community must allow freedom of creativity and the chance for exploration. If the type serves merely to create an objective aesthetic argument, the result might just as easily be rejection and then anarchy.

Knowing from the outset, therefore, that numerous creative and technical minds would come into contact with the work, MetaDesign sought ways of allowing designers and others to use the solution with variety rather than mere reiteration. Type, by and large, is here for a purpose, and in all cases should be designed with that purpose in mind. In the case of a typeface that must 'brand' an event of the scope of Glasgow 1999, it would be unrealistic to suggest that the typeface alone can do this. What will develop this character are the materials on which the typeface is employed: printing, stock, layout, and distribution which all support the typeface in its work. Our rôle broadened into suggesting applications for the work and the typemark, giving us the opportunity to control the interim use. But, in the end, it is the responsibility of the individual designers to sustain the integrity of the design.

The initial invitation to MetaDesign to participate in the Glasgow 1999 typeface competition came in the form of a fax, late in 1996. Some weeks later, following a request for credentials, we received notification of our selection to move into the second phase of the project wherein a handful of designers and type-design specialists would receive a development fee to produce an outline treatment of the phrase *Glasgow 1999 UK City of Architecture and Design*. A cursory glance at this phrase shows that most of the critical letters required for the production of a typeface were present (26 characters in all). Within the time set for the second stage, all that we could realistically produce was a broad concept for a typeface but presented in a way that showed how, by way of application, the typeface would grow in character and support Glasgow 1999's communication needs.

The project from the outset was a collaboration between MetaDesign's offices in London and Berlin, giving us the knowledge and experience of MetaDesign's founder Erik Spiekermann, as well as the support of type designers in both offices.

The possibilities of the design began to open up when, in the early part of the year, Erik faxed over an outline concept for what would have become a phonetic alphabet. At its heart was a modest clipping from *The Guardian* claiming that nearly a quarter of conversation conducted in day-to-day communication was formed from just ten words (the, and, to, a, in, that, of, it, I and you). Then, of course, there are letter-combinations, diphthongs and frequent character-groups which could be turned into ligatures to save compositors time.

Here was an opportunity to design an alphabet which, through design, might echo these idiosyncrasies and oddities. Kurt Schwitters published his face *Systemschrift* in 1927 as an attempt to capture the sound of language. It denied a traditional idea of balance by representing vowels and other sounds in bolder type or by joining characters.

In a way, this would be a remedy for the lack of diacritical marks in our language, which distinguish between letter-sounds, thereby sculpting the noise we make when speaking. What we began to develop was an alphabet that would automatically represent such patterns and quirks. However, the realities of time were all too clear: the programming of such an exercise would require a considerable investment of time which was not available. So the concept developed at the final stage leaves phonetic representation to the designer's creativity and understanding. In the end, the complexity of application of our original concept was deemed overwhelming.

The brief from Glasgow asked for a typeface that was distinctive and memorable, that would reflect the spirit of a contemporary city. There would also be the need to create from the typeface a 'typemark' which needed to be applicable in its basic form as an identity for Glasgow 1999. Couple that with a desire to de-mystify the process of type design and the challenge became one familiar to many of those in the field of typeface design.

It might be easy to create a typeface that is memorable in isolation, but not so easy in its application that it doesn't become mannered and quickly date. The longevity of the typeface, achieved by a design that supports but does not dominate communication was a the key and a concern of Glasgow's that we had to focus on. The typeface had to be a supporting artist and not have so much ego that it dominated the message.

At this point, Ole Schafer, Director of Type Design at MetaDesign, started producing some really exciting outline ideas from Erik's original pencil sketches. Schafer joined MetaDesign in 1995. He worked on *FF Info* text and display with Erik Spiekermann. As designers continued work on the project, Ole came across a quote which encapsulated the ccntral focus of our work, both in the design of the type and in its application. Andy MacMillan said that 'Glasgow is Scottish in its stone, European in its urban pedigree, American in its grid-iron plan'. To add to the notion of industry, the following comment from Janice Kirkpatrick seemed appropriate: 'it (Glasgow) has a history as a manufacturing workshop where a good day meant making something'. At the point of presenting at the second stage, the rationale for our work was fairly clear.

Glasgow is Scottish in its stone, European in it

The face aimed to give shape and character to language itself, and by doing so bring character to Glasgow 1999 through its application by commissioned design consultancies. The approach taken was governed from the start by the anticipated future use of the typeface and the objectives of the organisers. The final design would have to reflect the past, but be firmly rooted in the requirements of contemporary type design.

It remained vital to us that an element of freedom was created within the design of the type. Therefore, the alphabet contained a number of variant sorts, ligatures, and underscores where letters can be bolted together by designers with the use of keystrokes. It was desirable to avoid rigid guidelines for use: the last thing we want to do is dump a solution on anyone without any prospect for them to interact with the face.

As we prepared our submission for despatch, we felt we had created a robust design, suitable for use in the bewildering range of likely applications. Showing the face against a range of background images, we hoped to create a vision for the judges of how this concept was going to work; we had to project snapshots of the future. When the theorising stopped, we submitted an interim proposal which we felt answered the brief, and which went some way to showing Glasgow 1999 the possibilities offered by a typeface designed under the rigours of a traditional process and in response to their brief.

Presentation to the judging committee followed our selection to proceed with the typeface to completion. The work was described by one of the judges as being the sort of alphabet you could 'take out for a drink on a Friday night' a comment we took as a compliment. The type made people smile probably because they could see it *in situ*, working and already responding to their concerns.

Our accompanying outline was, effectually, a statement of intent describing what the typeface could do. In trying to reflect the spirit of a contemporary city and of an event likely to bring it another period of sustained scrutiny, we did not entirely reject the past. Charles Rennie Mackintosh not only produced ground-breaking designs, he was also a key influence in the development of the Bauhaus and the Wiener Werkstätte whose pursuit of an understanding of the machine is in keeping with our exploration of a typeface that can be built – not just set. It is an industrial shape and structure, influenced by the heavy close-set metal typefaces of the 60s and 70s. It can be set very tight to give a look of solidity and strength: it has impact without shouting too loudly.

Since Glasgow's decision to select MetaDesign to proceed with the design of the typeface, we have been developing our initial proposal in a variety of weights with appropriate alternates. We have, at the same time, worked hard in partnership with Glasgow 1999 establishing a level of dialogue where all parties had a clear understanding of the process. Such a project could never be a case of just delivering. Why fail to engage the people for whom this design will represent so much, and who will use it as an important tool?

rban pedigree, American in its gridiron plan

This dialogue with Glasgow 1999 has meant we have had the opportunity to create some exciting applications of the interim typeface and typemark and we look forward to the time when designers throughout the region and beyond will get the chance to take what we have done and mix it up a bit. Perhaps no two Glasgow 1999 typemarks will look the same. We regard this as exciting and, communicated in the right way, should be a positive opportunity for all those involved to develop an understanding of the notion of 'brand' identity as opposed to brand 'personality'.

There are in the typeface a number of alternate sorts (three e shapes, numerous lines to bolt characters together, underscores) which when explored will provide a whole host of opportunities. But the alternates will retain the same basic character. Good designers fully appreciate that variety does not have to mean confusion. The materials available for Glasgow 1999 will have a robust charm, a creative excitement and a solidity of character which will serve this important event well.

The technology of type design today certainly brings some terrific advantages to this type of process, and efficiency is clearly one of them. But at the heart of the job is the design itself, and a design of integrity will never result from a massively hurried, ill-understood brief; but through careful planning, open discussion, and good ideas. Designing type for a purpose remains a highly skilled and time-dependent task. It is an intelligent pursuit, whose goal is communication and, in the context of a city, there can be no greater responsibility.

UK City of Architecture and Design

A hot dog in Japan is pretty much the same thing as in England: it looks the same, it tastes the same and it is the same word – not quite, actually it is a hotto doggu. You are not sitting in a restaurant but in a resutoran, your drink is a dorinku and the radio in the background plays the besuto ten toppu songu (non sutoppu).

Words of foreign origin are usually called 'loanwords'. In Japanese they are called 'gairaigo' – literally, 'language from the outside'. All languages extend their vocabulary with foreign words from time to time, but no language has adapted to this area of inter-national exchange to such an extent as Japanese. Thousands of English words have become part of the Japanese vocabulary and found their way into daily conversation. Some experts say that loanwords constitute approximately ten per cent of the Japanese language, and that the figure is increasing. This is all the more remarkable when one considers the large linguistic gap between Japanese and English, and the fact that few Japanese words have entered English.

Many English words were brought into use because there was no equivalent Japanese to express a concept. Other English loanwords became popular even though perfectly good Japanese words already existed for the concepts expressed. In fact, many of the borrowed terms have completely replaced their Japanese counterparts.

It seems that the Japanese back up Ludwig Wittgenstein's supposition that the meaning of a word depends on its use in language. Not only are English words pro-nounced very differently, they also go through a variety of semantic and structural changes. Loanwords are like emigrés, once they become part of another culture they develop a life of their own.

Word pray

English loanwords are spoken according to the rules of Japanese pronunciation, which does not offer the flexibility to accurately reflect their original sound. There are no chains of consonants in Japanese. Foreign words are automatically stretched out to form a greater number of syllables. 'Grapefruit juice' in Japanese becomes gurépufurétsu jésu and the city Amsterdam is pronounced as amusuterudamu. The Japanese are famous for their difficulties with l and r. In fact, there is no distinction between both sounds; the Japanese pronunciation falls somewhere between the two. As a result the

words 'writer' and 'lighter' become the same word: raitā. 'Glass' and 'grass' becomes identical in guarasu and a furai pan can either be a flying pan or a frying pan. Sometimes the shift in pronunciation is rather unfortunate. About ten years ago the word 'city boy' was introduced to signify someone coming from a big city and therefore considered sophisticated and smart. The trouble is that 'ci' turns into 'shi'. Young Japanese men proudly wore T-shirts emblazoned with the legend: Shity Boy.

Imèji chenji (image change)

For many years in Japan, modernisation was associated with westernisation. Having foreigners around and using foreign words somehow showed that progress was being made. Using English was modern. Loanwords were preferred to their non-loan equivalents because of their connotation: 'new, modern, and therefore better'. Many of the goods which Japan has imported from the West were entirely new to the culture and therefore were known only by their original names. A tea bag for example has certainly never been used in a traditional tea ceremony. The Japanese word for tea is (o) cha, but a tea bag is called tī baggu. In many cases it would not make sense to translate loanwords into native Japanese. The word hotto doggu (hot dog) for example would become atsui inu and refer to a real dog, sweating in the heat.

Today Western and traditional Japanese styles are mixed or exist side by side. Just as many Japanese houses have a traditional Japanese room while the rest of the house is fitted with a Western interior, many objects have two names – one Western in style, one Japanese. When you eat rice with chopsticks from a bowl it is usually called gohan, a Japanese word. But if you eat the same rice from a western plate with a fork, perhaps in a western style restaurant, you call it raisu from English 'rice'. A table in Japanese style is a shokutaku while the western equivalent is called tēberu which led to tēberu-supīchi (table speech) and tēberu-maná (table manners). With Western goods also Western ideas came to Japan. For example, no native Japanese word developed to express the concept of privacy. A traditional Japanese house has only paper doors between the rooms, indicating that the individual is considered less important than the community. Both the word purabashī and the concept had to be imported from the West.

Communication used to be defined as one-way in Japan. It always flowed vertically from top to bottom, eg, from teacher to student, from parent to child, and from government to people. The idea of communication as 'the interchange of thoughts and opinions' came with the new tide of democracy after World War 2. The loanword komiyunikē-shon holds this new democratic connotation, unlike non-loans such as dentatsu (the imparting of information). More recently the practice of speaking furanku (frank) became fashionable in Japanese society, where people have traditionally spoken and behaved with reserve. In the 1960s the word rejá (leisure) was introduced, disproving the cliché that Japanese people work hard all the time. For a while everybody was talking about the great rejā būmu (leisure boom).

Loanwords not only express modern concepts but also over-shadow and replace their Japanese counterparts. In most cases the meaning of a loanword and a native word are interchangeable, but the increasing reliance on Anglo-American English means that

older Japanese people sometimes find they can not understand their own language any more.

Fusion and confusion

Confusion over loanwords can actually lead to great linguistic creativity. The Japanese are highly inventive in coining new words, and may put English terms into combinations of which native English speakers have never heard. For example, who would have guessed that romansu gurè (romance grey) refers to an elegant older man with grey hair, or that hai misu (high miss) is an unmarried woman over thirty. A person's most attractive physical feature is called châmu pointo (charming point). Someone who has a driving license but never or rarely drives is a pêpâ doraibâ (paper driver).

Even combinations of English and native Japanese words are not unusual. Ningen dokku (human dock) is made up from ningen the Japanese word for 'human' and dokku which normally means 'dock for repairing ships'. But what is a human dock? Strangely, it means a complete check-up in a hospital.

Many loanwords only appear as part of compounds and are never used alone. The word bebî (baby), for example, is used in most of the terms related to a baby: bebî shittâ (baby sitter), bebî shûzu (baby shoes) or bebî fûdo (baby food) but the baby itself is called aka-chan, a purely Japanese word.

English words are not only used differently in Japanese, they can lose some of their original meaning or even turn into their opposite. For instance, how do thirty people fit into a one man car? No problem; in Japan a wan man ká (one man car) is not a tiny automobile as you might assume but a bus. The word simply indicates that the bus has no conductor. Feminisuto (feminist) does not signify a woman fighting for women's rights, but a man who is very kind to women. Atto hômu (at home) does not mean that someone is in his own place, it just describes a relaxed personality. An easy-going person has got an atto hômu character.

The expression furu mûn (full moon), related to hanemûn (honeymoon), refers to a trip by a couple who have been married a long time. The loanword was actually introduced by a Japanese company that organises such trips. The word baikingu shows perhaps the most radical change in meaning, from 'Viking' to 'all-you-can-eat buffet'. 'The Viking' was the name of Japan's first smorgasbord restaurant, which opened in 1962. Soon the word was stripped of its Scandinavian heritage and used to signify any style of buffet. Today it is common to find breakfast vikings, world vikings and even Chinese vikings. The accidental phonetic similarity between baikingu and baikin, which means 'germ' in Japanese, doesn't seem to have affected the popularity of these buffets.

The Japanese are partial to abbreviations. If a word is shortened in English already, it is usually introduced into Japanese in a similarly handy form. 'TV', for example, becomes terebi, and 'hi fi' becomes hai fuai. But there are also many new shortened words, made up from English, that are almost incomprehensible to the uninitiated outsider. For example, pan suto (panty stockings) are tights, but han suto means hunger strike. Similarly confusing are compounds with 'kon': paso kon stands for 'personal computer', and fami kon for family computer, but maza kon is not a mother computer as you might expect,

it's a mother complex. Abbreviating can even create new superstitions. Sutêki is used as an abbreviation of bîfusutêki (beef steak). The night before a big competition, Japanese athletes sometimes eat a sutêki together with a katsu (cutlet). The reason for this is that the meal allows a play on words: the phrase 'teki ni katsu' (steak and cutlet) also means 'beat your enemy'.

No kommento

Japanese is a very polite, sometimes formal language. People find it difficult to speak about unpleasant things or private matters. English words can be helpful here, since they don't have the same fixed connotations as Japanese words and therefore provide a less direct way of expressing something considered awkward.

A typical euphemism is seku hara (sexual harassment). The word has been often mentioned on the news lately and is probably used instead of a Japanese word because it is not understood by everybody. Another example is the word kanningu (cunning) which sounds much less unforgivable than its Japanese counterpart fusei-kôi (literally: unrighteous act).

Bâsu kontorôru (birth control) is a problematic subject too. Taking the pill is a very uncommon practice in Japan. It is forbidden by the government and usually associated with prostitution. Beside condoms, abortion is the most common way of birth control, but everybody avoids mentioning this.

Like most other big cities, Tokyo has its red-light district (Kabukichô). The establishments in this area usually have western names in order to veil their true purpose, even though everybody knows what is going on.

A bathhouse with prostitutes, for men only, used to be called toruko (Turkish bath) until the Turkish embassy complained. Since then, the name has changed to sôpu rando (soap land). Other establishments are called kyaba kura (cabaret club). In Japan the word cabaret has a quite different meaning from western countries. It refers more to a nüdo shô (nude show). Certainly, the Kabukichô area has several blocks that function as a rabu hoteru (love hotel) or fasshon hoteru (fashion hotel) with rooms rented by the hour and no questions asked.

The nau na féringu (now feeling)

English loanwords are trendy. Their usage is concentrated in the youngest part of the population. At an early stage, Japanese teenagers enter a hierarchical organised social system. High school is mainly seen as a preparation for the extremely difficult entrance examinations to one of the few prestigious universities. To graduate from a top university is almost a guarantee for a well paid job. For young Japanese this is the only way they can afford the high rents and gain independency from their parents. To succeed in the system they have to accept the established pattern of behaviour and communication. Loanwords suggest a temporary break from the conventions, they are fresh, intriguing and incomprehensible to elders. The advertising industry and mass media are introducing new English words on a daily basis in order to express a fasshonaburu (fashionable) and torendé (trendy) lifestyle. Important aspects of teeage life such as

fashion, music and love are almost entirely represented by loanwords.

Being kyûto (cute) is the ideal for girls whereas boys rather want to appear as tafu (tough). Every improvement in someone's personal style is noticed as imêji appu (image up) – a hai sensu (high sense) is synonymous with having a good taste in clothes. Being sumâto (smart) is not necessarily a question of character, the word rather means 'attractively slim'. Girls seek to surimu appu (slim up) or sheipu appu (shape up) in order to gain a dainamaito bodî (dynamite body).

For a romansu (romance) young couples meet at a dêto supotto (date spot). A kisu (kiss) in public might be châmingu (charming) but is still not common. On barentainzu dê (valentines day) mainly girls send a purezento (present) or a rabu retâ (love letter) to the one they fancy as their bôifurendo (boyfriend). About one month later on, the so called howaito dê (white day) comes the opportunity for boys to reciprocate, usually with white chocolate gifts.

Some Japanese are using loanwords simply to impress others or to show off. In order to appear more sophisticated they pepper their conversation with terms like nihirizumu (nihilism), konpurekkusu (complex) or narushisuto (narcissist).

Nobody denies that our perception of the world around us (and of our self as a part of it) is influenced by the language we speak. But to what degree does the increasing mix of languages changes our point of view?

During the Sixties, the American socio-linguist Benjamin Lee Worf developed the theory that speakers of different languages experience the outside world as physically different. What would that mean for the Japanese concept of reality? The influx of loanwords is not only the symptom of a fast changing culture it is also one of the conditions. Today, due to modern information technology, words travel fast, new trends and styles shape new phrases all over the world, the so called global village is already a modern Babylon; at least in Japan.

The typographies which relate to the languages of fifteen member-states within the EEC are eleven in number. Danish. Dutch. English. Finnish. French. German. Greek. Italian. Portuguese. Spanish. Swedish. The latin-based alphabet serves ten of the eleven languages, with Greek in a class of its own. Of the eleven, Finnish (or Suomi) is the only language which is outside the Indo-European linguistic grouping. Portuguese typography requires sixteen diacritically accented characters to augment both upper- and lower-case alphabets.

When the Slovak language joins the eleven at Strasbourg and Brussels, seventeen accented sorts will be needed to serve the typography of printed and word-processed documents. While there are only eleven administratively and politically privileged languages within the EEC, merely 110 processes of interlingual translation are needed to report what is being said or written about the pricing of strawberries across the continent. Within two or three years, there will be sixteen languages officially recognised within the EEC secretariat: the services of 240 interpreters will be needed while MEP's debate and resolve the problem of distilling sunshine from cucumbers. 120 bi-lingual translators will suffice for tasks such as converting a Polish document on chicken-manure into its Hungarian, Dutch and French editions.

You can see, by now, that here are problems which are too large, too complex, to be solved. However, might some of the problems be alleviated?

Research briefing

In 1987, we began our first review of interlingual communication. The origins and development of graphic systems of interlingual communication date to some seven-thousand years ago, and to somewhere in Mesopotamia (today's Iraq). Rule-governed strings of ideomorphic tokens evolving into structured suites of pictograms and abstract ideographs. There was a parallel use of herdsmen's tally-stones, complemented by the scribe/accountant's uses of the abacus. The various message-systems transcended interlingual barriers because they literally modelled the transactions to which they referred.

In 1988 we made a special study of C K Bliss's system of typographic interlingual message-exchange, *semantography*. Bliss (1897–1985) invented his system in the early 1940s and continually developed it throughout the rest of his life. Semantography

Light-emitting diodes (LED). Proposed scheme for improving public information display systems.

Top panel: Orthodox capital characters based upon standard matrices, each comprising 35 on/off diode-lights arranged seven high and five wide (the British Standard Institute specification). The top panel also shows upper-and lower-case charac-ters, each character assembled across the visual field from vertical slice-components, seven diodes high. The concept, and the alphabet *Gusto*, were developed by the author. Compare the BSI and *Gusto* versions for phrase-lengths, word-shapes, letter-widths, visual homogeneity and distance-legibility and foreshortened.

Middle panel: Variant-width character-sets within a proposed scheme for bus-blinds with double-height route-numbers and two lines of single-height route-information.

Bottom panel: Proposal for bus-blind switched to double-height characters across the whole field. Illustrations shown by courtesy of Peter Powell Design, Brighton.

comprises two sets of ideographs, augmented by alphabet and the ten indo-arabic numerals. The two sets of ideographs echo the written and printed notation relating to the Japanese language. Semantography needs alphabet for representing *names* (proper nouns). We set out to apply our understanding of ideographic systems of language notation to the problem of interlingual message-exchange. Parallel to our enquiry into message-exchange, we set out to improve message-displays which use three technologies: light-emitting diode (LED); liquid-crystal display (LCD); and videotext (broadcast teletext, and closed circuit viewdata).

Two project-briefings: the *Pangloss Project* oriented upon interlingual message exchange, and the *Dottiness Project* oriented upon multilingual message-display.

Dottiness project

There are alpha-mosaic, dot-matrix letterforms, prescribed by the BSI, for use with LED display. The forms are based on standard character-cells containing five columns of seven dot-LED's. Each five-column cell across the display-field needs to accommodate slim *and* wide letters. Between each character-cell is an inter-character spacing module which is equivalent to a single column of switched-off diodes.

The standard-width character-cells generate message-displays which are difficult to read fluently when reader and message are in motion relative to each other, particularly when the message is fore-shortened.

By 1992 we were proposing single-column *component-cells* in place of the five column

universal character-cells. The engineers said that it can't be done. We said 'If Jacquard, that French engineer, found a way to solve the problem in 1803, why can't you adapt his idea to control-circuitry today?' The engineers said that it *can* be done but the price would be too high, and who cares enough, any way?

By late 1995, (you might have noticed) a fair number of bus-blinds appeared on the streets using displays which exploit single-column component-cells so that upper-and lower-case characters have their proper width: slim for i and the full-point and the interword space, but broad for cap M and cap W. Two component-columns are all that's needed for the i and eight for the M. Earlier this year, Daimler-Benz Aerospace let us have specifications for their LCD systems of instrumental and gantry display. The module is single-column and we have found a way to exploit the principle for all eleven EEC typographies and for Anglo-American English on its own.

Finally, we have established the specifications for single-column LED and LCD modules which make the *minimal* uses of control-circuitry. The question is important: systems must be as simple and robust as possible to make, to operate, and to maintain. To display messages in all EEC typographies so that Greek and diacritical characters are accommodated, upper and lowercase, we need the ten-level single-column component-cell.

We have designed all of the character-sets needed to span all eleven typographies. A seven-level component-cell will serve Anglo-American English message-displays. Our system allows LED, LCD, and videotext displays to have access to sans and seriffed *designs;* standard, condensed and expanded *forms;* and standard, bold and massive *weights.* Imaging can be dark upon light field, *and* light upon dark field.

Moving into *double-height* displays, 21-level covers the EEC typographies, and 15-level covers Anglo-American English. We are examining extension into Chinese and Japanese typographies. Our character-sets including pi-sorts and punctuation. It should be practicable for up to five customer-designed pi-sorts to be fitted into systems and software. Future stages of Dottiness provide for cyrillic and arabic...

Liquid-crystal display (LCD). Part of a sketch-proposal for a condensed sanserif character-set. At furthest left is shown the basic component-cell: ten levels are needed to achieve at least eleven EEC typographies, including Greek, together with all diacritical variants of vowels and consonants. Applications range from multilingual public information systems and ephemeral message-displays to portable language-tutors. Daimler-Benz Industrie originally developed similar component-cells for their *proportionalschrift* character-sets within liquid crystal regimes.

Pangloss project

It is a fearsome labour to acquire a second language. Esperanto, and Bliss semantography, are difficult to learn, impracticable to use. Besides, we need a *multilingual* approach.

Bliss (and written Japanese) use two classes of ideograph. One class has a purely semantic and lexical function: noun or verb-root or adjective-stem et cetera. The other class of ideograph exists to *inflect* the meanings of the semantic ideographs. We have a set of ideographs which have semantic value *only*, complemented by a set of ideographs which have logical and grammatical value *only* (such as singularity, plurality, gender, diminutive, case, preposition, tense, mode et cetera).

About the time of Bliss's death in the mid-1980s, the technology of personal computers and major breakthroughs in software made it feasible for messages in Bliss coding to function as *source coding* for a system of interlingual message-exchange. If the source-coding were programmed for its *semantic and logico-grammatical* values, and if the source coding were entered into machine-memory under a strict regime, output-messages might be generated simultaneously in, say, all eleven EEC typographies.

While looking at a page of printed Japanese, we can sharply and unambiguously distinguish the pictographs with semantic value from the ideographs with logico-grammatical value. Deep in the internuncial processes of the central nervous system, the Japanese reader plays the two sets of values concurrently and according to the rules. She or he converts the combined coding into Japanese.

Early in 1991, it struck me that I was using my central nervous system as a means of transforming the rule-governed Japanese into rule-governed English. Using the same input (Bliss semantography or Japanese) an Italian might transform the code into her mother-tongue. If Maria and I stood side by side, looking at the same source-coding, the same ideographic notation, she will transform it into Italian while I am transforming it into English.

In other words: for many commercial purposes, learning one other foreign language or learning Esperanto or learning Bliss semantography might be redundant. Instead, we might have bureaux, possibly web-sited, where trained personnel can source-code your messages for computer-based internuncial processing towards, say, Russian and Chinese. Remember, however, we are not dealing with literature or linguistic subtleties. Just messages. Day-to-day transactions. Directives. Travel arrangements. Hotel bookings. Questions. Answers. Confirmations. Stuff like that. Mundane. Boring. *Useful.*

Key texts and further reading:

Informing the Traveller: Public Information Display Systems, A Bowyer and C Chizlett, Peter Powell Design, 1996.

Semantography, C K Bliss, Semantography Publications, Sydney, Australia, 1965.

The Cambridge Encyclopedia of Language, D Crystal, Cambridge University Press, 1987.

Structural Analysis of Modern Japanese, B Saint-Jacques, University of British Columbia, 1971.

The Earliest Precursor of Writing, D Schmandt-Besserat, journal Scientific American, June 1978.

The Origin of Writing, R Harris, Duckworth, 1986.

Foreign accent. Part of a sketch proposal for variant-width alpha-mosaic character-set for multilingual public information systems based on batteries of on/off light-emitting diodes. Shown here are the fifty-seven lower-case characters with which to cover at least ten European typographies. Also shown are ten non-aligning numerals, and ten *pi*-sorts. The matching upper-case, punctuation, and the Greek, character-sets have also been drafted. Variant-width characters would be achieved by combining component-slices: five for a, two for i, and eight for an m. Each component-slice would be a single column of light-emitting diodes.

1997 **Johann Cruyff, corporate America and a shortwave radio** Martin Perrin

The most important purchase to make when leaving England for a spell abroad is a shortwave radio. I prefer the digital variety – a little more expensive than the other sort, but with much better reception. I live in New York, a convenient five hours behind GMT. There really is nothing more rewarding after a hard week's work than lying in bed at 10 o'clock on a Saturday morning, cup of Earl Grey in one hand, digestive in the other, listening to English Premier League action. At 11 o'clock we receive live second-half coverage from the BBC Radio 5 team. It is nothing short of exhilarating when the commentator sends out a special welcome to 'World Service listeners'. Of course, one could lie in bed at 3 o'clock in the afternoon in England awaiting kick-off, cup of tea, etc, but somehow the ritual doesn't hold the same exclusivity.

I moved to New York three and a half years ago, shortly before the 1994 World Cup Finals were held in America. It would be a little unfair to suggest that between the inaugural match on June 17th and the final on July 17th I wasn't searching for employment with quite the level of effort that one might expect from someone with limited financial resources, and with no legal working status.

I had made the decision to leave London and transfer overseas a year or so previously (during the odious Graham Taylor regime). Having graduated from the Royal College of Art on the night that David Platt was busy knocking Belgium out of the World Cup in Italy, in 1990, I was now at a crossroads in my career. I didn't feel ready, or feel that I had sufficient knowledge or experience, to run my own studio but felt the need for a new challenge – hence the move to New York.

In London I had worked predominantly for arts-oriented clients, but in New York it seemed appropriate that I should make a complete change of direction and throw myself into working within corporate culture at its most extreme.

I began working at Straightline International in September 1994. Founded only two years previously, the company had a wide range of clients, both large and small. They took the rôle of communication and strategic thinking very seriously and saw design as only one aspect (albeit a very important one) of the overall communication process. Whilst not always agreeing with company philosophy, I have learnt a great deal about the development of a concept, and breadth of knowledge needed to convey my ideas to the client, than I had previously thought possible or even necessary.

Even as a lad I had been fascinated by travel and the idea of living and working abroad – namely, The Netherlands. Not for me the antics of Gert Dunbar, Hard Werken, Wim Crouwel and Total Design. No, it was 'Total Football' that I was obsessed with.

In the early 70's, the Dutch established a flexible, attacking style of play that culminated in the great club side, Ajax of Amsterdam, winning the European Cup three years in a row (1971, 72, 73) and the national side being narrowly beaten into second place in successive World Cup Finals (1974 and 78). Led on the field by the skills of Johann Cruyff, and off the field by the tactical brilliance of Rinus Michels, the Dutch represented a combination of sporting virtuosity, European sophistication and aesthetic brilliance.

When Cruyff led his team onto the pitch, sporting skinny-ribbed orange and black Adidas kits, it was the first time I had seen, and therefore contemplated, how important it was to make your product, whatever that might be, look good. The orange seemed to emphasize the energy and creativity of the team. It was as if the Dutch had created a totally cohesive graphic concept. The strategy being: we *look* brilliant and fashionable. Consequently, we are obliged to *play* in an exciting, modern way. New standards of style and content merged together emphatically. 'Total Football' had a very profound influence on me. It convinced me that football is indeed the 'beautiful game' and, more importantly, established an aesthetic code that I still adhere to. There was such an obvious link between the quality of the football (content) and the modernity of the image (style). Orange is definitely the futuristic red – relatively devoid of emotion yet appealingly bright, clean, efficient and attractively modern. Even now, as I kick off a new project, the predominant colour I use when considering my palette is a strong, bright orange.

Within a couple of days of moving to New York, I found myself playing football (or 'soccer' as I am now forced to call it for fear of being misunderstood as a fan of American Football).

A couple of jumpers thrown on the ground in a bumpy Brooklyn park and away we went – it was like the school playground all over again. I had played football on a regular basis, since my days at the Royal College, with Design Albion FC. Formed by a motley crew of designers who, in all probability, had reached their peak on a school playing-field some years earlier but were still eager to exercise their profound lack of talent. In England (and many other countries) football is a very important part of the national culture. People become armchair experts irrespective of whether they play or not (in fact, it usually helps if you can't play). In America, there is no substantial football heritage to speak of (due, in part, to the lack of a consistent league system and therefore, a lack of players and teams that have hero/rôle-model status).

The interest in discussing tactics and statistics over a pint or two down at the local pub really doesn't exist (Americans save that for baseball). Instead, those interested in the game tend to just get on and play. I began playing more regularly than ever in New York – you can pick up a game in any number of parks in the city or, content yourself by watching a game on satellite TV at one of the city's many Irish bars.

As a stranger in a strange city, it is often difficult to meet a group of like-minded people but, suggest playing or watching a game, and you soon gather an interesting

crowd. But football, being the great leveller that it is, soon turns vague associates into good friends.

For a long while my schedule was organized around playing football – two nights per week playing 5-a-side on Roosevelt Island, a playground on East 12th Street, on Sunday mornings, and not forgetting the trusty shortwave radio. I have played with people from all over the world – Americans (both male and female), Australians, Colombians, Croatians, French, Germans, Hawaians, Indians, Italians, Jamaicans, Swiss, as well as fanatics from all over the UK.

One can never take for granted the international language of football as a communications tool. Whenever one is in need of a topic of conversation, one can always rely on football. In America, where the game is just beginning to take hold (the professional Major League Soccer is about to reach the climax of its second season) I have had many conversations with fans about the possability of the USA winning the next World Cup (very slim!) and who still remember Pele and Bobby Moore playing for the New York Cosmos.

One of the biggest perks of working in the American corporate arena has been the acknowledgement by big firms of the need to spend money to develop their public image. For me, this has meant having the opportunity to travel widely, use world-class printers, real photography budgets, and the experience of dealing with a wide range of people at the highest level. For the time being, gone are days of travelling across London by Tube to deal with un-cooperative printers, asking photographer friends to donate their services and having to cope with clients who felt that the design firm being located 100 miles from their headquarters would somehow be detrimental to job-efficiency.

One of the highlights of my American career so far was to design the 1996 annual report for CCII, a cellular communications company, whose operations are based predominately in Milan, Italy. This job had all the ingredients required to make it the perfect

Annual report for CCII.
Photography by Fernando Scianna.
Printed orange and black.

project: the need to shoot in Italy; sufficient funds to use a great photographer (I worked with the Italian maestro, Ferdinando Scianna, of the Magnum team); and the chance to watch some decent live football.

Arriving in Milan on a Saturday morning, I immediately headed for the impressive San Siro stadium to stand in freezing conditions, slugging shots of espresso, watching a dreary draw between Inter Milan and Cagliari – it was brilliant! Scianna skillfully managed to capture the drama and tension of the crowd and I was only too happy to manage events. In fact, I repeated the pilgrimage later in the week, again experiencing freezing conditions, and watched the once great AC Milan get booted out of the European Cup by an impressively efficient Norwegian team whose name fails me.

Whilst I am sure that all I have described – finding enlightened clients who actively encourage creative work, and the obsessive nature of football and the resulting communities – goes on all over the world, it was in New York that I experienced the two phenomena side by side for the first time. I would encourage anybody to experience the challenge of following their hunches and having a shot at trying something within a new cultural climate. After all, it didn't take so long to work out that Americans call Association Football 'soccer'.

Design Albion FC carries on regardless, both in New York and London, although the original players seem to be rapidly dispersing to the farthest corners of the globe. I am now partially retired due to recurrent injuries and an all too obvious insufficient level of skill – and due to the fact that the football season unhappily coincides with the annual report season.

Of course, I still miss the back pages of the English newspapers but, with the internet and transatlantic calls at only 12 cents per minute, I can always get up-to-date accounts of tough away games, alleged big money transfers and niggling injuries. And there is always shortwave radio …

1997 **What do you consider to be cutting-edge graphics?** Liz Farrelly

The latest computer-generated, multi-layered, aesthetically ground-breaking CD cover? Well think again. For graduates of graphics courses who strive to become the design world's equivalent of pop stars but end up disillusioned and working for peanuts as an assistant to an assistant re-packaging breakfast cereal, there is an alternative.

Why not put those sophisticated communication skills to good use, to make a real difference to the lives and welfare of a vulnerable, under-privileged populace? That's what Royal College of Art graduate Chrissy Levett did when she got involved with the Mines Awareness Group (MAG), a non-governmental organisation which aims to clear mines and unexploded ordnance (bombs dropped from aircraft) in a number of war-torn countries. MAG train local people to detect and defuse anti-personnel mines so as to reduce the incidents of injury and death, and to enable economic recovery which is disrupted by the presence of unexploded mines. The majority of people living in close contact to mine-fields are subsistence farmers who have no choice but to starve or to risk their lives farming valuable land which is still scattered with the deadly debris of previous military conflicts. Sadly, the majority of victims are women and children, killed or injured while going about their daily chores.

Deterred by the graphics star system, that she saw operating in London, which is both male-dominated and computer-biased, Levett set off, to be a 'hippie chick' for a while. Finding herself in Cambodia, back in 1992, and in need of a job, she replied to an advert in the local two-sheeter newspaper, the *Phnom Penh Post*, requesting a helper for the Community Mine Awareness Programme based in Battambang Province, and got the job. From their initial work in Afghanistan, where Director Raw McGrath set up MAG back in 1990, the organisation was expanding into new territories with this awareness pro-gramme as their initial foray into Cambodia.

When MAG start work in a region they begin by gathering data, visiting hospitals and talking to mine victims, with the aim of mapping out the mine-fields. Only then do they organise de-mining teams and instigate education programmes. Levett underwent the same training as other ex-pat MAG workers and local recruits, learning to identify the vast number of different mines, being drilled in safe practice, and how to recognise the various signs which villagers themselves use to mark danger spots.

This is when Chrissy Levett's graphics skills came into use. Producing posters, stickers,

designs for exercise books, tee-shirts and caps. Levett had to hone down the dos and
don'ts of living with land-mines to the equivalent of a Green-Cross-Code for explosives.
'The quality of some of the information graphics I found was so poor they just complicated the issue. I concentrated on making bold, clear statements, using a hand and a
red cross to signal a warning'.

Where children in the West are taught about the dangers of playing with traffic,
children in Cambodia, Laos, Angola and Iraq are warned *not* to stray off the well-worn
path, play with colourful, ball-shaped bomblets, nor collect fuse-wire, to use as fishing
line, and unexploded bombs for their scrap-metal value.

As MAG's policy is to run their long-term operations independently of foreign staff,
Levett's next task was to train local artists to produce all the necessary visual material.
Off to Luena in eastern Angola in the summer of 1995, with a bag full of artists' supplies.
Levett began with the basics. Teaching by example, with no common language, was
frustrating, but revelations such as blue and yellow mixed make green, enlivened
the proceedings. Being aware of, and making concessions to, the differences in visual
language between Western and Eastern cultures was crucial to the readability of
informational images. As Levett explained, 'I realised that a table drawn in perspective
just looks like a load of flat shapes to a Cambodian who would draw a table as it is
constructed with a flat-top and four legs. But I *did* manage to wean the Angolans off
curly '70's typefaces'.

Another problem is the level of literacy, which can vary widely in different regions,
depending on the effect war has had on the educational infrastructure. The Angolan
refugees who have been in Zambia speak English but those who stayed behind speak
Portuguese. All these factors come to light through grass-roots research, and have to
be taken into account before designing awareness-raising graphics.

MAG personnel will visit and revisit, hundreds of villages in a designated area during
the course of the mine-awareness programme, staging open days which draw the entire
population together – over 200,000 Cambodians had seen the demonstrations by early
1995. Getting the message across without causing a general panic prompted MAG to
bring entertainment into the mix, principally by staging puppet shows for the kids –
Levett made papier-mâché heads and commissioned illustrator Andy Lovell to construct the jointed wooden bodies. Drummers and singers performing songs with
instructional lyrics turn the whole event into a positive experience which is important
in situations where MAG are informing refugees of the grim realities awaiting them
back home. There are Angolan refugees who've lived their entire lives in huge camps
on the Zambian border, who have to be told about the dangers of foraging for food
and collecting fire-wood in the Angolan bush. The UN are starting the process of repa-
triation, but the problem is if we scare the refugees they won't want to go back, and
then MAG may be banned from the camps and the returning refugees will walk
straight into a very dangerous situation.

Of course, all this effort is totally worth while, but the fact is that back in the developed world a number of countries are still supplying mines – the USA, Russia, the UK,
Italy, Germany, France and Austria are still supplying mines – to areas of conflict. These

suppliers are perfecting devices which are both highly sensitive and virtually undetect-able – the new plastic mines can't be located with conventional metal detectors. Taking a step back from field-work, MAG are ceaseless lobbyists, campaigning on behalf of those who have no access to the world's media or to the most influential politicians. Through publishing lists of companies who are involved in manufacture of land-mines, MAG request that Western consumers boycott their products. Back in London, Levett designs posters, leaflets and reports detailing the need to curb weapons sales, using statistics and documentary photography which spell-out in no uncertain terms the consequences of this amoral trade.

In Spring 1996, Chrissy Levett's next stop was Laos, where a new set of problems awaited her. Twenty years after the cessation of military operations, the populace has learnt to live with the colossal amounts of unexploded ordnance which litter every village, field and playground. Between 1964 and 1973, during the Vietnam conflict, the equivalent of a B52 bomber's worth of explosives was dropped on Laos every eight minutes, with a detonation failure-rate of 30%. People are so used to the presence of unexploded ordnance that they even build houses using up-ended, but extremely unstable, bombs as roof supports. This level of complacency presents a new set of problems for the education programme. For instance, villages keen to help will often present MAG personnel with bombs they have carried to the camps.

Chrissy Levett is modest about her rôle in all this, 'I am not a mad missionary, there's enough of *them* around, I just want to do something useful'. There is no doubt she's gone beyond the call of duty of what is expected of a graphic designer. Forgetting the fact that designers usually end up in the employ of commerce, selling the public goods it hardly even needs, here's a lesson in back-to-basic principles. Getting a message across is the real work of a designer, and through the skills of graphic designers, that message can be made truly effective.

1999 **Typography versus commercial lettering** Fred Smeijers

Perhaps a strange title since it suggests that typography is not commercial. In fact, typography started with a commercial thought, to reproduce texts faster than writing, thus
saving time – and time is money. It is true, of course, that this commercial goal is rarely
noticed by the average reader – quite the opposite intention of commercial lettering –
carrying urgent messages of a local enterprise with something to sell.

   The term 'commercial lettering' describes quite precisely what it is; the communication
of the fact that something, a product or service, exists and can be obtained, it might also
describe what a product looks like and what it does. Another important element of
commercial lettering is the need for it to have a wide public appeal and be able to
express itself with some force. It needs to communicate to the passer-by who sees it for
the first or the hundredth time. All this, plus the fact that commercial lettering is, of
necessity, limited to simple messages, might suggest that it is an undemanding craft
compared to the complexity of 'typography'.

   However, both make use of letters (often supported by images) and both are concerned with communicating a message as effectively as possible. The one wants to make
a firm impression on your memory and will enlist the help of any 'effect' to achieve
this, the other requires a quiet approach; an absence of unnecessary disturbance. Both
are intended to attain their goal as effectively as possible, principally, by the use of
these symbols we call letters. But it is the addition of visual 'disturbance' to letter-forms,
which occurred during the development of commercial lettering, that has been its
defining characteristic, and which, undoubtedly, later played an influential rôle in the
development of type design for use in printing.

   One might ask; which came first, books or signs? The conservative world of serious
typography (reading text, micro-typography) tends to think that type started from the
wish to make books (which is true) and consequently, all other developments in type
are branches of this main trunk (which is not true). Sign-painting, for example, is certainly the fruit of another tree.

   Traditionally, type-design was a very slow process, but during the last two hundred
years, we have witnessed an ever-increasing speed of production. However, the visual
richness of many fonts available today is rooted in everything except typography itself.
Handwriting and plain lettering, often executed by people who had no contact with

the world of printing at all, were the main sources of inspiration. Take, for example, the designs of Vincent Figgins or Thorowgood. These designers did not produce their fonts out of the blue. No, Figgins and his friends saw these designs on the streets first; the block-serif and the early sans-serif, hand-drawn and painted onto all manner of signs and buildings. Communication achieved by all means other than the typographic! The streets were banked left and right with such letter-forms before the type-founders thought that it might be commercially viable to translate these letters into equally strong, equally large 'real' type in wood and metal.

The simple forms that made up many of these letters were developed out of necessity. For the sign-maker, block-serifs and bold sans-serifs were easier to draw (and to make in three-dimensions or in bas-relief) than the delicate serifs found in Roman capitals. Guided by basic economic necessity, sign-makers therefore freed themselves from the formal style of accepted typographic norms. Block-serifs save time and time is money! The sign-makers saved even more time by adjusting the design of letters to avoid time-consuming problems such as delicate curves. This was achieved simply by constructing letters using only a straight-edge and compass. This not only made the letters quicker to draw, but also easier to space. Another important feature was that because these letters were made up of simple, calculated shapes, it was far easier to teach someone else how to construct them. This lowered the number of staff required, and thus provided an improved profit margin. Mean-while, the type-founder, watched these developments with interest. After all, the same practical and economic conditions which sign-makers faced were also relevant to him.

It is easy for the public to detect inaccurate letter-shapes, and the more 'traditional' the letter-form, the more difficult it is to draw correctly. The layman may not find it easy, or even possible, to explain *why* the letters are faulty, but certainly everyone recognises that there is something wrong. They breathe an air of clumsiness. 'These people must be amateurs', is the wholly appropriate conclusion. The sign-maker had both good

The cover of a French letter sample book for painters, clearly showing its decorative character. Probably late 1800s.

practical and business-oriented reasons to develop his own particular vocabulary.

Signs dated before Gutenburg hardly exist. By this I do not, of course, mean the well-known, letter-cut messages made by Romans or other civilisations. Instead, I am refer-ring to pieces of wood, stone or cloth announcing economic activities, organisations and a specialisation of craftsmanship. The development of complex, urban environments and the resulting vital growth of trade played an important rôle here. The more impor-tant these announcements became, the more demand there was for commercial lettering and so its growth, as a more specialist activity, was inevitable.

It is hard to imagine the first commercial sign-makers. When, exactly, and where did they work? What kind of sources did they use? Some sources are obvious, for example, the tradition of cutting letters into stone. These letter-forms were derived from written letters and, later, even (printed) type became an source of inspiration. But cutting letters into stone is something quite different from the relatively less permanent character of sign-making. Who were these early sign-makers? The engraver, perhaps, used to working on hard, tough material such as steel, copper and probably glass. Or the craftsman who made the decorated wine-glasses of the successful seventeenth-century merchant. With this proven skill, he might well be asked to engrave seals as well (or vice versa). In this way, the engraver of seals, essentially a 'mark' to symbolise an individual or group, pro-vides a direct link with 'branding' as we know it today. A seal provided a guarantee that the entitlement or purchase involved was genuine. The seal also made very clear who the sender or previous owner was and equally important, that nobody had touched its contents since. (Consequently, we occasionally find imitation seals on products today, a romantic, if wholly erroneous, suggestion of quality).

But the engraver soon had more to engrave than just seals. The design of the seals had to be enlarged and engraved into copper or wood from which prints could be made to serve as labels, thus playing an important rôle in the earliest packaging designs. For the engraver, working on small pieces of copper or wood, this work was similar to the

A page from a French letter sample book for painters (cover left) clearly showing that there was no fear of any visual effects which might be applied to the flat, painted letter.

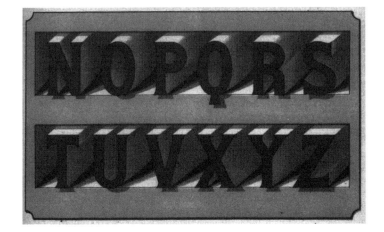

cutting of type in both scale and refinement. He could imitate written or typeset quality, and, perhaps, for some this work evolved into the cutting of punches from which to strike type-moulds.

So, for the engraver, calligraphic examples and typographic type were his sources. But, in the scale of work, as well as the materials and tools being used, the activities described so far are still a long way away from to the sign-maker as we understand and recognise him today.

Perhaps the gap can be narrowed by the craftsmanship of the interior decorators: painting fake marble and other elaborate architectural details onto plain walls or, perhaps, disguising cheap wooden doors as hardwood. These were skilled craftsmen, whose clients could not only afford the luxury of 'decoration' but who considered it a necessity.

Decorative painting was certainly not a new activity (it is an art-form as old as architecture itself) but there was an increasing growth of bourgeois clients who employed the decorative painter: from the magnificent country house down to the commercial establishments in the city streets, buzzing with economic activity. In business premises, the painters not only had to take care of the interior walls but also the sign outside, the glass-gilded windows, or even the exterior walls. These decorators had no connection with the world of printing and were, of course, facing an entirely different set of problems compared with the traditional engraver/punch-cutter. At first, the decorators might have attempted to imitate printed typographic letters, but soon realised that these did not ideally suit their needs. Instead, being used to inventing their own visual effects, they began to experiment with letter-shapes. All kinds of adoptions, adaptations and variations would be made to establish a stronger, visual presence and a better fit, simply by using the technical effects they had used as interior decorators. The 'drop shadow', for example, must surely have been introduced by such craftsmen.

Typography had virtually nothing to offer them; I am sure they did not walk around with a Fournier specimen-book to remind them of how the typographic trade considered decorated letters should look. Rather, I think it likely that it was the other way around; that Fournier saw hand-painted, decorated letters on the streets and made his own 'tasteful' interpretation of them. Typography is slow to evolve and only moves when the opportunity of commercial demand is available.

Inevitably, some decorative painters, eventually, started to specialise in sign-writing and the genuine commercial sign-maker was born. Like all other crafts, the knowledge and skills developed into traditions which were passed down, establishing styles and innumerable ways of manipulating letter-forms. In the mean time, type-foundries and individual type-designers have continued to steal and translate these styles into type right up to the present-day (while not forgetting to put a copyright label on it!)

Eventually, sign-writing became an established craft and a suitable subject of study. Sign-painters would have begun to utilise typographic conventions and the two crafts began to cross-influence each other and it is highly likely that sign-writers would use type-specimen books issued by type-founders (who had initially copied them from street signs) to use as reference material.

In time, the craft built up its own library of professional literature. There are many

examples of American, English and German titles, written at the beginning of this century or earlier. Germany, in particular, has a rich tradition of letters being used for street display purposes and still has strong connections with gothic script. The 'Schriftmaler', as these craftsmen were called, seemed to take a far more traditional attitude to their craft than in the rest of the world. German literature about the subject is of the highest quality and clearly demonstrates that these craftsmen were very knowledgeable of letters; how to make and how to use them.

Their knowledge, gained initially from their experience in the decorative trades, and later blended with (selected) rules of typography, is certainly worthy of our attention. Their creative achievements were made with minimal connection to the printing world. For type-designers, typographers and designers of this century, it seems the sign-writer and his products have been considered to be of inferior quality or simply not 'high brow' enough, yet the typographic world owes a great deal more to their achievements than is usually acknowledged.

1999 **The languages of design** Jan van Son

Working in Brussels means working in different languages. Dutch and French are
the two official languages of the Belgian capital, and European administrative centre.
English, as everywhere, is used by most people but German acts as the third official
language of Belgium. Relatively large minority languages in Brussels are Italian, Greek,
Spanish, Turkish, Arabic languages, and African languages. Altogether, an international
environment in which I need to use Dutch, French and English on a daily basis.

Whilst the terms typographer, printer and typesetter have quite specific, literary
equivalents in Dutch, French, English and German, the graphic designer is referred to
with words that are quite different. Similarly, the words that describe the products of
their respective work also differ considerably and these provide clues as to the varied,
perceived rôles of the graphic designer within the European Community.

The (graphic) designer is a '(grafisch) vormgever' or 'ontwerper' in Dutch, 'Gestalter'
or 'Grafiker' in German and '(dessinateur) graphiste' or 'maquettiste' in French. In French
'création graphique' is also used for 'graphic design', but I have not come across the
term 'créateur graphique', which would be a direct translation of 'graphic designer'.
Although the words are not used so consciously in their true meaning, the Dutch
'vormgever' is 'giving form' and the 'ontwerper' proposes a concept, the German
'Gestalter' is 'originating something'. The German 'Grafiker' is applying graphic
techniques, as is the French '(dessinateur) graphiste', although the word 'dessinateur'
is limited to drawing. The French graphic designer, as 'maquettiste', is making a reproduction model, the equivalent of artwork in the graphics industry, whilst the French
'création graphique' focuses on creating something new. I prefer to use the French term
'conception graphique' for my work, emphasising the conceptual aspect of my work as
a designer, but unfortunately this term is sometimes perceived as pretentious. The
English word 'design' is used in all four languages, although it is more closely associated
with 'industrial design'. Dutch and German also have their own words for industrial
design, whilst the French tend to just use the word 'design' for it.

I know enough of the four main languages to realise that there is little point in
trying to decide which expresses the practice of the graphic designer best. Besides,
deciding which is the 'best' is not a very sensible option when looking at different
languages and cultures. Instead, I will try to elaborate on these differences, and show

how they influence perceptions of the work done by designers living in these different European countries.

Would you call Gutenberg or Coster type-designers, printers, typesetters or graphic-designers? I suppose the terms to describe the different tasks within the printing process were nominated rather quickly as the first 'publishers' started diversifying tasks and employing assistants. For hundreds of years, whilst techniques improved, the process remained fairly simple: typesetting, engraving of illustrations, printing, binding. The primary goal of multiplying information only changed during the industrial revolution when typographic information started being used to advertise and 'brand' industrial products. This led, eventually, to the concept of visual identities for corporations. Illustration and photography started playing an increasingly important rôle. The tasks of 'art-directors' and 'type-directors', new words from the United States, where advertising started, entered the process, co-existing with typesetters and printers. The graphic designer remained the responsibility of the 'art-director' in advertising agencies, which primarily earned their commission-income from the buying of space in newspapers and magazines. Because the designers were not generating a significant income at that time, the advertising agencies did not try to prevent some of them starting up by themselves, as the first graphic design consultancies.

These consultancies first appeared in the USA and UK, and also, a little later, in The Netherlands. Advertising agencies sub-contracted work to designers, and 'graphic design' began to establish itself in the market place. Once graphic design was recognised by larger corporations at management level as an important contribution to their business, the (financial) value of design increased and advertising agencies began creating their own design studios again.

In the meantime, 'graphic design' (then more commonly known in Britain as commercial art) had established itself as a discipline in art schools, but everybody had their own interpretation of the task of the graphic designer, which was not as easy to define as that of the typesetter or the printer within the production process. During the 'photographic revolution' of the industry, the rôle of the 'art-worker' evolved and was soon to be found in every print-house, advertising agency and design consultancy. This person was employed to stick down text printed onto photographic paper during the transition period covering letterpress, photolithography and digital print production. In Brussels, advertising agencies started to use the Dutch word 'creatief' to describe their designers, implying the 'limited' rôle of creativity within the design process. Creativity can, and should, explore all possibilities, whist the design process tries to control this and set specific goals. Here in Brussels, I found this term used in both Dutch and French. The use of the equivalent term in English shifts 'creative' from the category of adjective to noun. In Britain and the USA, visualisers and copywriters might well have been called creatives.

I started my career working as a typesetter/art-worker in a small print-house in Haarlem, Holland, working with punch-tape memory on an AM Varityper and IBM Composer. For many clients, there was confusion over quality, techniques, and whether they should be approaching an advertising agency, a design studio, or simply going

directly to the printer for design work. I remember quite a few individuals and smaller companies, who still came straight to the print-house, where I worked, for the design of their letterheads and business cards, as they had done for centuries. Eventually, however, the printer could not answer all the questions nor provide all the new techniques. There was a gap in the middle of all this confusion that the graphic designer could fill with a knowledge of photography, illustration, type-specification, art-direction, design and print-production.

The process of change described above probably applies first to the United States and then, in my experience, to the United Kingdom and later, to The Netherlands. In 1990 I came to Belgium to work in the branch office of the London-based design studio Banks & Miles. So here I was, with my Anglo-Dutch design background, just 150 kilometres away from the Academy in The Hague where I had studied, to find that there was no word for 'graphic designer' and therefore, my profession might well not exist here!

Major design jobs were still being commissioned from printers, and major signing jobs went to sign-makers. The graphic designer here in Belgium at that time was called 'grafist' in Dutch-speaking Flanders, and 'graphiste' or 'maquettiste' by French-speaking Belgians. All these words referred to the final product of the work and not to the process of how the work was conceived. I discovered the term 'lay-out artist' being used in a request for a quotation from one of the institutions of the European Union in Brussels. This illustrates why it is important to define professions and tasks by the right name. Is 'layout' intended to signify the work of design, with 'artist' signifying the designer? In this particular case, the task turned out to be dtp work following already established design grids. It was actually typesetting that was being requested, and the job could have been done by a dtp-operator.

Unfortunately, the capacities of typesetters were underestimated. Thus the Brussels-based EU institutions that send requests for design to printers, designers, and even colour-separators, accompanied by conditions that have to be accepted and which do not recognise the principle of intellectual property. This is another subject, but I think it has everything to do with not understanding 'who does what' in the graphics industry. In my opinion, it is the industry itself causing the confusion by not being able to name the various tasks involved by single, appropriate titles.

Different terms in the different languages lead to different expectations from clients. Why should we expect our clients to understand all these terms, or understand the processes between a sketch and the final print-work? From a 'maquettiste' you expect artwork; the final reproduction-model. From a 'créateur' people expect something original. A design decision, for instance, to imitate a gossip magazine when developing an annual report of a magazine publisher, does not represent 'création', but can be a very functional design concept.

The fundamentally different words used to describe activities within the same profession reflect fundamental differences in approach and methods of working, to the point, at times, of completely inverting the accepted or notional hierarchy.

You might expect the position of a 'graphic designer' to be at the upper-most point of a pyramid, which then broadens beneath to take account of the different specialists

who take care of the graphic process. The 'maquettiste' would be part of this process when the essential design-elements had already been decided and defined by the client, or by a printer in relation to his press-capacity. This is also why I don't like the term typographic designer, which implies that the solution to the design problem lies in the use of typography. I believe in the importance of type and text, but prefer to call myself a graphic designer so as not to exclude other graphic means. I am aware, however, that not all the design problems with which I am involved are solved, necessarily, by graphic means.

The desktop publishing revolution caused even more confusion. The 'dtp-operator' seems a good word to me for a typesetter who is also expected to work with images, although it implies, unfortunately, the acceptance that typesetting requires of the operator more computer knowledge than typographical knowledge. The graphic designer would normally be able to control this process and provide the dtp-operator with the right instructions in order to preserve the quality of the typesetting. However, in practice, many designers now do their own typesetting, not only because the computer offers this option, but also for financial reasons, since good typesetting now appears to be both exclusive and expensive.

Since 1994, I have worked in Brussels, meeting both designers and clients in Belgium and France who were producing or commissioning design as I knew it. They were not, however, part of a design-stimulating culture, such as I had experienced in The Netherlands and England. Belgian art-schools produce very good illustrators, who are made to believe that they are, respectively, 'grafist' or '(dessinateur) graphiste', which to them is the same as graphic designer, because that is how designers in Belgium often sign off their work. As design education improves, so a design culture is emerging, especially in Flanders, and the Dutch words 'vormgever' or 'ontwerper' are replacing words like 'grafist' which was borrowed from French. Typography is, in general, largely ignored but the young Belgian 'designers' have jumped straight into multi-media and cyberspace. They do not, yet, have the need to call themselves something to describe their activities, they just 'do'; creating a new visual language that, perhaps, one day, will provide our European languages with a new word.

In France, where typography is taught as part of a design course, I have heard the word 'maquettiste' used less often as more designers present their work as 'conception graphique'. 'Création graphique', meaning 'graphic creation', is also used less, probably because it ignores the conceptual and 'problem-solving' part of the design process. In French, we are just one step away from the 'concepteur graphique' which would be the equivalent of 'graphic designer'. However, in France, since the emergence of 'infographics' there is suddenly the 'infographiste' whose job description is often that of a designer or a dtp-operator. During the nineties, the word 'infographics' appeared, describing designers/illustrators who made pictorial explanations of events. The 'event' that established 'infographics' as a serious specialisation was the Gulf War, when the American newspaper, USA Today, published detailed, illustrated pages showing various military actions. There was, of course, already 'information design', referring to designers who specialised in designing 'pure' information such as installation manuals, financial

reports and study-books. Within information design, graphic illustrations are often used to support and clarify what is discussed in the text. Since images are used increasingly as a primary source of information, good 'infographics' communicate without an explanatory text.

In between all these terms, the word 'concept' is suffering from serious abuse in French as well as Dutch and English. In Belgium the word 'concept' is used for sketches or design proposals, but rarely for the overall approach to a project. In the meantime, in the UK, the English word 'concept' sounds like the archetypal salesman's 'pitch' from the eighties, and might slowly be replaced by other words, although it does cover an essential aspect of the design process.

I have been focusing on these different terms because they illustrate how the profession of graphic designer is regarded in different countries and cultures. While the designer has some professional authority in The Netherlands or the UK, this is not so much the case in Belgium and France. I know that organisations such as the BNO in The Netherlands and the STD in the UK have contributed to a better perception by the public of what it means to be a graphic designer, what to expect of a graphic designer. But what really established graphic design as a profession were the public service companies and multinationals who commissioned substantial design projects, thus contributing strongly to the status of our profession.

Whilst printing is specific, graphic design is fluid; the design tasks change, with each project requiring fresh thinking, new techniques and new uses of appropriate media. There is no need for alternative words to describe printing, since there is no confusion about this industrial process in any language. Whilst the fluidity of graphic design causes some to worry about its future, creativity will always be needed as an aid to communication. However, designers of the future will not only be designing for print, and will be required to know much more about computer programming. In the future, biologists will have a rôle in the design profession, connecting neurons in our computers for specific communication tasks. New words for graphic designers will emerge, suggesting new tasks and status within the communications business. Some words are certainly going to disappear.

On our computers, we can already see a new, international language evolving, exclusively using symbols and icons instead of words.

2000 **'Real World'** Jeremy Tankard

This phrase has always amused me – eyes rolling upwards: here we go again, another lecture about what you are supposed to do after graduation (that is, if you decide to stick to design). But if you say the 'real world' is what happens outside college, what, then, is education – the 'fake world'? Hmm.

Well, no illusions here. 'Outside' is a very different place, in many different ways. No amount of work experience can prepare you for the difference because at the back of your mind, when the placement is over, you know you will be back to the cocoon of college life. My first placement was at Conran Design Group, at that time situated above Heals Furniture Store on Tottenham Court Road. I worked in corporate design for three to four weeks. I did not do much apart from play with the new (and then) novel colour copier. I remember a designer there telling me he wanted to be dead by thirty. I never worked out the thinking behind this, but you can begin to understand as times goes by and you are stuck in a highly repetitive rut! Following that stint of deathly silence, I floated for a week doing nothing, eventually turning up at the environmental graphics department. This was the closest I came to a concept of design whilst on placement. Another 'holiday' placement was with Wolff Olins Hall. This was a dreadful experience which resulted in being given a free ticket to the D&AD dinner as compensation. Other holiday jobs were with The Thunderjockeys and the Ellis Sutton Partnership. All very different experiences; from big to small studios.

I finally graduated in 1992 with the obligatory 'student debt' wrapped around my neck. No joking – this is a good incentive to 'get a proper job'. I was one of the lucky ones to be offered work which came in the form of business cards rammed between the pages of my comments book; which for the most part consisted of toilet humour by mouthy friends. The choices were Minale Tattersfield and Partners or Addison Design Group. Marcello Minale, who had left his card with an instruction to call, was on holiday, so off I went to Addison.

A few days later I found myself being inducted into a strange, alien world. There was carpet on the floor. There were people wearing suits. There were people who did not do design. There were old people. There were hierarchies. There was no music. There was a telephone with a unique number on it that was mine. There was a computer on my desk. Then there was the work and with it came deadlines, commitments, justifications,

meetings. It was very weird and for the first week I was mentally and physically useless, upset and very stressed.

I have often thought about this period and tried to understand the differences.
College does not prepare you for the non-fake world. College time is pretty much your
own time, your own work, your own illusions. You can turn up or wander off, cocooned
in your own creativity. Suddenly, your time is the client's time, the client's money, and
the design belongs to the team. You are just another pair of hands, hired because you
arrange things nicely or because a lecturer recommended you because you turned up
at college regularly and were therefore deemed trustworthy. But at the end of the day,
you are a lump of playdough ready to be moulded into a way of thinking and designing
that has very little to do with your design education.

I followed the route of corporate design. A holy grail that could, potentially, open up
a whole world of design possibilities. With corporate design (and the right brief) you
can design anything, any size, any colour, any sound, any space. It could be a new TV
channel. A millennium exhibition. A new shopping experience. Interiors. Exteriors. Local.
Global. Or it could be an estate agent.

My indoctrination into this fantasy 'real world' was at Addison and I wouldn't have
had it any other way. I hated it to begin with, but you learn quickly. College seemed
a world away and a pretty useless experience. The methods and practices of the 'real
world' were different from college, the computer programs were different, the design
briefs were different (they actually had a purpose and were real). Addison had a workshop in the basement. The integration of a working company must be the envy of
every college. At college there is so much red tape to get anything done, in the 'real
world' it gets done and done quickly.

The first thing I worked on at Addison was Sabena Belgian World Airlines. The team
included consultants, senior designers, junior designers, product designers, project
managers, there were people who specialised in textiles, in signs, in talking. I'd never
designed a plane before; college was more about being arty and making a statement,
oh and the occasional idea (as long as it was graphic). The final design for Sabena was
(as is normal in the corporate world) a compromise of everyones' ideas. It landed on
my lap to oversee the application of the identity on the plane fleet, draw up the logotype and think about the tail fin. The first plane we did was an Airbus 310 and involved
working between London and Brussels. All very glamourous. No, not really, at the back
of my mind I was more confused about design than ever. The design world covers a
huge variety of disciplines, college didn't. The closest I had come to this kind of design
was at Conran Design Group and the Environmental Graphics team.

Suddenly design is really interesting. In the 'real world' you can be a sculptor, an
architect, a musician, its all design. In corporate design you can take an idea in many
directions, only stopped by your imagination. There are sacrifices and these are different
for each person.

Two years later Addison radically reduced their staffing levels. I had just signed a
contract with Wolff Olins. So all was fine and dandy. Wolff Olins was a very different
place again. No workshop, instead, a restaurant. I started working with the embryonic

New Media team who were creating a video-conferencing system for British Telecom. This was pure intelligent design. A useful thing that would enrich people's lives. The potential of this technology was, and is, astounding. Unfortunately it was never really taken seriously at Wolff Olins (as far as I know there is no slide-presentation of it). These jobs are very rare, 99% of new media feverishly buzzes around website design; a glorified Exchange & Mart of blips and spinning logos.

The learning curve after graduating college increases sharply. It keeps increasing. I never presented to a client whilst I was at Addison (thankfully). However, this pleasure arrived swiftly at Wolff Olins. No excuses, never done public speaking before? Never mind. Take your keys out of your pocket, don't fidget, get on with it. I now enjoy this aspect of the design process. It is your work and you have to present it, explain it and be ready to defend it in a clear, simple, understandable way. That can be difficult, especially if you are passionate about something. Some things you don't win. Some you do. Not every job carries the design 'gold star' seal of approval. Good design doesn't have to. It is a very subjective business. But with a little creativity, the ordinary can be made extraordinary.

As time went on, I moved more toward my interests with type design and typography (both very different disciplines that are often confused and misunderstood today). The more I eased into the daily routine of the 'real world' the more I drifted into the world of type. It was hard to do type at college. It had to be pigeon-holed; type for books, type for advertising, type for signage. My world of type is whatever I wanted it to be and, working for myself, this is where I am today.

College gives you the confidence and determination to continue. Not much else. After all, it is by self-definition, the 'fake world'.

The six years I spent working in corporate design have given me a unique understanding of type design and use. Through working in the environment of a design office, you learn about your needs as a designer, your aims, ambitions and weaknesses and how to act on them.

I wonder if that designer at Conran lived past 30?

Technology

1971 **Standard Specification System for Print** Maurice Goldring

It is argued that traditional, informal, practices of specification for print production
are becoming obsolete. The need for the creation of a standard specification system is
expounded. Such a system – to be imagined as a handbook, loose leaf file, card index,
or computer data-bank – would contain comprehensive descriptive lists of materials,
equipment and production processes as well as statements of performance requirements. This information would be compiled and formulated as data-groups which would
be appropriately classified and notated. A standard job specification would be obtained
by extracting the relevant information items from the standard specification system
and listing them following a standard procedure. It is then suggested how, and by
which organisations, work on and the funding of such a project could be undertaken.

Examples of successful approaches to introducing a standard specification system in
the construction industries of Sweden and Britain are described. The beneficial effect
classification and notation could have if applied to the whole field of technical and
trade literature, in helping to make it more manageable and comparable and thus more
usable, is appraised. 'Standardisation is not an impediment to the development of
civilisation, but, on the contrary, one of its immediate prerequisites. A standard may be
defined as that simplified practical example of anything in general use which embodies
a fusion of the best of its anterior forms.' (Walter Gropius: *The New Architecture and
the Bauhaus*)

Traditional specification practice

Designers, typographers, editors and printers in the technologically advanced countries
are becoming ever more aware that the traditional practices of specifying for print
are no longer adequate in relation to management and production techniques in the
printing industry.

The traditional practice of specifying can best be characterised as informal. The information needed for the production of a job is transmitted using various visual modes,
usually in specification notes, letters, and memoranda, and in annotations to authors'
copy, designers' layouts, and printers' proofs. Such information is also transmitted
verbally, perhaps at second hand, as telephone messages. Information is not transmitted
in a comprehensive, coherent form from the outset, but by degrees. This can and does

work so far – at a cost – but what are the disadvantages and limitations of this practice of specification as opposed to a more formal approach, such as would be possible by the application of a standard specification system as we will call it, which will be outlined below?

At present, printers meet with unnecessary difficulties and uncertainties in scheduling, planning, and co-ordinating their operations, also in estimating their production costs reliably. Traditional specifications usually have to be assembled and transcribed, and sometimes translated by someone other than the specifier for use at the various levels of skill and by the various trades involved in the print production process. This represents a potential source of factual error and misinterpretation of the designer's or print buyer's intentions. Moreover, the duplication of effort incurred is wasteful.

Such specifications do not facilitate consistency of specified information, especially in the event of amendments and alterations. Nor do they facilitate effective and systematic quality control or reference for further use.

One of the most urgent reasons for considering a standard specification system is that the traditional practices of specifying are not compatible with computer applications and with the requirements of the evolving new techniques in printing.

The limitations listed above not only concern designers. All members of the design/production team (author, editor, designer, publisher, printer) are affected by them as well as the manufacturers and suppliers of materials, machinery, and equipment.

Proposal for a standard specification system

Let us now consider what a standard specification system is, how it would be applied, what it could offer, and how it could be brought about. We shall then see how the construction industries in two countries benefit from standard specification systems in their field.

A standard specification system for print production would be both a method and a physical object. As a method it is the simplified, rationalised means by which a standard job specification as we will call it, can be arrived at.

As an object it can be imagined in the form of a handbook, loose-leaf file, card index (possibly edge punched), or even a computer data-bank. It would need to be concise, presenting the information in the verbatim form required: easily accessible, permitting the relevant selections of information to be found rapidly and to be extracted neatly. It has to be flexible, allowing for amendments to be made.

The standard specification system would contain the following main kinds of information: comprehensive descriptive lists of materials, equipment, and print production processes. It could also contain statements of performance requirements. For example, a printing ink's lightfastness rating, say LF3, or its spirit varnish resistance rating, say SVR5: both maximum ratings (according to British Standard BS 4321: 1969 Methods of Test Printing Ink), could be seen as qualities of an existing ink, and as performance requirements for an ink that has as yet to be found or to be made up. A maximum permissible tolerance, for example, of typographic measure, could also be seen as a performance requirement and be specified as such.

The information contained in the standard specification system should be of high technical quality, presented in concise, clear language. It should be the most comprehensive assemblage of such information available. It should therefore list all materials, equipment and processes that are in use, and all attainable performance requirements.

This information would be presented in the form of standard specification data-groups. From these data-groups the appropriate items would be selected and be incorporated verbatim into the standard job specification.

The standard specification system would also contain a set of recommendations as to its proper use in assembling a standard job specification. For instance, in what sequence the data-items should always be placed, etc. It is possible that a standard job specification would be assembled in a manner so that each production section (typesetting, illustration-processing, printing, binding, trimming, etc) could receive its own extracts copied out of the standard job specification document. This master copy could also be agreed to have a contractual function in conjunction, of course, with the layout-drawings, artwork, estimate, and production schedule.

A typical sequence out of a standard job specification, a sequence dealing with the paper to be used, and which has been assembled from information contained in the standard specification system, might read as follows:

Stock	Wood-free off-machine coated
Size	SRA1 (640 x 900 mm)
Weight	$120 \, g/m^2$
Colour	White
Coating	Air-knife, trailing blade
Surface	Super-calendered, high-gloss, two-sided
Sizing	Hard, engine-sized
Printing	Letterpress
Cutting	Guillotined four edges
Wrapping	Kraft wrappers

Variables such as the brand name of the paper, price, quantity required, etc would also be written into the standard job specification where necessary.

The items given in the example above follow the pattern long established by the British trade journal *Paper Facts & Figures* which is now generally accepted by paper manufacturers as providing a good basis for the presentation of factual, comparable information on paper and boards.

Classification and notation

The standard specification data-groups would be classified and notated using an appropriate notation system (possibly alphanumeric). This would allow the data-groups to be arranged systematically for storage, selection, and retrieval.

Such a system of notation would provide a shorthand method of specifying where, instead of the full data-group, only its notation might be given. This would be useful

in many ways, for example: where production in a foreign country under foreign language conditions was involved.

Presupposing that a standard specification system could be agreed, eventually, on an international basis, a job could be specified, say, in the German language version of the system, referred to by notation and produced, say, in Britain using the English language version corresponding to the notation.

This necessary approach of classification and notation should also – and most urgently – have an exemplary effect on the whole field of technical information related to print production, especially on the disparate body of manufacturers' and suppliers', trade literature, and on sample distribution. Trade literature is, of course, competitive in its nature but nevertheless it can become co-operative to the extent of offering itself pre-classification and bearing the appropriate notation. It would also be an advantage if the format of such trade literature could be standardised to the A4 size and be pre-punched for filing. The user – designer, print-buyer, technician – could thus much more effectively shape all the available source material, or have it shaped for his use in a library, into a ready tool of up-to-date reference and learning.

Moreover the materials, processes and products which competing manufacturers offer in, their promotional literature appearing under the same notation would invite and facilitate comparison.

A way to create the system
How could a standard specification system be created and how might it be accomplished at a national level?

In Britain, the first step would be to hold consultations with the representative professional, research, and trade associations of the industry to agree the need for such a system, with such bodies as the Institute of Printing, British Industries Federation, Research Association for the Paper & Board, Printing & Packaging Industries (PIRA) the Society of Typographic Designers and the Society of Industrial Artists and Designers.

Having reached agreement both on the need for and the feasibility of a standard specification system, the next step would be to define the scope of the research which would need to be undertaken to determine the system's information content, structure, presentation, and use. At the same time, the research necessary to create the related classification and notation system would also have to be considered.

Thought would have to be given at this stage to what agency should commission the research, who could carry it out, and what it would cost. It would then be possible to put forward an application for financing the research to an appropriate funding organisation such as the Office for Scientific and Technical Information (OSTI) of the Depart-ment of Education and Science. Once the standard specification system and its related regime for classification and notation were created, an organisation responsible for publishing them and for promoting and supervising their use would need to be set up. This could either be an independent organisation or, possibly, one integrated into an existing professional association such as the Institute of Printing.

Another industry's experience

One of the main problems is the complexity and diversity of the printing and associated industries. How has a comparable, though larger, industry which has to face a similar challenge started to deal with the need to rationalise its methods of specification? The Swedish construction industry lead the way with the publication of Bygg-AMA in 1950. This is a general specification of building materials and workmanship which was agreed and adopted throughout the industry. It is recognised in Sweden that it has proved valuable to use a unified general specification, and that it has been beneficial to get a common pattern of specification for all trades.

Apart from the Swedish Bygg-AMA being the first standard specification for the construction industry to be adopted, it also pioneered the use of the SfB system for the arrangement and coding of its contents.

The SfB system is a method of classification and notation devised for all aspects of building. It uses a series of alphabetical and numerical symbols denoting conceptual groups covered by tables which form the basis of all permutations of the system. The SfB system originated in Sweden after the Second World War. Within a few years it spread to the other Scandinavian countries and to Britain, where it is now thought to have its widest use. The system is also in use in many other countries throughout the world.

Twenty-two years after the Swedish initiative in publishing Bygg-AMA, the British construction industry will, in 1972, be adopting its own standard specification system, the National Building Specification (NBS). This is being prepared by NBS, a subsidiary company set up for this purpose in 1969 by the Royal Institute of British Architects. The NBS has the support of the representative organisations of the construction industry. Its aim is to improve the quality of job specifications, making them more consistent, relevant, and reliable. Standard specification clauses will be provided which can be incorporated into job specifications. They will be classified and notated using a development of the SfB system – Cl/SfB. The NBS will be suitable both for manual and for computer applications.

As the construction industries in two countries find that a standard specification system brings many advantages, the time seems to be appropriate for serious consideration to be given to the creation of such a system in the printing and associated industries.

1975 **The field of a majuscule** Anthony Froshaug

1 William Savage: *A Dictionary of the Art of Printing*, pp. 179-180, article 'Composing' London 1841.

2 Jan Tschichold: *Typografische Entwurtstechnik*, p. 10, (reproduced below) heading 'Versalien?', Stuttgart 1932 (translation, right, by Anthony Froshaug).

1841 William Savage
'In setting a line of capitals, a careful workman will pay attention to the bearing off of different letters, for many of them when they fall together stand as if there were a space between them and produce a bad effect: to remedy this inequality hair spaces, or bits of paper, are required between those letters that stand close'.[1]

1932 **Jan Tschichold** [Translated by Anthony Froshaug from the illustration below left]
'The right width can be defined fairly accurately: capitals should stand just so far apart, that the verticals of the wide characters H, N stand in even relationship to the areas between the stems.
NOT BALANCED (Completely inadmissible)
PULLED APART
BADLY BALANCED (CH, AU, LI too wide; with HL, GE, GL, HEN too narrow)
CORRECTLY BALANCED
    It is not enough, simply to be guided by the rule that the space between the characters must be the same. They are the same in the word HUHN, but the word is more difficult to read than when balanced. The areas inside the characters must be made inconspicuous through sufficient balancing. Not till then will the word be readable.
wrong: HUHN right: HUHN too wide: HUHN
    An O must not appear as a hole, but must be neutralised in its effect:
wrong: OHNE right: OHNE too wide: OHNE
    In so doing, one must not overlook the fact that the two uprights in, say H are pulled together by the horizontal stroke joining them.'[2]

Die richtige Weite ist ziemlich genau bestimmbar: Die Versalien sollen so weit auseinanderstehen, daß die Senkrechten der weiten Buchstaben H, N noch gegenüber den Flächenräumen zwischen den Staben zusammenstehen.

NICHT AUSGEGLICHEN (durchaus unzulässig)

AUSEINANDERGEZOGEN

SCHLECHT AUSGEGLICHEN
CH, AU, LI zu weit; HL, GE, GL, HEN zu eng

RICHTIG AUSGEGLICHEN

Es genügt nicht, sich bloß nach der Regel zu richten, daß die Räume zwischen den Buchstaben gleich sein müssen. Im Worte HUHN sind sie gleich, doch ist das Wort schwerer lesbar als das ausgeglichene. Die Flächen in den Buchstaben müssen durch genügendes Ausgleichen unauffällig gemacht werden. Erst dann wird das Wort lesbar.

falsch: **HUHN**   richtig: **HUHN**   zu weit: **HUHN**

Ein O darf nicht als Loch erscheinen, sondern muß in seiner Wirkung neutralisiert werden:

falsch: **OHNE**   richtig: **OHNE**   zu weit: **OHNE**

Dabei darf man nicht übersehen, daß die beiden Senkrechten etwa im H durch den Verbindungsstrich zusammengezogen werden.

1945 Anthony Froshaug

The process of learning to read is more than the identification of individual characters. It demands learning to see words (and later, groups of words) as complete wholes, as configurations, Gestalten, rather than as a sum of their component letters. Any juxtaposition of letterforms which favours the reading of single letters or of unintentionally grouped letters, rather than of words, tends to unreadability. For this reason, the 'good gestalt', the assembly of a line of characters which appears to the eye as an evenly patterned whole, is an aim in typography:

minuscule	even visual spacing [see editor's note]

Lower-case letters, minuscules, respect this requirement. Indeed, one of the criteria for judging the readability of a typeface is regularity of 'fit' between pairs of letters, irrespective of the combination in which they may occur. Thus in a 'good' type, lowercase letters hardly ever require any extra compensating spaces to be placed between them; only when unforeseen letter-combinations arise (such as the fk in Kafka), or when the design employs a display rather than a book face, need the compositor regard the bearing-off of individual characters – and then mostly in larger sizes, which are often cast with minimal shoulders.

　　Capitals, majuscules, are so cut and fitted on their respective bodies that they may assort well with the minuscules of the majority of words in which they occur – words set with a preliminary capital, followed by lowercase:

Majuscule and Minuscule	even visual spacing

To ensure this, a capital A or T or V or W or Y is so cast that the face of the letter is almost co-terminous laterally with the metal body on which it stands; the body width of an H or I or M or N or U includes considerably more shoulder. Unfortunately, the amount of bearing-off which is suited to words set in a combination of upper and lowercase is insufficient for, and not necessarily appropriate to, words set in capitals only:

MAJUSCULE	no visual spacing

Lines of capitals therefore invariably require letter-spacing to enable them to be read as words rather than summations of letters:

MAJUSCULE	even visual spacing

Some compositors are satisfied by the insertion of equal spaces, usually 1 pt or 2 pt, or a certain number of Monotype units, between each majuscule, in text composition sizes:

MAJUSCULE	one point spacing throughout the word
MAJUSCULE	two point spacing throughout the word

Editor's note:
The original text for this article was photoset and Froshaug set his spacing specimins (for example, MAJUSCULE) using 9 point *Gill Sans 262* Monotype metal. These were then incorporated within the original artwork. For the purposes of this reprint, these examples have been set in 8 point Monotype *Gill Sans* using QuarkXPress, with tracking values aimed to provide a visual correspondence to the original examples. Froshaug's references to these have not been changed.

This practice, particularly favoured in keyboard setting of lines of small capitals (often used in running heads), can not be regarded as an adequate substitute. Visually even spacing demands the use of spaces which vary according to the printed shape of each letter-pair – even though small capitals approximate to a more rectangular contour than do full-size caps, and consequently, the insertion of physically equal elements between each does not lead to such an obviously unevenly patterned whole as occurs with majuscules.

It is, of course, possible to give the eye an impression of visually-even spacing by the use of such large constant spaces between capitals that the resulting visual space is so great as to neutralise the effect of the slight variations which still remain:

MAJUSCULE   en-quad spacing throughout the word

The letter assembly may then appear to be of even pattern; but this assembly no longer reads as a word. A word-whole can only be obtained by the closest possible spacing compatible with evenness. This evenness is conditioned by two factors:

1 the visual space resulting from the contours of the adjacent strokes of each letter-pair;

2 the extent to which the counter of any letter demands attention at the expense of the form of the letter as a whole, as a figure on a ground.

Factor 1 relates to the fact that two letters with verticals adjacent to each other (for example H, I) stand closer together than can two letters of angular contour (W, A), since type is almost invariably cast on bodies of rectangular form.

Factor 2 relates to the fact that even when a word does not include the extreme case of two adjacent angular contours, and it may seem possible to set it without extra space, since the visual areas between the characters appear equal, even so, sufficient extra space must be given to kill both the counters and the semi-enclosed areas. The minimum amount of spacing is therefore just so much that not only is the counter of an O neutralised, but also the semi-counters between the open stems of A, H, K, M, N, R, U, V, W, X, Y do not take precedence over the figure on its ground. And this minimum is also the maximum: a minimax.

All this implies that it is possible to determine a correct amount of space between each letter-pair for each size of each typeface.

Now, this extra inter-letter space might be considered as being formed from two components, one from each shoulder of the adjacent letter-pair. If this were so, it would be possible to cast capitals and small capitals so that they would emerge from the composing stick or caster already visually spaced, just as do lowercase characters. For those majuscules which form part of an ordinary fount, in which they are chiefly employed in combination with minuscules, such additional set-width would naturally be a disadvantage: the conflicting constraints of close fit to lower-case in upper- and-lower-case setting, and of visually-even fit to other majuscules when used in lines of capitals, are irreconcileable. It is therefore not proposed that ordinary capitals be altered in fit. But in the case of titling founts, and of small capitals, which, no matter where they occur,

need visual spacing, there would be great advantage in so casting each character that it was automatically, ex-foundry or ex-matrix, a self-spacing element.

Given that the amount of space between letters depends on the letter-pair, it is necessary to classify majuscules into categories according to their forms, and then to consider the spacing needed between specific examples of each category in the various combinations of letter-pairs.

The chosen classification considers characters in terms of their gross symmetries, ignoring serifs or visual compensations such as the difference between the sizes of the semi-enclosed areas of an S. Each character is assigned a notional midpoint, about which it may be rotated and through which pass axes of horizontal or vertical symmetry reflections. The symmetry categories are then five:

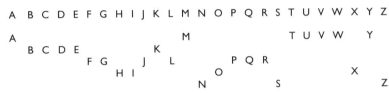

	A B C D E F G H I J K L M N O P Q R S T U V W X Y Z
reflective vertical symmetry	A M T U V W Y
reflective horizontal symmetry	B C D E K
no symmetry	F G J L P Q R
reflective vertical and horizontal symmetry	H I O X
reflective and rotational symmetry	N S Z

Also, the majuscules must be categorised according to the form of their lateral edges:

one/two visually angular lateral edge(s)	A L T V W Y
one/two irregular lateral edge(s)	B C E F G J K P R S U X Z
one/two rounded lateral edge(s)	C D G O Q
one/two vertical lateral edge(s)	B D E F H I J K L M N P R

Combinations of these categories sort the majuscules into equivalence classes:

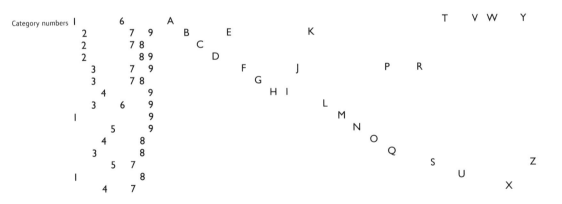

Category numbers	1 6	A
2 7 9	B E K
2 7 8	C
2 8 9	D
3 7 9	F J P R
3 7 8	G
4 9	H I
3 6 9	L
1 9	M
5 9	N
4 8	O
3 8	Q
5 7	S Z
1 8	U
4 7	X

For composition sizes of type, a grosser sortment distinguishes three basic classes of majuscule:

1 two letters of categories 1,6: A T V W Y
2 one letter from categories 1,6: A T V W Y juxtaposed with one letter from categories 1/4/5, 9 H I M N
3 two letters of categories 1/4/5, 9: H I M N

If no extra space is added to the shoulders of majuscules in class (a), and sufficient extra space is added to majuscules in class (c) to ensure that they stand correctly together when juxtaposed, then, when combined as in class (b), the correct amount of visual spacing will automatically arise. In smaller sizes of type, this principle may be extended to other characters. Thus, in the instance of 9pt *Gill Sans 262*, used for the examples here it is possible to indicate the amount of space to be added to the shoulders of each majuscule, using half-point and one-point spaces when the majuscules are juxtaposed:

A   B   C   D   E   F   G   H   I   J   K   L   M   N   O   P   Q   R   S   T   U   V   W   X   Y   Z

yielding the following spacing for the word:

½ ½   0 0   0 ½   ½ ½   ½ ½   ½½   ½ ½   ½ ½   ½ 0   ½ ½
M   A   J   U   S   C   U   L   E

M   A   J   U   S   C   U   L   E
½   0   I   I   I   I   I   ½

which, when set, appears:

MAJUSCULE   automatic visual spacing

(9pt *Gill Sans 262* was, of course, chosen as an example since it is 9 set: each Monotype unit thus corresponds to half a point.)

Obviously, the grosser sorting into classes which is used in this last example could easily be refined, if typefounders were ready to collaborate; an obvious necessity is to determine how much shoulder each character bears in the normal fount. A first approximation might well be made by setting brass rule between each majuscule, and working from repro proofs.

1975

The text above was written thirty years ago [in 1945]. It was never published – indeed, those members of the printing trade with whom I discussed it then (mainly at the Monotype Corporation) dismissed it as the complicated fad of an impractical maverick.

It is true that cold metal titling founts and small caps, bought from type foundries, would cost more, since type is priced by weight; but this constraint does not apply to hot metal composition, where the jewelled characters are eventually melted down again to lead, antimony, tin and dross.

My concern, though, was also with economy of labour: the production of an end-

product which would automatically conform to the principles of good typesetting, without the compositor needing to spend a disproportionate number of hours on inserting hair spaces, either when first setting from the case, or when running Monotype machine-set matter through the stick again. However, the view of the trade has (too frequently) been to produce just what the customer will accept, and no more. Often less. If some self-styled typographer demanded visual spacing of lines of caps or small caps, then of course the trade would do its best, charging accordingly.

It is a matter of respecting the forms of letters – and the perceptual apparatus of the human being. It is a matter of whether tradition is to be respected by examining the conventions of the past, and developed within the particular social and technical constraints of the time. It is a matter of determining whether such tradition still offers a necessary foundation on which to build in our time, within a changed environment, not by pastiche but by using it to discover new forms appropriate to present needs. (Though I do not think that human perception has changed much since the year 1440, when 'there was a golden year, and men began to print').

In 1945, the problem of fit of minuscules did not arise: lower-case letters were so cast on their bodies that they automatically assembled into word-wholes – if they did not, the typeface concerned was condemned at first sight.

In the intervening period, photosetting and computer control of typesetting have developed into a challenge to typographic printing surfaces. This challenge is two gloved – economic and aesthetic. To mention a well-set text is to make an aesthetic judgement. What has changed is who determines how to print, with what, and to whom. The cult of technical excellence has been misdirected into a zomboid fulfilment of unnecessary and undesirable constraints, apparently culled by mechanical and electronic engineers from the twisted housestyles of those who have survived the Procrustean bed of justified setting. Obsessed by this technical problem, the engineers proudly proclaim that their equipment can set justified type to almost any measure – it can actually letter-space lower-case words, or juxtapose characters so closely that any setting fills or fits the measure: rubber type at last.

In the late nineteenth century, the Monotype machine restricted the free choice of set-widths of characters (which the founder's adjustable mould could allow) to a system of unit widths. Each character was constrained to a certain number of units, 18 of which units made up the em quad. (In practice, no character was less than five units wide, and the 16 and 17 units were not used.) Effectively, the choice was limited to 12 possible set widths. Types were redesigned to fit (in old-style modern, the r, s wider, the h, k, n, u narrower, the a, o much narrower, the e unchanged). Only in the early years of this century did the concept of the set-em and the later addition of automatic unit-adding allow a greater flexibility (in 9pt *Gill Sans* and *Italic 262* with *Gill Bold 275*, for example, the 9 set matrix-case arrangement permits 14 possible discrete widths of character).

A small experiment in perception can be made. Select a number of matches, throw them on the floor, and ask the experimental subject to take a quick glance and say how many there are. Up to seven is a foregone conclusion; with fourteen or so, incorrect assessments arise. The result could be guessed, in fact, from considering those separa-

tions of categories which are made in everyday life: the grammatical threefold good, better, best; the income-group fivefold A B C D E; the educational sevenfold alpha plus alpha, alpha minus, beta plus, beta, beta minus, plus gamma.

It is typical of our present setting machinery, that IBM has thought fit not only to design the Selectric Composer on a 9 unit system, of which 7 unit widths are used, but also to attempt to force well-established type designs into such a system, rather than designing a new type within these meagre constraints.

Even worse, the cheaper photosetting machines pay scant regard to letter fit. (Paradoxically, the huge capital investment in machine-tools, machines and ancillary equipment obliged the Monotype Corporation to adapt their hot metal casters and matrix cases to photographic images, rather than starting afresh; but the comparative sophistication of their given equipment has resulted in Monophoto setting being far superior to many systems conceived in terms of photosetting.)

The problem of designing a new minuscule letter may yet be found susceptible to an extension of the ideas expressed in the 1945 section above. The difficulty is that the lateral outward shapes of miniscules are far more various than those of inscriptional characters: roundness seems nearly all. To consider all the possible combinations of juxtaposition (even allowing for mirror-image characters, the b and d, p and q which all apprentice compositors must learn to mind) would yield an upper limit of but little less than 676 = 26 x 26. But courage; it might, after all, be supposed that certain letter-pairs or diagrams do not arise in a particular language, such as English. The digram qb might be thought not to occur, for instance. In fact, it occurs in the previous sentence. Apart from such sports, the most commonly appearing digrams may be tabulated in a matrix, according to their frequency, in order to reduce the problem.

The following matrix is compiled from a count of 25,000 trigrams, made for crypto-graphic purposes, and lists the 109 most frequently occurring digrams in the English language. The digram TH was counted 1582 times (6.3 per cent), BU 100 times (0.4 per cent) in the original research. Since human perception appears to follow a roughly logarithmic scale, the original data has been converted to such a form for this table, and the resulting logarithms divided into seven equal intervals, numbered 1–7, interval 1 representing the most frequently occurring. The first letter of the digram appears in the vertical column on the left, the second letter in the row along the top of the table.

	A	B	C	D	E	F	G	H	I	J	K	L	M	N	O	P	Q	R	S	T	U	V	W	X	Y	Z
A	·	·	·	7	·	·	·	·	6	·	·	5	7	3	6	·	·	3	6	4	·	7	·	·	·	·
B	·	·	·	6	·	·	·	·	·	·	7	·	·	·	·	·	·	·	·	7	·	·	·	·	·	·
C	6	·	·	6	·	·	7	7	·	·	·	·	·	5	·	·	·	·	7	·	·	·	·	·	·	·
D	7	·	·	5	·	·	·	6	·	·	·	·	·	·	·	·	·	·	·	7	·	·	·	·	·	·
E	5	·	6	7	·	·	·	7	·	·	6	7	3	·	·	·	·	·	4	7	·	7	·	·	·	·
F	·	·	·	·	·	·	·	6	·	·	·	6	·	5	·	·	·	3	·	·	·	·	·	·	·	·
G	·	·	·	7	·	·	·	·	·	·	·	·	·	·	·	·	·	·	·	·	·	·	·	·	·	·
H	4	·	·	3	·	·	·	4	·	·	·	·	·	6	·	·	·	·	·	·	·	·	·	·	·	·
I	·	·	5	7	·	·	·	·	·	·	5	·	2	5	·	·	·	7	6	4	·	7	·	·	·	·
J	·	·	·	·	·	·	·	·	·	·	·	·	·	·	·	·	·	·	·	·	·	·	·	·	·	·
K	·	·	·	·	·	·	·	·	·	·	·	·	·	·	·	·	·	·	·	·	·	·	·	·	·	·
L	5	·	·	5	·	·	·	5	·	·	6	·	·	6	·	·	·	·	·	·	·	·	·	·	·	·
M	5	·	·	6	·	·	·	7	·	·	·	·	·	6	·	·	·	·	·	·	·	·	·	·	·	·
N	7	·	6	5	5	·	7	·	7	·	·	·	·	6	·	·	·	·	7	4	·	·	·	·	·	·
O	·	·	·	·	7	·	·	·	·	·	7	·	6	4	·	·	·	·	4	7	7	4	·	·	·	·
P	6	·	·	6	·	·	·	·	·	·	7	·	·	8	·	·	·	6	·	·	·	·	·	·	·	·
Q	·	·	·	·	·	·	·	·	·	·	·	·	·	·	·	·	·	·	·	·	·	·	·	·	·	·
R	5	·	·	3	·	·	·	5	·	·	·	·	·	5	·	·	·	·	7	·	·	·	·	·	·	·
S	7	·	·	5	·	·	·	6	·	·	·	·	·	·	·	·	·	·	7	4	7	·	·	·	·	·
T	5	·	·	3	·	·	1	3	·	·	·	·	·	6	·	·	·	6	·	·	·	·	·	·	·	·
U	·	·	·	·	·	·	·	·	·	7	·	6	·	·	·	·	·	6	6	6	·	·	·	·	·	·
V	·	·	·	5	·	·	·	·	·	·	·	·	·	·	·	·	·	·	·	·	·	·	·	·	·	·
W	6	·	·	6	·	·	6	6	·	·	·	·	·	·	·	·	·	·	·	·	·	·	·	·	·	·
X	·	·	·	·	·	·	·	·	·	·	·	·	·	·	·	·	·	·	·	·	·	·	·	·	·	·
Y	·	·	·	·	·	·	·	·	·	·	·	·	·	·	·	·	·	·	·	·	·	·	·	·	·	·
Z	·	·	·	·	·	·	·	·	·	·	·	·	·	·	·	·	·	·	·	·	·	·	·	·	·	·

This, then, is the next sieve of approximation. We must play rationally where we see we can; after that, and only after that has first been done, may our imaginations and our judgement take command.

1983 **LOGOS: letterspacing with a computer** David Kindersley

The object of spacing text is to cement letters into words so that no inter-letter space can be confused with word-space.

Space is needed to separate words.

Words rather than individual letters are read. To achieve a balanced and cohesive pattern within a word is therefore of the greatest importance. Close letter-space means closer words. One is now free from spacing letters within rectangles. This new freedom has left compositors and typographers without the feeling of safety that metal type once gave them and consequently many disasters occur in text. Our aim has been to find out how the eye assesses the characters' space which was done so easily by the early professional scribe who had no problem in placing the second letter in a word so that it looked in the middle between the first and the third and so on throughout pages of text with appropriate word spaces.

(below left) Spacing letters within rectangles (letterpress).

(below right) Finding the centre of the letter.

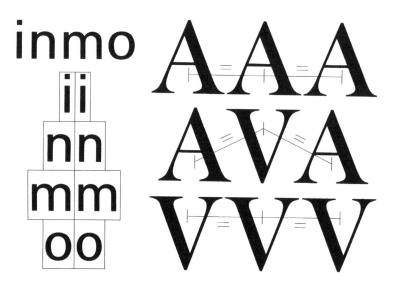

TWENTY QUEER MANHATTAN NAVVIES MAROONED IN THE IRRAWADDY WITH FOURTEEN VERY PUZZLED SEXY JIVING BROWN BAALBEC SKIVVIES

The centre of the letter

The eye processes a letter by judging the distribution of black around an optical centre. That which surrounds the centre we speak of in terms of weight. Thus the black of a letter which lies at some distance from the centre will have a larger computer weight than that close to the centre. It follows that any shape when computed in this way will have a space which equals that which, having a different shape, has the same computation. A rectangle is easily measured, but a letter is not easily measured but a rectangle that has a similar computation to a letter gives us the space for that letter. These rectangles we call canonical characters. They resemble letters in that their horizontal and vertical strokes match those of the particular alphabet.

Using simple mathematical progressions, such as 2nd, 3rd and 4th moments, it will be readily understood that the centre point of a letter will vary its position according to the weight and the distribution of the black. For example, an A will have a relatively low centre whilst a V will have a relatively high centre (illustrated left).

Our system of spacing joins the centres of letters and is the result of one half of the canonical value joined to one half of another generally with a constant added. The virtue of this lies in the resultant putting together of letters with widely differing centre heights such as A V, whilst two As or two Vs will remain suitably apart. In lesser degrees all letters vary their space relationships in a similar manner. This method of spacing letters we call 'Daisy Chain' and dispenses with any idea of a letter being spaced in a fixed rectangle.

Space with weight in mind

The mind always reaches for what it knows and what it knows is in three dimensions. For this reason, letters have to be spaced with weight in mind and all that that entails –like increasing force as distance increases from a centre. There is no joy to be had from thinking two similar letter strokes should always have the same space between them. Take two capital Is; they will always need more space between them than capital Hs. The reason is obvious, an I has no space within whereas an H has plenty. Those differences apply throughout all characters to a greater or lesser degree in the most subtle manner.

The complete alphabet, illustrating the results of daisy chain spacing.

Working with film-setters

It became obvious to me that with film-setters, none of the structures of metal were being solved. Indeed, some manufacturers prided themselves on their ability to achieve the quality of spacing they previously had done rather badly in metal type. Their failure was inevitable any way, as ink applied by pressure to paper could never be matched by photo composition! Our concern was the proper spacing of letters and text whatever the technology, and here, at last, was an opportunity with film-setters for compositors to put right all that had gone wrong during this century. Computers are coming to the rescue of the printed word as they are programmed to deal with the finer and more subtle variations of letter forms. For many years now, it has been possible to tap away at a keyboard like a typewriter and proof-read before passing the work on to a film-setter which will set the pages in the type of your choice. Programs exist which deal with dozens of conventional layouts – pagination, paragraphs, notes etc. The computer memory takes care of the spacing, but the spacing has to be provided by the designer of the alphabet or a technician in the company that supplies the film-setter and the alphabets. That all this may work, the designer's letters have first to be digitised.

I suspect that existing measurements are scrutinised but few changes are made to the spacing of pre-digitised alphabets. The designers of new alphabets may fare better – but is it fully realised that the task is immense? Just take one letter, the capital A.

1 This must fit with all other capitals of the same alphabet at least on two sides.

2 It must fit with every lower case letter, again on both sides, because, of course, the last lower case letter in the previous word must fit exactly.

3 It must fit with small capitals.

4 It must align optically in the margin at the left and at the right when the text is justified.

5 On occasion, it must fit with italic lower case.

If all these fine adjustments were considered worth while in the past, surely now that it is so easy with digital type it should be done. With LOGOS, all the above are achieved with one formula, and, at the time of designing with the aid of a computer and I have only mentioned capital A. The problem has been finding the eye-preferred centre of all shapes of characters with one formula. It always seemed likely that the computation for this would yield each correct space. For some years now, we have been achieving text spacing better than that produced by any computer driven film-setter but there is lack of interest shown by an industry still backed by advisors who believe in metal as the golden standard for all time at best.

The typographer today must deal in programs if he is to have any real impact. For a long time now, because the typographers are not willing, or able to be at the most central point of the new technology, they have little to do but select a typeface and choose a grid and offer a few indents here and there – perhaps insist upon justified or ranged right text or what have you.

Letterforms with a stylus

Another program has been devised for the designer of alphabets which enables letters

(facing page) Pen plotted detail of a variety of *Bembo*. 'The spacing formula works with anything'.

IT WOULD SEEM THEREFORE THAT WHEN ENGRAVERS
WORKING FOR BOOKPRINTERS RESORTED TO SCRIBES
FOR THE PATTERNS OF THEIR PUNCHES THEY WERE
NOT OBLIGED BY TECHNICAL REASONS TO DO SO.
ON THE OTHER HAND MARKET AND MANUSCRIPT
CONDITIONS WOULD INEVITABLY ENCOURAGE THE
ADOPTION OF CALLIGRAPHICAL MODELS. THIS HOWEVER
DOES NOT PROVE THAT PRINTING IS OR WAS OR
OUGHT TO BE BASED ON CALLIGRAPHY, ONLY THAT
PRINTING THEN AS NOW WAS A BUSINESS. THE COPYING
OF CALLIGRAPHY IS MORE DIFFICULT PERHAPS THAN
THE ASSIMILATION OF INSCRIPTIONAL MODELS BUT
THE CALLIGRAPHICAL RESULT ACHIEVED BY SUCH
IMITATIVE MEANS IS ARTIFICIAL. AS A PERMANENT
METHOD IT SHOULD HAVE BEEN REJECTED BECAUSE
IT IS INCONSISTENT WITH THE NATURE OF PRINTING
WHICH IS A DEPARTMENT OF ENGRAVING. THE
IMITATION OF CALLIGRAPHY IS EXCUSABLE IN THE EARLY
PERIOD OF PRINTING BECAUSE IT WAS INEVITABLE.
BUT WHILE IT IS ONE THING TO EXCUSE THE PRINTERS
OF THE FIFTEENTH CENTURY FOR DELIBERATELY COPYING
HANDS FAMILIAR TO THEIR PUBLIC IT IS IMPOSSIBLE
TO BE SO INDULGENT TOWARDS THE SIXTEENTH
CENTURY PRINTERS WHO REPRODUCED THE FASHIONABLE
HIGHLY FLOURISHED GERMAN CALLIGRAPHY.
Fourth moment thirty percent
Diamond formula
Daisy Chain spacing

to be drawn very much in the conventional manner. Here one uses a stylus and draws on a tablet, flat or slightly raised like a drawing-board, but what you draw appears on the screen in front of you. The slight dislocation one feels at first soon vanishes. Indeed, there are advantages. A list of all the usual equipment is at hand and selected at once by a touch of the light pen. Rough sketches can be made, altered, stored or discarded at will. Parts of letters in an alphabet are often similar and much time is saved by recalling bits and pieces. A letter can be drawn to completeness or generated from a skeletal form. One alphabet can be swiftly expanded, elongated or slanted. From any alphabet whole families can be generated. All the time, the LOGOS system, which has been stored in the computer memory, is at work spacing and will display the unique space of a letter if asked, or strings of letters. LOGOS ensures life to the word. In fact space *is* life. The eye, such a marvellous organ, deserves the best we can give it.

A final word

It has been found that the works of great composers of music mysteriously yield to mathematical analysis. Their music is not rendered less by such research! The fundamental laws that underlie many of the greatest works in architecture also show an awareness of such laws. However it is never quite enough to assume that a maker or composer applied such laws. Were it so, life might be very boring. Creativity requires only a sense of such things rather than knowledge with absolute certainty. To know in advance is to use only a part of oneself and this is never enough. All things must be done with all one has. Some of us have more than others but we never have enough. At best, we are good guessers.

1981 **Typesetting principles that are academic** Fred Thompson

Apart from the newspaper industry, typesetting in the United States can be categorised into several areas of specialisation including advertising, book, technical (chemical, mathematical), legal and financial, catalogue, and data-processing files. Many firms have found that they can specialise successfully in two and possibly three areas. Most are content to master quality and service in but one area.

One US typesetting firm which has successfully found its niche in these carefully demarcated fields of specialisation is Graphic Composition Inc of Athens, Georgia. GCI has narrowed its marketing sights to serve primarily university presses and other academic and scholarly publishers.

Before 1970, most university press titles in the US were still being typeset in hot metal. In 1973, William E Loftin, owner of Heritage Printers, Inc in Charlotte, North Carolina, and Fred Thompson, the design and production manager for the University of Georgia Press, saw the potential for selling photocomposition in the university press marketplace. The company began business in April 1974 with just three employees, including Thompson. Loftin continued to operate Heritage Printers in Charlotte and serve a sustained demand for high quality Monotype and Linotype composition.

Graphic Composition began serving its customers with a Mergenthaler VIP driven with an Automix perforating keyboard and terminal. Offering most of the standard book typefaces, Thompson placed marketing emphasis on high character quality, good letter fit, and the use of true-drawn small caps and old style figures with all appropriate typefaces. Since book typographers in the US often spring from a wide variety of backgrounds, many typesetting houses do not have the designer's appreciation for the use of old style figures and small caps and consider them a nuisance.

Finding considerable success in the academic publishing community, the company was forced to find a more efficient means of keyboard input. Having previous experience with optical character recognition (OCR) systems, several IBM Selectric typewriters equipped with OCR typing elements were acquired. Using an OCR scanning device which produced TTS perforated tape, input was doubled and tripled.

Since character positioning on the VIP phototypesetter is electromechanical in nature, the typographic fit of individual character combinations leaves much to be desired. Using the on-board computer in the scanning device, Graphic Composition designed

character-fit combination tables for each type family in its inventory. With the limitations of the computer's memory, a separate memory load was required for the character-fit table of each type family used. This attention to fine typographic detail earned for the company a reputation for quality.

In early 1978, production volume required planning for new hardware. After studying the need for a front-end computer system to drive the VIP on-line, GCI personnel visited many sites where front-end systems were in operation. Management purchased Data General computers with Penta Systems software. The following year a Mergenthaler Linotron 202 was added to the system and the VIP was retired. In 1980, four terminals designed by Penta systems and Data General specifically for quality typography, replaced two standard Beehive terminals (a standard data processing terminal).

While placing great emphasis on high quality equipment, the management at Graphic Composition has placed at least equal emphasis on qualified personnel. In many plants, the input and terminal operators are trained to look at book composition as word processing. At GCI all personnel are taught typography in an on-the-job training pro-gramme. After being employed a few months with the company, the common complaint heard from a new employee is 'I simply can't read a book any more for looking at its typography.'

Since the advent of computer controlled composition, personnel in many typesetting plants have lost their typographic orientation in the face of the overwhelming power offered by large computer systems. The people at Graphic Composition consider them-selves typographers first and computer operators second. Computers are viewed as a tool to aid in the production of fine book composition. For example, computer formats have been written and stored in the system to automatically produce sunken initials based on the point size and the number of lines the initial is to be sunk for a chapter title page. Using the kerning tables available on the Penta software, hundreds of char-acter fit combinations have been stored to improve the typographic fit of any given type family. When a new typeface digitally stored is received on a floppy disk from Mergenthaler, GCI typographers analyse the character fit as it is initially typeset with-out refinement. Character combinations are checked and minute spacing adjustments are stored in the kerning table for that typeface.

Perhaps the most critical area of expertise in a computer typesetting plant is the planning and markup department. It is necessary for a markup specialist to understand fully the operation of the computer software but, at the same time, to be a typographer. It is his responsibility to interpret the designer's specifications into computer formats and control codes. Graphic Composition normally typesets sample pages for publishers, including all typographic elements and textual apparatus found in the manuscript. The markup specialist oversees a job through the system.

Initial input after markup is done by cottage keyboard operators. Typists working at home normally put in five to six hours a day on an IBM Selectric typewriter. The pre-requisites for being a keyboard operator are good typing and language skills. It takes approximately one week to train a keyboard operator so that he or she may begin key boarding the simpler manuscripts produced at Graphic Composition. Some systems rely

heavily on keyboard operators to produce text-streams which are later code-edited at terminals. At GCI, the input operators are trained to insert all the codes on the first typing. The markup specialist tests all formats during sample page production to ensure that the job will run smoothly.

Before any job is seen for the first time by a customer, it is proofread twice. Input from the OCR typewriters is scanned for storage on hard disk systems. It is then listed on a lineprinter without hyphenation or justification for the initial proofreading. After proofing and corrections are made on a terminal, the stored file is then processed through the computer again for hyphenation and justification. A justified printout is obtained for the final proofing before the job is typeset. Proofreaders are trained to check for typographic niceties, the publisher's house style, and careful adherence to the author's manuscript. To qualify as a proofreader at Graphic Composition, an applicant must have a minimum of a bachelor's degree in English, arts and sciences, or the humanities. Each applicant takes an extensive proofreading test to determine if he or she can 'find four-leaf clovers.' In addition to being a good speller, and having other general academic skills, a proofreader must simply have a knack for discovering errors. Some can find them and some can not.

Pagination is the last step in the production of finished pages. Pagination is accomplished both manually and through the computer software. Manuscripts which have the standard textual apparatus with little non standard material are entered into the system for computer pagination. Books which have oversized layouts, heavy illustration, or highly technical material are assembled on a light table using templates.

The success of Graphic Composition is reflected in its customers. GCI has served approximately half of the seventy university presses in the United States. This number includes such prestigious publishers as Cambridge, Oxford, Yale, the Metropolitan Museum of Art Virginia, California, MIT, Duke, and Cornell. In commercial publishing, Graphic Composition serves such publishers as Time-Life Books and the C V Mosby Company (a medical publisher and a division of Times-Mirror).

1980 **Creative design and the computer** F H K Henrion

The design process

My definition of a designer is someone who helps, in a small way, to replace the past by the present by having his eye on the future, which, after all, is tomorrow's present. A designer has to make himself aware of what is in the wind, what kind of experimentations and achievements are going on in related fields which might influence his field of action, and which field today is not related to design? The designer's malaise is caused by a vague knowledge, or at least uneasy awareness, that computers have entered the design field, especially in the area of design planning. In French, the computer is referred to as 'ordinateur,' the ordering machine. Now it can be said that all design activity is an ordering process, an attempt at reducing chaos, or, as it has been put by N Wiener, negative entropy. Entropy is an elementary law of nature based on the fact that everything organic and inorganic is gradually running down, being reduced and dissolved.

It is the 2nd thermo-dynamic law which has been expressed colloquially 'you can not win!' Every positive human activity is an attempt 'to win.' It is like rowing against the current of a river, where the strength put behind the oars must be greater than the strength of the current in order to move up-river. A pause, how-ever short, allows the current to take over and undo previous strokes, the quantity depending on the length of the pause and the strength of the current. Design is, therefore, rowing up-stream and, in so doing, replacing the chaos found by at least a measure of order. This measure of order depends on the amount of simplification and unification achieved in a given situation. Mies van der Rohe put it: '...design is doing more with less.' This often quoted maxim holds a lot of general truth and can almost always be used as valid criticism when comparing design solutions and when choosing one alternative in favour of another, which is relatively simpler, which in fact does more with less.

It could be applied to textile design, a poster, a piece of typography, a package design and equally to a locomotive, a space rocket or a wristwatch, an electric shaver or a building. In this sense, the designer could be described as an 'ordinateur', which at least, in French, would equate him with a computer.

The creative process

A designer does, of course, a little more than create order, simplification and unification. If he is good, his new and better order can also be arrived at intuitively, by a kind of free association, by lateral thinking, which makes him combine ideas or elements which have never been put together before because they did not seem in any way connected. To quote F C Bartlett, '…the most important feature of original experimental thinking is the discovery of overlap and agreement, where formerly only isolation and difference were recognised!' Invention and innovation come about when seemingly unconnected things can combine to make something completely new.

This can happen as the result of long endeavour or happy accident, usually both; somebody realises it is happening and demonstrates the phenomenon and its implications to himself and others.

Thus Heidegger defined the creative act as 'Aufweisendes Erkennen', which freely translated means 'communication of insight'.

Creativity is not restricted to some particular content. C R Rogers assumes that 'there is no fundamental difference in the creative process as it is evidenced in painting a picture, composing a symphony, devising new instruments of killing, developing a scientific theory, discovering new procedures in human relationships, or creating new formings of one's own personality, as in psychotherapy.'

This creativity caused the invention of the wheel, the concept of the pyramids, Archimedes 'Heureka', the Venus de Milo, Picasso's 'Guernica', a space rocket or the few examples of outstanding contemporary architecture.

There is only one difference between the last two examples and the others; while all the former were based on the insight and concept of one man, the last two have

In 1525, Durer devised methods to design objects and people in perspective. The man standing, points the end of a string to a point on the lute. The string from the pulley to the pointer represents a single ray of light and passes through the picture plane. As the man with the pointer fixes different reference-points on the lute, his assistant measures off the vertical and horizontal co-ordinates and plots each new point on the drawing. When there are enough points, he joins the relevant ones and completes the drawing.

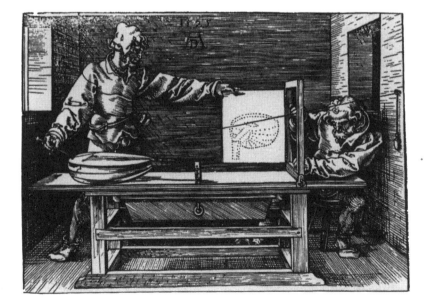

been the result of team-work, which means a combination of insight and concepts by many people. Team-work becomes essential in the solution of contemporary industrial problems, which usually involves one or more technologies. Technology implies the gathering of many bits of information and applying and relating them appropriately to the job in hand. Everybody knows that this is one of the primary functions of a computer, into which an enormous amount of information can be fed and retained in a memory and appropriately related through correct programming, with the result that the output is almost instantaneous. The quality and pertinence of this output is entirely dependent on the quality and pertinence of the program. It is also generally known that the input depends on information which can only be gathered by identifying subjects and sources through penetrating analysis. Systems analysis means identifying a system, component parts, and its purpose.

Systems approach

At this point it becomes essential to define what is a system: to speak of a system is to speak of the coherence of sub-entities, called parts, of that system. To identify the collection of entities as being coherent is defined by intelligence, it is an act of insight. It has, in fact, been said that 'design is intelligence made visible' (Frank Pick). An internal combustion engine is clearly a system. All the bits and pieces which make it up have a relationship to each other. We can, in fact, recognise a pattern of relatedness: a systematic pattern. Because we acknowledge this relatedness we call it a system. But what matters is that the relatedness of all parts are relevant, because it has a unifying purpose, namely – to work.

Thus a system must have relatedness, pattern and purpose. It was the English philosopher Locke who for the first time saw clearly the importance of relation. According to him '...knowing the relation rightly is more valuable than knowing rightly which things are related'. This was the beginning of the philosophy of the environment, that the connecting lines are more important and meaningful than the bits they connect.

Today, we all realise that everything is connected to everything else which in turn makes each item with which we are concerned one of immense complexity. If we look at a chair we try to find out the different materials from which it is made, how they are made, how they fit, and how they are joined together.

As this chair is only one bit of furniture in a room, it matters how it relates to other bits of furniture, to the space and colours of the room; and how the room relates to the other rooms in the house, and the house to other houses in the street, the street to other streets, to townscape and landscape and so on. Simultaneously, all these hierarchies of physical items are connected with corresponding hierarchies of people on all these levels.

Even if all these relationships are acknowledged, the system can consistently offer related items whose relatedness is relevant. Thus a system identified as relevant to the town planner will be different from the one which seems relevant to the interior architect or designer.

The town planner and the interior architect or the industrial designer select from

an infinite number of relations between things, those which seem relevant to their particular problem area. It follows that the recognition of a system is a subjective matter. Two people will not necessarily agree on the existence, or nature or boundaries of any system they have detected. But a person can nominate a system by pointing out the relevance of relationships others have not noticed, pointing out their coherence, pattern and purpose.

Professor Bernal asserted that, in 1896, there were perhaps 50,000 people in the whole world who, between them, carried on the tradition of science. Not more than 15,000 were responsible for the advancement of knowledge for research. Today the total numbers of scientific works in industry, government and universities is over 3.5 millions. It is true to say that 90% of all the scientists and technologists who have ever lived are alive today. Statistics of the actual rate of technological change include, in the last century alone, that our speed of communication was increased by 107, our speed of travel by 102, data handling (and this means computers) by 10^6, energy resources by 103, and weapon's power by 10^6.

Computers are used in all these areas, in fact they have substantially contributed to this frightening increase in speed, intensity and power.

The architecture machine

The computer can create shapes in 2 and 3 dimensions. It creates perspective projections from any desired angle. It can multiply a shape at will, it can form a pattern by repeating the shape in all directions, the pattern can be symmetrical or asymmetrical. The distances between the shapes can be increased or reduced until they overlap to

Systems: Each of the well-known international organisations shown here can be seen as a system in itself. For instance, vw through its organisation, administration, design and development and sales activities through agents and dealers, forms a related, patterned and purposeful system. Another system could include only the multinationals like Ford, BP, Shell, ICI, etc. Another only the motor car manufacturers in all countries; and yet another would consist only of French, German, British and US organisations and so on. This is to demonstrate that number of different relationships between elements can be seen as systems depending on their relevance in a given context. But every system presents a high degree of complexity.

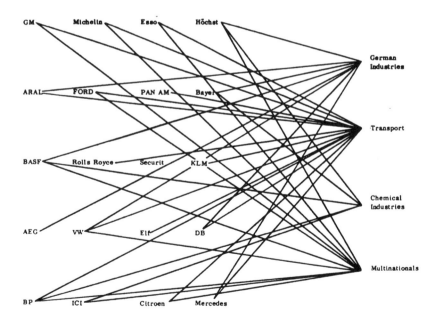

(below left) Simulation of perspective views. It is possible to generate the projection of the same town seen sideways, from above, nearby and from street level. This makes it possible to simulate townscapes before they are built, in order to consult with people who have to live in these buildings. Public consultation is possible before final decisions have been made. This technique, which can show buildings from all angles and from varying distances, is used to train pilots to land on oil platforms at sea and conventional airports.

(below right) Rotation of typefaces and repetition at will has become possible. Once a unit, letter, flower or a geometric symbol has been created, it can be repeated symetrically, asymetrically, staggered, in rows or rotating in different sizes, forming any desired pattern. It is possible to draw a motif on tracing paper, manipulate and multiply it at will, decide on a dozen colour-ways and put this programme on punched tape so that a computerised knitting machine with different coloured yarns can weave samples in several colour ranges.

any required degree. Any shape or form in 2 or 3 dimensions can be rotated 360° in all directions. Any form or volume can be built up from its most simple elements and again be reduced from greatest complexity to nothing at great speed. Each element can change in scale, projection, even proportion: the square can be made, by degrees, into a rectangle, the architect's basic building module, for instance, one room unit, can be extended in height, length and width, repeated vertically and/or horizontally. Windows and any other details can be added and the whole building rotated so that it can be seen from any angle of approach.

A model of any mass-produced product can be put into a numerical form and be transferred to computer tape, so that the computer, through a drawing machine, can produce all the plans, sections and elevations of any scale, in a precision which eliminates human error.

If the fields which make up a pattern are numerically listed (digitised) they can be filled with any colour (up to 64) or texture at will in any combination. Any pattern or form can be transformed into any other pattern or form in controllable degrees. For the making of animated cartoons, the computer can fill in the phases between each given key drawing using the computer's capacity for transformation.

But it can only do what can be numerically defined. When I spoke about systems I emphasised the importance of relatedness. Providing these can be numerically (mathematically) stated, the computer can show the visual form of such a relation.

If a designer understands the principles of the systems approach, he will welcome the computer as a useful tool which is likely to enrich considerably the number of

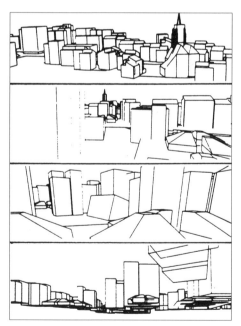

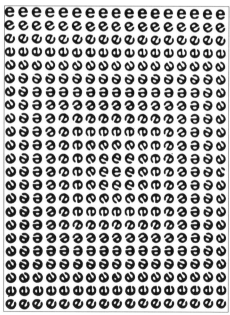

choices during the process of decision making; the computer is likely to increase precision and speed of output through addition of colour, texture, shadows and light-angle into any suitable perspective view. This is equally important for interdisciplinary team-work where one specialist may have difficulty in following the other's intention, and for designer/client communication which is so often a source of considerable misunderstanding.

The importance of clear communication between these specialists becomes essential for successful team-work. The power of the computer to help visualise could be crucial. Lastly, it must be remembered that the computer can record and memorise anything it shows, so that however many choices of shape, form, colour, proportion are visually offered, each is reproducable and capable of being specified for production.

Thus, I have seen the Sci-tex computer at work at Derek Healey International, a large fashion consultancy firm. There, the computer is connected to two knitting machines with the amazing result that every design, pattern, colour-way shown on the computer screen can become a knitted sample within a matter of minutes. The creative designers there have no feeling of competition, only one of enormous help, especially as all the creative work, as well as the final choice, is made by them.

A great deal of research has been done to design programmes for architectural space-planning as this was the first major area in architecture to receive attention from computer-minded people. Some think that now it should perhaps have been the last, as space-planning is one of the most difficult and creative aspects of design and, as such, the least suited for automation. The reason why researchers tried this first, I suppose is, that it is the most exciting and appealing, and also for the reason that conventional methods seemed inadequate. However, computers are best suited for well-defined, routine, tedious and repetitive tasks, such as quantity surveying and structural analysis, ergonomic analysis of equipment, and possibly draughting plans and perspectives. The visual simulation of the environment to be designed is clearly another good application. Future areas might be automatic detailing. The last area of all will be computer aids for initial sketch design and layout, although this might happen any day and be useful eventually. The fact that, historically, a lot of effort was put into Automatic Space Planning, has meant that, initially, designers were led to expect too much from computers, both positively, in terms of better, more 'optimised' designs, or negatively, in terms of being replaced by machines.

Then what actually has happened came as an anti-climax since none of the space-planning systems turned out to be very useful, so some went to the other extreme and decided that computers were no use at all and should be avoided. From all this, in archi-tecture at least, the conclusion is that professional designers should not be threatened by them but rather be helped. Possibly design assistants, technicians and draughtsmen may legitimately be scared of losing their jobs. Further, the increasing use of expensive machines, expensive software systems, is going to give additional advantages to large and rich design practices at the expense of the smaller organisations. In engineering this is already happening.

Without mathematical understanding, it is easy to imagine that every increase in

connections of a system adds vastly to the mathematical complexities to describe it. The required length of time and the cost of involving such sophisticated computers makes such applications usually far from cost effective.

Obviously, the designer spends a great deal of time designing (often by trial and error). After he has formed his concept satisfactorily, and he has made a choice between various alternatives, he still has to carry out his ideas in detail, which is a very lengthy process. Whilst the computer could do most of this very much faster, the research, analysis and design of a suitable programme takes much longer and therefore costs a great deal more than the conventional solution of a design problem by a designer.

At all times it is important to consider the costs involved (in the design activity) in the light of likely benefits to the eventual design.

However, the price of computers drops every year (some manufacturers claim as much as 25%) and computers, once installed, are available 24 hours a day but are rarely fully used. So it is possible, in large industries or government departments who own a computer, that there is often 'play time' available for experimentation and development.

In all cases, the designer will be part of a team, when he or she will have to work along with a computer specialist. It is in this context that the designer will learn and benefit from this collaboration as he is forced to verbalise his problems to a degree to which he is not normally used. The usual design brief will have to be broken down into goals, objectives, constraints and criteria and their inter-dependence have to be described. Objective design methods have to be evolved using mathematical decomposition techniques for analysing the structure and ordering of complex problems. The problem must be represented by a set of elements with a quantified association or degree of inter-action between all pairs of elements. This is called the 'inter-action matrix' or 'association matrix'. The definition of a problem must be a unique representation of this problem. Design can be seen not simply as a synthesis of form but, at the same time, as a synthesis of problem.

Problem and solution are indivisible. Most design methodologists agree that a more self-conscious approach to design will lead to improvement.

My own experience has shown me the validity of my assertions. For the last 15 years I have worked with Alan Parkin, a designer who has a degree in mathematical logic. Together we have made surveys and written design briefs for large organisations for whom we have been acting as consultant designers on their total design policy. Amongst them were KLM, BEA, Blue Circle Cement, and the British Post Office. In each case, the exact number of design items was not known, yet had to be established. It was also important to find out which people were likely to make decisions on the design of these items. A systems approach proved most helpful to make a list of all design items; in the case of the Post Office, from a television tower to a postage stamp, including all telecommunication equipment from Telstar to Telex, all graphic applications from advertising to stationery and forms. At first, all these items had to be listed through a search strategy for obtaining all relevant data.

Questionnaires had to be drafted in such a way that they described all facts and contingencies about each item, both quantitively and qualitively. When this data was

to hand, these items were put into related groups like street furniture, architecture, and so on, making fifteen basic categories, which, in turn, were broken down into sets and sub-sets, which eventually contained all the items. In that way, they could be shown as a system where all categories related to each other, a number of sets related to each category, and even a larger number of sub-sets to each set. Subsequently it was attempted to trace the administrative hierarchy of people involved in design decisions at the Post Office as a complete system in itself. This system of people involved in design decisions was then related to the new system of things so that the very many and contorted connections between both diagrams were sufficient proof to show that a unified design policy was not possible unless procedures were changed. The network of lines between people and things had to be simplified in order to produce better designed items.

The systems approach is also helpful in much smaller contexts: any range of products or furniture must be related, and to express this relatedness in words or figures is useful, even more so for mass produced goods where the same component parts are common to a number of models, as in motor cars. For example, Volkswagen today attempt such a policy along with all major car manufacturers; all their new models, together with those made by Audi-NSU, are different yet have a large number of component parts in common. Thus a systems approach contributes to successful design, achieving a wide variety made up largely of identical component parts – a difficult equation which faces all mass-production industries.

In order to find computer languages which can be usefully employed in design areas, computer experts study the sequence of thoughts and actions of the design process in the human designer. This is done in the hope of finding new, objective design methods which can be converted into computer programmes.

My suggestion is that the designer in turn might benefit from studying the scientific attempts of describing the design process. The designer will be helped if he understands this emerging methodology and applies it consciously to his own work. This in itself would establish a constructive interaction matrix.

Creativity, defined earlier as combined ideas or elements which have never been put together before because they do not seem in any way connected, can now be seen in system terms as finding new relations between ideas or elements which did not exist before. Personally, I am confident that this most important aspect of Man's unique contribution to change is unlikely ever to be challenged by the computer, but that will be vastly helped and enriched.

In Heidegger's term 'communication of insight' the computer can communicate but the creative insight is likely to be Man's alone.

1982 **Designing for Prestel and after** Mervyn Kurlansky

The challenge for a designer in this field is to see what is really new in the electronic medium. But in order to communicate we have to do more still; we have to relate what is new to what is familiar.

This double challenge was central to the work I was asked to do on the British Telecom viewdata service, Prestel.

The word 'viewdata' signifies a system whereby information is passed from a central computer data bank, down ordinary telephone subscriber lines, to be displayed on a specially modified domestic television set. Subscribers call up the central computer which holds all the data, by means of a simple keypad. The information originally comes from a variety of commercial and official organisations. A key element of the Prestel system is the index – or routeing system – provided by British Telecom itself. This enables the subscriber to choose and find the required information, either by topic or by provider.

My task was to design the pages for the routeing system. This involved decisions about the layout of information, typestyle, use of colours, hierarchies of headings and the overall 'look' of the pages.

By the time I was invited to contribute to the system, the matrix for the screen had already been established by the BBC and IBA: they were using the same matrix for their teletext transmissions. This was a pity, because the matrix was a prime example of com-puter thinking unchecked by design considerations. The main idea had been to cram as much on the screen as possible. Up to 960 characters could be shown on a single page. This was no doubt a technological achievement but in reality, the matrix could never be used to its full capacity, because a screen packed as densely as that would be virtually unreadable.

Not only the matrix but the alphabets were predetermined. The basic alphabet was known as *Alphanumerics*. Designed by engineers, this was formed on a 10 x 6 grid, and as you can see, the letters were extremely crude. A finer grid would have permitted letterforms with much better definition. Even with the given matrix, however, more readable characters could have been achieved if type designers had been consulted

In addition to *Alphanumerics*, we had at our disposal another building block based on the same matrix. This was called the graphics mode. It offered a total of 64

permutations to produce images on the screen. But the units were relatively large, and therefore allowed only very limited shapes to be made.

There was one other pre-programmed alphabet, derived from the graphics mode I have just described. This was called *Alphagraphics*, and was designed primarily to be used by all information providers for headings on their own pages. It is a hideous alphabet. It is impossible to achieve the effect of continuous curves or diagonals, with the result that most of the characters are extremely clumsy and difficult to read.

We embarked on an exercise to attempt to over come these limitations, but at best, we could only achieve marginal benefits because of the constraints of the system. And, in some cases, we could make no improvements at all.

One experiment that did partially succeed was with the *Alphagraphics* mode. We incorporated serifs. This helped the eye accept the awkward diagonals, which, because of the building blocks of this mode, looked like staircases. Perhaps because the serif is rather like a step itself, it seemed to finish off the letters and provide cohesion.

None of these improvements came near to tackling the real problem presented by the Prestel brief. It is a problem I would like to dwell on because it raises important issues.

As graphic designers we are always involved in many layers of communication: informing, persuading, identifying and so on. Prestel ideally needed a range of typefaces and graphic possibilities. Only in this way could the pages for each information provider have been given a distinct and appropriate character. The necessary use of the same alphabets, colours and graphic elements creates an undesirably uniform appearance.

The primitive resources offered by widely used screen data systems like Prestel make such distinctiveness impossible. In terms of typography, you could say that we were faced with limitations that put us back 2,000 years. Nevertheless, we did our best to give Prestel's own pages as individual an appearance as possible.

We anticipated that the information providers themselves would produce rather cluttered pages making maximum use of the seven available colours, the two alphabets and the graphic mode. Many of them would also probably attempt to recreate their existing logos in rather crude form on the screen.

For the Prestel pages, we generally used only the three most legible colours. Further-more, we used the basic *Alphanumerics* alphabet almost exclusively, and usually only in capitals to achieve maximum legibility.

Having decided to use a single alphabet, it was important that individual items of information could be rapidly located. So we a!so introduced horizontal lines to isolate each heading and each section of information.

One of the peculiar aspects of the Prestel matrix was that it produced in the basic alphabet, space between words that was greater than the space between the lines. This made reading difficult, because the eye tends to grasp words in groups rather than one at a time. The effect of the odd spacing was to create vertical groups that were visually stronger than the horizontal groups. Now of course, to make sense of a line of writing, the eye must be encouraged to travel horizontally. We tackled this by stipulating that whenever possible, double line spacing should be used. This rule supplemented the separating effects of our horizontal lines.

The cumulative effect at which we were aiming on these pages was authoritative, uncluttered and yet distinctive.

Prestel could not identify itself simply by the look of its pages. It also required a logo-type or symbol. The special interest in designing this was that the mark would appear not only on the screen but also on the advertisements, brochures and other printed matter that would promote and explain the service. In other words, we had to come up with a design that would prove equally effective in the old media and the new.

Now we could have reproduced the name 'Prestel' in the pre-programmed *Alphagraphics* alphabet, or in some special configuration using the graphics mode. But somehow, all the possibilities that these solutions allowed had the look of compromise. The limitations of the system were always apparent and became even more so when we attempted printed versions. Furthermore, solutions of this kind looked similar to those being produced by others using the system. Prestel needed to be different.

So we took another look at the basic alphabet – *Alphanumerics* – and the available colours. We noticed an interesting coincidence: the name Prestel had seven letters – the same number as the colours in the system.

So we tried showing the name with each letter in a different colour.

The letters were spaced wide apart. The reason for this was that, in order to change colours, the computer at this stage in its development required the user to skip one letter space. We felt we had arrived at something different, but not yet immediately striking. The eventual solution was to arrange the Prestel letters into a diamond shape: we had created what we wanted, a unique trademark [see page 191].

On the screen of the visual display unit that we were working with – they have advanced since then, of course – the background was invariably dark. To translate this into print and other uses, we set the logotype within a black diamond shape. It was then ready for application – either in colour or black and white – to stationery, vehicles, dealers' windows, illuminated signs, labels and tickets, promotional literature, advertisements, promotional items, and finally the inevitable badge and sweatshirt.

(below left) Example of page layout.

(below right) Display alphabet: *Alphagraphics*.

(facing page) detail of matrix and letterform.

On the screen, the mark is true to the medium, yet quite distinct from the usual type of computer data symbol. Off the screen, it appears comfortable in print and other applications, but is still appropriate to the service it identifies.

Throughout the Prestel project, we fixed our attention on the qualities we were trying to achieve, and everything we did was subordinated to those goals. A lot of decisions about the designs amounted to self-imposed restrictions. When one is working with a new medium it is essential not to feel obliged to show off everything the medium can do. This is particularly relevant to information technology, because computer engineers, quite understandably, tend to be dazzled by all that they have achieved in an incredibly short space of time. Left to themselves, they would naturally be inclined to pack their screens with spectacular demonstrations of technique.

Designers are, or should be, preoccupied with communication, not technology. We have to be sparing, and refuse to be too easily impressed. This is an ideal, of course. In reality, designers too get caught up in the headiness of a new breakthrough.

I would like also to touch on some of the advanced and sophisticated screen work that is being done today in universities and commercial institutions; in a sense, the progression of our efforts with Prestel, these computer graphics are evolving toward a new art form.

It is now possible to programme impressions of three-dimensional objects that are almost alarmingly realistic. Not only can complex objects be built up on the screen, they can be revolved, viewed from different angles, and twisted into new shapes.

We are, no doubt, seeing here the birth of new visual language, neither film nor graphic design, but owing a lot to each. The point I wish to make, however, is that so far, little has actually been said in this amazing medium. The content of these images for example, is effectively without any communicative purpose at all.

A small child scribbling with a crayon is more fascinated by the activity of the crayon on the paper than the image created, let alone what the image might convey.

The important thing is not to get stuck at this stage too long. The content and quality of communications must quickly become our priority. The medium is not the message, but the servant of the message. If we insist on this, we stand a much higher chance of influencing the ways the technology develops. It isn't enough for design to keep pace with new techniques. New techniques must be developed to meet the requirements of good design.

If on the other hand, we allow ourselves to be seduced and dominated by technology, we are in danger of surrounding ourselves with much that is brilliant in its way, but at the same time empty and ugly.

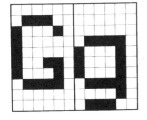

1987 Maintaining standards with medium to low resolution digital typefaces David Saunders

We have reached a watershed. For half a decade or more we have been scrutinising and manipulating bit-maps. Now, quite suddenly, we realise that effective solutions have been found for most of the problems of digitising typography at low dots per inch resolution. Consequently, we find ourselves with the need to address the problems of the practical use of digital type rather than to confine ourselves to the examination of the technical minutiae of its production.

With continued improvements in printer technology, such as higher resolution and better edge definition, the problems of character representation will continue to recede, and the elements of document typography will come to the fore. We must first recognise, however, that typographical awareness is not confined to the expert.

Typographical awareness is acquired from an early age. For example, as children we recognise our own books; and we soon learn to recognise children's books in general. But it is interesting to note that although a book set in a slab-serif face that is very similar to a conventional typewriter face, we would not accept the latter for bookwork. In fact, even as children, we would have recognised the difference!

It is not surprising, therefore, that the letterforms of early electronic printers were unacceptable, nor that continued exposure to them has done nothing to make them acceptable; figure 1. No more acceptable are our distortions that defy the normal proportions of our alphabets, making recognition difficult. In figure 2, no provision has been made for lower-case descenders. In the early days of low resolution printers it was not uncommon to find manufacturers making fundamental decisions on formats before the typographical aspects had been fully appraised. Even the shortening of the A to include the circumflex above, although not impairing recognition, is irksome to the reader; figure 3.

The problems of representing adequately an analogue design figure 4 at low resolution are now well known. At 1000 dots per inch figure would represent a 4pt character, but at 300 dots per inch it would represent 12pt. Such a coarse rendering at 12pt will have a considerable effect upon the design. In figure 5, we see detail being lost progressively as fewer dots are available. Even so, it is possible to produce designs that are of acceptable appearance; and here we must be realistic. Not only do we acquire a typographical awareness through life, but we also acquire a recognition of

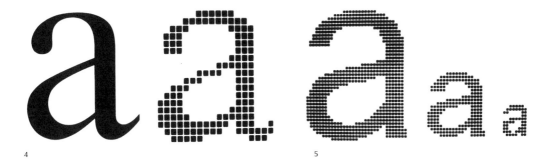

4

5

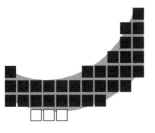

6

7

fitness for purpose. We seem to develop a scale of values which we apply visually; for instance, we would expect a higher standard of printing for a wedding invitation than for a car park ticket. Used in the appropriate context, the lower resolutions can produce results that are quite acceptable.

Let us examine a few of the technical problems, and see their solutions. One of the better known optical effects apparent in typography is the size relationship of round and square characters. It is important that these all appear to be the same size but, in fact, the o projects below the square base line, and the top similarly will project above the square tops of the lower-case. The essential feature is that the round and square characters should appear to be the same size as each other, and that they should appear to stand on a common base line. What things appear to be is the reality.

If we examine the digested interpretation in figure 6 we see the shaded areas representing the true shape of the character while the square represents a low resolution interpretation; but the grid is too coarse to interpret correctly the small difference needed to create the required illusion. The problematical area is represented by the hollow squares. If these squares are incorporated into the bit map, the round character will be too large, and will be seen to be too large. If omitted, the character will base align with the adjacent square elements and appear to be too small. In this case however we can invoke a deception. By omitting the three pixels in question we will give the rounded character a somewhat flattened appearance, which will then match visually the adjacent square character. It will at the same time, if designed carefully, still give an acceptable representation of the design.

We find that sloping or italic designs can digitise quite well, contrary to what might be expected, figure 7. It is less surprising, however, if we think about the way that we represent our bit-maps. Figure 8 [overleaf] shows a number of possible representations. Notice how different they appear. Only that at the bottom right-hand side comes anywhere near to a realistic representation of the character in its output form.

The somewhat diffuse edges of most of the product generated by low resolution output devices do in fact soften the worst of the effects created by the 'jaggies' on sloped or rounded characters.

When viewed in the form of a bit-map based on a regular, squared grid, the attempt

to produce the italic version seems crude and ineffective. Seen in the correct context however, the low resolution version of *New Berolina*, even at 6pt, figure 9, displays the essential characteristics of the design. In metal, such designs are not often made in sizes below 14pt. The diffused edge can not, however, be taken too far as a solution to the problem of 'jaggies'. Made too diffuse, the eye will interpret the text as being out of focus. Unable, apparently, to bring the text into focus, the eye will find this diffusion more distracting than bad shaping.

This brings us to the important point concerning the way we see things. The whole of our representation of the printed word is closely related to the mechanisms of our eyes and our brains. It is unlikely to be pure inertia that has caused us to retain our conventions of printing for so long; our capital and lowercase alphabets, our black ink on white paper and our rectangular formats, to name a few.

Our expectations also play a part in the way that we see things. The bit map figure 10 reveals a lack of symmetry in the rings of the percentage sign. Scrutinizing of the output would also reveal this, but our experience will lead us to expect symmetry, and the eye passing over at a small size will accept that symmetry exists, figure 11.

We are sometimes asked if there are typefaces that are inherently easy or difficult to digitise. In practice, the problem doesn't seem to work out this way. Rather we find that it is individual characters, perhaps in individual point sizes, that will create a problem. I recall a fount where most characters, including the lower-case o, were rendered with little difficulty. Contrary to what one might expect, it was the capital O that proved the most difficult character to portray satisfactorily.

Another aspect of bit-map construction arises when we compare the effects of different output technologies. Figure 12 shows the same bit-maps on different output technologies. To make both texts appear the same, an appreciable thickening needed to be made to the thinner fount; figure 13.

It might be, however, that at times we are too concerned about such discrepancies. The differences between litho and letterpress have been with us for many years, as exemplified by the comparison in figure 14.

Screen founts present another area where considerable improvements have been achieved. The alphabet in figure 15 need never have been as bad as it is. In particular, far too much height has been allocated to the ascenders at the expense of the x-height. Lower-case a, e and s are almost indistinguishable. Already, however, we are beginning

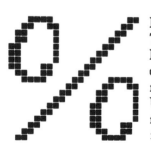

8

Pack my b
quick brown
require the

9

PQRSTUVWXYZ
ᵡxyzßﬀﬃﬁﬄﬂﬀﬆﬁﬁĳœœ
⅛ ⅞ ′″ % °%₀
[ ] † ‡ ¶ •
> ± ≤ ≥ ≠ ⌑⌦ ¬

10

%

11

PACK MY BOX WITH FOUI
THE QUICK BROWN FOX
Pack my box with four dozen i
quick brown fox jumps over th
require the use of Compact Spa
Unusual Sizes, Weights and Pr
needed to improve appearance
rifling coffiin a:fflict effect

12

to see screen founts with a true typographic identity, giving on-screen displays a document appearance.

These are only a few of the many problems that arises in digital type representation, but it is evident now that most of the practical problems of producing acceptable, convincing type in digital form at low resolutions have, to a large extent, been solved; so where do we go from here?

We saw at the beginning that typographical awareness is by no means confined to experts. Standards of printing are remarkably high, particularly when viewed in terms of the job that they have to do, and the economic realities. These are the standards that have already been set, and they have already determined our expectations. Documents such as that in figure 13, currently printed by litho or some other traditional process, will in the future be produced by non-impact printers of some sort. The publishers of such documents are already expending considerable effort to make them look good. They are unlikely to look favourably on systems that although offering economy and versatility, compromise such benefits with a marked drop in quality.

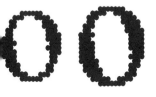

13

We live in a culture with a high typographic awareness. Books, magazines and advertisements present us daily with thoughtful and imaginative use of typography. We cannot 'unsee' the things that we have seen. What we see around us will compel manufacturers to develop their printers still further to match our expectations. And the final step? The users of the ever increasing range of low resolution non-impact printers, having been presented with the ability to set quality type, will find that they need to use it with care.

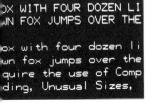

14

As we present users with an ever expanding repertoire of quality typefaces, they will need the discretion to use them well. Used badly, the results will be as bad, or perhaps worse, than that produced with mono-spaced typewriter founts. At least they had coherence.

We know now how to produce digital type to a high standard; but we will be presenting it to users who will in all probability have no typographical expertise. The task for the future is to enable them to use it effectively.

15

1984 **A new breed of designer?** Martin Poole

Unlike micros, the more sophisticated colour terminals rely on a host computer for their processing power and the main application of the systems available is for business graphics and engineering. The business community apart, the designers who have benefited most are those working in specialist areas such as TV. Such is the surfeit of computer graphics on TV that it needs no description here, but the technology is now filtering down to more prosaic applications. Animations have been a 'natural' for computer graphics and it is by extension that one acquires the ability to interpolate and derive one image from another.

In all this the creative typographic designer has, perhaps, remained somewhat in the background. Brian Reffin-Smith from the RCA is certainly not presiding over a huge academic budget to research into some obscure graphic goal. His (postgraduate) students at the College have to improvise, and far from using megabuck computers he started with a BBC model B (for which he has written a popular program available from the BBC) and a 380Z – the machines you are most likely to find in a primary school classroom. These programs are a useful introduction, if a far cry from the £100,000 one can spend on a full system.

While for many purposes the micro can be considered as the only computer you will ever need, the requirements of the serious graphic designer are such that it is perhaps better to regard a small micro as a training aid. You can use it to find its limitations, the better to define your needs. Having done this, you can use the same micro for your accounts or word processing and you will really know what you want if you set out to get yourself a fully-fledged system.

Many people I meet, who find out that I now do my graphics on a computer, would like to think of me as part of a 'new breed' of designers who have 'crossed over' or made the transition to a digital medium. These are clichés and should be avoided. There is no reason to react to this medium any differently from how we all reacted to the advent of phototypesetting, Letraset and PMT's, etc (ie distrust, suspicion and irrelevant comparisons with existing methods). It is just another tool for designers to use in getting the job of communicating done. It is also just as absurd to ask if computers will appear on every desk allowing non-visual people to take over your job or somehow replace hand-done work? Not so, there is too much invested in hands already.

I use my digital painting station, and as an illustration, logotype development and audio-visual machine. It enables me and my clients to put ideas into visual reality with a speed and flexibility that I have not found in my 15 years' past experience as a graphic designer. We can change colours to anyone of 16.7 million, do airbrushed areas in seconds, distort to shapes, overlay type, and change the size and orientation of anything on or off the screen. In short, it allows us to make our usual aesthetic decisions, implement them immediately, view the results within minutes and backtrack or push forward as necessary without the inhibiting consideration that it's too much like hard work to try this or that.

Nevertheless, I'm regretfully aware that the push for computer graphics has come from the client side rather than from designers themselves, many of whom – prompted by their more technologically aware clients from TV, films, publishing and the business world – have dragged themselves along to us with a brief to produce their next report-cover or illustration via computer.

Our company, 'Digital Arts', operates a bureau service at £50 per hour including trained operator (me in fact!). Designers can direct the operator just like a photographic session. Most single images, report-covers, magazine illustrations take from 1 to 6 hours. Pencilled-out images can be traced in through the digitising pad or photographed by a digitising rostrum camera or from video. The images can then be manipulated via the menu selections on the pad in almost every way. Then output to video or a special film recorder that smooths out the dots and other TV screen aberrations so that the transparency can be put through the usual four colour reproduction process without any moiré effects, and with good colour fidelity.

As the hardware only costs about £15,000, we've sold the painting station to designers and graphic design courses at art colleges. The students, of course, are not burdened with our preconceptions so it looks as if they'll come out with a good knowledge of digital design techniques and they'll be able to take advantage of the increasing number of jobs in this field.

Okay, the type still has little lumps on it, but don't wait forever to try it out. I still remember a man I worked with in the late sixties who wouldn't use phototypesetting because it couldn't do his favourite joined up script. In fact, he said, it would never catch on.

Many designers in print and films seem to be waiting until computer graphics changes to meet their view of what it should be: higher resolution, no jagged bits, better type, but what's needed is an exchange of views between graphic designer and software writer and hardware builder. If designers and typographers won't get creatively involved then they can't complain if the medium is not growing up the way they'd like to see it. Also, the longer you leave it before you have contact with it, the harder it will be to catch up. So come on! Be the first on your block to do a computer graphics piece!

1982 **Who does what – and why?** Colin Cohen

These days, when we talk of demarcation in typesetting we are normally thinking in terms of who is fighting for the privilege of slogging through an indifferent manuscript pecking out the keystrokes. Those who try to convince the National Graphical Association (NGA) that their skilled members are destined for higher things suggest that compositors should confine themselves to clever activities like entering the codes needed to give the right sizes, measures and faces on a photosetter – entering these codes on a text already 'captured' in one way or another by someone less skilled, but who has to type the whole thing anyway. When these matters are discussed seriously, it sometimes seems as though it's the NGA versus the rest – while in Fleet Street it is the NGA v the NUJ (National Union of Journalists) – never mind the fact that the two unions have been debating a merger.

The argument in favour is simple, one of need. The designer knows what he wants and what he expects something to look like and so should have the means at his disposal to execute his wishes. So far so good – no one is in the least put out as long as a designer simply marks instructions on a typescript in pencil. Few will mind, even if this is done in marked up keystroke codes rather than in plain English (as long as he uses the correct codes!). Further, it is rare that anyone complains, or is particularly concerned, whether or not a designer or typist is a member of a union. That, how-ever, is about the limit.

While one can see the designer's desire to get behind a keyboard, and make up pages on-screen, one can see many reasons why this is not such a good idea – and is likely to be too complex, technical and also too expensive for some time to come. For these reasons, I have some reservations about the generally excellent SIAD courses at the London College of Printing. Having dealt with designers for years when buying print, I have often wished that designers had a better idea of how the end result was obtained in phototypesetting. Anyone who attempts this training is risking, however, taking a wrong turning: it is, in part, a question of a little knowledge being a dangerous thing and, in part, the fact that, in an industry which accommodates a huge range of type-setting equipment, a decision has to be made as to which plant will be used for instruction. Will it be the *right* plant?

The SIAD is probably in a better position than any school to construct such a course,

as not only does it represent its members in a way that the educational establishment
never can, however hard it tries, but it can be more flexible in changes of syllabus.
In the world of printing colleges, any but the smallest change in syllabus can involve
endless committees, and the Local Education Authority. In a period of quite extraordinary change, an institution such as the LCP is unable to respond such shifts of direction
and is glad to be involved with outside bodies on an evolving syllabus that can adapt
to changing needs. It is teaming up with the SIAD over the last couple of years that has
certainly produced a popular course.

I attended one of the whole day sessions at the LCP, the fifteenth in a series that
have all been fully booked and promises to remain so for the forseeable future. Devised
by the SIAD Education and Training Board, the day is divided into two main sessions: in
the morning the small groups are instructed on a variety equipment by LCP composing
department staff – while in the afternoon session the SIAD's Graham Stevens, practising
designer, leads a more theoretical session followed by a very active discussion period.
The course is intended only as an introduction to the basics of computer-aided typography (which effectually means all phototypesetting these days), but during 1982 more
ambitious courses will be run at Watford College on their advanced Ferranti CS7 front-
end computer system: only those who have attended the LCP course will be able to
enrol for the latter. In light of the fact of the fall-off in the number of trainee comps,
and the fact that there are now four to five times as many designers being trained as
there are comps, the quality of such courses is of vital importance.

In constructing such a course there is choice of making it equipment specific or
sticking to theory and just explaining the principles of modern typesetting. The SIAD
have decided on a compromise; we have already mentioned: the morning session takes
place in the composing department. Here the restrictions of a college, even one as well
equipped as LCP, become apparent. Even if the LCP were better equipped (ie with more
modern and more varied kit) there would be a limit to what one could handle in morning session – but with a limited range of photosetters there is a real danger that students
could gain the impression that what they have seen is representative of the range
available. The LCP can offer a reasonable range, and some of it, like the CompSet 4560,
is up to date. Other equipment, such as the Monophoto System, 1000 Photon, and Linotron, are a representative of certain major sectors of the industry, but can hardly be
said to represent the 'state of the art' in phototypesetting technology. The LCP is also
very fortunate to have an early model of the Xenotron page make up terminal as it
is an early model. However, its software has long since been overtaken by later issues,
which limits its scope; and as it is programmed to drive the College's Photon, many of
the faces and sizes that are, in theory, available on the screen are in fact barred from it.

If this seems somewhat negative comment, it does raise a question to be considered
when trying to teach the rudiments of setting to working designers: that is, that when
they are shown what can (or cannot) be done on a particular machine, they might think
that this applies to all machines. What is more, with the advent of digital machines (at a
price that ordinary typesetters can afford, that is) none of these constraints apply. For
instance, there are hundreds of Linotron 202s and C R Tronics in the country as well as

the Alphatype CRS, Monotype's Lasercomp and Compugraphic 8600. All of these offer what are considered to be acceptable image quality and virtually no limitation of size or face mixing. Indeed, rather than the machine imposing a discipline on the designer, it is more a case of the designer having to restrain himself from using all the goodies available at virtually no cost penalty. What price then, what we were told about one system only having x lenses (and thus sizes) readily available to the operator? No need, either, to worry where the optics are (will a face look the same at the middle of the line as at the ends?) rather, the designer has to grope with such problems as copy-fitting in 9.25 points on a 56 mm measure or the presence of 'sloped roman' as a substitute for italic on some systems (not necessarily mentioned) or the fact that some modern faces are designed to be sloped (not mentioned, but perhaps it might be acceptable).

As I have said, there seems to me to be a very real risk of becoming too device dependent when there is such a vast and changing array of equipment at the designer's disposal. This brings me to another point. Many designers are not actively involved in the buying of print or typesetting, in that they freelance for clients who do this for themselves or work in organisations that have their own buying departments. In these cases, the designer will probably never know on what system his work is likely to be set: indeed he will just have to put up with whoever's *Baskerville*, *Times* or *Univers* he gets and hope that it is more or less the same size and colour as the one he was expecting. The SIAD's Fountspec helps – but only if the designer is allowed contact with the setter. Apart from the fact there are buyers who are bloody-minded enough to consider that specifying a system is outside the designer's remit, it is often not practicable to specify the system in advance. For a large number of jobs where price or timing are sensitive, it may have to be a last minute decision. Where the system is known there are also problems. It was said at the LCP (after speaking of Monophoto's superior quality) that the 18-unit system was no longer good nor flexible enough for modern standards. But for the designer to move away from the 18-unit system seems to me to be risky. 96 units were mentioned as being increasingly popular and while this is true for the Lasercomp, for example, it is by no means standard. The Linotype Library faces, which set standards that many would consider the equal of Monotype, is available in 18 or 54 unit systems, while the Alphatype CRS works on 144 units. Typesetters are used to being asked for 3 units space and automatically translate it to the unit system they are using from the 18-units system that they assume designers are working with. But it seems to me that a designer who specifies any other unit basis has to be very certain of the system to be used – not only for output but as a front end.

At the more theoretical afternoon session, talk was mostly on what is involved for the designer who specifies typesetting. Much of the time was spent on format codes. Here we enter the complex area of front ends. Many people consider that the front end has more effect on the quality of setting than the 'back-end'. Certainly it can have a marked effect on the ease with which complex work can be done, and in some cases the ability of all the unit widths on a phototypesetter to be used might be affected by the front end.

In the area of formats and marking up, there is undoubtedly an important rôle for

the designer. My feelings, however, are that it is vital for the designer to make his requirements clear. All relevant details need to be shown: type face and sizes, spacing requirements (both vertical and horizontal) and any fount changes. Most important, perhaps, is for any changes that take place in the body-text to be clearly indicated, as these are the sort of instructions that it is easiest for the typesetter to overlook. While I fully agree with the SIAD on the need for the designer to understand how different systems work (perhaps so that they can understand why some things are more difficult than others) there are some things that are best left to the typesetter. It seems to me that the construction of the sometimes complicated character-strings that are needed for formatting are best left to the person who actually taps them or someone in their department who is thoroughly familiar with the system. This is because only the slightest slip in such a code can have a devastating effect. After all, it is not just like any old typing error: one error in a format code could for example double the measure or change the whole job from one face to another. The SIAD, together with the STD and some other interested bodies, feel, however, that designers should know the possibilities available.

Another reason for not straying from plain English in mark-up is the increasing availability of 'soft' keys. Such keys are available even on £300 home computers, where keys numbered 1–10 can be allocated any function. As a result, key 1 can be 10pt Times Roman to 18ems, while key 2 is italic, key 3 bold and key 4 is 12pt to 37ems. While it may seem easy for the designer to learn and use these codes they don't stay still! The comp can (and has to) change the codes from job to job. After all, if there are only ten keys they soon get specified. While this is therefore a useful facility it does seem to me to be best used by the typesetter rather than the designer.

Finally, on the subject of demarcation, the SIAD, quite rightly, sees certain advantages in its members being involved in some aspects of keyboarding. Here again I can foresee problems. Few designers are going to want to get involved in text keyboarding – and as a member of the advanced 'search and peck' school of typing I know why. There would, however, be very real advantages to be obtained by designers who develop the skills to use page make-up terminals. I can see nothing more logical than the modern designer using electronic 'cut and paste' techniques.

I hope the day will come when the NGA recognise the designer as a legitimate user of these machines – as well as perhaps the NUJ or even just anybody. One problem will remain if this happens, that of cost. Page-view terminals will always be considerably more expensive than more straightforward keyboards. Thus they will need to be heavily utilised (perhaps even on two or three shifts) to be economic and this is not likely to happen in anything but production conditions.

1992 **When will we see what we get?** Andrew Boag

In any analysis of the representation of type on screen the term 'WYSIWYG' will inevitably be heard. The letters, of course, stand for 'What You See Is What You Get'. But the fact is that this is a meaningless term at present: it is a dream yet to be fulfilled.

Vendors define WYSIWYG computer systems as those which give an exact, image on a preview screen of one's final paper or film-output. All WYSIWYG system users, on the other hand, know that such a statement is somewhat inaccurate.

The need to display type on computer, screens has inevitably been influenced by our expectations, based upon five hundred years of typographic history. Some typographers have claimed that the limitations of the computer screen demand completely revolutionary letter forms, but this has never been seriously entertained. Therefore, many of our familiar typefaces have been distorted – some almost beyond recognition – in order that they can be represented on computer screens.

Typefaces which we view on our screens today are generally crude representations of what type really is. And, since they are crude representations, what you get, in the form of paper or film-output, can not be exactly like what you saw on the screen. In effect, computer screens play a dual rôle: they render visualisations of work in progress, but in doing so, they obscure the real appearance of paper output.

All of this raises three important questions. Why does type on screen look relatively crude? Why do we put up with it? And will we have to continue to put up with it?

The first two questions can be dealt with fairly quickly. Each image of a document on a screen is built up out of rows of dots which are, on average, one seventy second of an inch in diameter – low resolution. Paper documents are built up of rows of dots which these days are generally at least, one three hundredth of an inch in diameter – medium resolution.

The main reasons for this difference are: the practical limitations of finite spot size, the amount of random access memory needed to hold screen images, and the economics of processing speed needed to create screen images. This large difference in resolution is the reason why type on screen looks crude.

We put up with it because we want to preview our documents so much that we are prepared to accept lower standards of preview quality compared to final output quality. This makes common sense – we know that current standards of crudeness on an Apple

Macintosh screen, for example, are sufficient to allow us to carry out work interactively which we would not be able to do if we were to use a typewriter and which we would not be able to do so with as much flexible control if we used a scalpel and Cow Gum.

In addition to this, the way in which a CRT (cathode ray tube) screen displays type helps to make us more tolerant of its low resolution. To display a dot, a beam of charged electrons is fired at the phosphor coating on a CRT screen causing the phosphor coating to glow. The phosphor glows with high intensity in the centre where the electrons hit but the CRT spots are not the same intensity across their width. Because the phosphor glows with decreasing brightness the further away it is from the centre of the spot, CRT spots are soft-edged and fuzzy.

This fuzziness has the effect of improving the 'appearing quality' of low-resolution character descriptions. Hard-edged spots output on paper would have to be much smaller and much closer together if they were to have the same 'appearing quality' as 72 dpi soft-edged spots. Although this is a reason why we are relatively tolerant of screen images, the difference in marking characteristics between screens, laser printers and typesetters is, of course, also a reason why what you get can not be exactly what you saw.

My third question – as to whether we will have to continue to put up with relatively crude screen representations – demands rather more consideration.

Computer, technology is improving at considerable speed. Interpretations of type on screen have improved as computers have enjoyed wider acceptance. But, to get an idea of how far we have come and how far we have yet to go, I would like to compare the development of computing and the representation of type on screen with the early development of printing and type manufacturing.

Gutenberg, by inventing the adjustable mould around 1450, is generally acclaimed as the inventor of printing from moveable types. He, and other early printers, were primarily concerned with imitating hand-written manuscripts. Naturally they were influenced by both their own and their users' expectations about the nature of books.

Type design and manufacture were the same. (Gutenberg's types imitated the textura written forms of the time. The Italian types of Jenson and Aldus of the 1470s and 1490s, landmarks though they were, were typographic renderings of existing hand-written and sculpted forms. The small letters were based upon the humanistic minuscule and the capitals on the roman inscriptional letter.

Typography came of age in the 'golden age of French typography' in the sixteenth century, especially with the work of Robert Estienne who became printer to King François I, around 1539. In Estienne's books, we can see for the first time a celebration of the possibilities offered by type as a medium in its own right. He was the first printer to introduce a system of biblical verse numbering, and he was innovative in his use of typographic variants to distinguish elements of complex dictionary and encyclopædia entries. Estienne was an information designer and, in the words of Elizabeth Eisenstein, his work was 'a miracle of lucid arrangement'.

Type design and manufacture came of age around the same time. Claude Garamond was also patronised by François I for whom he cut the *Grecs du Roi*. Garamond cut

many roman and italic types between 1530 and the 1550s and Robert Estienne made extensive use of these. Garamond's types were the first, truly typographic renderings of the humanistic minuscule. In D B Updike's words, 'Garamond, in his new roman, was no longer reproducing a manuscript, but, creating letters considered independently as types'.

This shows that the legacy of the manuscript tradition had a firm hold on the early printers and type manufacturers. It took another century before printing and type design developed in their own right.

Coming up to present times, it seems to me that Estienne's innovations, as a typographic designer in conveying information in printed form, have a parallel in the development of interactive multimedia systems which provide a means for the innovative use of the computer in the communication of information in electronic form. Also, Garamond's types have a parallel in the digital type designs created specifically for low resolution CRT displays, a good example of which would be Bigelows' and Holmes' *Lucida*.

Though the rate of change is considerably faster in the twentieth century than it was in the fifteenth and sixteenth centuries, we can deduce that the development and application of computing to the communication and presentation of information are still in their youth. Personal computers and screen rendering techniques continue to be heavily influenced by our non-computer driven experiences of the world. Consider, for example, the desktop metaphor, and the large numbers of traditional type faces which we attempt to render on the screen.

All of this implies that we will have to put up with crude screen resolutions for some time. It will be a long time before technology advances to a stage where users no longer demand interactive feedback via a screen display. Developments like that demand a technological leap beyond the bounds of our imaginations.

Before then, our screens will be improved considerably. NeXT computers already use 92 dpi screens as standard, and they show improvements over 72 dpi screens. Other manufacturers have even developed 165 and 300 dpi screens.

Nevertheless, a number of factors suggest that 72 dpi will continue to compromise the match between paper and screen. These factors include the memory and processing speeds mentioned earlier, the hardware costs, the large investment that users have made already in dedicated 72 dpi systems, and the inability of the computer and television industries to agree standards for high resolution display.

Given that we are going to be faced with the problem of crude screen resolutions for some time, how can type be rendered on screen to best satisfy the needs of users, especially DTP users involved in the production of paper-based publications? The activities of these users can be divided into two broad categories: word processing and designing.

When DTP users are involved in word processing, the legibility of type on screen is paramount. We know that the luminance of CRT screens can induce eye strain. This, coupled with user's general preferences for interaction with paper-based documents, means that reading screens for accuracy is something which our visual and mental

processing systems find particularly difficult to handle at the moment.

I do not suggest that users should proof-read, or even read lengthy passages of text on screens. When users are having to perform tasks which inevitably involve some reading for meaning and sense, the characters rendered on screen should be optimized for decipherability and not for their approximation to typefaces designed for high resolution rendering. As Charles Bigelow has pointed out, 'at very low resolutions (72-120 dpi)…letters are struggling for their existence as legible entities; failures are not merely ugly, they are illegible'. In the final analysis, 10 or 12 point characters rendered at 72 dpi can be no more than decipherable.

Some excellent work has been carried out by type designers and manufacturers in this area. When using word processing applications, DPI users should be encouraged to use type faces like *Lucida* for which the hand-edited screen fonts were optimised for legibility on the screen. The *Geneva* bit-maps supplied with Apple Macintosh computers might also be recommended.

A number of software improvements could assist users when a job has progressed to the design stage but continues to require editorial amendments – last minute corrections or changes are inevitable. Page make-up software could be adapted to restrict the display of a document to a minimum, legible size as soon as the user makes an editorial change. This would mean that users would not, try to read text which is too small to be rendered legibly on screen.

Alternatively, page make-up software could he adapted to render generic fonts on screen: hand-tuned bit-maps whose character widths would be the same as the type-face required for final output, but whose shapes would be optimised for on-screen decipherability rather than for specific typeface representation.

Another option might be to force the user to call upon a separate text editor, like the one in PageMaker 4, when making editorial corrections. The editor would then display the text in a restricted number of typefaces suited to the editorial task.

It is more difficult to suggest how screens should be rendered to improve the design process. When designing, users want, to be able to make decisions about visual rela-tionships. For example, a user might want to examine the visual qualities of a typeface, compare typefaces, see how typefaces combine, compare the relative appearance of different text elements, examine the relationship between pictures and text, or get an overall impression of the appearance of a document. Designers have always needed to perform these tasks.

For screen-based designing, the consequence of this is that users want screen images to match paper output as closely as possible. As I have already discussed, our screens can not faithfully represent medium and high resolution output because of their resolutions and their marking characteristics. Researchers have, therefore, repeatedly emphasised that users must not make final decisions while viewing preview screens. Fine judgements and final decisions must be made while examining samples of paper output produced at the intended resolution.

A brutal approach would be for all screens to render generic bit-maps of typefaces. This would improve legibility as I have outlined before, and might force users to view

paper output instead of being seduced by inadequate screen renderings.

Generic screen fonts might show clear differentiation between typeface variants but would not cater for the subtlety of design decision-making. Users might regard this as a decline in viewing standards, and could well be confused by the even greater differences between screen and paper output.

At the opposite end of the scale, some type designers and manufacturers might hold that, as with all technological change, the hardware will eventually catch up. However, instead of us all having to 'just grin and bear it' until screen resolutions improve dramatically, we must consider making more use of greyscale technology in the interim.

Most type on screen is currently rendered by black and white pixels. Greyscale technology allows pixels to be black, white, or a number of shades of grey. Many screens are capable of displaying up to 256 levels of grey per pixel; we can assume that, before high resolution screens are common place, we will all be viewing greyscale display screens. The impending popularity of multimedia and the ability to manipulate four-colour separations make this a certainty.

10 pt characters displayed at 256 levels of grey on a 72 dpi screen can be remarkably accurate representations of high resolution typefaces. They provide a quality of feed back which could enable users to make more accurate preliminary design decisions on the basis of what they see on their preview screen. However, the result of greyscaling is that characters are even more fuzzy at their edges. Research seems to suggests that our eyes find it difficult to focus, on this fuzziness. As a result, greyscaled characters may be useful when users are designing but not when they are word processing.

This is a sample of 10 point *Times New Roman* output at 600 dpi on a *Monotype PaperMaster*.

This is a representation of 10 point *Times New Roman* as seen on an Apple Macintosh screen at 72 dpi, with the screen set to black and white. A dump, or picture, of the screen image has been taken and this has then been output on a *PaperMaster*.

This is a representation of 10 point *Times New Roman* as seen on an Apple Macintosh screen at 72 dpi, with the screen set to 256 levels of grey. A dump, or picture, of the screen image has been taken and this has then been output on a *PaperMaster*. The dump was imported into *QuarkXPress* and output with a screen ruling of 100 lines per inch.

DTP software breaks down traditional boundaries, enabling users to carry out the activities of word processing and document design and make-up on one computer system. More significant though, is the fact that users can mix the activities as they work, switching from one to the other as a job progresses. And even more significant is the fact that many users may not even make a distinction between the tasks. From this it is clear that no one method of representing type on low resolution screens can satisfy all the needs of users.

Any long term solutions to problems of screen rendering at low resolutions are dependent upon tailoring type to specific tasks and educating – or limiting – users as to the typefaces they should use for specific tasks and the procedures they should follow when decision-making. Evidence so far accumulated suggests that many users do not make wise decisions about the typefaces they use for writing, editorial and design tasks.

DTP users have been given the freedom to use any typeface at any stage in the production of a document. Although any limitations on this might be seen as a backward step, there is little doubt that semi-intelligent, or responsive interfaces, could go some way to improving the current state of affairs, by providing screen renderings suited to the circumstances of use.

Whatever happens in the coming years, we can be sure that until we are all able to preview our documents on high resolution screens – and possibly until we cease previewing screens altogether – what we get will continue to be somewhat different from what we see and the screen will continue to both enhance and restrict the interaction.

Sources included:

Bigelow, C. *The Principles of Digital Type*. The Seybold Report, vol 11, no 11, 8 February 1982, pp2 – 23.

Eisenstein, E L. *The Printing Revolution in Early Modern Europe*, Cambridge University Press, 1983.

Updike, D B. *Printing Types, their History, Forms and Use*. Oxford University Press, second edition, 1937.

1991 **Let typography look like type** Jenny Towndrow reports the lecture by Matthew Carter at Typo90

Matthew Carter believes that technology has had only a transient impact on type design until now. And today, in the age of digital composition, its real impact is often misunderstood.

He acknowledged that there have been instances in the past where the impact has been significant, citing the development of *Excelsior* in 1931 as an example of a design that 'was driven entirely by technical pressures'. The first special purpose newspaper face, it solved the problem of ink-trapping which had dogged newspaper printing for decades before.

The introduction of photocomposition in the early 1960s was actually 'a technological liberation' for type design. But, as so often happens when technology is still in its infancy, type designers tend to underestimate the technology's potential for improvement. As a result, they can be lured into over-compensating for perceived deficiencies or limitations. Matthew Carter admitted that he had fallen into this trap.

'I remember talking to Adrian Frutiger in 1969 about the *Univers* family, which had been completed by then. We discussed the problems with the heaviest and the most condensed versions of the family. They suffered from a technical problem inherent in the photosetting, when very heavy complex forms like W gained weight because light passing through them overflowed the image. To compensate, very deep crotches had to be opened. I remember experiments were done with entirely new forms of W – we did away with oblique strokes completely and used wholly rectangular forms of W. It was all deep crotches. But, of course, no sooner had these been drawn than the engineers fixed the optical system. The technology advanced so that it accurately reproduced the design. All the design compensation was suddenly made obsolete by a piece of clever engineering'.

Matthew Carter had a similar experience in the early 1970s with the CRT. Because this set type very quickly but changed fonts very slowly, only one font was used. Condensed, extended and italic versions of the font were created synthetically within the system without loss of speed.

'The results were extremely ugly. *Futura* or *Helvetica* were not designed to be distorted. So we studied the problem and came up with a new sans-serif family which stood up much better to being distorted than traditional sans-serif. The result was a

whole new typeface called *Video*. Has anyone heard of it? No! Why? Because the digital technology improved. Font-changing became extremely fast. Everyone went back to true italic, true condensed, true expanded. *Helvetica* looked absolutely wonderful and *Video* died. It was a short-term solution for a technical problem that was soon corrected.'

'That episode taught me a lesson. It was a self-obsolescing typeface. Technology changes much faster than design does. Type is very adaptable. When the technology does show shortcomings, it's because it's underdeveloped. Technology is perfectible. Humans are not. Most readers are still human.'

So where does this leave the type designer with the new technology? Quoting Zuzana Licko, Matthew Carter said 'you no longer have to concern yourself with the technology of how a typeface is going to reproduce'.

'It's not that you no longer have to concern yourself with the technology, you can not even if you wanted to, because the type designer does not know any longer how a typeface will be reproduced. If you buy a font of a typeface I have designed, I can not possibly predict how you will use it – on a laser printer at 300 dpi, 400 dpi 600 dpi, on a typesetter at 1,200 dpi, 2,000 dpi or, as Rene Kerfante predicts by the millenium, 4,000 dpi. It could be on a screen – monochrome or colour – or a film recorder, broadcast video system, TV, architectural sign-making system or whatever. All are digital. All use the same font. But I have to assume – and any type designer has to assume – that sooner or later our typefaces will be used in all of these things and probably some others that haven't been invented yet.' He said that the only time a designer now knows how a typeface will be reproduced is with faces, like *Bell Centennial*, designed for specific purposes at specific sizes.

This led him on to what he called 'the text of my sermon' – namely, 'suspicious of theories that relate the shape of letters to the way they are made or which claim a truth to "materials" in type design of the sort you can find in a fine art such as sculpture or architecture.' To emphasise this point, he compared two letters: one chunky, coarse and wooden, and the second 'with all the sensitive modelling you associate with very fine metal work'. But appearances were misleading since, as he explained, the first was made with steel punches and copper matrices and the second was cut in wood and cast in sand models. 'Beware of seeing sculptural pictorial qualities in type. They are often illusory. As Eric Gill said: "Letters are things, not pictures of things".'

He made another comparison between two black-letter characters. One was 'a contemporary Postscript letter form showing the obvious influence of the Bezier technology. The other was a sort of original black-letter model, hand-cut in resistant material of steel, which had that indefinable spark of light from the human which the machine can never capture.

Well, I'm lying in my teeth. Both these letters were made from Fontographer with Beziers. The first one is Zuzana Licko's *Totally Gothic*. The second was done for the purpose of the presentation. The same technology, the same program, probably the same release of the same program. So what made them different is not the technology. It's the designers. They're different because the designers wanted them to be different.'

He explained that there was another paradox about black letter, reminding delegates that Zuzana Licko had said 'black letter was at one time more legible to people than humanist typefaces'.

'Black letter is technically the perfect digital typeface. It decomposes perfectly into a mosaic on a computer screen. There are beautiful bit-maps. It's even self-hinting. It's so perfect for the digital medium, why has it not supplanted roman in our current all-digital typography? Roman makes very indifferent bit-maps, I can assure you. Hence the business with hinting. It's not historical authenticity nor suitability to the prevailing production tool that determines the viability of a typeface. Black letter is perfectly digital but not perfectly legible, at least not nowadays as Zuzana Licko has noticed'.

Matthew Carter then moved on to other aspects of digital composition. In particular, the benefits it offers the type designer. One was the ability to interpolate additional weights to get obliques – a very useful feature in designing italics. Another was the way it displayed options instantaneously, enabling proportions and spacings to be compared at actual size and to be adjusted accordingly. It also offered considerable potential with contextual letter forms, a vital consideration for non-Latin types since these are closer to their calligraphic roots than Latin.

But, as Matthew Carter explained, the benefits were even more fundamental than that. For centuries after the invention of printing, there was no distinction between designing and making type. But, from the eighteenth century, the designer had to rely increasingly on a specialist punch-cutter to render his designs into type. Baskerville, for example, was one of the first not to cut his own designs. Apart from rare exceptions like Goudy and Rudolf Koch, the separation between art and craft became complete.

'But now we've come full circle. The supply of type is no longer tied exclusively to the supply of typesetting equipment. The independent foundries cast pixels nowadays not lead alloy: the same opportunity exists also for individual designers. Software programs, such as *Fontographer, Ikarus M* and *Font Studio*, have done for type design what page layouts and illustration have done for graphic designers. They put them in control of the production of their own work, if they wish to be in control. Designing, making and setting, even selling type are now back within the reach of the individual. And now that personal computers and laser printers are being installed in art and design schools, the teaching of type design has become a practicality'.

While reunifying the art and craft functions, the new technology has also 'democratised' the industry, leading Matthew Carter to conclude that 'we may be on the verge of a diverse and more vernacular style'. Many new personalised faces are now being developed. He wondered whether any of these would be assimilated into every-day mainline typography and asked if there was a classic face lurking among them which we did not yet appreciate? He reminded his audience that today's classic typefaces were not always recognised as such when they first appeared.

'People thought Baskerville's types by comparison with Caslon's were so sharp and bright that they would make people blind. My own research has revealed that only 47 per cent of professional typographers can distinguish *Baskerville* from *Caslon*. We don't think of *Baskerville* now as a weird typeface but in 1757 it struck people as barbarous.'

The new typefaces, he said, are in keeping with the whole ethos of the personal computer as a means of self expression. He pointed out that 'the aim of working with and understanding technology is to liberate yourself from it – it's very hard to design if you're intimidated by your tools'. So where does Matthew Carter draw his line?

'What I ask of typography is that it should look like type. What does type look like any longer? It's hard to say. I find that my idea of what type is is expanding at this conference, it's pushed against boundaries. That variety does not militate against my own critical standards of what is good.'

1991 Forget hot metal – this is hot chocolate! Jenny Towndrow reports the lecture by Gerard Unger at Typo90

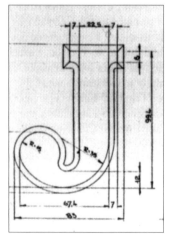

Gerard Unger's presentation in Oxford Town Hall was certainly unique. It was, for example, the only event at Typo90 which carried an advance health warning – those planning to attend were advised to refrain from consuming desserts at lunch beforehand. The title of the lecture was 'Chocolate Alphabets of Holland', although Gerard Unger felt that another title, 'And Swallow the Message' was actually more appropriate, since delegates had the opportunity to digest his type at the end of proceedings!

Chocolate alphahets have been a cherished tradition, associated with the celebration of the feast of St Nicholas in The Netherlands for about a century.

Gerard Unger, Dutch designer and teacher, traced the history of this tradition back to its roots in Asia Minor, now Turkey. Little is known about the legendary figure of Nicholas apart from the fact that on his death on 6 December about the year AD 340, he served as Bishop of Myra.

For two centuries he appears to have been forgotten until his name became linked with a number of popular legends – for example, he was supposed to have saved the inhabitants of Myra from famine and to have rescued sailors from drowning.

'Within a short period, he had become the patron saint of sailors, fishermen, shipbuilders, grain and wine merchants, perfumers, bankers, lovers, students and also children,' Gerard Unger explained. 'Today, he is mostly known as the patron saint of children. In 1087, his remains were kidnapped from Myra and brought to Bari in Italy, where he is now believed to be buried. From this point onwards, he was an official saint in the Catholic church.'

In the meantime, missionary endeavours had spread Christianity to northern Europe. Around the year 600, Pope Gregory the Great had decreed that images of heathen gods were to be transformed into those of Christian saints where possible. This edict meant that Odin, a god of the Teutonic peoples, was transmuted into St Nicholas.

'The qualities of St Nicholas fitted the popular image of Odin remarkably well, although St Nicholas never rode a horse. So Odin's spear was replaced with a crozier, the helmet with a mitre. Later, in Scandinavia and Germany, Father Christmas got some of these characteristics.'

The veneration of St Nicholas also took over another Scandinavian tradition associated with Odin. Letters made of bread were offered in thanksgiving to Odin when

grain was harvested and made into flour. This custom was assimilated into the celebration of St Nicholas's anniversary, as was the reading of poetry – Odin was the god of poetry. These traditions became firmly rooted and have continued to this day, even surviving attempts by the post Reformation church in The Netherlands in the sixteenth century to ban them.

'Each year, about three weeks before his anniversary, St Nicholas comes to The Netherlands by boat from Spain – he is now supposed to live in Madrid. Thousands turn out to see this event. At the same time, chocolate letters appear in confectionery shops, groceries, supermarkets and department stores.'

The other strand of this Dutch tradition is the history of chocolate. Cocoa beans first appeared in Europe in the early sixteenth century. By the beginning of the next century, chocolate, in its liquid form, was already known to the wealthy and later became popular. In 1825, a method for making solid chocolate was invented in The Netherlands – known as the Dutch Process, this is still used today. About 1890, the first chocolate letters appeared for the celebration of St Nicholas's anniversary and were an instant success. Up to that time, pastry letters were used.

Gerard Unger showed his audience a variety of chocolate letter forms with names like *Sint Nicolaas 5*. These included serifs, sans serifs, plain and ornamental – even ones incorporating whole hazelnuts! The Dutch, however, have firm ideas on the typography they prefer.

'Since the chocolate letters are associated with homeliness, cosiness and a good bite, the public prefers solid, traditional letterforms. Other faces, it is claimed, don't taste as good. You no longer have to worry about legibility. Edibility is what matters!'

'All the letters have to be same weight. This means there is no I. It also means that the stem width of a W is very much compressed compared to that of a J and the depth of a mould for a J is deeper than that for a W. I design bold type on my Mac with Ikarus. Unfortunately, the program does not give the third dimension I need for chocolate type!'

Nevertheless, those who attended the presentation had the privilege of being the first people outside The Netherlands to see Gerard Unger's revolutionary contribution to chocolate typography – a chunky, semi-modular M which, he claimed, was the world's first digital chocolate letter.

'It's not a joke,' he said, defying his earlier explanation about Dutch preferences for traditional letter forms. 'This is a real leap forward. It will be marketed from the middle of November this year. One of the advantages of these letters is that they are easier to break up into smaller pieces!'

(facing page) Varied stem width and height to maintain the same weight in chocolate.

(below) Bamboo mould by Keuter & Co. Circa 1930.

(bottom) Varied stem width and height to maintain the same weight in chocolate.

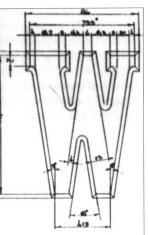

1996 **Due to increased dynamic range, raise the volume above average: Play it Loud** Teal Triggs

New consumer paradigm [1]

Technology has become hip [2]

Advocates of new technology tells us that 'education is entering a new era'[3]. Computers are firmly established in every classroom, from early pre-school learning centres to higher education institutions. Students are now rising through the educational ranks with a high degree of computer literacy. Meanwhile, tutors find it increasingly difficult to keep up with the latest software developments. Recently in the *Times Higher Educational Supplement*, Chris Hutchison warned us that while we are being seduced by 'glorious technologies' in educational environments, we must also take time to think through the 'social and pedagogic implications.'[4] Computers have redefined traditional working relationships and standard teaching practices. In this period of transition thoughtful educators have raised difficult questions: should they teach *'about computers, or through computers, or by the way of computers'.*[5]

In certain ways, the computer has become a 'natural' extension of the physical self. We appear to be plugged in permanently, with the mouse as an extension of our hand, the keyboard our fingers, and the screen, our eyes. The next logical, if fanciful, step is the virtual realm where the screen is accessible to total sensorial interaction. 'Virtual classrooms' with online electronic resources are not as distant as we might think. In the United States increasing numbers of university professors deliver classes on the Internet. For example, The World Lecture Hall website, housed at the University of Texas at Austin, provides links to a wide range of courses ranging from Advertising, Design Inquiry, Internetting Skills to Cyberspace Composition. Each course provides access to specialist tutors from all over the country who 'hand-out' course syllabi, assignments, and lecture notes, as well as provide online tutorials and examinations. Courses on the Internet related specifically to art and design are currently under development by academics in Germany and the United Kingdom as part of the Erasmus (Socrates) programme. Deliberations is a new site devoted to teaching and learning issues in art and design for tutors who are interested in developing their teaching skill-base in the non-virtual world. Online access means they can engage actively with educators from Middlesex University to discuss art and design teaching methods and learning strategies.

1 New Consumer Paradigm is advertising speak on the Internet for 'market'.

2 Clifford Stoll. *Silicon Snake Oil: Second Thoughts on the Information Highway*, Pan Books, 1995, p.10.

3 Chris Hutchinson. 'Snares in the Charmed Circle'. *Times Higher Educational Supplement*, 12 April 1996.

4 Ibid.

5 Theodore Roszak. *The Cult of Information: The Folklore of Computers and the True Art of Thinking*, Lutterworth Press, Cambridge, 1986, p.50.

Temporal Ghetto [6]

A good piece of technology dreams of the day when it will be replaced by a newer piece of technology. This is one definition of progress. [7]

Technology is ephemeral, but determining and defining forces of the 'machine age' have given way to a 'post-machine' age where technology has supported a new 'information culture based upon instant communication services'. [8] Conventional forms of communication technology have included the telegraph, telephone, and more recently the fax machine. Entry into the digital computer domain has created new devices. As each new device is superseded, the way in which people think about, send and receive information is re-assessed. As designers grasp increasingly more sophisticated and highly complex systems and structures, new ways of representing ideas and information, either though text or image, must be found which are appropriate to that medium. [9]

While the computer has enabled a greater freedom to explore conventional forms of communication and visual expression, the digital realm has opened up new possibilities. Interactive design and the structure of new information and communication networks (eg the Internet, e-mail and discussion groups) presents new conceptual and practical opportunities for graphic designers and typographers. Within these networks, information has become a valuable commodity. [10] This is especially true within the international corporate realm. As information increases in value, so too are the designers who are trained to create new visual digital landscapes.

The greatest scope for developing visual design would appear at the moment to be in developing new and appropriate visual languages for screen-based mediums. There is also great scope for experimenting with new communication models. Some critics proclaim that the digital computer will bring us to the 'end of print' while others compare its importance to the advent of the printing press. The visual and verbal language employed by designers for use on the computer does not necessarily belong in either the print or digital worlds; the language is conceptual – perhaps a meta-language. The way we think about and represent ideas and information is fundamental. It is the application of this language to the 'new' computer medium that is still fluid. Computers may allow rapid access to information, but this is no substitute for the creation of ideas. This is where educators can make their greatest contribution, or as Theodore Roszak explains, the rôle of educators is to *...teach young minds how to deal with ideas: how to evaluate them, extend them, adapt them to new uses...* [11] When graphic design educators come to review their curricula, this component must remain in the foreground and receive proper emphasis. A balance must be achieved between developing ideas and the pragmatics of technical training if we are to achieve the desired result, Chip Jewellery. [12]

Numerous heated debates questioning the computer's function within communication, typography and graphic design production have arisen. Despite increasing sophistication, some still argue simplistically and dogmatically that 'creativity emerges out of technology'. Others who are more sober advocates see the computer as an integrated 'tool' of the design process. Legibility and readability, visual aesthetics, function verses decoration, designers as authors, are all issues which evoke great passion and are some

6 Computer slang for the particular mental space entered into while stuck in the past.

7 Coupland, Douglas, *Microserfs*, Flamingo, New York, 1995, p.179.

8 Lovejoy, Margaret, *Postmodern Currents: Art and Artists in the Age of Electronic Media*. Prentice Hall, Englewood Cliffs, 1992, p.76.

9 Alan Kay argues in 'The Infobahn is Not the Answer' *Wired*, May 1994, pp.76–77, that we ...need a better sense of how to transcend the psychological and social limitations of being human in order for change to be positive.

10 The notion that information is a new and valuable economic consideration is discussed by a number of authors including Theodore Roszak.

11 Theodore Roszak, *The Cult of Information*, p.88.

12 Computer jargon for old computers destined to be scrapped or turned into decorative ornaments.

great distance from resolution. Whatever the viewpoint, the computer is recognized as a standard and accepted object of every graphic design studio and, for the moment, every design educational institution.

Like all universities, art and design colleges have their problems. Drastic cuts in government funding and student grants have created a climate of uncertainty. Many institutions have been forced to increase student numbers dramatically and/or create part time provisions to compensate lost revenues. Teaching hours are dissipated as actual taught weeks decrease. Budgets for already scarce physical resources are cut, affecting the maintenance and development of existing computing facilities. At the moment, graduates of British graphic design departments are entering the workplace with competence. They possess computing skills and are literate in programmes such as Freehand, Quark and Photoshop. But will they be equipped to solve increasingly complex design problems? It is imperative that educators review fundamental programmes in graphic design, typography and related academic studies. Conventional apprenticeship structures and one-to-one studio tutorial systems are no longer economically viable. New and innovative teaching strategies must be adopted to maintain educational quality. There are vehicles that may be developed to create sustainable alternatives that are linked to teaching students to become self-reliant.

Approaches to teaching and learning may have more to do with shifting notions of what graphic design practice is today. With developments in digital technology, graphic designers may have more to do with co-ordinating teams of technical specialists than in the past. Project briefs should be set which enhance students' understanding of team situations. For example, areas may include the development of negotiation, interpersonal and management skills. Cultivating students' abilities to be designers but also to effectively co-ordinate activities lies in part, within design education.

Jitterati [13]

A random and persistent disturbance that obscures or reduces the clarity or quality of a signal [14]

Tucked away on the back of the liner notes to Lou Reed's most recent album is a short set of instructions: due to increased dynamic range, raise the volume above average. *Play it loud.* Technology in the music industry has long provided musicians with opportunities to explore the expressive qualities of sound through machines. For example, a 1970s experimental Lou Reed album, *Metal machine music,* recorded the 'screeching feedback' of metal machines. In Rob Reiner's cult film, *This is Spinal Tap* (1983), one of the heavy metal band members reveals that the sound level on his guitar amplifier can go as high as a setting of 11. As far as he was concerned, this was one better than the conventional setting of 10 and would therefore enhance the overall quality of his performance. John Cage, on the other hand, allowed random chance in the immediate environment to determine sound in his piece *4:33* where the pianist sits silently behind the keyboard. In a similar fashion to the generation of musical dissonance, typographic 'tones' may question conventional notions of beauty and their relationship to form. [15] It is in this concrete sense that students must grapple with new

13 Computer slang for the digital generation tanking up on too much coffee.

14 'Noise', as defined in the *American Heritage Dictionary.*

forms. Design in the 1980s and 1990s illustrates the problems.

Many critics have described the 1980s as the 'designer decade'. Simple matt black products may have lined the studio walls of self-proclaimed design darlings but on the 'street' the visual world was viewed differently. In almost Blade Runneresque scenes, information was available everywhere you turned. Complex informational layers were adopted by many young designers who sought to question conventional ways of reading. Despite the introduction of computers into design studios, much of the early visual 'style' associated with the technology was generated by hand. The early work of Nick Bell, Jonathan Barnbrook, and Why Not Associates are cases in point. Yet design reflected the complex layering of typographic information often associated with the manufacturing of computer technology.

The 1990s are responding against visual noise in favour of a new form of fragmented and distressed typography. Designers such as David Carson and Tomato are readily employing technology which reflects a breakdown of a computer generated visual languages. In this seemingly contradictory state, typography – like the best-selling Levi's blue jeans – has become 'distressed'. They are washed so much that the letterforms are worn down and deteriorating. Ideas are clearly more important than the medium. Visually, the computer – machine – is negated.

In the transition from a culture of print to a culture of digital screens, reading and writing are redefined. Although many of the basic communication models will remain the same for the graphic designer – sender/mediator/receiver – the underlying assumptions of communication will take on new significance. The greatest effect will be upon the idea of time, narrative structures, and the organization of given information. As Sven Birkerts stated in The Gutenberg Elegies: *The context cannot but condition the process.*[16]

15 Stephen Holtzman, *Digital Mantras: the languages of abstract and virtual worlds*, MIT Press, Cambridge, Mass. USA, 1994, p 261.

16 Sven Birkerts. *The Gutenberg Elegies: the fate of reading in an electronic age*, Faber & Faber, 1994, p.128.

2000 **A new medium** Nicky Gibson

Typography has undergone massive changes. New dimensions have been added that weren't there before. Type can now alter shape, size or colour upon command, or as a result of users' interaction. Before, methods of emphasis were based on type-weight, leading and placement on the page. In the new media, words and information can be called up when needed, animated into position, be placed, re-sized or written on-the-fly by the user. With the introduction of motion and morphing, type begins to take on its own personality. A far greater degree of emotive expression can be added to a statement, whose type may also act as an interface, leading the user around a relational content structure. With such a plethora of options, there are, of course, huge new challenges to the designer. Each day, the interactive designer is constantly bombarded with an ever widening palette of tools. With so many factors in question and new techniques emerging everyday, the construction of a solid concept, with appropriate aesthetic and functionality, is a difficult task to master and perfect.

But is there still a place for two-dimensional words on a four-dimensional stage?

www.typographic56.co.uk A web-site designed in 2000 to accompany the publication of (the conventionally printed) *TypoGraphic 56*. Designed by Nicky Gibson, Richard Kwok Wah Ho and Mike Reid at DeepEnd, London.

Transition – the reality of design limitations

The typographic standards and processes have been imported from the history of print and are changing and evolving in this new environment. Something that is hard for the traditional print designer to do is to let go of control over the exact outcome

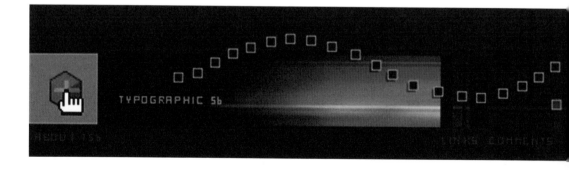

of the final visual. In print design, the issue is how to translate what is seen on screen exactly onto paper to the finest detail. Typographic on-screen design, especially in web, does not permit that luxury. Designs must be constructed to allow for variation in font-size, colours, alignment, and especially space. Even the simplest function, the fact that browser windows are stretchable by the user, means that flat html sites will always be at the mercy of individual user's defined preferences.

Realisation

With the advent of KPT filters in the earlier days of *PhotoShop*, a gross and blatant over-use of these effects cheapened a quite revolutionary change in the use of *Photo-Shop*. The innovations made by Kai Krouse in experimental, intuitive interface design had inspired debate in themselves. Technological advances creating greater choice of software, are driving design solutions to constantly evolve and progress.

Today, the temptation to over complicate or over design a site by layering it with as many new features and gadgets as possible is greater than ever. The Internet over-all is not ruled by great aesthetic design, but streamlined information design. The race for technological prowess often means that good ideas and visual design sense get left to the last, and are often neglected. But the designer who can produce both pixel-perfect imagery and operate within tight technological constraints is a good designer.

To design effectively in this new medium, the typographer has been forced to refor-mulate conceptual boundaries and take inspiration from the design process of product designers. The design solution not only has an audience but also *users*. As a result, the Web designer today must be a combination of information designer, graphic designer, and product designer.

Although typography still plays a strong visual rôle as communicator, the interactive product often has varied purposes and needs, depending on its user base. With sites varying from e-commerce solutions, to product and brand promotion, news and infor-mation portals, e-zines, games, discussion groups and forums, Web communities, and a wealth of personal and corporate home-pages, a combination of advertising and multi-media approaches are used.

The right balance of creative skills, spatial design and narrative story telling, forms

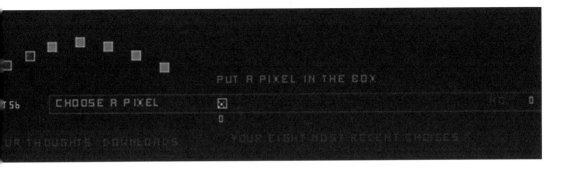

the conceptual focus of an effective site, around a backbone of confident technical production, fused with precise information design and slick visual persona.

Tools for directions

The potential of the Web is only now beginning to be fully realised. After a settling in period, visual designers have begun to rethink their approach to interactive and animated environment design. Browser plug-ins such as *Flash* and *Shockwave,* have allowed previously impossible functionalities to be incorporated into the Web. Harking back to the early advances in multimedia design, there are now many more opportunities open to the typographer, working in a far more flexible and liquid design medium. *Flash,* especially, has proved to be an effective tool for visual designers. A combination of animation, interactivity and type handling has combined the two previously separate disciplines of coding and graphics that are so definitively separated in director production. The thought of programming reams of code is not appealing to every designer, *Flash* has simplified the process of combining type and interaction, the essential ingredients that are at the core of navigation in the on-screen environment.

For a while, there were technical restrictions limiting typographic design on the Internet. In recent months, innovative functions, introduced in *Flash,* have grown and flourished throughout the Web. The advantages of keeping a fixed layout within any browser, has returned control back to the designer. From animated typography, to on-line cartoons, and complex three-dimensional interfaces, the final rôle of type in such a flexible playground has yet to be identified and established.

In the past year, many new and exciting ideas have emerged from *Flash4 Action* scripting. The *MONO** crafts site has pioneered some of the most innovative Web inter face designs to be credited on the Web to date (http://www.yugop.com) combining fluidity, beautiful design and deceptively masked creative coding. Others, such as *Praystation* (http://www.praystation.com) have developed similarly influenced experiments but from a more mathematical visual perspective.

(below and facing page) Two 'pages' from www.typographic56.co.uk a web-site designed in 2000 to accompany the publication of *TypoGraphic 56.* Designed by Nicky Gibson, Richard Kwok Wah Ho and Mike Reid at DeepEnd, London.

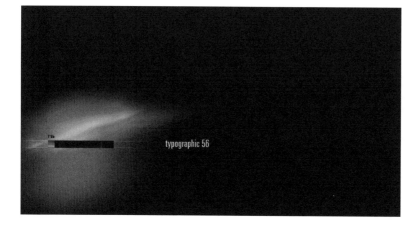
typographic 56

Flash community 'shockfusion' has proved to be a valuable centre point for *Flash* designers, providing a forum to share ideas and gain (often all too) honest criticism from fellow designers and competitors. *Shockfusion* was the first, fully functioning, *Flash* generated chat-room and instant messaging system.

A site with an interesting comment to be made about the nature of the web is *Soulbath* (http://www.soulbath.com). It reflects what the Web designer experiences day today, pointing out the use of code, but uses metaphors and styles from the grey, operating system styles in a clean, logical and minimalistic way.

Changing boundaries

In past html designs, type was used in bite-sized, fixed chunks, echoing magazine formats in print design: the advantage being the ease of updatability in coding. With recent developments within *Flash*, type can now be instantly updated by the producer or user: a feature previously impossible in the sealed unit of a *Flash* 'swf' file. The advent of *Flash Generator* and *Shockwave* multi-user features now means that many more sites in the future will offer two-way communication between visitors, again, producing a new kind of typographic design challenge.

Reflective design – pixel typography style

Only when technology becomes accepted, as part of daily life, do the iconic metaphors created to represent real life situations themselves become metaphors for new idea.

One of the main influences to be seen growing in Web graphic design is icon pixel graphics. This pixel style has turned from technological constraint into a graphic and fashion statement in itself. The most successful *Interaction* designers on the web are those who have taken what were seen as imperfections by the print designer and created a whole new visual style, based on functional graphic devices. The creation of desktop icons has been taken to an art form, each and every pixel of the 32 x 32 grid, has become crucial.

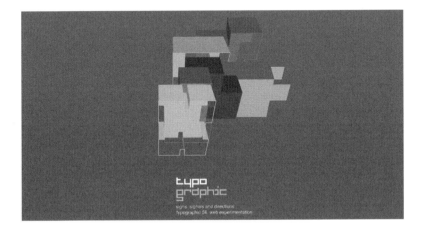

Influences from the graphic style of the desktop – the art of icons – have encouraged the evolution of 7pt pixel on-screen typefaces adapted from their print counterparts. Aliased text is quite popularly perceived as more readable than anti-aliased below 10pt on-screen. The fact that we are seeing more and more on-screen specific typefaces being designed today is a positive indication of the developments we may see in design specific to the genre.

Historically, effective print fonts use serifs to help enhance the shapes for readability. When type is applied to paper the eye finds the shapes easier to recognise, as the resolution is high. When fonts are converted for on-screen use, even the standard *Times* 12pt becomes blurred and hard to read when anti-aliased. Aliased screen fonts such as *Geneva* 9pt are far more readable because the edges are sharp and crisp.

Today you can see a many examples of graphics on the Web whose style is based around aliased elements. The embracing of the technology, rather than working around it, has encouraged a typography to evolve that is specific to this medium.

Interaction design draws very heavily on the influence of computer game graphics as they share many common functional design issues. Graphic characteristics of consoles such as the *Gameboy* are paid homage to (and imitated) on many websites because of its history of success with minute typography, and character animation.

In a reaction against the flatness of *Flash*, and in remembrance of classic computer games, the humble pixel has become the focus of attention.

Signs + symbols + directions = navigation?

'Signs, symbols and directions', describes the palette of the interaction designer.

It describes the process a user goes through to access and digest the information from a non-linear medium such as Website, CD rom, or real-life situation. As information in these environments can often be followed via a non-linear path, careful navigation design is even more imperative than in the linear medium of design for print.

Signs and symbols within print graphics are used to convey the order and hierarchy in which people access the information from a flat page. Users of a book can access each page individually but have the choice of reading them in any order or to chose only small parts to read or skim to gain an overview of the content: titles, for example.

Signs and symbols within new media are about navigating the user through information in four dimensions, using spatial depth and time to expand the canvas with which we work. Directing the user through levels or panoramas of information is often achieved through the use of iconic symbols based on metaphors drawn from real life scenarios, or developed versions of existing symbolism.

Even though the content of a commercial Website or CD rom is likely to involve (mainly) type, the most important question is, how to structure that information so that the user can get to what he wants to know? Essentially, we are information designers.

The issue of type and 'content' distracts designers of commercial websites from examining new interactivity, as html limitations force them back into the constraints of grids, gutters, and Web 'pages'. It is a shame that designers get trapped into seeing the white space in front of them as a series of two-dimensional pages to click through,

when, with the advent of *Shockwave* and *Flash,* the limits of this virtual space are only the limits of a creative mind.

There is a lot more we could do with interactivity. There are endlessly interesting situations we can create using depth and fluid motion that have not nearly been fully explored. In the near future, we will see more amorphic and spatial graphic environments, in *Flash* especially, where animated scaling of graphics has been made more practical with vector elements. The use of layers to create space, a more familiar visual mechanism popularly used in *Photoshop*, will gradually become utilised more creatively in the *Flash* design medium. I hope those designers who so readily embraced *Freehand* as their tool of choice several years ago, can now take their ideas forward into this, a new dimension in graphic design.

We must explore the possibilities we have open to us in creating more intuitive and realistic interaction, and forge a new visual language through the evolution of typographic design. Through the shedding of the restrictions of two-dimensional design and embracing the challenges of the new medium, we are now free to examine the future rôle of 'new typography'; another paradigm shift is upon us.

ISTD student award scheme
assessment in progress, 1982.
TypoGraphic 19.
Although the scheme has evolved
since it first began in 1975, it still
takes, on average, an hour for each
student entry to be assessed.

Education

1998 **J H Mason, typography, and the art school ethos** David Jury

1 *The Monotype Recorder*, May – June 1928, p 7.

2 Why Technical Education, *British Printer*, May –June 1901. 'Our street hoardings are emblazoned with American-printed posters... In our print-sellers' windows ...chiefly bear the imprints of Saxony, Bavaria and Germany. The vast majority of children's story books in this country are designed here and yet are printed in Germany, America and Holland.

3 Technical Training for Printers, *British Printer*, July and August 1897. T E Tailor, of the London Society of Printers '...we all know that there are a large number of so-called journey-man compositors whose knowledge of the trade does not extend beyond a pair of cases...'. Also: 'The Prevailing Incompetency of Workmen', *Printers Registrar*, 6 March 1878, '...We pick lads who can not read books to make them'.

4 Master Printers' and Allied Trades Association, minutes book, 1891. 'The improvement of machinery of every kind is going on at a rapid rate, but the question may very properly be asked, are working men improving at the same rate and to the same extent? Many of the improvements in machinery have actually had the effect of lessening knowledge and skill of workmen'.

5 Christopher Frayling, *The Royal College of Art: One Hundred and Fifty Years of Art and Design*, Barrie & Jenkins Ltd, 1987, Part 1, 'God Help the Minister that Meddles with Art'.

6 Inefficient Workmen, *Typographic Circular*, No 424, 1888.

[7 and 8 overleaf]

At the end of the nineteenth century the printing industry, the second largest industry in London at the time,[1] was under tremendous competition from abroad,[2] the failure of the apprenticeship system was forcing standards of workmanship down[3] whilst the very nature of the printing process and its products was under-going radical changes.[4] In 1896, the Technical Education Board of the London County Council was able to report that: '…a Central School of Arts and Crafts had been set up to fill certain unoccupied spaces in the field of education'. Even so, it was a further nine years before printing was included in the curriculum.

W R Lethaby was considered to be the natural choice for the job as principal. Emery Walker and Sir Sidney Cockerell persuaded him to put his name forward, and testi-monials were obtained from, among others, William Morris and Edward Burne-Jones. Lethaby had worked for many years as a successful architect, was profoundly influenced by William Morris, and had worked with Morris for the Society for the Protection of Ancient Buildings, alongside other champions of the Arts and Crafts Movement.

Art schools in the 1890s had tended to be rather dilettante institutions with little or no vocational bias to their work or purpose.[5] Lethaby described them as 'teaching how to swim without water'. Technical colleges, on the other hand, aimed to simulate indus-trial working practices and conditions, including all the inbred dogma.[6] To establish the required balance of academia and training, Lethaby had the innovative idea of appointing only a small core of full-time teachers, whilst employing practising artists and designers on a part-time basis. An interdisciplinary approach to study was insti-gated as students were encouraged to 'see how stained-glass windows are made, and books are bound and gilding done'.[7] Students and teachers were expected to undertake 'live' projects which might be self-generated or commissions from outside the College. All of these were bold policies which gave Lethaby and the Central School of Arts and Crafts a growing, and eventually world-wide, reputation; ideas absorbed and employed by, among others, Walter Gropius[8] during his initial years as Director of the Bauhaus at Weimar.

An unusual fact about the Central School of Arts and Crafts was that students, during these early years, were not subjected to examinations, nor were certificates or diplomas awarded, it being considered sufficient to have a portfolio of work that demonstrated

a student's abilities. Lethaby did not conceal his distaste for the competitive nature of commerce and industry; '…education need not…be conceived as an introduction to the competitive scramble'.[9]

In 1905, some nine years after the Central School had opened, evening classes in printing were started at the Central School of Arts and Crafts, and John Henry Mason, at the recommendation of Cobden-Sanderson and Emery Walker, (who both served on the London County Council Consultative Committee to advise the Council on these subjects) was invited by Lethaby to be responsible for them. Mason thus became one of the very first teachers of typography in an art school. Walker and Cobden-Sanderson were eager to see the improved standards achieved by the private presses reflected in general trade printing. Mason was appointed to teach two evenings each week. The following entry appears in the 1906 prospectus: 'Printing.[10] A class will be established in typography under the direction of J H Mason on Mondays and Wednesdays from 7.00 to 9.30. This class, which is intended solely for apprentices and journeymen actually engaged in the trade, aims at supplying instruction in the highest type of bookwork to the exclusion of mere advertisements, trade cards etc. It is felt that in view of the recent revival in printing, the establishment of such a class, which would co-operate with the classes in bookbinding, lettering, black and white design to form a complete school of book production, should do great service to the craft generally'.

Trade union pressure had made the proviso concerning sole entry to the course by apprentices and journeymen essential but that bar would be dropped by 1916. The statement '…exclusion of mere advertisements and trade cards' is interesting because it clearly reflects Mason's contempt for an activity within the printing trade that was growing at enormous speed. By the end of the century, jobbing-work represented by far the largest part of the printing industry's output. The rich range of new typefaces, or 'freak types' as some called them,[11] created for the jobbing printer, was proof of the considerable commercial growth of this area. The term 'jobbing-work' described any-thing other than book-work; all forms of advertising and other promotional material such as posters, leaflets, programmes, tickets, catalogues and brochures. As the term implies, jobbing-work had always been considered to be of a 'lower order' to book-work, but as the use of advertising and related promotional items became more wide-spread, so the demand increased.

Unlike bookwork, where a clearly defined dogma existed, jobbing-work had no precedent and, to be effective, required all the traditional typographic skills plus a flexibility in the application of those skills. Jobbing-work existed to demand attention and, therefore, to work effectively needed to extend typographic norms and language. Nothing in the traditional training scheme prepared the young print apprentice for such work. Besides, the general attitude among printers, as employers and employees, was that such material was handled under sufferance. Real printing still meant books and, if it wasn't a book, the same rules were applied regardless![12] Mason's refusal to incorporate jobbing-work into his course is understandable given that the aims of both Mason and Lethaby were to lift the standards of the printing trade to that of the private presses, but it also suggests a denial of the state of the printing trade at that

7 L T Owens, *J H Mason Scholar-Printer*, Fredrick Muller Ltd, 1976, p 43.

8 When Walter Gropius was a refugee and resident in England during the thirties, he became a member of the Central School of Arts and Crafts Advisory Committee.

9 L T Owens, *J H Mason, Scholar-Printer*, Fredrick Muller Ltd, 1976, p 41.

10 Until the first quarter of the nineteenth century, the dictionaries equated printer with typographer and Samuel Johnson's terse definition, Typographer: a printer, explains why there is no mention of printing in Mason's 'printing' classes.

11 Sayers and Stuart, *Art and Practice of Printing*, Vol. 1, Pitman, p 243 'With regard to some freakish type-faces now in use, little need be said…. Novelty there must be in this restless age, but illegible and ugly types, popular as they may be for a time, soon pass away'.

12 Beatrice Warde, *Typography in Art Education* p 73, 'Every apprentice-compositor is, or should be, taught in the shop how to make a handbill look like a handbill… (but) it has never been the printer's business to make anything look "different", nor has he had much to do with changes and improvements of the "recognisable" style'. Also Charles L Pickering and Beatrice Warde, *Training for Tomorrow*, published for the IPEX exhibition, 1955, 'Since the sixteenth century (printers) have been depended upon to know how a given book, pamphlet or broadsheet ought to look – in effect, how to prevent it looking "different". The notion of actually encouraging lads to ask irreverent questions about the look of print… is alien to the atmosphere of the normal printing office'.

time and the direction in which it was inevitably moving.

Mason's experience of the general printing trade was limited to his years at the Ballantyne Press in Covent Garden where he was an apprentice compositor from the age of thirteen. This appointment was to prove important because the Ballantyne Press was not a publisher-printer, but still printed a lot of bookwork. Of special interest to Mason were Ballantyne's links with Charles Ricketts, an admirer of William Morris, and founder of The Vale Press. From 1895, Ballantyne reserved a press and pressman to work exclusively on The Vale Press books under the direct supervision of Ricketts. To Mason this proved that 'fine' work could be produced by an established 'trade' printer to the demanding standards of a private press.

Mason's employment was abruptly ended by a fire which destroyed the Ballantyne Press in 1900, but after a short break, Mason was recommended to T J Cobden-Sanderson, who, with Emery Walker, appointed him to work at the newly formed Doves Press. Mason found working at The Doves Press quite a culture-shock; '…this is a new and beautiful world after commercial work…' although, importantly, working at the Ballantyne Press had been far from the 'competitive scramble' of a typical printing office of the time.

The Doves Press continued until 1916, but Mason had moved on to a new sphere of work at the Central School of Arts and Crafts in 1909, when Lethaby offered him the opportunity to join the full-time staff, and to organise day classes in printing.

The 'Day Technical School of Book Production' began with the clear intention of utilising Mason's knowledge drawn from his research and experience of the private presses. The School was open to boys who had been awarded scholarships plus a certain number of free admissions, as an alternative to normal secondary school. The first year was divided between printing, bookbinding, and academic work which had a bias towards the needs of young printers. The next two years were devoted to printing or bookbinding and more advanced academic work. Drawing, lettering, design for book-binders and wood-engraving were taught throughout the three year period; '…forming

J H Mason, at the age of 25 in 1900.

elements of a broadening culture'.

Mason explained the benefits of the Day Technical School in the first issue of *The Imprint*, 1913; 'The general education of the boy is not arrested at fourteen, but is con-centrated more or less onto the work which he is taking up for life. Further, the habits of discipline which have been inculcated with untold labour in the elementary school are in the case of these boys further strengthened in the technical school: so that when the boy leaves at sixteen there is a strong reason to hope that they may be among the permanent lines of his character'.

After three years spent at the School, the boys would be apprenticed for five years in the regular way and become journeymen, normally at twenty-one. These classes found favour with, as Mason put it, 'enlightened companies' such as the St Clement's Press and the Baynard Press, who began taking the majority of their apprentices from the school as the trade unions allowed the concept of time spent at technical school to form part of the apprenticeship scheme. Of his approach to teaching and learning Mason wrote: 'first, my aim was educative in a wide sense as industrial specialisation

had had the result of giving the printer a minor part in the work as a whole..[13] To meet this I aimed at giving the young student a complete framework of knowledge of his trade, into which the content of his later experience could be placed with a sense of its place in the whole order of the trade. Secondly (or simultaneously) I wished to give him a love for, and a delight in, his trade as a means of self-expression and as a mode of life and as a joyous activity, closely linked to my third aim which was workmanship, and the sense of satisfaction resulting from mastery and conscientious work'.

Mason's approach to education was student-centred; instill the need to know and the student will be motivated to do the rest. Put into an industrial context, Mason explained it thus; 'The printer's need of verification will lead him to history and literature. Art and aesthetics will open wide and attractive fields before the youth who is interested in illustration. The inevitable interest in kindred or ancillary trades and activities will widen his range still further, and from the relations he will trace every-where between the special activities in his own trade and that trade as a whole with other trades, will open the study of political economy – the chain is unbroken, it leads to ethics and philosophy. A trade is, or should be, the true university'.

This philosophy, emanating from the Central School of Arts and Crafts, had many admirers, particularly abroad, but in the UK it also had its critics. Complaints usually concerned inadequate training with modern technology and the absence of realistic working methods. But some, surprisingly even from within education itself, considered the time and effort spent on 'aesthetic issues' a waste of time. J R Riddell, principal at the London School of Printing, wrote in the *Monotype Recorder*, 1928; 'Some of those associated with art schools... have contended that if the prospective printer were thor-oughly trained in aesthetic principles a higher standard of printing would be produced ...a claim unsubstantiated. Whilst the printer must, of necessity, have some knowledge of the proportions, balance and the most suitable type for the job, in this mechanical age his work may be said to be more scientific than of an artistic character... Best results... will come speedily if those engaged in the industry will insist that the courses of instruction in the schools be so arranged that they meet the needs of the craft, and do not blindly comply with the views of "visionaries," who may be genuinely interested in education, but do not understand what is required in a modern printing office'.[14] This view was shared by many in the trade and was fuelled perhaps, by Mason's criticisms of commercial printing standards in *The Imprint*.

The first issue of *The Imprint* was published In January 1913. Mason, along with Gerard Meynell, a pioneer in the revival of printing, and two of Mason's colleagues from the Central School of Arts and Crafts, Edward Johnston, who taught calligraphy, and F E Jackson, who taught lithography, shared the rôle of editor of this new monthly typographic journal. It was aimed principally at the trade, with the offer of genuine exchanges of knowledge and experience within its pages. Mason certainly made full use of *The Imprint* as a mouth-piece; his critical views of the typographic skills and working practices of the contemporary printing trade became a regular feature and he was never less than brutally frank. In his review of *The Mask*, a quarterly journal of the Art of the Theatre, Mason, having criticised the choice of type, the layout and poor

13 Alpha, *Printers Registrar*, 6 October 1880. 'Many printing offices inherently do not afford a fair chance to an apprentice learning his trade in its entirety...the division of labour in large establishments (confines) a lad to one item of his business in which he becomes wonderfully expert to the exclusion of all other training'.

14 Training the Printer of the Future, *Monotype Recorder*, May–June 1928, p 10–11.

press work concludes, 'The whole thing typographically looks to me like the untrained piecemeal conception of the amateur printer. I haven't the patience to go over it in detail; for there is a matter of excellent printing, and it drives me wild to see it fooled about in this way'. On the use of type itself, Mason gave the following critique of 'The American Printer'; 'So printers and advertisers aren't content to use print as God Almighty meant it to be used – quietly and honestly – but strain the beautiful instrument into discordant forms that repel all finer minds, and bring the craft into contempt. What regard or dignity has the printer nowadays? The craft has become an industry, and the industry one of the least esteemed'.

His criticism did not always go unanswered although Mason's resolve remained absolute. His review of 'The Fellowship Books'; 'A rather pretty series of priggish little books…', goes on to say 'these books… might have passed with a stream of pretty pettiness, except that on page ten of the prospectus there was a claim of, 'excellence in format' by the publisher'. This was clearly too much for Mason who then tore in to his subject with characteristic venom. James Guthrie, the publisher in question, complained that the reviewer was not prepared to make any allowance for the necessary creative thinking that a new task brings, that he was denying the existence of new and significant printing, the result of which would be to relegate design forever in the past. A reasonable response perhaps, to which Mason replied; 'I don't deny (new and significant printing), but I deny that it's good…and if it's significant, it is significant generally of bad taste and want of knowledge, or worse'. The industry he describes is that for which he was preparing his young students. No wonder Mason advised those who showed promise to go into education rather than the printing trade.

It should be no surprise to learn that Mason, unsympathetic, and becoming progressively more hostile to the printing trade, was more successful at preparing boys for a career in education rather than industry. Owens describes how out-standing students, Leonard Jay[15] and Charles L Pickering[16] to name but two, would be singled out to take up teaching posts, as many colleges sought Mason's guidance and help in recruiting their teachers.[17] To Mason's mind, his best students would be wasted by an industry where there was little opportunity for the intelligent student to fulfil his potential. Mason's earlier, generous view of the print industry being 'a true university' had been short-lived.

According to Owens, Mason's students were aware of the new typography coming out of Germany. Mason himself worked, both before and after the First World War, at the Cranach Press, based in Weimar, Germany. So it is unlikely that he was unaware of Gropius and his work at the (Weimar) Bauhaus. In London, Bertram Evans gave a lecture on the Bauhaus at the Royal Society for the Arts, and Charles Peignot had lectured on his new typefaces. Eric Gill had designed his Sans Serif to great acclaim, and had pioneered the use of ranged-left, ragged-right setting, at least in the UK. What Mason's supporters might call his 'highly disciplined approach' others would describe as narrow-minded and singularly dogmatic. Anything conceived outside his ideological frame of reference was dismissed with absolute contempt; 'We are quite satisfied that oblong books are not desirable.'

15 Leonard Jay became Head of Printing at Birmingham college where he established an international reputation with his bookwork and the journal, Torch.

16 Charles L Pickering became the first HMI to be appointed as a national specialist for printing subjects.

17 L T Owens, J H Mason, Scholar-Printer, Frederick Muller Ltd, 1976, Page 67, 'Many young aspirants received their first invitation to undertake some part-time teaching, for printing schools from a wide area sought Mason's guidance and help in recruiting their teachers'.

Mason saw himself as the defender of typography against the threat of falling standards of workmanship caused by the mechanisation of a printing process offering little
opportunity, in his view, for the printer to practice his craft. Alternatively, Gropius, after
initially experimenting with ideas similar to those pioneered at the Central School of
Arts and Crafts, went onto take the opposite view, and the Bauhaus, famously, embraced
technological progress and all forms of mechanisation into the design process.

I can find no reference by Mason concerning his views of the Bauhaus, but Mason's
friend and colleague, Stanley Morison,[18] complained that the Bauhaus was; '...making
an art out of something that should be a service, violating tradition, convention, ortho-
doxy'. Doubtless Mason would agree since he also believed the typographer was in the
service of type, its history and the great names who created it. The upholding of standards meant that there could be no deviation from the methodology incorporated by
the 'classic' works and that to deviate would let down 'typography'. No doubt to Mason,
the Bauhaus experiments had not the remotest connection to typography as he understood the term.

After Lethaby's move, in 1909, to the Royal College of Art as Head of Design[19] his
teaching ideals, so successfully implemented at the Central School of Arts and Crafts,
came under attack from the members of the 1910 Departmental Committee, established
to report on the function and constitution of the Royal College of Art and its relations
to schools of art in England. It had been noted that Royal College of Art design students
had, over a considerable period, been virtually unemployable as designers.[20] It was
no surprise[21] when the committee had completed its deliberations that it reported of
'...detailed criticisms which have reached us...it is maintained that (Lethaby's students)
spend too much time in making imitative studies in the museum and then acquiring
a "stock-in-trade" of motifs for future use; and, as a corollary, that their exercises in
inventive design lack originality, and are pieced together from the models they have
reproduced. In so far as they receive a definite artistic bent, it is described as "medieval".'
In 1918, Lethaby was 'retired' on the advice of the board of education at the age of
sixty-one. The usual expressions of regret are completely absent from the Royal
College of Art's files but at least the students in the Design School clubbed together
to buy him a farewell gift – a bicycle.

The latter years of Mason's teaching career however, were marked by a national
recognition of his services to education and to printing. In 1936 Mason was named
as one of ten Royal Designers for Industry, (Eric Gill was another recipient). Mason's
distrust of Modernism was not just tolerated, but revered. It should be remembered
that the thirties were a time of mounting national concern about political events taking
place in Europe, and a period for reflection of all things British was, perhaps a natural
reaction. National identity required a boost and was acheived by scouring the past.
Mason's stand for the *status quo* was perceived as heroic.[22]

The Hambledon Report on Advanced Art Education in London, 1936, was also com-
plimentary of Mason and the work emanating from the Central; '...this large and highly
successful institution, with its reputation and the excellence of its teaching attracts
students from a wide area...its highest branches perform work more appropriate to a

18 Stanley Morison first met Mason
in 1913, when Morison, then a bank
clerk, successfully applied for a post
working on *The Imprint*.

19 Lethaby had, in fact, accepted
the appointment of Head of Design
in 1900 (re-titled Professor in 1901) at
the RCA and until 1909 he divided his
time between the Central School of
Arts and Crafts and the RCA.

20 The 1910 Departmental
Committee reported (3 July 1911) the
extraordinary statistic that 'only 26
alumni had become "designers and
craftsmen" in the first decade of this
century'.

21 It was well known that the 1910
Departmental Committee, led by
Lewis Day, was going to be highly
critical of the RCA and in particular
of the Design Department led by
Lethaby. In a letter, written prior to
the inspection, to Sir Robert Mount
of the Board of Education, Day
wrote, 'Design and ornament, so far
as they are taught at all, are taught
in relation to architectural decoration,
so that in reality ornament is very
little considered and its practical
application to industry is entirely
neglected. It could not be otherwise
with Professor Lethaby and his staff.'

22 The question as to why Mason
was so revered whilst Lethaby was
so heavily criticised, when both held
the same views concerning design
education, is beyond the scope of
this article. Clearly Lethaby was in
a much more public position as one
of the four professors at the RCA. But
perhaps, more importantly, prior to
1945, typography in the UK remained
a highly conservative activity with
no industrial body willing or even
believing it needed reform.

national than to a local institution...' In fact the Central was held in such esteem that the Hambledon committee considered the possibility of it amalgamating with, or even superseding, the Royal College of Art as the National Institute for the advanced study of applied art.

It was in 1940, after the Central School had already been evacuated to Newbury, that Mason decided to retire; '...I gave up printing mainly because of my sight; but partly because of the economy regulations which precludes good design'. After the war, he returned to Putney where he died in 1951 at the age of 75.

Shortly after the end of the Second World War, mass communication became a reality. Multinational companies needed to communicate in so many ways to so many people that an infinitely more flexible approach to solving design problems was recognised as a priority. The new situation was addressed by a generous restructuring of Higher Education provision which took place in the late forties to 'Get Britain Moving'. Design for print, now called 'graphic design', was to be taught as a subject quite separate from the print process, and there were not many, on either side, who were sorry to see the split. The symbiosis of the design and printing processes that Mason had nurtured had come to a very abrupt end.

Printing schools took the view that their work was now science and technology based. Whilst graphic design courses, now housed within fully fledged art schools, and liberated from direct links with the printing industry, took a very different approach. Here, design students looked towards European ideologies of which they had been starved prior to the war.[23] Whilst links with printing departments were maintained, with the intention of providing a 'practical' element to the design process, these tended to be rather difficult to implement. Old habits die hard, and printing departments did not like the idea of letting outsiders into the print rooms,[24] particularly 'art' students, 'flashy little stylists',[25] who would, eventually, be in the market for clients who had previously been exclusive to the printer. Not surprisingly, art students exhibited certain feelings of antagonism, even suspicion towards the printing departments, often to the point of suspecting sabotage when-ever the finished printed job did not come back the way it had been planned.[26]

The stratification of design and print areas had been implemented quickly and thoroughly. James Holland, in 1955, described the situation thus: 'It is doubtful if any country has built up a more comprehensive structure for art and design education, at greater expense, than Britain. There is a real danger, however, that in the stratification of further education, the planning and creative skills, allocated to one level, may become unreasonably detached from the implementing techniques, which in their own way are no less demanding of skill and understanding yet are relegated to lower-level institutions with few links with creative design studies... so a situation has arisen in which the graphic design student may be edged into academic isolationism, while his printing counterpart tends increasingly to become a machine minder...'[27]

As Beatrice Warde had predicted, the printer had become the hod-carrier, and the graphic designer, that 'flashy little stylist', the architect.[28]

23 The Modern Movement's post-war proponents at the Central were Jesse Collins, Anthony Froshaug, Nigel Henderson, Herbert Spencer and Edward Wright.

24 James Holland, *Penrose Annual* 1955, pp 77 and 79, 'The drawbridge from design to the production area has for too long been out of action... The demarcation between design and printing in education as well as in industry has done nothing for the international image of the British industry, and may have been a minor contributory factor in the proportion of British work that goes abroad'.

25 Beatrice Ward, *Typography in Art Education*, p 84

26 F H K Henrion FSIA, Design for Production, *Printing Review*, Vol 14, No. 47, Summer 1948, p 5, 'It too often happens that the printer says to the designer "You do your job then hand it over to me and let me take care of it" and then, when the designer compares the original work with the final printing, he complains wistfully "Look what they have done to my design"'.

27 James Holland *Penrose Annual* 1955, p 81.

28 Beatrice Warde, The Pencil Draws a Vicious Circle, *The Crystal Goblet*. The Sylvan Press, 1955.

With thanks to St Bride's Print Library and Central St Martin's Archive.

1998 **A time of change: an introduction to the Working Party for Typographic Teaching** Justin G Beament

The first meeting of the WPTT took place in Geoffrey Bensusan's office at Bowater House in Knightsbridge in the late summer of 1966. It is hard to remember everyone who was there, (although I certainly recollect that Michael Twyman, Ernest Hoch, Don Warner, Edward Wright and Fredun Shapur were there from the start) I turned up at the meeting, fresh-faced and just a year out of London College of Printing.

There was a strong feeling at the time that the teaching of typography, and its place as an important graphic language, was being neglected. This coincided with a major shake-up in design education – the transition from the National Diploma in Design (NDD) which supported specialisation to the new Diploma in Art and Design (DipAD) where the emphasis was put on a broader, more liberal, visual education. It was also a time of major change in print and composition technology, an expansion of graphic design into television media, along with the fast-moving cultural changes of the 1960s.

The Working Party, which was supported by the STD and the Society of Industrial Artists and Designers (SIAD) later renamed the Chartered Society of Designers (CSD) was concerned that good quality typographic teaching, with an emphasis on form following function, was not being properly addressed. This view was supported by both the publishing and printing industries and was very strongly articulated by Christopher Bradshaw, design director at Eyre and Spottiswoode. Christopher was a real champion for those of us who believed passionately in typographic teaching, and in the rôle design should play in the managerial process in industry.

The WPTT set up two working panels, the Methods panel being conducted by Felix Gluck and Fredun Shapur, with Cal Swann and Anthony Helliwell (WPTT Secretary) conducting the Syllabus panel.

First provisional report

A provisional report on Equipment, Staffing and Facilities was published in February 1967 carrying the initials of Don Warner (Senior Lecturer in Typography at Brighton College of Art). Considerable emphasis was placed on the recommended acquisition of a composing room, with at least two full families of type, along with proof press, and adequate technical support. Facilities for mechanical composition were considered to be a desirable addition.

The composing room was seen as an integral part of the teaching, learning and design process throughout the course. Sadly, many institutions abandoned their composing rooms in the 1980s due to economic and technical support constraints, and they have since greatly regretted this. The use of the composing room greatly benefits in laying down the basics of alignment, spacing, detail, and specifications.

The WPTT report gave typography tutors genuine support in making our case with the principals and governors in obtaining funds to set up composing and print facilities. This support was often backed up by two superb HMIS: Charles L Pickering and David Rutt, who were ever conscious of the need for sound typographic teaching and the part that workshop experience played in the learning process.

The teaching recommendations placed much emphasis on establishing a sound design methodology based on careful problem-analysis, problem-solving, using sound typographic principles, evaluation, development and refinement, and finally realisation. It was recommended that the subject be taught in a sequential manner, working with limited typographical elements, and adding to these as the student gained confidence and experience. The drawing of letters it was felt should also be studied and practised.

Typographic design was seen as a broad subject area encompassing stationery and forms design, publications, catalogues, books, magazines, exhibitions, signage, and interpretation. Emphasis was given to the importance of technical theory, cost implications of design decisions, and the need to produce clear typographical layouts which were properly specified, not only to communicate clearly to the compositor, but also to underpin understanding by the student.

The development of skills and the acquisition of first-hand industrial experience with printers, publishers and design groups were considered to be important stages in the education of the aspiring designer. Background knowledge of the history of printing, lettering, and the major design movements and trends were another important educational element recommended by the WPTT.

First WPTT conference

The first WPTT conference, titled 'Creative Teaching in Graphic Design', was held at Central School of Art, London, in October 1967. The aims of the Conference were to explore logic and invention in typographic teaching and to stimulate a greater exchange of experience among teachers of typography in graphic design education. Notable speakers from industry were Christopher Bradshaw, Bernard Moriarty, chief typographer at Lintas Advertising. Peter Burnhill of Stafford College of Art made a major presentation which demonstrated the fact that Stafford was well established in the teaching of typography. Edward Wright from Chelsea School of Art reflected his teaching philosophy on the subject and showed various examples of his students' work.

HMI David Rutt gave a controversial speech forecasting, correctly, that many Colleges of Art would be combined with Colleges of Advanced Technology to form Polytechnics. We were in a time of change (when haven't we been in a time of change?) in art and design education.

The aims of the WPTT were successful in raising the profile of typography as a subject

in the design education agenda. Within a relatively short time, Dr Michael Twyman and his team established a first degree in Typography and Graphic Communication at Reading University, which became an important centre of study in the subject, whilst the establishment of the STD Student Assessment Project was instrumental in regenerating both staff and student interest in the typography with, the production of challenging projects, assessed to rigorous professional standards of communication, function and creativity.

Thirty years on...

How healthy is typographic education today? In addition to Reading University, we now have specialist degrees in Typography at the University of Plymouth in Exeter, and, more recently, at Swindon. Both the London College of Printing and Stafford College have excellent HND Typography courses. The diversity and quality in typographic teaching in more general graphic design courses can be demonstrated in the STD Student Assessment's submissions.

Electronic typography has produced both benefits and some undoubted horrors. The results can often produce strong arguments in favour of the need to raise awareness of sound typographic foundations, both in teaching and practice. Typography is a visually expressive medium, but it is primarily about delivering, with sensitivity, content that meets the needs of the user and reader.

Many people expressed concern at ATypI at Reading University last September [1997] about the need for improving typographic education in graphic design degree and diploma courses. As we move towards the 32nd anniversary of the establishment of the WPTT, should we not be considering seriously that it might be time to revive it?

The Working Party on Typographic Teaching: interim report, October 1968 Michael Twyman

1 The Working Party

1.1 Origins of the Working Party on Typographic Teaching

The Working Party on Typographic Teaching was set up in October 1966 by the Society of Industrial Artists and Designers, with the active support of the Society of Typographic Designers, in response to repeated criticism from assessors, teachers, and spokesmen from industry that much graphic design work in colleges of art and design was let down by an immature approach to typography. Since then, the Working Party has become an independent and permanent body with nearly fifty active members drawn from departments of printing, colleges of art and design, universities, and a number of branches of industry. Amongst them are representatives of leading national and international organisations and societies connected with typography and graphic design, heads of graphic design and printing departments, and teachers (both full- and part-time) from many parts of the country. A full list of working party members represented is appended.[1]

1 List of Members, October 1968:

Michael Twyman BA PhD, (Chairman) Lecturer in typography and graphic design, Reading University.

Gillian Riley MA (Secretary) Private practice.

Anthony Helllwell ATD (Conference Organiser) Brighton College of Art.

Harold Bartram, Private practice and London College of Printing.

Justin G Beament BA ATD MSIA Private practice and Norwich School of Art.

Geoffrey Bensusan FAIE MSIA, Publications Officer, The Bowater Organisation.

John R Biggs MSIA ATD NRD FRSA, Head of Graphic Design, Brighton College of Art.

Roy Boothby C&GFTC (Prg), Brighton College of Art.

Kenneth Briggs, Private practice and Ravensbourne College of Art and Design.

Peter Burnhill ATD, Head of Design, Stafford College of Art and Design. Dennis Cheetham.

Clive Chizlett C&GFTC, Brighton College of Art.

continued overleaf

1.2 Terms of Reference

The initial terms of reference were to consider the place of typographic design in graphic design courses and to suggest means of improving the quality of the teaching of the subject. As work progressed it soon became obvious that the traditional meaning of typography (printing) would have to be extended to include all visual communication systems involving the use of words, numbers, and other symbols. It also became clear that we were really concerned with the fundamental issues of the design process which, in our experience, can best be approached through the study of an industrial design discipline such as typography – engineering or architecture would serve equally well, but typography is the obvious choice in graphic design courses.

1.3 Regular Activities of the Working Party

The organised activities of the Working Party are of two main kinds: regular monthly meetings for members, and a series of national study conferences. The monthly meetings usually take the form of demonstrations and descriptions of projects which members have undertaken with their own students: and these have provided valuable points of

departure for the discussion of general ideas about what we want our students to learn and the value of the teaching methods we use. Other meetings have been conducted as discussions introduced by a member of the group or by a visitor. Among the topics covered have been the teaching of engineering design, courses for teachers of typography and graphic design, and the place of the study of the history of typography, technology and design. In addition, the Working Party has set up special study groups to consider in more detail a number of such aspects of the teaching of typography.

1.4 National Conferences

Two national study conferences have been held, and a third is planned for this November. The response to these has confirmed our belief that the dissatisfaction with the present structure of courses and the approach to the teaching of typography and graphic design is widespread. Over 300 people attended the first conference 'Creative teaching in graphic design' which was held in London in October 1967, amongst them practising designers, teachers of typography, principals of colleges of art and design, representatives from the printing and allied industries and professional bodies connected with printing, and an observer from the Department of Education and Science.

Allan Cooper MSIA CGLI, Private practice and Camberwell School of Art.

Ken Dickinson MSIA FSTD MAA AMIPA, Art Director, Alfred Pemberton Limited.

Geoffrey Dowding, Hobson, Bates & Partners Limited.

Howard Dowding MSIA, Wace Group.

Felix Gluck MSIA, Private practice and Hornsey College of Art.

Maurice Goldring MSIA Cert HfG (Ulm), Private practice and Chairman of the SIAD/STD Typographers' Computer Working Group.

Miriam Goluchoy ARCA, Private practice and Brighton College of Art.

Brian Grimbly, Royal College of Art.

Philip Hadley, Head of Printing, Camberwell School of Art.

Ernst Hoch, Private practice and Chairman of the ICOGRADA Commission on Standardisation.

Michael Hutchins, Camberwell School of Art.

Roydon Jenkins C&GLI, Stafford College of Art and Design.

Alan Jones, Publicity Manager, The Monotype Corporation Limited.

Jock Kinneir FSIA, Private practice and London College of Printing.

Francois de Mauny MSIA, Merchant Adventurers Limited.

Leslie McCombie FSIA, Private practice and London College of Printing.

1.5 Aims and Intentions

These organised activities have gone some way towards making the aims of the Working Party known, but perhaps its most valuable contribution to date has been in providing an opportunity for the informal exchange of views amongst members with a wide range of professional and industrial experience. Contacts of this kind have enabled us to clarify our ideas and learn from one another; in this respect a particularly important rôle has been played by those members working in industry.

One of the original intentions of the Working Party was to produce some kind of document outlining basic requirements in relation to courses, staffing, equipment, and so forth. It soon became clear, however, that such a document would be premature, and possibly approaches to one area of design education; too specific proposals at this stage might even have the effect of inhibiting further essential experiments. What is clear is that we need a situation that positively encourages new and varied kinds of courses to emerge. Secondly, we believe that courses should be designed to suit the genuine educational needs of students for the benefit of society as a whole, and that they must be shaped to some extent by the interests of particular teachers and by local considerations both inside and outside the teaching centers.

A few examples may help to illustrate this last point. Some study of cybernetics, linguistics, and perception seems to be essential to an ideal course in typography and graphic design, but we do not suggest that these subjects should be obligatory at this stage in view of the difficulty of re-training existing teachers and finding suitable new staff. The history of printing may be most profitably studied, particularly where original material exists locally in a good library, but the history of technology may prove quite as rewarding when studied in an area where interest can be aroused and nurtured by contact with actual examples of engineering from the past. Practical

involvement with modern printing machinery may be a most valuable part of a student's course, but it is not absolutely essential, and the nature of the contact would certainly depend on the size and type of the educational institution and the attitude of local industry.

1.6 The major issue.

This report is therefore mainly concerned with general ideas and principles. Though it has been prepared by members with wide experience of the organization of courses in typography and graphic design, it dwells primarily on the need for a new approach to design education and, as an example of this, the relation of typography to other subjects. The design of courses must stem from these fundamental propositions.

2 The Art and Design Conflict

2.1 Foundations of design and design teaching. In our examination of objectives and teaching methods we have found that inadequacies in typographic design teaching mostly stem from the treatment of the be perfectly legitimate in painting and sculpture, but is a distortion of typographic designing and, for that matter, any other designing. The most effectively developed methods we have seen have been those that have rejected the use of typography as a form of applied art and have concentrated on the functional, technical, and economic factors which are involved in its use as a means of communicating information within a prescribed brief.

We contend that so long as the purposes of art are allowed to dominate the study of design, students will be robbed of an opportunity to develop the knowledge and attitudes required to deal with design problems in the area of visual communication. We believe that design problems are different in kind from those associated with the practice of either art or craft and require different forms of training from those which are traditionally associated with art and craft. The designer is no longer confined to creating aesthetically satisfying objects within prescribed areas of activity and is becoming increasingly concerned with planning and co-ordination as a major function.

2.2 Implications for Secondary Education

The changing rôle of the designer also requires that potential design students in secondary education should be given a clearer idea of the new kinds of subjects which they will be required to study on design courses and when they practise as professional designers. This in turn means that the designer's function has to be understood by those responsible at secondary level for advice about future careers. We believe that the view of industrial design held by teachers and pupils in secondary education is still largely based on the concept of the designer as an artist, and design courses as means of refining the 'artistic ability' of students who show promise of this kind at school. We believe that this view must be changed if students with the right attitudes and potential are to come forward. For this to happen, design education in colleges of art and design must be seen to be concerned with matters other than those of the art and craft room.

Ian McLaren, Private practice and Ravensbourne College of Art and Design.

Bernard Moriarty MSTD, Chief Typographer, Lintas Limited.

James Mosley MA, Librarian, St Brides Printing Library.

Keith Murgatroyd FSIA FSTD MInst Pkg Private practice, Manchester College of Art and Design, and Chairman of the ICOGRADA Audio/visual and Library.

Geoffrey Powell AMIPtgM MIHE, Head of Department of Printing, Graphic Arts and Educational Technology, Garnett College of Education.

Peter Rae FSIA MSTD, Private practice and lecturer on graphic design and typography.

Angela Reeves MSTD, Private practice and Secretary of the Society of Typographic Designers.

John Salsbury C&GFTC, Bournemouth College of Art.

Fredun Shapur ARCA MSIA, Private practice, London College of Printing, and St Martin's School of Art.

Bob Miller-Smith MSIA MSTD, Duncan of Jordanstone College of Art.

Graham Stevens MSIA MSTD, Liverpool College of Art.

continued overleaf

2.3 The Social Rôle of the Designer

The prevailing confusion over design education has important social ramifications. We believe that the present educational pattern does not encourage the design student to appreciate the significance of the rôle he has to play in the community at large. Much too much importance is attached to personal satisfaction arising from self-indulgence rather than from the reward of seeing a design problem satisfactorily solved for the benefit of others. This is only too clear in the case of typgraphic education where the tradition tends to encourage certain kinds of jobs which are superficially treated and involve no more than visually exciting images. Other areas of designing, of more consequence to society, are neglected. Furthermore, the emphasis on so-called originality often results in mere stylishness which disguises a complete absence of original thinking. Consequently, many extremely important but unspectacular areas of typography and graphic design, such as educational books and other visual aids, scientific papers, government regulations, reports, instructions, forms, and directional systems, all of which play an important part in our lives, are usually either not designed at all or are designed very badly.

2.4 Economic Considerations for the Country

Cal Swann FSIA MSTD, Manchester College of Art and Design.

Bernard Thurlow MSTD, Garnett College of Education.

Walter Truman-Cox FSIA, Private practice, Berkshire College of Art and member of the Southern Regional Advisory Committee for Art.

Don Warner MSIA ATD C&GFTC, Typographic Workshop, Brighton College of Art.

George Webb LSIA ASTD FRSA, Exeter College of Art.

Peter Werner ARCA ASIA (Ed), Head of Graphic Design, Ravensbourne College of Art and Design, Chairman of the ICOGRADA Education Commission and member of the NCAD Advisory Panel for Graphic Design.

Fred Whitehead, Ravensbourne College of Art and Design.

Edward Wright MSIA MSTD, Head of Graphic Design, Chelsea School of Art.

Brian Yates FSIA, Private practice industrial and graphic design, and Head of Graphic Design Central School of Art and Design.

HMI Mr David Rutt accepted an invitation to attend the meeting as an observer.

We believe that, on economic grounds alone, this country cannot afford to tolerate bad design education any longer. Our concern here is with the rôle of the typographer, which is perhaps rather a special one since printing and other visual communication systems are central to the machinery of government, industry, trade transport, education and scholarship. The efficient working of all kinds and levels of society depends to a large extent on communication by means of the printed word. We cope with an enormous quantity of material of this kind, the effectiveness of which depends to a large extent on the ability of the typographer to understand its content, order it meaningfully, and find a suitable medium for it. A pattern of design education based primarily on cultivating personal expression does little to come to terms with this problem. Most students leaving colleges of art and design this year will be ill-equipped to face up to the needs of industry today, let alone the future.

3 The Work of the Typographer

As stated earlier, we believe that design method in general is best studied through a specific industrial design discipline, and as far as graphic design is concerned we believe that typography is the ideal one.

The function of the professional typographer is to communicate specific information as efficiently as possible within the limitations imposed by his brief. In the first place, the typographer must be capable of analysing 'copy' and, if need be, re-ordering its structure. A thorough understanding of the use of English is essential for him to handle efficiently any material given to him. He must equally be able to advise a client as to the appropriate means of communication. A general knowledge of systems of communication as a whole is therefore necessary, together with an understanding of the psychology of perception. The need to be able to discuss and analyse projects and problems

with keen minds from business and industrial fields suggests that the typographer
needs to be articulate as well as literate.

Because the typographer must produce creative and compelling solutions to the
problems that are put to him, we must stress at this point the importance of stimulating
the student's imagination as well as training his analytical powers. A course which
neglected this in favour of purely scientific and technical studies would be grossly
unbalanced. We recommend that any complementary studies designed to avoid this
imbalance should be connected where possible with the student's main field of study.
To quote a single example, an historical topic can on its own be a disciplined and
imaginative field of study, but when related to the typographer's other activities it
can enrich and expand his appreciation of them.

Having studied a client's requirements and having, from his experience in this field,
arrived at an efficient and creative solution to the problems raised, the typographer
will next advise the client on production methods in relation to such factors as costing,
budgeting, quality control and allocating priorities. The typographer, and thus the
student of typography, has to be informed of every aspect of the printing and allied
industries, methods of typesetting, printing and binding, materials, processes, trade
services, and so forth. The typographer will be acting as planner and co-ordinator of a
multiplicity of processes and the link between them and his client. He must therefore
be conversant with the theory and practice of them all.

Summing up, the practice of typography is not only a matter of intuition or flair, but
essentially a discipline and combination of skills and functions capable of analysis.
On this basis, typography can be taught in a way that can be professionally and
educationally valuable, while at the same time demonstrating the principles of design
practice as a whole.

4 Related Disciplines

We do not propose a rigid structure of studies relating to graphic design, but it is very
clear that many new disciplines need to be introduced, and that they would open up
the possibility of worthwhile advanced work in a variety of fields. The desirability of
introducing new disciplines naturally has some bearing on the plans to incorporate
many graphic design courses into the educational work of polytechnic institutions. We
believe that the following subjects are amongst those which have a direct relevance to
the education of typographers and graphic designers, and indeed most other designers:
English, Mathematics, Management Studies, Psychology, Linguistics, Cybernetics,
Technical Studies, and History of Design.

4.1 English

Any designer needs to be capable of writing and speaking clearly and objectively on
various aspects of design. The preparation of visuals, storyboards, process artwork, and
working layouts has to be augmented by concise, but comprehensive, written and oral
data. A designer who is responsible for fact-finding in relation to a project must be able
to present his findings in a form in which they can be used by others. Furthermore, the

typographer is closely involved with editorial decisions and must have a clear understanding of the meaning of his copy before he can begin to order it. For these reasons,
we recommend that all courses in typography include provision for students to develop
fluency and clarity of expression in written and spoken English and that, where ever
possible, this should be linked with practical work in design.

4.2 Mathematics

Calculations and measurements are normal routines of typography and demand a
competence in simple mathematics. The preparation of specifications is an important
aspect of design, and students of typography must be familiar with methods of calcu-
lating costs and quantities and in the ways in which these can be expedited by the use
of formulae and slide-rules. The typographer is also concerned with communicating
statistical data, and this means that he must be able to understand the general principles of statistics and statistical graphs. Descriptive geometry, augmented by practice in
technical drawing, is clearly of value to graphic designers who frequently work in three
dimensions. Particular areas of mathematics, such as mathematical logic, analogue
geometry, and binary notation, are linked with cybernetics. We believe that mathematics
is as central to typography as it is to many other areas of design and technology.

4.3 Management Studies

Definitions of management are often synonymous with definitions of design. The
functions of management have been defined as planning, organising, directing, co-
ordinating, and controlling. These are also important functions of the designer, and it
is commonplace for designers to fulfil executive rôles in organisations. Training in the
principles and techniques of effective management, administration, and planning is
valuable to the young designer because such principles are analogous to those of good
practice in design. In a number of colleges, students of graphic design are already being
taught the principles of particular management techniques of analysis and planning.
Through such studies, students can be helped to develop their own design philosophies:
they can learn something about organisational structure, acquire insight into the rôles
and activities of managers, and learn to appreciate that implementation of a project is
equal in importance to, and more complex than, its visualisation. Management studies,
including matters of finance, law, and modern techniques of planning should be integrated with the study of professional practice in typography and graphic design courses.

4.4 Psychology

We believe that the study of the processes of conceptual thought, learning, perception,
memory, cognition and other aspects of human behaviour are of great importance to
the typographer and graphic designer and should be included in his education. In particular, all students should have some understanding of perception in relation to reading
and should be familiarised with work that has been done in the field of legibility.

4.5 Linguistics

The typographer is primarily concerned with ordering verbal information and ideas.

Until recently the traditional ways of ordering such material had changed very little, but the development of algorithmic methods for the presentation of information during the last decade has opened up entirely new approaches which should be very much the concern of the typographer. Similarly, the typographer has much to learn from the new discipline of linguistics, which is concerned with the study of the function and structure of langauge in general. Typography can legitimately be seen as 'visual linguistics' and should be studied in relation to the wider use of language.

4.6 Cybernetics

The inter-related fields of cybernetics, computing and automatic data processing are the leading edge of contemporary technology and are central to a large and important sector of typographic engineering. Unless students of typography are introduced to the principles of cybernetics, they run the risk of becoming redundant within a few years of leaving college. Access to a computer is desirable but not essential in order to train students in the principles of computing and programming. Such simple apparatus as a typewriter and stencil-duplicator can be used for a communication system which can provide a basis for introductory experience in the disciplines of systems analysis and systems programming.

4.7 Technical Studies

For many reasons this is perhaps the most difficult kind of study to implement in full-time education. We are conscious that some teachers attach little or no importance to technical studies, and we know that many teachers are largely ignorant of technical matters and are not in touch with recent developments. We believe that technical studies in typography should not be limited to the operations of printing but should extend into other areas of the communications industry. It seems to us absurd that design students in any field should be uninformed of relevant equipment, materials, processes, standards, conventions and technology.

5 Implications for Higher Education

As mentioned above, this document is not concerned with making specific proposals relating to the implementation of courses, but more with general conclusions that have emerged from our discussions.

5.1 Entry requirements

We do not wish to state categorically which subjects should be required of students who enter design courses, or what level of achievement should be expected, but we do believe that some requirements will have to be made. We make three general observations.

Firstly, there is at present a tendency for good applicants with scientific interests not to look in the direction of design. Ways must be found to change this situation if students with such potential are to come forward.

Secondly, the new approaches to teaching science and mathematics in primary and

secondary education are particularly relevant to the thought processes which will be required of designers, especially in relation to the inter-disciplinary character of design operations demanded by new technological developments and managerial techniques. We are certain that unless students have a foundation in these disciplines at school, higher design education can not properly fulfil its rôle.

Thirdly, design education must provide opportunities for mature students who need to change direction. We believe that provision for such students must become a feature of design courses, and that high level studies will benefit from an infusion of maturity (as was shown during the immediate post-war period in many areas of further education). Clearly, entry requirements demanded of this type of person would not be solely dependent on formal academic qualifications.

5.2 Equipment

A generous supply of elaborate and expensive equipment is no substitute whatso-ever for a sound, imaginative approach to teaching typography and graphic design. Many of our members have been disturbed by the undue emphasis placed on prestige equipment in some schools and have found that this can so easily obscure some of the more essential thought processes of design education. Machinery and other major items of equipment can, and ideally should, play an important part in the education of students of typography and design, but the first priority should be to discover what they are needed for. Only then will it be seen what kind of equipment can be most satisfactorily used to serve the educational purposes in mind.

5.3 Links with Industry

We are very much in favour of forging strong links between educational establishments and the printing and allied industries. Such co-operation would go some way to solving the problem of familiarising students with modern industrial processes without the need for schools and colleges to incur enormous and unnecessary capital costs. It would also help students to understand some of the social and organisational problems of industry. Students should spend some part of their vacations working in a variety of branches of the printing and allied industries, and ways must be found for students to spend periods working under supervision in industry as part of their courses.

6 Urgency

We welcome the current re-appraisal of design education and can not overstress the urgency of dealing with these problems.

1973/4 **Standards** E Carr

The educational design concept is the cultivation of the student's capacity to achieve enduring values in design principles in both intellectual and moral realms of experience, whether it be in his place of work or the world in which he lives and operates during his waking hours. Typographic solutions seem to evoke varying responses from different people. Who is to say which response is the more appropriate? Who indeed, unless we believe that there are objective aesthetic values, in which case we may choose to rely on the decisions of experts as to what is good typography.

We may judge good typography by using criteria said to be authoritative, and may claim that any work of a typographic nature which scores low on these criteria will have difficulty finding a place in our good design dossiers. Textbooks on typographic design rely on these standards when informing students on matters involving appreciation and assessment. The fact, however, that critics of typography differ widely when assessing work brings me back to my previous question. Who is to say which response is truly appropriate? There seems to be no rational answer to the problem of the judgement of typographic design. Should the arrangement of type be representative or should it be the product of the creator's imagination? The first view depicts the typographer reflecting the scene around him in printing, its materials and processes and is related to his literal and visual experience. He must employ his mental agility intellectually in analysing, synthesising and employing a systematic approach which projects a professional outlook on to decisions.

We try to develop the basic design skills in the young student by making him more aware of colour, form and the appreciation of the reality of texture, and take him back into the evolution of our alphabet and its letter shapes. Subtle appreciation of colour and its effects, and shades/tints seem to bewilder him and hence the question of 'good and bad' design rears its ugly head.

One can not transfer thought and analysis and visual experience, but only an awareness of what, in our opinion, is technically a sound, aesthetically pleasing, visual solution, bearing in mind the cost. This is dependent on the teacher's constant intake of stimuli in the form of his reading, example, tours and contact with fellow professional designers, industry, his research and his own empirical design flair. The comprehension of the stimuli becomes systematic and here the danger could evolve in the interpretation

of the good and bad elements. Should we allow the student to be governed by his own intuition in his decision making in relation to design solutions, bearing in mind the environment in which he operates and the pressures of customer, user and manager in his visual thought patterns? The mature teacher and designer has a very large mental computer-bank of design information, which he identifies and recognises at a glance and to some extent he anticipates the typography and designs he encounters, categorises them into cubicles of 'good and bad' criteria in the brain, but these criteria may only apply for a short period in history. This is evident when one can identify a solution as belonging to a certain historical period in design thinking, related positively to changes in media, materials, machines and demand and, in some cultures, religions and politics. Unfamiliar designs can be perceived only through a process of deep analysis, the extent of which depends on the degree of unfamiliarity. Parts of the solution may be partially familiar, but it can prove of little value as a cue to the perception of the whole design solution. Should we not ask the student for his understanding of the meaning and leave him to the visual interpretation as his perception of sensory skills develop and mature during his life span?

Many researchers have uncovered aspects of design and typography which have stimulated many arguments in respect of views of 'good and bad' standards. I take their stand in assessing student design, especially their research into legibility, aspects of distance, speed of perception, eye-movement, blink-rate, visual fatigue, peripheral vision, visibility etc when I assist a student in finding a solution. These are the real issues I perceive and not the emotive values of likes and dislikes. M A Tinker, says, 'habit, experience, and the subjective ease of perceiving the design is one thing, performance seems to be another'. Students identify fashion and habit, but we try to help them to analyse beyond the impact on the market into how and why it performs and its function in society. In the analysis stage of a design the designer is a solitary man if he is not to be influenced by his environment but led by good and bad standards. He creates out of his personal drives and experiences, and this can be the only good or bad example to a student. He expresses his feelings by projecting, with the clients consent, what he thinks the solution should be. In this capacity the designer enjoys unlimited freedom to use his pen, brush and rule in a way that fulfils the creative urge within him.

Some teachers believe education should acquaint the young designer with the many apparent levels of design, the ugly, the abhorrent, the grotesque and the unique. Others are adamant that they should perform a social function, communicating to all individuals of their time, and not trying to emulate and please a tiny clique.

Should he be destined to please, and be in harmony with me, and appeal to my interpretation of good and bad typography? The feeling is of guilt that he has bent to appease. The designer who has pleased his critics is probably at the end of his inventive powers, for critics tend to judge in accordance with accepted standards of the time. Indeed, the young designer rejected by his teacher/assessor may well be the true innovator in the next generation of designer/typographers.

1976 **Vocational courses in graphic design** A J Marshall
A J Marshall was Education Officer for the Society of Typographic Designers in 1976,
the second year of the STD Student Award Scheme.

Vocational courses are defined as courses directly aimed at employment and as presently constituted they fall somewhere between BA degree courses and recreational courses. In recent years there have been many changes in design education, and the situation is still in a state of flux. Many STD members may remember that the National Diploma in Design (NDD) was replaced by the Diploma in Art and Design (DipAD) as a result of a report published in 1960 by the National Council on Art Education (NACAE). This report recommended the establishment of an independent body to administer the new award (which was to have the status of an honours degree). This body, the National Council for Diplomas in Art and Design (NCDAD), was established under the chairmanship of Sir John Summerson and the first courses leading to the new diploma were started in selected colleges in 1963.

When the DipAD was announced, the majority of colleges running design courses applied for validation to run DipAD courses, but, for a variety of reasons, many of these applications were turned down. Some college enrolments were considered too low to ensure continuity, other colleges lacked the necessary facilities, and others were turned down for reasons not immediately apparent.

This creation of a degree course elite, together with the ending of the former NDD, left many colleges without a validated course. These colleges reacted in various ways. Some sought regional validation, others awarded their own college diplomas, and others sought recognition by the Society of Industrial Artists and Designers in an attempt to obtain professional recognition for their vocational students. This is reflected in the enormous increase in the number of colleges running courses leading to LSIAD assessment and the rise in student numbers seeking such recognition. Table 1, left, shows that from three colleges and twenty-seven students involved in SIAD assessment in 1964 there were thirty-eight colleges and 369 students so involved in 1967. This increase continued so that the 1975 figures were seventy-six colleges and 1,132 students.

The figures given (in table 2, left) are the totals for all areas of design. The SIAD has some twenty-five categories in which students can be assessed. These can be divided into four main groups: graphics, fashion/textiles, interior and product design. A break

year	colleges	candidates	%pass
1964	3	27	52
1965	16	144	58
1966	34	292	63
1967	38	369	61
1968	42	454	74
1969	45	519	75
1970	42	419	75
1971	58	634	73
1972	64	831	74
1973	66	898	78
1974	68	1034	80
1975	76	1132	78

Table 1

area	candidates	passes	% pass
graphic design	2818	2134	75
fashion/textile	878	715	82
interior design	1027	709	69
product design	552	432	78

Table 2

down of the nine-year period 1966 to 1974 is [also] described in table 2.

Many readers will remember that the DipAD ran into trouble when students, teaching staff and employers started to comment adversely on the content of the course, the entry requirements and the final 'product'. This led to the NCDAD setting up a working party to review the DipAD structure at about the same time that NACAE were considering vocational courses. In view of the fact that modification of any one part of the art and design structure would affect the whole, the councils of NACAE and NCDAD established a joint committee to review the whole art and design scene in 1968. Their report, The Structure of Art and Design Education in the Further Education Sector, was published in 1970 and recommend a number of changes in both the DipAD structure and in vocational courses. It recommended the setting up of a central body to be responsible for planning a national network of design technician courses, and to undertake their validation and coordination. Upon receiving the 1970 report, the then Minister of State set up a working party to, 'look into the provision of vocational courses in art and design below advanced level in colleges of art and other FE institutions, to consider the extent to which the provision meets employment needs, and to propose a pattern for the future having regard to the joint committee's recommendations on design technician courses and relevant developments in further education generally'.

The Gann Report
This working party, under the chairmanship of A S Gann, reported in 1974. Some of its major recommendations were that:
1 The Secretary of State should undertake the establishment of a separate national body for vocational courses in art and design.
2 This should be autonomous and have a title fully reflecting this status.
3 Its functions should in scope resemble those of the Technician Education Council and the Business Education Council.
4 The membership should reflect the interests of education, industry and relevant professional bodies and allow also for regional involvement.
5 Reciprocal participation should be sought between the TEC, the BEC and the art and design body.
6 There should be consultation with the TEC and the BEC with a view to the national body being brought into a formal relationship with the TEC and the BEC jointly.

The Gann Report also recommended the establishment of a two-tier vocational structure for the two main outlets into employment, one at eighteen-plus, the other at twenty-plus. In most cases, these two courses would exist in the same colleges and that the junior course would prepare students for various employments requiring design knowledge and ability, while the senior course would lead to professional qualification.

For school leavers of sixteen-plus, full-time courses are suggested as follows:
1 A two-year course for those with suitable qualifications, leading to a certificate or diploma comparable in status to an OND.
2 A course for other students, not so qualified or motivated, leading to a certificate

serving a different purpose. Solely for the purpose of identification within the report, the terms Course 1 Certificate (C1) and Course 2 Certificate (C2) are used to describe these respective qualifications. Openings for further study should be avail able to C1 Certificate holders not wishing to enter employment immediately. As one possibility amongst others it is hoped that there could be eligibility for a BA place but as the main opening for further study, a course leading to a Higher Certificate of the validating body is suggested.

The Gann Report has been widely accepted. If implemented, the proposals would tidy up the confused vocational sector of design education, and provide a national qualification to replace the present assortment of courses at varying levels.

Two main criticisms have been levelled at the report. One is that the professional design societies and academic interests are not happy at the prospect of coming under the Technician Education Council, which has made a bid to take over design education. An independent council is preferred. The second criticism is about the delay in government action. It took only eighteen months for the Gann Committee to collect and investigate the evidence and provide the Secretary of State with its report. In the light of this, it would be surely reasonable for the Ministry to make its views known.

The Technician Education Council has established a committee on Visual and Graphic Communication which is to be directly involved in several areas of graphics (Printing Subjects including Design for Printing; Audio-Visual Technicians; and Technical Graphics are but three examples). These committees contain very little professional representation and are neither what Gann recommended nor satisfactory to the professional design societies.

Assessors at the 1976 student assessment scheme. Walter Bath and John Biggs.

The SIAD Direct Admission Scheme has, in the past ten years or so, become the main validating body for vocational courses. The SIAD's views on the Gann proposals are, therefore, important. The SIAD has a lively Board of Design Education and a dedicated education officer, James Holland, who was a member of the Gann Committee and therefore a signatory to the Gann proposal. The SIAD, aware that its views on recent developments coincided with those of other professional bodies, acted as convener of an informal meeting of representatives from professional associations, held in London on 4 October 1975. Of the thirty-one bodies invited twenty-five sent representatives for an initial exchange of views and ideas regarding design education. This meeting provided a lively discussion on the current scene and a great deal of extremely pertinent comment upon the general standard of vocational design education. The meeting decided to send a joint letter to the Secretary of State regarding the concern felt about the delay in commenting upon, or implementing the Gann Report. Part of the text of this letter stated: 'the delay in announcing any decision on the future of vocational design education (following the 1974 Report and recommendations of the working party on vocational courses) is seriously hampering the work of colleges and those professional bodies who take some part in this'.

'It was also urged that you should resist the continuing pressures being exercised in favour of the Technician Education Council assuming responsibility for this area of design education'.

As a result of this first meeting, a small working party was set up to propose any future liaison and action. As the twenty-five societies fell into eight broad areas of activity a representative of these interests was invited to attend the first working party meeting on 4 December 1975. At this meeting, Terms of Reference were drawn up for verification by the individual societies, and a standard letter to Conference participants requesting precise details of their involvement in design education.

A further meeting of this working party was held on the 13 May 1976 at which it was decided to recommend to the participating societies the setting up of a joint committee on design education. This joint committee would pool opinions on all aspects of design education and, it is hoped, unify policy regarding the current problems in design education. At the time of writing [1968] this proposal has not yet been ratified by the individual societies.

As yet no information is available regarding the Ministry's views on the Gann Report. If the report is implemented there will be many changes in the present provision of courses. The report, for example, makes no mention of Foundation courses which, at the moment, are a feature in many colleges and which are taken by many students, whether they are going on to a BA degree course or a vocational course.

This, it seems, is deliberate, for in answer to a question raised at a conference at Coombe Lodge, Mr Gann stated that 'it was implicit in the suggested C1 and C2 courses that they would be available for entry without an introductory course'. Many teachers have serious doubts about the validity of foundation courses but this is the first time that doubt has been expressed from an official source.

Vocational courses, as noted earlier, are concerned with preparing students for full employment, and a measure of the success of such a course is how successful it is at providing industry with educated and trained personnel.

SIAD Assessment Scheme

It is worth outlining the assessment procedures of the SIAD and the STD before we discuss the criticisms made by various professional bodies of vocational courses.

The SIAD assessment for Licentiate Membership takes the form of an assessor who visits the college to inspect the work of each candidate. The assessors are specialists in the particular category in which the student is being assessed (in 1975 there were 100 assessors). The projects are set by the college but the SIAD states, in broad terms, the type and number of projects which it expects the student to prepare for assessment.

In addition to inspecting the work, the assessor interviews each applicant individually, discussing the work in detail. As part of the assessment, the assessor marks the student's work in ten areas, five in the creative section and five in technical and professional:

Section A – creative

1 Does the student define and analyse design problems intelligently and is this apparent in his work?
2 Does the work show creative ability?
3 Has the student, in interview, given evidence of aesthetic awareness?

4 Has the student developed the scope and quality of his work?

5 Does the technical skill and presentation match the creative standards?

Section B – technical and professional

1 Is the student knowledgeable about methods of graphic reproduction, materials, printing and manufacture?

2 Do the design projects show appreciation of costs, commercial or industrial limitations?

3 Do working drawings and specifications convey production requirements clearly and accurately and is there evidence of professional responsibility in the handling and presentation of the projects?

4 Is there evidence that the student can express himself clearly, orally and in writing? There must be at least one project report.

5 Is the thoroughness of thinking and research established by note and sketch books? A pass of 50 per cent in both section A and section B is necessary for the acceptance of a candidate for licentiateship of the SIAD.

As a result of his visit to the college the assessor prepares a report, which is sent to the college, outlining his observations of the work assessed and indicating the strengths and weaknesses of the work and the course.

With such a detailed examination of students and courses over the years, the SIAD is extremely well placed to comment upon the general standard of vocational courses. Over the years, assessors have made the same comments: that far too many students lack the necessary technical knowledge which is required to be a successful designer, and that the same deficiency is found in professional knowledge. In an attempt to put these matters right, particularly the lack of professional knowledge, the SIAD ran a number of conferences for college lecturers a few years ago which sought to draw attention to these weaknesses and to offer advice on ways of correcting the situation.

STD Membership Entry Assessment Scheme

A few years ago the STD received a number of requests from colleges seeking recognition by the STD. As a result of this, the STD launched a pilot scheme last year to enable students to gain recognition as Associate Members. The STD has no desire to compete with the SIAD, and indeed many designers are members of both societies.

The STD felt it set a very detailed project which would involve a great deal of work and which, if successfully completed, would clearly indicate both the student's creative ability and technical competence. The STD also sought to assess each student's work in detail and to return a detailed report to each student whether successful or not. In this way the STD hoped to give the student the views of practising designers on his work which would be of value in subsequent design projects.

Projects

The first project was for a catalogue/brochure for an agricultural chemical manufacturer giving details of his range of chemicals to farmers. This year's project was for a

sales brochure/technical data leaflet related to kitchen units. Both projects involved the student in a great deal of work and required them to submit the following items:

1 Finished layouts for client presentation.

2 Working drawings and full typographic specifications, sufficient for the job to be produced without further reference to the designer.

3 Copy preparation and type mark-up.

4 Platemaking instructions for the treatment of illustrations.

5 Initial scamps/roughs.

6 Case history of approximately 200 words explaining the interpretation of the brief, methods of production and whatever else the student would wish the assessors to know about the submitted design.

In the first year's pilot scheme, seventy-five students submitted work from a total of twenty colleges. Six students were awarded Commendations and twenty three others gained Associate Membership.

In the 1976 assessments 164 students submitted work from thirty-eight colleges. Eight gained Commendations and forty-five have been awarded Associate Membership.[1]

Each student was supplied with a brief, copy, drawings of kitchen units, a planning chart for kitchen layouts, and photographs of a typical kitchen arrangement. The brief involved the design of a brochure, planning chart, hire purchase application form, logotype, etc, for production within the stated technical facilities available within the company which, the student was to assume, employed him.

The assessment is carried out by a team of Fellows and Members of the STD, working in pairs, who assess each student's work in detail, awarding marks for:

1 Analysis of problem and interpretation of the brief.

2 Standard of presentation.

3 Typography (including the selection of typeface/measure/paper/ink and the exploitation of available plant).

4 Craftmanship (eg lettering).

5 lllustrative ability: vision and technique.

6 Accuracy in casting-off copy.

7 Copy preparation.

8 Typographic drawings and specification.

9 Creative ability

A total of 60 marks is required for Associate Membership, and 80 for Commendation.

What of the resulting work? On the basis of only one year's projects it is of course dangerous to draw too many conclusions. Nevertheless it is obvious that while there is much to commend about graphics courses up and down the country, there is also much that is disturbing: '...the greatest weakness was in the lack of technical knowledge shown in many entries. Some students seemed totally ignorant of the processes by which their work is produced and some of the specifications were unbelievable. Copy-fitting was either very accurate or else an uninspired guess, and it seems that many students would advocate the use of rubber type! With so many students applying from a wide range of courses, it is inevitable, although sadly so, that the technical

1 Since the assessment scheme was launched, a number of inquiries have been received from colleges requesting guidance in strengthening the weaknesses indicated in the assessment reports. The Council applaud this constructive attitude and is anxious to help in any way that it can. A number of possible avenues are being explored, including the possibility of a travelling exhibition and/or a conference/seminar at which the work could be displayed and discussed. This would provide college staff with the opportunity to compare their students' work with that produced by other students from colleges all over the country working on a common project.

knowledge displayed should reflect wide differences in the subject matter taught and, one supposes, the importance attached to this essential area of a graphic designer's training. The Society of Typographic Designers is concerned about this lack of technical knowledge and deplores the fact that some colleges seem unable or unwilling to give this area of study the attention it must be given if students are to be designers in the true sense of the word, and not merely creators of pretty but incompetent work.' (STD assessors' report 1975)

Criticism from the Institute of Printing (IOP)

Criticism has also come from other quarters, including the Institute of Printing. The IOP Design Committee, under the chairmanship of Mr Brooke Crutchley, has issued a report which is very critical of graphic design in general, and graphic design education in particular: 'It is probable that (the designer) has no deep understanding of production methods and materials, costing and estimating, marketing and management techniques, since little attention is usually given to these in training for his job, and it is unlikely that he will be afforded any opportunity to acquire knowledge of them in his working life. The result is that his usefulness is limited and he will be incapable of exploiting the available resources in the most efficient way from the manufacturer's or the customer's point of view. Also, there is a danger that he will issue inadequate or impracticable instructions.

A designer must have an appreciation of costs and of estimating procedures, and because his design must eventually satisfy a customer he should have some knowledge of selling and customer relations. In addition, since in the end his design or production plan must fit into the total operation of a factory, or factories, he must understand management procedures. The foundations of all this knowledge and the understanding of their interdependence should be provided in college courses, leaving experience on the job to develop and perfect them.

More fundamental is the need for design and production to be fully integrated in a college course. This means that suitable courses could best be offered where there is a fairly extensive printing department and where design and production students can make the fullest use of each other's resources. The superficial investigation of printing processes and materials which forms part of so many high-level graphic design courses is totally inadequate and is clearly failing to reach the objectives set'.

What is to be done?

The purpose of this article is to invite practising designers, who employ or work with the end-products of vocational graphics courses, to offer constructive suggestions for improving the quality of students leaving such courses. If the Gann Report is imple mented and a Design Education Council (DEC) established along the lines of the TEC and the BEC, it is to be hoped that it will seek the views of the professional bodies which serve the profession. The STD is anxious to play a full part in any such discus- sions and for this reason the education committee is interested in gaining the views of STD members. The Council firmly believes that graphic design students must receive

an education which incorporates a detailed study of technical production planning, business methods and professional practice. Far too many courses are too fine art oriented. A designer, unlike an artist, has to be involved with production and should be knowledgeable about all aspects of modern production and business methods. This knowledge should be acquired at an early stage of his education and not left, as all too often happens at present, to chance.

A personal statement

In placing before you an outline of the recent past and present provision of art and design education, I have attempted to be objective. However, since I am inviting you to submit your views, perhaps I may now be allowed to state mine.

Before stating the policy and organisation which I would like to see being implemented to administer and validate vocational design courses, I must enter the usual cave at that my views are personal and do not necessarily reflect the individual or collective views of the STD Council. They're based on my experience as a practising designer, twelve years in design education, and upon the many discussions I have had over the years with designers, students, employers, clients, educationalists and representatives from other professional societies.

It seems to me that the first requirement in any future plan is to end the association which has grown up over the years between 'art' and 'design'. In many people's minds they are synonymous terms, but to those of us who earn our livings as designers they have only passing similarities. For far too long, art and design have been officially seen as the same subject whereas they are in fact nothing of the sort.

As I have already hinted, I am not in favour of vocational courses in graphic design falling into the hands of the Technical Education Council. In company with most designers and educationalists, I would like to see a new Council – the Design Education Council. Picking up the wording of the Gann Report, 'The membership should reflect the interests of education, industry and relevant professional bodies, I consider that the DEC should be made up of representatives from professional bodies engaged in various areas of design, together with representatives from industry (CBI and TUC); from education (secondary as well as further); and perhaps also from an organisation having some interest in design but which would mainly contribute a layman's attitude – one of personal concern rather than vested interest. This Council would be served by a number of committees, each for a particular area of design which would be responsible for organising the syllabus for the three levels of courses proposed by the Gann Report (C1 and C2 plus the advanced course proposed to follow C1). They would be responsible for setting the examinations/assessments and for issuing validations of courses and students.

I would like to see these committees consisting of members from appropriate professional bodies. For example, in technical communication design, the committee would contain, say, three representatives from the Institute of Technical and Scientific Vocational courses in Graphic Design.

Communicators, and the Association of Illustrators, together with a representative

from associated professions such as the Institute of Printing and others. The committee responsible for graphic/typographic design would contain, say, three members from the STD and the SIAD, together with a representative from the IOP and the Institute of Incorporated Photographers, etc. In this way the examining and validating body would be a specialist committee representing the professions most concerned with the individual areas of specialist study, together with representatives from associated professions. The opportunity would exist for any professional body seeking to involve itself in design education to make representation to the Governing Council for either membership of an existing specialist committee or else for the setting up of a new committee to establish courses and validation in a new area of study.

Governing council
Consisting of chairmen of specialist committees; industry; education; and laymen.

Specialist committees
Consisting of representatives from professional bodies, together with representatives from associated professions: Graphic design, Technical communication, Photography and Film, Illustration, Interior design, and Textile and Fashion. I see no reason why, within these broad divisions, subsections could not flourish so that, for example, someone studying graphic design could select an option such as book design, packaging, etc.

As regards examinations, my view is that these should be in three parts, all of which would have to be passed to qualify. The three parts would be:

1 An assessment of work undertaken upon the course (in the manner of the existing SIAD scheme).

2 A detailed assessment project (on the lines of the present STD project).

3 A written paper on the technical and economic aspects of the specialist area of study.

Such a scheme would go a long way towards correcting the weaknesses of the present courses and examinations.

1985 **Graphic designers or typographers** Mafalda Spencer

Typography, or rather typographic design, is currently enjoying a new vogue, especially among the young. This is largely thanks to publications such as *The Face* magazine and the prevailing fashion for 'neo-modernism'. As in most cases, students tend to be one or several, steps ahead of their teachers. Normally this situation would be a healthy and, indeed, normal state of affairs, but the current practice (due to ever-decreasing education budgets) includes phasing out part-time staff who have always been used as the specialistist in a college. They can be employed for their specific knowledge or skills as and when the students require them. Much teaching of typography is achieved in this way. A large proportion of full-time teachers were employed in their current positions during the 1970s, a time when the trend in graphics was towards the graphic image (pictures) rather than type. The result is that many of the staff in our art schools today are illustrators or very broadly-based graphic designers; few have a strong typographic background. Another reason for this is, of course, that it is conceivable (and advisable) to carry on working in one's field as an illustrator but extremely difficult to run a typographic design practice whilst, at the same time, having a four days a week commitment to teaching.

One cannot level too much of the blame on the staffing systems in colleges – modern technology has not been as beneficial, at least in the field of typographic teaching, as was first expected. Photocomposition allows a student with very little knowledge or understanding of type to use it, but problems arise when students use this system without ever having handled metal type itself. They do not understand the point system and, not illogically, they assume that the point size relates to the cap height, and assume too, therefore, that all 12 point type is the same size. Obviously this misconception is not held by a majority of students but it is not rare either.

By handling type I mean actually using it, on a reasonably regular basis. In doing this one develops a certain understanding and feel for typography which can not be achieved by using any system which uses a keyboard. For some reason, the keyboard seems to have the effect of raising a barrier between the user and the type. Most people, even those who are more visually aware, will deliberate for hours on the benefits of one typewriter keyboard layout, etc, but few will pay much attention to the typeface it produces.

Admittedly allowing students to use cold metal has disadvantages: a proofing press has to be inked and cleaned every day, type goes missing or is neglected, and dissing often consists of opening the nearest type case and tipping the contents of a galley into it. On the other hand, students will often be held up for hours while they wait their turn on the photocompositor, often just to set a couple of words.

The fact that the use of cold metal has generally been phased out has given it an air of the old-fashioned, the dusty, even the inferior. With the current interest among students for the typography of the inter-war years has come a wish to recreate some of the effects then achieved with woodletter. Instead of going down to the composition room and proofing some woodletter they will often spend hours adulterating a piece of photosetting to make it look like the genuine article. Those however who have discovered the joys of handling type often become almost hooked on it – finding it therapeutic, but many never experiment with it simply because they feel unsure about the process – they feel they ought to know how to set type but never quite get around to asking someone to help them.

The handling of type is only the beginning of understanding letterforms, one needs to draw them. As with all skills this takes a great deal of practice. The first results usually look extremely clumsy – a very demoralising situation for a student who, by virtue of being on a graphics course, must have ability in drawing. This apprehension often leads them to avoid hand-rendering at all costs, spending vast amounts of money on transfer-lettering instead.

It is unfair to expect a student to be able to master hand-lettering just by practice. They need encouragement and a general build up to it. When children learn the piano, for instance, they are not made to practice a complicated piece endlessly in the hope that they will eventually master it; they would soon give up, bored. Instead they are given small, relatively easy pieces to perform, gradually building up as they improve their technique. The same applies to lettering. Basic calligraphy is not particularly difficult to master and is a good introduction to hand lettering, also having the benefit of self expression. Unfortunately, calligraphy is now little taught in art schools. It too has been dropped by the wayside as being old fashioned. This is a pity as it is not only an excellent way of teaching an understanding of letterforms but is also a skill worth mastering. It is always pleasant to come into contact with beautiful handwriting.

The cutting of letters into stone is also now hardly ever taught, either in practice or in theory – this was another craft of great benefit for those learning typographic skills and understanding.

Modern drawing implements, while having many advantages, also have a great many disadvantages. Apart from costing a good deal more, a felt pen always has the habit of running out at the most inconvenient time. At least with a pencil one is well aware of when it is time to buy a new one. Rotring pens are marvellous when they are running smoothly, but they are prone to hiccupping. If one wants to use a different colour of ink one has to clean it out, or own several; mapping pens, on the other hand, while not only producing a line that is sympathetic to letterforms, need only to be wiped off and have the benefit of allowing the user to fill it with ink or paint (especially useful

where extra cover is needed). Ruling pens also carry this advantage.

The design history courses in many art schools are spending more time on graphic design and typography. This is a good omen as most people learn by example, and, in time, I think that this will spur students on to wanting to know more about the old crafts. It is a difficult subject to make interesting to the layman, and students are, at least at the beginning of their courses, laymen when it comes to typography. However, the example I gave earlier of woodletter is not isolated, there is an increasing interest in crafts such as marbling and hand-made papers. These crafts became rare earlier than hand-lettering and type, they have a certain appeal that the latter two have not yet gained, but no doubt will in time.

Most courses have now introduced computers, many are finding that they are already needing to replace them with machines capable of far more complex functions as students soon use them to their limits. They are wonderful tools but students often begin using them in the typographic field when they have not yet mastered the art of letters. The results tend frequently to be clumsy and the computer is often wrongly blamed. The problem is that too often the art of lettering is not equated with the art of drawing, a skill that art students have probably always had a natural talent for, but they have also worked on improving it for many years before they arrive at college. The same applies to the history of art, a part of daily life – but who, outside the field has ever heard of the history of typography, except of course of Gutenberg and Caxton?

1982 **Are present day design courses really necessary?** Philip Turner

Gutenberg, Plantin, Garamond, Bodoni, Caslon, Elzévier, Fournier, Jenson, Ratdolt, Geoffrey Tory, Baskerville, Van Dijck. These, and others, were the giants of fine printing and typographic design which thrilled and energised many of us in my student days. We were to see breathtaking examples of their work at the British Museum, Gutenberg Museum, Plantin-Moretus Museum, John Rylands Library, and St Bride's. Such was our enthusiasm that it was quite normal for us to discuss in manic detail the comparative merits of *Bell*, *Bulmer* and *Bembo*. And we enjoyed the sympathetic patience and shared enthusiasm of such luminaries as Beatrice Warde, Ellic Howe and dear Turner Berry. The museums for the great printers, their work-places and libraries, were the repository of five hundred years' achievement in fine printing which, I have grown to realise, is now virtually locked away in history.

When I was a student it did not seem difficult for academic staff and others to relate to the qualities of fine printing and typographic design which we so revered. After all, we shared techniques and the cultural, aesthetic, and emotional styles of our common endeavours. Indeed, we realised, that our design teachers were themselves part of a continuing tradition, and were passing on the standards and tastes which they themselves had inherited from earlier times.

The tragedy facing design education, and especially typographic design education today is not merely that most connections have now been severed with the beauty and skills of the best printing which has gone before us, but also that the electronic revolution and the microprocessor have not yet brought in compensatory advances in qualitative design. We are, it seems to me, caught in an unproductive hiatus between the vanishing expertise of the past and the revolutionary – and as yet largely unproven – techniques of the future.

The rarity of typographic design courses is a sign of the times. The advertising profession has taken over the major rôle in influencing the direction of typographic design. No longer, it seems, is any real depth of typographic design of understanding achievable in the majority of colleges and polytechnics. The courses themselves, at the lower levels, are almost totally geared to an immediate vocational objective, frequently, in the short term, directed towards finding a job in advertising. There seems to be no time to take a medium term view. Typographic courses (where they exist) seem to be

regarded as something of a specialist indulgence, with the consequence that most typographic design in advertising, and indeed in other fields, falls well short of the qualities achieved by designers and printers in earlier centuries.

Although heavy coffee-table books can show examples of high quality typographic design (much of it rightly admired in design education and elsewhere) a more accurate reflection of current standards can be seen in what are, to me, horrendous places such as the new Covent Garden complex where the boutiques (shops of course) seem to be stocked with products whose style of packaging and typography is reminiscent of earlier times, and strives, self-consciously, to evoke nostalgia for a world that never really was. Besides – the texts are usually too small for comfortable reading. British design is awash with *pastiche* and we are in danger of mistaking this for good taste. Alas, not many are able to tell the difference.

How does modern typographic design education relate to this tendency? Many problems are being identified and more and more questions asked. Can we afford (should we afford) specialist courses in typographic design, spreading perhaps over four years and extending beyond the students' late teens? Yes, because, typographic design needs certain qualities of mind found more frequently in the relative maturity of the early twenties than the late teens. Is the microprocessor and its varied techniques going to make classroom learning almost obsolete, undesirable even, in the training of typographic designers? Is the pursuit of professional survival and self-protection going to tilt the quality and kind of design education towards the interests of academic staff, as cynics claim it already has? Can the 'reality gap' (which seems to be increasing) between what is appropriate in education and what industry really needs be closed, and can the quality of design teaching be revolutionised?

Will it be, as some of us think, that the skills and knowledge of something like 25% of design teachers, if not already largely obsolete, will become absolutely so, well before the end of this decade? What is going to happen to them? Already many design teachers are incapable of catching up. As a consequence, many design courses cannot rise above the staffs' incompetence. The claims made to support such courses are increasingly unconvincing.

Will the mistake of separating so-called vocational from professional designers be rectified, and will designers become mainly creative people with increasing access to, and influence on, electronic processing? If these and other activities cannot be retained and undertaken to the degree of satisfaction that society demands it will surely be that the users of design and print will themselves increasingly bypass designers and have access, even by direct entry, to the printing process; including facilities on their own premises.

Design departments in colleges and polytechnics are surely going to have to be involved much more in mid-career learning, distance learning, retraining and a constant updating of knowledge, in a world which moves forward in a technical (if not necessarily fruitful) sense with accelerating rapidity. Some will not survive. Many are not surviving now. Frequently, local authorities are not making the degree of financial commitment to maintain design teachers at a level of educational competence. Staff

development in general continues to be a mockery. Local authorities will need to invest if they are to continue to have viable departments.

We can recognise that even printing, as we have known it, is destined to undergo major changes and various commentators have described the probable future well enough. It is likely that many local authorities will quietly decide not to keep up with the investments needed for appropriate education until the course atrophies. Shared investment with industry, however, will surely become commonplace, thus liberating typographic design education from its present outdated traditional institutional confines. This will take typographic education into printing locations outside the colleges and polytechnics as it becomes increasingly accepted that modern techniques of printing are easily learnt. Conventional design education seems destined to remain relatively static whilst the world outside is poised for lift-off. Careers and jobs may be in disarray in the short term but the potentialities of the new technologies in the 1980s make the microchip as exciting as the twenty-six soldiers of lead ever were.

1982 **Students who don't read** Don Rooum

A typographic designer needs a lively interest in written communication. That is a stultifyingly banal statement, rather like saying a fashion designer needs a lively interest
in clothes, or a theatrical designer, a lively interest in theatre. Or more accurately, it is
stultifyingly obvious to anyone who knows what a typographic designer does. Many
applicants for places on typographic design courses do not know, and for some of them
the connection between typographic design and writing is going to be a nasty surprise.

The reason, I suspect, is the invisibility of much good typography. You can read a well-
designed text, or fill in a well-designed form without being really aware of its visual
structure. Users of typographic design need never know of its existence, unless it is
called to their attention.

One can imagine a person who is keen on written communication joining a typographic design course without knowing what it is about. Such a person, as he or she
comes to an understanding, may well become very enthusiastic about the idea. But there
are many young people, intelligent, visually aware and completely literate, who find
reading and writing a boring chore to be undertaken only when necessary. Such persons
might make excellent pottery designers, display designers, illustrators or sculptors, but
they can never be typographic designers. They do not care to learn the rules of spelling
and punctuation. Nit-picking niceties of style and spacing, intended to produce minuscule improvements in communication, will merely try their patience. The prospect of
reading the same passage again and again, to compare the legibility of different settings,
will be for them a frighteningly tedious prospect. The whole endeavour of typographic
design will strike them not as a creative challenge, but as a hideous creative hindrance.

Attitudes change, of course. Someone who thinks reading is a bore may suddenly
discover that reading is fun. But such conversions are rare, and colleges have no means
of producing them. It is neither ethical nor prudent to enrol people as students on
courses where they have little prospect of success. Those who are not keen on written
communication, no matter how talented visually, should never be enrolled on typographic design courses.

The problem is how to stop such unsuitable people from applying for a course, and
if they apply, how to distinguish them from the suitable applicants. It is not at all easy.

The first and most obvious line of defence is to send out to everyone who requests

an application form a letter, or a leaflet, which explains the course and sets out in clear and unequivocal terms, the qualities and attitudes required in a student. Suitable applicants will read such documents thoroughly before sending in the application form. Unsuitable applicants, on the other hand, will not read them. They never read bumph; that is what makes them unsuitable.

Oral explanations given to applicants at interviews, are marginally less useful. They are understood by neither suitable nor unsuitable applicants, though listened to with every sign of keen interest. The applicant at an interview is keyed up, eager to convince the interlocutors and in no mood to learn anything. As to subsequent recollection, the offer of a place is liable to drive all cautious advice from the applicant's memory.

Questions and answers at the interview are notoriously poor indicators. It is difficult enough to distinguish the stupid from the shy, or the brilliant from the glib. Attempts to distinguish whether or not the applicant is keen on written communication is even more difficult. For instance, the question 'What kind of things do you read?' may elicit an impressive reading list or a non-committal answer. The impressive reading list may indicate, either that the applicant is an impressive reader, or that the applicant or an adviser has anticipated the question and prepared an impressive response. The non-committal answer may indicate either that the applicant does not read, or that the applicant is an avid reader of works on popular music, or science fiction, or something else which could give an unfavourable impression, or that the applicant in the tension of the interview is forgetting to mention a splendid collection of railway timetables. Other things being equal, the applicant with the impressive reading list will be preferred, but the test is not reliable either way.

At some colleges, graphic design students of all sorts begin with a common course, then, after, say, a year, when student and college have come to know each other, the student opts for either illustration or typography. This may be a good scheme for selecting illustrators, but to judge from the final exhibitions of some option courses, it does not select students with the right attitude to learn typographic design. Those who opt for typography tend to be those who cannot draw; and there is no positive correlation between interest in written communication and lack of drawing ability.

A more promising strategy is to impose entry requirements. The requirement for DATEC courses (and most of the earlier 'vocational' courses) is three GCEs at O level. CNAA degree courses require three GCEs at O level plus two at A level, or for Art and Design degrees, the successful completion of a DATEC diploma, or have GCEs at O level plus a year of Foundation studies. None of these requirements constitute absolute minima; colleges have the discretion to waive entry requirements in whatever they deem to be suitable circumstances.

Student registration forms for DATEC record whether the student has more or less than the requisite three O levels. In time, no doubt, the DATEC computer will calculate whether possession of three O levels is a useful predictor of success, and what it will find in the cases of furniture design and painting I have no idea. In the case of typo-graphic design, however, it seems obvious that shortage of O levels is a fair indicator of unsuitability for the course. When a college decides to waive the standard academic

requirement, it is probably because the applicant is perceived to be more intelligent than the academic performance suggests; and if poor academic performance is not due to dullness of wit, it may well be due to a lack of interest in reading and writing.

It does not follow that success in GCEs always shows a love of reading and writing. All GCE passes are evidence of intelligence and application, and Art GCE more than some others, because the candidate is required to do a longish project in addition to the three-hour paper. But one may actually gain a top class pass in both O level and A level Art without reading anything at all, other than the examination paper. The same is true of many Art and Design Foundation courses. At present, the applicants for typographic design seem to offer Art more frequently than any other single GCE subject.

Colleges may, of course, impose entry requirements of their own. Christopher Bradshaw once advocated[1] that nobody should be accepted on a typography course unless he or she has a university degree in classics. He explains that in typographic design an ability to use words is needed. Now classics was good for this, because students are assessed on *how* they write as well as *what*. An English degree isn't so good, for instance, because the object is what you write, not how. This strategy would no doubt work if it were practicable, and it might conceivably be practical for a publisher's in-house training scheme; but it could not be worked in colleges. It is quite ordinary for typographic design students to have better qualifications than the standard requirements, and there are university graduates among them. But, certainly for the moment, there are not enough classics graduates among the applicants to fill a course in any particular year.

The known strategies for excluding non-readers, then, are imperfect. It seems inevitable that a few unsuitable people, under the misapprehension that 'design' is synonymous with 'not reading', will find themselves on typographic design courses. Those who cannot stand it will withdraw, and hopefully find a more appropriate place.

The more resilient, albeit they are on the wrong course, may nevertheless get some value from it. No full-time course consists exclusively of typographic design studies. Printing techniques, drawing, photographic techniques and artwork preparation are offered as useful supplementaries. The intelligent anti-typographic student may learn enough to work as a layout artist, an instant printer or a studio technician. There are also non-readers with good creative powers, who use art schools as a source of liberal education. Mostly they go for fine art, but a few join typography courses and come to no harm as a result. I know a model, an athlete, and two musicians, none of them in the least interested in written communication, but all of them former typographic design students who wafted through the course on charm alone.

Whether such people are helpful or otherwise, to their more committed fellow students, is another question.

Happily, the number of applicants who are interested in written communication seems to be increasing, perhaps as a rather remote result of the change in printing techniques. Teenage intellectuals are more likely than before to see references to typographic design in popular science articles and television programmes. Hopeful writers, browsing in *The Writers' and Artists' Yearbook* may now find typographic

1 Working Party on Typographic Teaching (WPTT) 1969, confirmed by personal communication, 20 February 1982.

design mentioned in the articles on copyright law.

There is still no shortage of applicants for typography courses who really want to be artists. But among young people who would like a career in some literary field, there is increasing awareness of typographic design as a career option.

1996 **Typography is too important to be taught to designers** Cal Swann

The dimension of graphic design has changed dramatically in the last five or ten years due largely to the impact of electronic systems and some consequent social shifts. The two major effects are that professional design groups require far fewer human resources to do far more work, and, most importantly, graphic design for print (in particular) is done by everyone with desktop publishing facilities. To add other new facilities which are developing at an incredible rate, multimedia and the World Wide Web, the picture becomes totally different from the traditional, professional consultancy world of graphic design.

Currently, in most graphic design courses, the model is one that is based on the art school 1960s model, despite the various changes to that environment which have occurred since then. Firstly, the Polytechnic takeover, then the Council for Academic Awards (CNAA) taking over the DipAD to award BA Honours degrees, and finally the University establishment of the so-called level playing field for us all (which happened in Australia a few years ahead of the UK). All of which should have heralded a dramatic re-thinking. Despite those changes, the course models have not changed much… it's just got much more difficult to teach that kind of course in the new climate of economic rationalism. If we take the first paragraph seriously, and no sane person is going to quibble with such a self-evident 1990s scenario, remarkably little has changed to the typographic instruction which is based on form over function (see Heller, 1995, and many others).[1]

An expressive/visually dominated graphic arts course is not what the community needs for the 21st century.

But a stirring in the pot is beginning. A succession of recent articles (Bernhard, Bonsieppe, Buchanan, Margolin, Swanson, Wodicka,[2-7] et al) and conferences such as 'Edmonton 95: charting the future of graphic design' (August 1995), and 'New Era: new typography' in Manchester (November 1995) as two recent examples of educationalists getting together – and this issue of *TypoGraphic* [issue 49] – at least indicates a new awareness that we have a problem.

New problems require new solutions. The 21st century graduates need to have many of the graphic skills we now foster, mainly the ability to conceptualise the form that communication must have in order to be absorbed through (principally) the eye/

1 Steven Heller, *Fashion follows function*, Communicating Design Batsford 1995.

cognitive route to understanding. But the emphasis must be on making reader-access to information as easy as possible, not making the form a vehicle for artistic 'authoring' (Rock 1996). The new graduates must have an attitude where the graphic/author – and by author I mean the author of the message – has the choice either to make information accessible to the reader or to use graphics as commercial art in the tradition of McKnight Kauffer, Wolfgang Weingart, etc. The new communications graduate must have a broad knowledge of communication theory, linguistics, semiotics and information technology, and have writing skills at the same level as the 'graphic form' we assume to be the knowedge/abilities base for graphic design graduates.

The interesting part is that we already have these programmes – courses in communication media in most Humanities faculties normally offer information technology, media and cultural studies and, as often as not, professional writing. As Dauppe[8] said, maybe we should just talk to our neighbours. What humanities is missing is that essential limb of visual communication – in what is primarily a visual medium. The combination of the above disciplines together with information technology as interactive electronic media and global communication systems would be formidable. Career opportunities for graduates would be very diverse – in government, commerce, publishing, broadcasting, multimedia, education, etc.

Specialisation in more professional areas for graphic design, public relations, broadcasting, etc can happen at postgraduate level. The idea is not new. The Society of Typographic Designers was instrumental, with the Society of Industrial Artists (as it was then) in setting up the UK Working Party on Typographic Teaching which, as long ago as 1968, recommended: 'Similarly, the typographer has much to learn from the new discipline of linguistics, which is concerned with the study of the function and structure of language in general. Typography can legitimately be seen as visual linguistics and should be studied in relation to the wider use of language.'[9]

In 1972 Weingart said: 'Certainly in the future, a study of typography must include a study of the meaning of text… we will need input for new fields such as sociology communications theory, semantics, semiotics, computers and planning methods.'[10]

Some response to these calls resulted in a handful of BA courses springing up in the UK that were titled 'Information Design' during the seventies and eighties. These all turned out in the event to be quite traditional graphic design courses and whatever claims may have been made, the students and staff were sucked into the eighties post-modernist era of self-expression. They, like Weingart (who went on from his statement quoted above, to confuse semantics, which is the meaning of words, with the graphic form of words) and some design historians, have been busy inventing high-sounding but highly fallacious, misguided theoretical connections to Deconstruction, in their attempts to intellectualise the egotistical pursuit of producing graphics for self gratification.

Lest that last paragraph be interpreted as a swipe against 'theory', let me hasten to point out that the curriculum which I am advocating is for considerably *more* theory, and less practising *ad infinitum* the easily learned skills of typography and layout. My point is that the theory would be substantially improved if much of it came from the standpoint of those who study the media from a critic's or real deconstructivist's

2 Bernhard, Stephen A, *The shape of text to Come: the texture of print on screens*, College composition and communication, number 2, Volume 14, 1995.

3 Bonsieppe, Gui, *A step towards the reinvention of graphic design*. Design Issues number 1, volume 10, 1994.

4 Buchanan, Richard, *The changing culture of communication design*, Paper for Charting the future of graphic design education conference. Edmonton: GDEA/ICOGRADA.

5 Margolin, Victor, *Design studies and the graphic designer*, Proceedings of the Graphic Design Education Association, Symposium, USA, 1990.

6 Swanson, Gunnar, *Graphic design education as a liberal art: Design and knowledge in the university and the 'real world'*. Design issues Number 1, volume 10, 1994.

7 Wodicka, Ulrich, *Information design: an emerging discipline*, Graphic design journal, Issue 3, Society of Graphic Designers of Canada, 1995.

8 Dauppe, Michele-Ann, *Why we should talk to our neighbours*, Eye Magazine number 16, volume 4, 1995.

9 *Working Party on Typographic Teaching*, (interim Report) Society of Industrial Artists & Designers and the Society of Typographic Designers, London, 1968.

10 Weingart, Wolfgang, 'How can one make Swiss typography?' Octavo 87–4, 1972.

position, rather than those who are deeply involved as, or with, the 'creatives'. The information society is now upon us, and whether it will be 'informationless'[11] or a better world for an easier and democratic access to information, it is theresponsibility of the education sector to initiate a new curriculum, preferably with the help of the professional community of designers. It will not make that creative education leap whilst the art school culture remains the dominant paradigm. Teaching typography to designers to become artists is an elitist indulgence that is ultimately a communications cul-de-sac. It is more important to teach typography to the users of the communications technology now available to everybody.

Perhaps we are headed for a split in the ranks of graphic designers and teachers of the so-called discipline of graphic design. The split has actually happened in that larger world outside the elite world of graphic design. As stated above, desktop publishing and the World Wide Web has spawned a whole new world of communicators who mostly just want to say something to whoever wants to listen, and now have the means to accomplish their goals to a massive audience beyond the wildest dreams of Gutenberg or even McLuhan. As one of my how-to-do-it books bought recently on 'creating cool web pages' says on the cover 'No graphic design experience necessary'. Courses in 'information science and management' in the humanities and information technology areas in the universities are already teaching multimedia and desktop publishing to undergraduates, teaching by teachers who have had no training in graphic design.

The growth of 'information design' as a distinct branch of communications in such organisations as The Communications Research Institute of Australia, The International Institute for Information Design in Austria, the Information Design Association, and *Information Design Journal* (which has been around for nearly twenty years now) demonstrates a body of knowledge and specialisation that is established and capable of embracing the technological advances that have been made for all people in a democratisation and demystification of printing, publishing and design. Richard Saul Wuman (1989) is concerned with 'information anxiety' and refers to himself as an 'information architect' in mapping out the structure of information so that the anxiety is reduced.

The calls for a new kind of graphic design course from Bonsieppe, Buchanan, Margolin, Wodicka, and many others including myself at the ICOGRADA Conference in Lisbon last year, have so far fallen upon deaf ears in the majority of the design courses in the UK, Australia, America and elsewhere. It would appear that the expressive impulse in those quarters is too strong to allow a rational design approach to re-enter the scene, at least for the moment. Indeed, one is made to feel a graphic heretic for voicing such ideas.

My appeal is for a marriage of the two camps, or at least for a *defacto* cohabitation that could bring together visual creativity and the information science that enriches both domains. It's time for a revised Bauhausian concept of art and technology to be entwined, because technology has suddenly outstripped the graphic designer we have nurtured for the past 40 years. The circle has turned fully round again and we have art school mentality in the so-called graphic communications cradle of education.

11 Sless, David, *The Informationless Society*, papers from the seminar Canberra: Communications Research Press 1995.

If the marriage is incompatible, then let's be honest about the differences. Let the graphic design courses (and the professionals that make their living that way) come clean and talk straight about the hero-worship of artistic individual achievement, and not pretend to be communicators except to that cult audience of surfers, teen-agists and those wired into whatever sub-culture of the world to which they wish to belong. Weingart made his position clear in the same polemic as quoted previously when he stated: 'I feel strongly that this new typography must also – and I emphasise also – be the result of a very personal thought-process in design. By that I mean those efforts based upon individuality, imagination and artistic qualities.'

His example could be followed more widely.

1996 **Is 50% creativity enough?** Jonathan Doney
Jonathan Doney is currently Education Officer for the ISTD.

When application was made for membership of the British Typographers Guild the ability of the candidate was measured against known industrial criteria and working practice. At that time, the skill of the submission rested on a difficult copyfitting and layout exercise which was subsequently measured against a proof based upon the candidate's typographic specification. Simply placing the layout over the proof confirmed the accuracy of the submission. The inherent skill was undoubtedly that of the hand, and depth of knowledge was tested via the specification. The original Guild was a pioneer in typographic education, instituting examinations in typography long before the Master Printers started their Gold Medal competition and before the City & Guilds Institute examination in typographic art and science.

As typographic working practice was highlighted in the ensuing years it became apparent that there was much industry criticism of the teaching of typography in colleges. The Society responded to this by starting a student assessment scheme with the intention of raising standards to those that industry required. The pre-requisites were still based on sound working practice that would be found in any industrial situation and work would be assessed against these known criteria. During this time emphasis was still placed on accuracy of specification and layout. Hand skills such as type rendering were vitally important as 'finished layouts' were given to clients as being clear indicators of the final product.

This practice continued for some time as the method of type production changed rather than the presentation methods of the designer. Computer assisted typesetting machinery began to evolve and it was important for the student to be aware of these changes in order that accurate specification could continue. The start of the decline in assessable hand-rendering skills that had prevailed for so long is probably attributable to the introduction of lettering systems such as Letraset and the development of associated products concerned with improving the visual presentations of designs, resulting in another 'hand' skill that had to be defined and catered for. Unfortunately, student skills in Letraset usage were not good and were condemned in favour of a return to hand-rendering, which was still seen as an essential craft within the student typographer's/designer's repertoire. It was not only a valuable skill but also taught the fundamental aspects of letterforms. Improvements in technology have made an impact

only in the last five to six years. The 'Mac Revolution' has caused a swing away from hand skills and those typographic specifications concerning accuracy of copyfitting. The ability of the computer software user to fill a given space with type is well documented. The technological age has added electronics to the old compositor's phrase of 'set to width, leaded to depth'. However, the emergence of computing power in the graphic and typographic design industries does not preclude the student designer from those essential practices found in the work place. The Society has had to change the way it receives and assesses submissions now that computers are commonplace in both industry and education.

The once taught tactile skill of hand-rendering, on which the Society had placed great emphasis, has almost totally disappeared in favour of the computer print-out, which will give consistently better and faster results. However, printers and print-outs differ quite markedly so that the quality of the print-out cannot be taken into consideration. Invariably screen images which boast 'what-you-see-is-what-you-get' often get translated on the print-out as 'what-you-see-is-nothing-like-what-you get.' This is especially true of colour, where the screen and the printer must be balanced or matched so that the transmitted colour from the screen matches the printed colour on the paper. In the first instance, it is taken into account that the student may not have any choice or control over the print quality because the institution has elected to buy a particular piece of equipment, but with regard to the colour-matching this can be achieved with technical support. Placing yourself in the shoes of a client, it is better to see something in the right colour knowing that the type definition will be perfect rather than trying to visualise a colour that is not there.

The sophistication of software now makes it possible for the student to control

Assessors discussing a proposed website design during the 1996 student award scheme assessment. Left to right: Freda Sack, Cliff Pyne, Peter Rea, John Harrison, Julian Lesage, Gus Hunnybun and Geof White.

spacing variables within type to great degree. In the days of the Guild and before phototypesetting became industrially accepted, it was not possible for candidates to kern or move baselines as they can now. As a computer must show you something when it is switched on and a key is pressed, it must also set characters in a line according to predetermined settings known as defaults. Most default settings are poor and candidates are now asked to specify all spacing variables in their typographic specification. This encourages them to critically analyse the copy they are working with, placing themselves in the position of the reader.

Through all this, the creative process is still looked upon as being the most important. Students now develop inexorable links with computers and rush to them as soon as they are faced with any design problem. The exploration of ideas and the development of creative thinking, including risk taking where necessary, can only be judged against some form of visible evidence. The rough, the thumbnail, the layout, the visual and other reference material show how problems have been approached and resolved.

Essentially, greater emphasis, more than 50% in fact, is being placed on the creative solution, its form, its function and its suitability to the target audience.

Computing power has led to easy access to a proliferation of styles which rarely student designers absorb and reproduce sometimes inappropriately or non-critically into everything they propose. There is an argument which says that the computer provides you with a creative medium only limited by your imagination. But this is nothing new, as the imagination of a designer has always been the limit no matter what technology was employed at that time. It is not enough to produce work simply because the software enables you to do so as this is the point where you have lost control of the task. There should be considerable evidence of thought, planning and preparation prior to allowing the keyboard and screen to finalise the process. Unfortunately many submissions to the Assessment Scheme hide behind a facade which outwardly looks superb but shows little depth when analysed.

Presentation skills have been redefined from the hand-rendering elements to that of organisation and visual presentation commensurate with the needs of industry. Specific typographic analysis is important to avoid unwanted irregularities and defaults. With the erosion of typesetting trade unions over the last twenty years, and the decline in the numbers of specialist compositors who instinctively knew when something was wrong, more reliance is being placed upon the typographer/designer to ensure that all the data they supply on disk for production is fully accurate. The staged process of design, layout, typesetting, artwork, film, plate, proof, print has been reduced to design, disk, plate, print, giving less opportunity to identify any errors.

As a professional body, the Society has, and must maintain, a watchful eye on the Assessment Scheme's educational content and its industrial relevance. The Scheme has an international reputation for the standard it maintains and industry recognises it as an exemplar of quality. There has been change, and there will continue to be changes in working practice and technical innovations together with shifts in trends and culture. They must all be recognised so that the educational policy of the Society matches the needs of both the student and their future employer.

1998 **From now on everything will (continue to) change** David Jury

The problems currently faced by design lecturers in higher education arise from the fact that successive governments have imposed mass accessibility upon a system whose internal values remain élitist.

Mass accessibility has resulted in increased student numbers – a good thing if it were not accompanied by severe financial cuts resulting in almost halving the number of hours students are taught, and hitting hardest, but by no means exclusively, the part-time lecturer input. It naturally follows that the 'élitist' values, by which I mean lecturers simply being able to talk to individual students, are under severe strain. Those of us involved in the education process would like to maintain this close contact with students – nurturing individual lines of enquiry and offering appropriate technical support – and, surprisingly, so do the consecutive governments who have imposed mass accessibility.

In fact, everyone; students, parents and government, want the same thing from higher education, and nowhere is this better illustrated than in the propectuses which college marketing departments are distributing at this time of year. In these you will find statements constantly referring to 'family' and 'community' and photographs portraying a similar, benevolent relationship between lecturers and students. Whilst colleges understand the consequences of mass access to higher education currently experienced by students, they also recognise that what, in fact, everyone *really* wants is the opposite, and so continue to sell the close contact and individual attention experienced by previous generations of design students. This puts lecturers in an impossible position. As UK colleges have been swept up into the competitive and entrepreneurial environment, marketing has become a self-legitimising force which runs dangerously close to undermining the fundamental purposes of education. Litigation is already a problem, especially since colleges do not have the funds either to defend themselves or to pay costs and/or damages, and it will get worse as students, not unreasonably, compare what has been promised with the reality they experience.

What is *the reality?* Most courses now consist of approximately eighteen 'taught' hours per week, although final year students often receive less, usually fifteen hours.[1] Of these fifteen, eight hours might be studio-based, that is, time spent on current design projects with a lecturer present. Apart from any group discussion about work in hand,

1 The first course I taught on – an Ordinary National Diploma (OND) course in graphic design in 1980, was allocated 32 hours per week, and included two evening classes.

or if a lecture or demonstration is considered necessary, teaching will normally be
in tutorial form. With an average size group of thirty-five students this works out at
about fifteen minutes with each student, or a popular alternative is to work in groups
of four or five to increase student / lecturer contact. Another five hours will be in a
specialist workshop, for graphic design students this usually means the computer suite.
This period is 'tutor supported' but is, essentially, to provide the third year students with
priority access to specialist equipment. Obviously there are not enough computers for
every graphics student, in fact there will probably not even be enough for all of one
year-group. Finally, two hours for complementary studies, usually delivered as a
programme of lectures to three or four specialist groups at a time ensuring the lecture-
theatre is filled to capacity.

Fifteen hours is two and a half days of standard college time. The paucity of tutor
contact will be justified to students as 'time to reflect' or to encourage 'self-manage-
ment skills'. Not surprisingly, those students who can afford it will buy their own computer and work at home on all days except studio and complementary studies time. It
is not unusual for students to arrive in time for a tutorial and then immediately disappear once the session is finished. Since 'hot-desking' was introduced, students do not
have their own work-space any more and so there is no incentive to look upon the
studio as their working base. In fact, the studio is now more like a class-room; as one
year group leaves, another comes in and the limited access to the computer suite, and
the pre-booking system for machines with specific facilities makes it difficult to justify
spending money to get into college if a student has a computer at home. On top of
this, for most students, part-time 'casual' work is now an essential part of student life
and often makes attendance outside their nominated fifteen hours (perhaps for guest
lectures, special meetings or group trips to exhibitions and to professional contacts)
impossible for many.

In the early 1990's government funding for higher education in the UK was not
ungenerous by international standards. Such comparisons are always problematic but
figures produced by the DES in 1991 showed that UK higher education expenditure fell
into the middle range of the thirteen industrialised countries which were compared.
However, a more detailed look at the figures reveal that whilst the UK had the *highest*
expenditure on student support and welfare, (ie student maintenance grants) it had
the *lowest* expenditure per 'qualifier'– that is: lecturers, technicians, support staff,
buildings, equipment, libraries etc. Since these figures were published, student enrolments have increased by more than 40% and yet support (qualifier) costs have continued to be *cut* yearly. Perhaps, in an attempt to redress the balance, UK governments in
the last three years have also made substantial (real) cuts to the student maintenance
grant of 10% per annum and the current Labour government has stated that it will
abolish the student maintenance grant completely. This year, the government also
introduced the policy requiring all higher education students to pay £1,000 towards
the fees for each year of study. This is means-tested but there is no additional 'student
bank-loan' provision.

There has not been a significant drop in the number of applicants to higher education

courses since the government introduced student payment of fees. The hurried introduction was unimaginative and crude but, in time, parents will learn to save for their
children's education just as they do in most other countries. So, should we be concerned
that we have lost what 'most other countries' have envied for so long? Since the 1960's,
going on to higher education, has been, at least financially, an easy, almost natural
progression. It was simply a matter of ability. The ethos was one of fairness and social
equality. In the 1990's however, the competitive market for students, the development
of consumerism, of students' awareness of themselves as 'purchasers' of higher education, and of their value to university budgets, are beginning to encourage demands for
'value for money' from students. But not, or so it seems, from the design industry which
higher education serves.

David Pocknell, currently Chairman of one of the judging panels for the RSA Student
Design Awards, and a former Director of the CSD, is angry at what he has seen
happening to design education. He is particularly concerned about the lack of
industrial contact now that part-time lecturers virtually no longer exist, 'Courses
are in danger of becoming ever more immersed in academia, and as the paperwork
to evidence the mechanics of courses increases, it is hard to see where the few
remaining full-time lecturers, having to cope with huge increases in students, can
find the time to keep in touch with what is happening outside education. I have
heard judges at the RSA Student Bursaries exclaim, "Where are the tutors? Who
is leading these students?"'.

He is also in no doubt that standards have dropped. Course-leaders would agree
but hesitate to make their opinions public for fear that it might stigmatise their own
course and damage the future prospects of their students. But it is a fact that whilst
the best students remain as good as ever (and of course, these are the ones that win
the prizes and generate praiseworthy PR copy for higher education) course-leaders are
aware that the *overall* standards are being forced down. It is the average and below
average students – the very students courses are being forced to recruit in higher
numbers in order to hit specified (increased) targets – who need more attention and
encouragement and who are hardest hit as a result of government policies.

Rod Springett, of Springett Associates, has been closely associated with a number
of colleges as external assessor and advisor and is also a member of the RSA's Design
Advisory Group. He describes 'design' as a 'people' business – an intellectual process;
part thinking and part doing, but most importantly, it is a process that can not be done
in isolation. 'Certainly, a by-product of current policies is that students are not only
losing contact with their tutors but also with their fellow students. People influence
people. In fact, course structure is an irrelevance when compared to the people who
run it and take part in it. Every designer working today can think back to a tutor who
gave a them an important lead, but these days tutors are finding it increasingly difficult
to function at all as educators. It appears to me that their job has become a mixture of
administration and councelling'.

So why isn't the RSA or the CSD protesting about this situation? Well, the fact
is, the government has been steering a wide berth of the industry-bodies knowing

full well such organisations could not support their policies. Brian Limbrey, who was Director of the CSD when the Deering Report was being formulated, drafted a submission for Deering which described the current state of design education and outlined its needs for the future. He told me that his concerns at the time were, '…that whilst teaching standards across the country might be variable, there was no doubt that design education at HE level had an excellent track record, world-class in fact. But education needs to keep abreast of developments in industry and I was concerned that the particular needs of individual subject areas, such as design, were being eroded. I wanted the autonomy of design education to remain intact.' Unfortunately, the remit given to Deering was to focus on the wider issues of finance and structure, and so the CSD's submission, which, of course, had not been invited in the first place, was ignored.

With incorporation (independent status) came the green light for all colleges to set up their own HE courses. Of course, there are quality controls to be satisfied and adhered to, but in my own experience of being on validation panels, whilst assurances have been sought as to academic rigour and course management, the course team's general knowledge, understanding and personal experience of design and genuine contact with the professional design industry appears to be less of a priority. More than a hundred additional HE courses in graphic design have been set up throughout the UK, but whilst the number of students attending foundation and advanced GNVQ courses has also increased, it certainly has not kept pace with the huge increase in places available at HE level. Despite graphic design and graphic media courses being among the most popular specialist subjects, there can be very few FE 'graphics' students left without an offer of a place by the beginning of the academic year.

In the circumstances, there are many in education who are convinced that educational institutions have been building courses to make money rather that to serve either a local or national need (inevitable when a free-market philosophy is applied to education). As the influence of executive-class administrators grows, it appears to lecturers, who are expected to deliver the courses as promised, that their rôle has become considerably more subservient and the particular needs of their specialist area of study often ignored. In fact, many believe that the result of this preference for executive hierarchy has led to the end of education-based decision-making, few lecturers now regard their colleges or universities as being education-led any more.

The last major expansion of higher education was in the sixties. Then, administrators had influence but not power. Their aim was to maintain the delicate balance of being responsive to local (college and community) needs but responsible to a local or regional authority to balance the books. Heads of departments held a great deal of power because they were deemed suitably close to the lecturing staff and the students, often with teaching duties built into their timetable, yet also had a direct route to the highest administrative levels. The emphasis of administration was then on support of academic staff. However, in the nineties, this situation has been turned on its head. The unprecedented demand for data by government bodies has led to the creation of bureaucracies

within universities who, with control of information and its distribution, have delusions of competence along with the undoubted power they now wield, changing the managerial style from supportive/consensual to tactical/combative.

New ideas, such as students paying supplementary fees in order to gain access to privatised, specified levels of provision within libraries, computer facilities, even careers and counselling services, have been aired, but so far with little response from potential providers. Perhaps administrative services could also be privatised and contracts developed for services such as finance, legal advice, 'customer' analysis, market research etc. To anyone teaching in higher education, there would be nothing fantastic about any of these suggestions, indeed we already have supermarket elements reflected in prospectuses as catalogues, home delivery in distance learning, consumer guides and tele-sales. If the entrepreneurial university can do better than its ivory-towered predecessor in exploiting the potential for synergy in higher education then I am all in favour. Indeed, if students contributing to the payment of their fees meant a stop to further cuts in the quality of the product they are 'buying' perhaps they would also be in favour. However, some of those in positions of power have forgotten what we are all in education for, and as a result, students, despite paying a high price for their courses, are beginning to feel distinctly irrelevant.

What are the dangers of current government policies regarding higher education? The effects of cutting student support and the introduction of payment of fees, certainly in the short-term, will be that full-time enrolments will fall, the hardest hit being mature students seeking part-time access. Whilst a few art colleges will be able to charge significant 'top-up' fees, generating income which will create a premier league of colleges for the few students who can afford it, the majority of colleges, particularly if government view the payment of fees by students as an opportunity to cut yet more expenditure to higher education, will find themselves in a further downward spiral of resources, narrower student intake; increasingly local, desperately trying to maintain quality, yet lacking the capacity or resources to innovate. They will be compared, unfairly and unfavourably, with the performance of the more expensive and truly (in the financial sense) élitist colleges. Opportunities for full-time higher education away from home will be restricted to those students with parents in the upper income groups. This is already happening as a result of the cuts to student maintenance grants, and the trend has been exacerbated by the introduction of higher education on a fee-paying basis. It follows that HE courses will be encouraged to offer programmes of study that are more generalist in nature in order to cater for an essentially local student intake. More specialist design courses, such as typography, which need to recruit nationally, will find it progressively more difficult to find sufficient students of the right calibre, or indeed, of any calibre at all!

If the previous ten years have been about the advent of mass higher education in quantitative terms, the prime concern of the next ten years must be about coming to terms with the qualitative consequences. It is easy to say that, on the whole, design education has not failed. Yet. That our commitment to intellectual rigour, technical dexterity, and a refusal to train professional 'quick-fix' fodder has not been lost. And

yet, everyone admits, at least in private, that general standards are plummeting. But, with one or two notable exceptions, there appears to be little concern from either government or industry leaving design course teams feeling distinctly isolated and certainly vulnerable to still further 'efficiency' measures. However, support might yet come from a source that has, until now, been remarkably placid during this dramatic period of change.

In the last ten years, power has moved away from the lecturers and their departmental heads and towards the administrators. Now, with the government's introduction of fee-paying students there has been another fundamental shift of power. There has been little effect so far, just a few isolated examples of litigation, low rumblings in the student refectories. However, in Paris, during the sixties, violent protests were ignited because tuition-paying students could not see their tutors often enough, could not attend lectures due to lack of space, and could not use essential equipment because there was insufficient access and technical support. This air of revolt also took hold in the UK, more specifically at Hornsey, Guildford and Brighton Colleges of Art, but these actions never became as intense as those witnessed in Paris. And why should they? The sixties were a time of comparatively generous funding for higher education in the UK. This has now drastically changed. Students have been remarkably indifferent to the state of higher education during this recent period of intense cuts. Perhaps now, having to pay for what they receive will awaken them from their stupor.

Key References:

International Statistical Comparisons in Higher Education: Working report. DES, 1991.

Thinking Ahead: Ensuring the expansion of higher education into the 21st century. CBI, 1994.

The Changing University. Edited by Tom Schuller. Open University Press, 1996.

2000 **Designing the real world** Alan Robertson

At a mundane level, what practitioners usually mean by the 'real' of the 'real world' is money. Time is money and there isn't any of it for 'pussyfooting around', for empty talk, for fancy idealism. 'A job in industry', 'making a living', or paying off a student loan or a mortgage – these are real, and are a part of the 'real world'. In the 'real world' your ideals will turn to custard before the might of money and even you, the original talent, the precocious rebel, the cool designer, will be corrupted. Dollar ranks big time, and no-one it seems, can stand up to it. Yet there must be more; surely there must be 'a real' meaning for the 'real world' which is at once representative of something deeper, and yet also accommodates the glib certainty of economic determinism. If one view of the 'real world' is that it is the place where 'reality' is the black and red of profit and loss, then such an unbalanced and limited vision itself represents an implicit failure of the dominant reductionist outlook of the past two hundred years. Life, even in the real world, can not be that simple. In fact, life is so complex that any attempt at reductionism must be viewed with the suspicion that it actually serves more as a tool for conceal-ment and denial than of understanding.

Yet typographic design exists to reduce the complexity of visual communication into accessibility, by way of simplicity; to eliminate confusion and visual 'noise' from the focused clarity of intent. The quality of that simplicity is deceptive. Not only does the simplicity conceal the effort and process-complexity of research, conceptualisation, synthesis and realisation, but it reduces all the complexity of the cultural landscape of the every-day (which it plunders for the purpose) down to a self-serving, and instru-mentally simplistic, 'message'. This process, while it serves at once to constitute meaning for designers as practice, also purports to deliver meaning (albeit as the graphic hegemony of the commonplace) to an 'audience' in the 'real world'.

Hitherto the 'real world' was implied to be where self-interest dominates because 'survival' depends on it. In the 'real world' (of commerce, business, self-interest) it was suggested that there is no room for ideals, for ethics. In the 'real world' there is no room for anything except the relentlessly amoral drive towards profit. This, apparently, is why the 'real world' is so tough. An unmitigated, mono-directional drive to self-interest is a hard row to hoe. It's risky in the real world because you might 'lose your shirt' unless you're 'realistic', 'pragmatic' and 'hard-nosed'; unless, in other words, you

take more than you give, on a 'me-first' basis. This is curiously narrow and conveniently indulgent because one critical paradox of 'reality' is that, as a social construct, it is contingent on other-interest as much as self-interest. Relationship is all. But admittedly it is tough working at relationships. It is difficult integrating your needs and wants (ambition and greed) with the needs and wants of others. It is a struggle reconciling with others the ambiguity, uncertainty and indeterminacy of 'real world' contradiction and confusion. So it follows that if the real world is contingent upon relationship, then self-interest will seem an easier option over the short-term. A handy ideology indeed!

Praxis means practising critically and responsibly within the public sphere. The personal process of designing involves all the conceptual, reflexive, visual, and technical activities of doing, making, and knowing. In the public sphere however (and all visual design performs in the public sphere) praxis involves others. Praxis may not even exist without others for it is fundamentally exoteric, other-seeking, dialogic. Praxis is the transformation of practice into a more responsible form of cultural production. Through their capacity to reflect on their actions within and upon the public sphere, and through the purposefulness of their reason, intellectual professionals like designers become free to intervene in their own reality. Design praxis means making itself accountable to others in the public sphere. But is this place called the public sphere the same place as the 'real world'?

The 'real world' is not just private, it is public too, and as such can not be a place governed by self-interest. Rather the public sphere is where 'disinterest' must be exercised with critical responsibility for the good of all. 'Disinterest' is not lack of interest, or indifference, or apathy. 'Disinterest' means altruism, an absence of self-interest, the impartiality by which one is not influenced by one's own advantage.

If we remember Victor Papanek's version of the 'real world' in *Design for the Real World*, it was diametrically different from what we have described above. We have here an interesting contradiction. The implicit meaning of the phrase 'real world' seems to have shifted from a place where real (ordinary, poor, non-elitist) people live, to a place where money, patronage and self-interest govern everything. In his seminal book, Papanek points out the iniquities of useless, low-quality, unsafe, expensive design as it impacts on society. For him, most designers, especially graphic designers, were more committed to designing for other designers than for ordinary people (the 'audience').

The real world is poor, uninformed, exploited, disadvantaged, unwired, and home to five of the six billion inhabitants of spaceship earth. Thus, only 5% of the world's population own a phone, only 4% a personal computer, and only 1% are connected to the Internet. The real world then, is about six times larger than the 'real world' of design practitioners. The latter 'world' is an almost wholly-owned corporatist subsidiary, concerned more with squeezing maximum profit out of its one billion over-consumers by selling them things they don't need, can't afford, and whose globalised manufacture and branding further damage both the natural and cultural environments on which the majority of planetary citizens, who are not able to 'participate', depend for their sustenance. And this money rollercoaster is called 'success'! It seems that the real world is very badly designed indeed.

Clearly, there is plenty of opportunity for design praxis in the real world. Clearly, there is an enormous 'market' for the design of communication ecology, and an emancipatory vision of social change. In fact, it would seem that the real world not only needs design praxis, but itself needs designing from the garden up! But Papanek's critique of graphic design focuses on the social products of design, the social rôle of designers, not on the processes of designing. He was quite correct to criticise 'the profession' because the profession pursues profit with every bit as much single-minded zeal as the next business-person. The profession is reluctant to engage in real world praxis, to examine critically its central rôle in the perpetuation of an ideology of corporatist domination and consumerism which is antithetical to democracy and planetary life. But, notwithstanding that, surely the process and practice of designing is a fundamental human activity worth preserving, even if the 'profession' as it stands is not. This is why I believe more in the real world of design education than the unreal world of professional design. It is way past time for the design profession to get real. Design might well be too important to leave to the 'professionals'.

The new Monotype department
of the Oxford University Press,
built 1925. *TypoGraphic* 52.
Photograph courtesy of the
OUP archive.

History

1971/2 **Facts concerning the origin of the STD** Vincent Steer

Vincent Steer was a founder member of the ISTD (originally called The Typographers Guild.
In 1953 the Society changed it's name to Society of Typographic Designers and, in 2000, this
was modified to International Society of Typographic Designers.) This text originally appeared
on the letters page of *TypoGraphic* 2.

Having received my copy of the STD's new magazine *Typographic* I am writing to inform
you of the true facts concerning the origin of the STD before they are 'Lost in the
Shadows of the Past'.

My interest in typography began in 1911 when I joined the Artistic Typography
classes held at the Camberwell School of Arts and Crafts. While there I designed and
set the title page for the school's year book. Through one of the teachers I obtained
specimen copies of the *American Printer* and the *Inland Printer* where I first saw
mention of the typographer. I printed myself a business card where I described myself
as an Advertising Typographer. In the Patents Office library in Holborn I read the
back numbers of the *Inland Printer* where there was published a study course in
Advertising. I copied this out word for word and studied it diligently. Then I went to
sea as a ship's printer for about five years which resulted in 39 round trips between
Liverpool and New York. In 1914 at a kiosk in West 23rd Street I purchased a copy of
the *Inland Printer*. When I opened it I found that they had reproduced my title page
and they described the *Camberwell Year Book* as an example of the finest printing
ever to come out of England.

After serving in the army, I emigrated to Canada and, having joined the Toronto
branch of the International Typographic Union, obtained a job in the advertising
department of the *Monetary Times*, where I had to set up advertisements in accordance
with the layouts supplied by New York advertising agencies.

When I returned to England, I rejoined the Camberwell School where I first met
Stanley Hayter who had started a class in Typographical Layout which I joined. Then
I obtained a post at Stephenson Blake's where I was engaged in producing the firm's
mammoth type specimen book for which I wrote the imaginary copy, prepared my own
layouts and set the type. After two and a half years on this project I obtained a post
as copywriter with Caribonum Limited and when I had exhausted the subject of typewriter ribbons and carbon paper I joined Saward Baker where the typographers were

called 'copy clerks'. After six months I left and went to work at Spottiswoode Ballantyne's where Stanley Hayter and Wilson Philip were employed as typographers. Actually I took Wilson Philip's place, for he had just left. One of the jobs we hated there was modifying the agency layouts which we called 'soleing and heeling'. I submitted an article to the *Advertiser's Weekly* entitled 'Let the Copywriter Stick to His Job', which they published. It foretold the coming of the typographer. I suggested to Hayter that we ought to form a society where the candidates would have to pass a rigid test in layout design and technical proficiency and he gave me the names of Wilson Philip and Alfred Vernon as possible members. I wrote to them and seven of us met at the Sicilian Restaurant in Holborn, and the original Guild was formed.

Actually, we could only find five practising typographers: myself, Hayter, Philip, Vernon and Hoath. Hayter brought along two of his students Arnold Jones and Edward Burrett, to make up the magic number of seven, inspired by the original Council of Seven, presided over by the Doge of Venice. When Charles Hoath died his place was taken by F G A Scott who did invaluable work as Secretary during the formative years of the original Guild. His name seems to have been forgotten. He should have been made a Fellow, but he retired from the COI when the Guild held its reunion in 1945. In 1934,

(below) The original layout.

(facing page) The first proof. Both from Printing Design and Layout by Vincent Steer 1934.

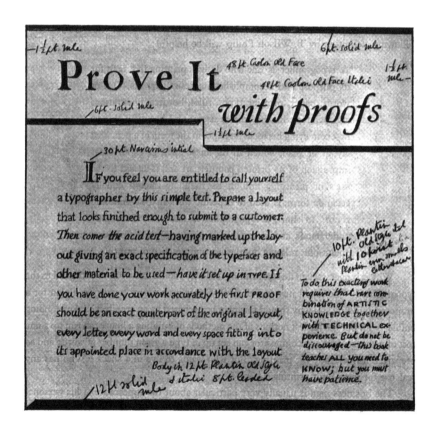

when my book was published I gave Wilson Philip's definition of a typographical layout but made no mention of my own name as founder of the BTG. Six thousand copies
of my book were sold before the outbreak of World War Two. When the second edition was published in 1945 I included the name and address of the Secretary of the
Society and in that year we had 700 applications for membership, but only 12 could
pass the test. Altogether in the years from 1934 to 1958, when my book went out of
print 18,000 copies were sold and it must have played a big part in arousing interest
in typography. It became known as the 'Typographer's Bible', due no doubt to its black
cover. In a review the *Inland Printer* called it 'A Complete Study Course in Typography',
and Sir Francis Meynell said that it was a better book than the one that he wrote.

   I was the first President of the BTG and when the Guild held its reunion I was elected
President for the second time, but the council made a new rule, the President was to
serve for one year only. The rule was rescinded at the next AGM and Caspar Mitchell
served for several years, I was never asked to serve again. When the name of the Guild
was changed to the Society of Typographic Designers, I reminded the Council that when
we originally discussed a name my suggestion was the Society of Typographers, but
we were overruled by Wilson Philip who fancied the British Typographers Guild after

Prove It
with proofs

IF you feel you are entitled to call yourself
a typographer, try this simple test. Prepare a layout
that looks finished enough to submit to a customer.
Then comes the acid test—having marked up the layout, giving an exact specification of the typefaces and
other material to be used—*have it set up in* TYPE. If
you have done your work accurately the first PROOF
should be an exact counterpart of the original layout,
every letter, every word and every space fitting into
its appointed place in accordance with the layout.

*To do this exacting work
requires that rare com-
bination of* ARTISTIC
KNOWLEDGE *together
with* TECHNICAL *ex-
perience. But do not be
discouraged — this book
teaches* ALL *you need to
* KNOW; *but you must
have patience.*

the old Guilds of the Middle Ages. The members were very fickle at that time. On one occasion when Mrs Beatrice Warde was due to address the Society, before she came they voted to exclude any member who could not pass the test, but after she had addressed them they reversed their previous decision, and the Society was opened to Graphic Designers. I was unable to attend the meetings regularly about that time, for I had been very busy on the second and third editions of my book and also I was admitted to hospital with a duodenal ulcer where Wilson Philip and Stanley Hayter came to visit me.

In 1960, on my 72nd birthday, the STD held its exhibition. I came along but could find none of my work on show, although I had submitted a batch of specimens. I remarked on this fact to Sir Francis Meynell, then President. He said to me, '…you ought to have opened the exhibition'. The amusing thing was that all the exhibits were from members of the Council, and they were all of a very bookish nature. There is no doubt that Wilson Philip did a great deal of invaluable work for the Society but on one occasion he offended the Master Printer's Association by telling them the truth. It was the occasion of a lecture delivered at St Bride's Institute. He compared the modern master printer with the early master printers, who were their own publishers and who employed university professor's to read their proofs. The printer, he said, had fallen from his high estate. I was sitting next to one master printer, who said to me 'If that 'man was in my employ I'd give him the sack'. Wilson Philip was forthright where as, in fact, you have to be diplomatic. It was one of three lectures. Hayter gave the first, entitled 'Printing begins with the Pencil'. The second was given by me, the title being The Seven Principles of Design'. It was very well received and I was invited by the Eastbourne Master Printers Association to repeat the lecture. But they were a little soured by Wilson Philip's address and started their own Gold Medal competition.

I am now in my eightieth year and my eyesight is not what it was. But I may be the only person alive who knows the true story of the forming of the STD.

1986 **The formative years of Dutch graphic design** Pieter Brattinga

Cleanliness is next to beautiful

Cleanliness is almost a proverbial Dutch virtue. So deeply rooted is it in the cultural heritage that in the Dutch language before 1930 there exists but one word (schoon) to define both notions of 'clean' and 'beautiful'.

   In a famous essay on De Stijl, Hans Jaffe quotes a Dutch philosopher, Schoenmaker: 'It may be suggested that these similar trends which we have tried to describe, in Calvinism and in De Stijl, are not due to incidental parallelism, but to the fact that Calvinism is part of the spiritual heritage of every Dutchman and makes its influence felt even in spheres which are not closely related to theology and even in persons who have no longer have any ties with the Church or with the Protestant community in their practical life'.

Design and advertising

The Dutch were rather slow in recognising the revolutionary new values which were being accepted in the advanced centres of the world. Looking back at a time of tremendous change in political, spiritual, artistic and commercial values shortly after the end of the First World War, The Netherlands could, for instance, hardly accept a new 'sinful' medium called advertising or the idea that a self-respecting artist could put his talent on view for a large public instead of a reputable gallery. A situation which is still reflected in contemporary Dutch relations between design and advertising. In The Netherlands one does not find one society or association which has members working in both advertising and graphic design. There is no link nor any federation between the graphic design association GVN and the Art Directors' Club Nederland. A situation which is rather ridiculous, since the Art Directors' Club issues its art directors' annual every year but receives no support from authorities and has no official representative on any of the numerous Dutch committees on design or the arts sponsored by the ministry of culture.

Art versus design

This situation has been in existence in The Netherlands since the beginnings of the century. In 1905, R N Roland Holst, an important artist of that time, attacked a poster

printed for a Delft firm of salad oil manufacturers. The respected Dutch painter Breitner had given permission to use one of his paintings for a poster showing two cart-horses on a building site. The painting had been carefully reproduced in hand coloured lithography and an imitation picture frame had been drawn around it containing an advertising text. Roland Holst criticised the fact that the trade lithographers had been forced to imitate a painting. Instead of the formative years of Dutch graphic design being allowed to make an original print, they had been set to copy the broad strokes of the brush; this was seen as a betrayal of artistic principles.

In 1917 a discussion took place between Roland Holst and Albert Hahn, an important socialist and political cartoonist. The occasion was an exhibition in the Amsterdam Stedelijk Museum on the theme of art in advertising. Roland Holst published his thoughts in a trade paper: 'There are two things an advertisement can be. It can either be a simple piece of information or it can be a shout… there is no need to shout out the truth because it can be stated quietly without having to be over-emphasized'. This was followed by a plea for craftsmanship, pure and simple, in which he put forward the need for designers to draw the designs straight onto the lithographic stone. Albert Hahn retaliated; 'Art in advertising is a type of art seen by everybody, and one whose very nature enables it to influence even those people who care little for art and who, as a rule, would never consider entering an art gallery or an exhibition. It is street art, pure and simple, and, as such, an out and out popular art'.

Later, in a political article, he stated: 'We live, unfortunately, in capitalistic circumstances still, our world is still one of competition. Under the social conditions in which we live, things are not produced in order to satisfy human needs, but on the contrary, in a manner that is utterly anarchistic'.

Hahn continued with an examination of the task of advertisements under such a system of production and arrived at the question: 'Why not a shout, if that is what is needed? If the artist is a genuine one, even his shouting is beautiful… according to what he is asked to do… the artist will 'shout' or make his point emphatically in some other way. In doing so he will usually make use of strong contrasting colours and simple shades since these make the most immediate appeal'.

'De Stijl' and 'Wendingen'

Theo van Doesburg, the editor of the periodical *De Stijl*, wrote in its first issue of October 1917 that the journal intended to direct itself against current fashion, as he saw it manifested in the work of the organic architect H P Berlage 'archaistic confusion and the "modern Baroque"'.

Also in 1917, another magazine was published in Holland. Called *Wendingen*, it was founded on the initiative of architect H Th Wijdeveld for the society 'Architectura and Amicitia' in Amsterdam. The design and content of the magazine will later also be classified as Amsterdam Expressionism. Together with *De Stijl, Wendingen* gives a clear reflection of the aims of Dutch design of that time. *De Stijl*, on one hand, with a progressive, rather than revolutionary attitude in architecture and design, and *Wendingen* on the other hand, with a plea for decoration through material in building or in design.

I contend that this division which sometimes overflows into other design areas still exists today.

Graphics for political movements

Because of the new social awareness and the growing power of labour unions, a tremendous amount of design was produced for political themes. Labour unions were divided into Catholic, a Protestant and a general union. Albert Hahn, for instance, designed his political cartoons and posters for the Social Democratic Workers Party and for its affiliated union only.

Dr J F van Royen

Influenced by the developments in Great Britain and especially the writings by William Morris, some Dutch artists specialised in typography, as they began to realise that type rather than decoration was paramount in a book. Again one sees a purifying influence in a sector of the arts.

In 1910, a number of young poets founded a private press called 'De Zilverdistel' and they were later joined by Dr J F van Royen, a civil servant of the PTT, The Netherlands Post and Telegraph office. Between 1912 and 1913, van Royen published a number of significant articles. Such as one about bad design in governmental printed matter. He wrote, 'The printed material for the government is ugly, ugly, ugly, in other words three times ugly in typeform, typesetting and in paper'. In 1917 van Royen becomes general secretary of the PTT. Being responsible only to the director general of the PTT, he was in a position to introduce designers to shape and design the postal vehicles, signs, letter covers, rubber stamps, lamps and so on. He had the courage to commission a number of designers to create items for the PTT, even when their way of designing was not according to his personal preference. It was van Royen who commissioned Piet Zwart to produce designs which still have a great influence on graphic design internationally.

Type and typographic design

Around 1912, a young designer called S H de Roos had joined the Typefoundry Amsterdam and designed a new typeface called *Hollandsche Mediaeval*, [see page 290] a development similar to the change in architectural design from neo-classical styles to 'honest' designs. Also at this time, the type-designer Jan van Krimpen was working for a typefoundry. In 1923 he joined the printing and publishing house, Joh Enschedé, as a typographic designer, and worked at producing books which were soundly constructed and worth reading. His principle was that all deliberate attempts at achieving typographic beauty were to be shunned since they only succeeded in diverting the reader's attention from the text on which it should be focussed. Here was further direction into a purer presentation of contents, rather than form.

Both De Roos and van Krimpen, were a great influence on the design of Dutch books before 1940. Interestingly, De Roos was very clearly an artist with strong social feelings which resulted in his membership of The Netherlands social democratic party. De Roos and his colleagues were aiming for a just, peaceful and happy society filled with

ABCDEFG
HIJKLMN
OPQRSTU
VWXYZ
abcdefghij
klmnopqrs
tuvwxyz!?
1234567890

beautiful things and right thinking. Van Krimpen, on the other hand, was an intellectual, with an aristocratic background, who found his satisfaction when the right kind of text was produced in a neat manner so that it could be read by civilised people.

Piet Zwart

Graphic designers like Schuitema, Huszar and Zwart were, through their work and philosophy, closely related to the so-called functional architects.

Piet Zwart writes about postage stamps (commissioned by van Royen) 'l think that by stating the elements which played a rôle in the design of a stamp, I made clear that the primary goal of the design was not the designing of a so-called beautiful stamp; the aim was to design a stamp by using the, for our time, characteristic technical possibilities, composed in a reasonable manner with functional elements and post office use in mind'.

Piet Zwart designed furniture, interiors and textile design. When he had moved from northern Holland to a suburb of The Hague, he became a neighbour of Huszar and the architect Jan Wils. Since they had both been involved with *De Stijl* it was a natural request that Piet Zwart was asked to join the group around *De Stijl*. He was reluctant to join however, and protested against the assumption that he had something to do with the group. He was a more practical solver of form problems than the editor of *De Stijl* magazine Van Doesburg, who, as a person, was merely tolerated by Zwart. In 1919, Piet Zwart became assistant to Jan Wils and thus joined the architectural profession. After two years, Zwart became a senior draftsman with Berlage. This lasted until 1927 and Zwart worked, among other projects, on the new plans for The Haag's Gemeente-museum and the Christian Science Church. At the same time, either through the office of Berlage, or on his own, Zwart designed new crockery, lamp-posts, benches and interiors. Zwart's first typographic composition was made towards the end of 1921, and his major work in typography began in the spring of 1923 when he started working for the Nederlandse Kabelfabriek. Much later, in 1970, he would write about these designs: '…and then I figured it out with the young man during lunch-hour how we would realise my little sketch. I really had to learn the profession of typographic arrangements. I did not know any of the terminology, I did not know anything about the methods, I did not even know what upper and lower case was'.

The choice of typeface, was, of course, dependent on what the printer had in his cases. During that period, only among the most progressive designers was there any tendency to do away with superficial decoration and use, for example, sans serif faces as type-faces. In 1923 Zwart learned how to make photograms and photography and photo-grams were used in his work for the Nederlandse Kabelfabriek and other projects.

Through the force of his personality Zwart became a very strong and able designer. To design as Zwart did, was only possible if one was strong minded since the commu-nity at large did not accept these new brutal and harsh designs and his work did not necessarily find favour with his contemporary designers.

(facing page) *Hollandsche Mediaeval* typeface designed by S H de Roos.

H N Werkman

A completely different creator with typography was H N Werkman, a printer in Groningen, a town in the extreme north of The Netherlands.

In 1908, Werkman had started his own printing works in Groningen but had to dismiss his workers in 1923 after a series of financial set-backs. In the same year he published a magazine and started to work on prints involving the type and technology of his printing company. Due to poor business results, Werkman had reduced his printing work even further by 1927, and in the face of financial set back concentrated on his print series. By the end of the thirties, however, an exhibition of Werkman's work had been arranged in Amsterdam and in 1940 he began a series called De Blauwe Schuit (The Blue Barge) which incites the readers to put up a spiritual resistance against the Occupation. Recognition came to him during the war but in 1945 Werkman, probably under suspicion of having printed illegal matter, was arrested by the Occupation forces in Groningen and was shot.

The main body of work by Werkman was made with the ink-roller as well as with the help of typographic material and through means of painting paper with the hand-roller while putting a cut stencil between the roller and the blank paper.

The promise of the post war-period

One of the most notable graphic designers of the post-war years, W Sandberg, had

(below left) W Sandberg. Poster for an exhibition of posters, 1960.

(below right) Piet Zwart. Advertisement for the post office.

been, during the war, a member of the Resistance group which had blown up the citizen's registration of Amsterdam. He had gone into hiding and produced during that time notable typographical experiments. Another post-war designer of German Jewish origin, Otto Treumann, was also in hiding and meticulously copied bank notes which would be exchanged by bankers in the resistance, for real notes. Many designers were, to various degrees, engaged in supporting, or had active rôles in, the Resistance. During that time the togetherness of those Dutch who considered themselves 'good Dutchmen' naturally led to dreams and plans for the post-war years. It was felt that the bureaucracy of the pre-1940s as well as the overwhelming power of political parties and the church should be changed. A new society, more egalitarian, should be established and a pure, democratic system should be initiated. In the arts, there were dreams of forming a federation consisting of the various specialist groups like the filmmakers, dancers, graphic designers, photographers, actors and so on. A new umbrella organisation would be set up which would encompass the various artist groups and thus form a new power within a new community after 1945. This dream was actually realised and Sandberg, one of the most active post-war designers became the first president of the federation of arts at the insistence of Queen Wilhelmina who, as a gifted amateur painter, was also a member of the new federation. Later Sandberg's presidency was confirmed by democratic means.

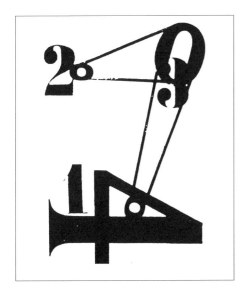

(above left) H N Werman. Type inspired print, 1924.

(above right) Poster by Wim Crouwel for the Jongkind exhibition, 1960.

Sandberg and the Stedelijk

Sandberg was a curator of the Stedelijk Museum of Amsterdam before the war, He had reached this position through his freelance activities in organising exhibitions of applied art for art societies. He was originally a designer who had been trained in pictorial statistics. After the war, Sandberg became director of the Stedelijk Museum and introduced new visions and concepts of art to that museum. Through his exhibitions and also through his outstanding design for the catalogues of the Stedelijk Museum, he made it one of the leading art centres of the world.

The post-war years

Among the graphic designers who became members of the so called 'GFK' (the F stands for Federation and the G and K for applied art) there were many with sympathies for the political left and the extreme left. In the GFK there were a number of unwritten rules about designers' behaviour, not only political but also the behaviour in the community as well as co-operation with certain industries, magazines or clients. These un-written rules were rather strict and often the annual meeting of the GFK ended up in heavy discussions about collaboration with capitalism in one form or another. Members of this association were unlikely to be working for advertising agencies, which were regarded as the tools of capitalism during that time. There was another association formed called the VRI which was not a member of the federation. Its members did work for advertising agencies and clients which did not belong to the approved group for which the GFK members were working.

If we turn back to 1945, we see that before long designers like Sandberg, Elffers (a former student of Piet Zwart) Jan Bons, Nicolaas Wijnberg, Wim Brusse, became active in a situation where paper was scarce, photo-lithography had not been introduced on a large scale and many type-faces were not available. Very strong feeling for renewal possessed these designers, manifested by their desire to use sans serif typefaces and be honest in their work. A similar spirit was inherited by the generation active from the mid-50s onwards (Dick Bruna, Wim Crouwel, Han de Vries, Mart Kempers, Alexander Verberne) also expressing an aspiration towards honesty in graphic design.

1990 **Patriots, philosophers and printers** Colin Banks

1 For a brief history of this famous press, see p 917 Bulletin 17, Printing Historical Society, by Colin Banks. For more extensive accounts, see the numerous publications in Hungary by Tibor Szántó and György Haiman.

(below) From the Monumenta Literarum. Twenty-four limited editions of world poetry. 1921–22 Lajos Kozma and Imre Kner.

Throughout this century, Hungarian book design has witnessed a series of revivalist movements. They have grown out of the constant need for Hungarians to reassert their national identity. So it should not be surprising if folk pattern and a carefully mannered rustic style sometimes still bring freshness to the printed page.

The need of the Hungarians to make a distinctively Hungarian mark in the world is as important to them now as it has ever been. The last forty years of Hungarian book design seem to me a story of the laying on of hands by those who had some experience of the 1930's, down through successive generations. In this way, the traditions of the painters (eg the Gödöllö school), other architect/illustrators (eg Kozma), and the scholar typographers (eg the Kners[1]) have been kept alive.

However, there have also been strong Modernist influences: from outside, through Tschichold; and from the Hungarians themselves, Lajos Kassák, Marcel Breuer and László Moholy-Nagy. Budapest was known as the Second Bauhaus. Since the 1939–45 war, the most fortunate postgraduates from Budapest completed their graphic design education in that best of schools, the Hochschule für Grafik und Buchkunst at Leipzig in East Germany.

The most influential post-war book designers and teachers in Hungary have been Lajos Lengyel, János Erdélyi, György Haiman and Tibor Szántó. Haiman and Szántó are

both scholar/designers who have contributed to the world's bibliographical knowledge:
Haiman especially to the fascinating history of Nicholas Tótfalusi Kis, the progenitor
of the *Janson* typeface; and Szántó to the history of Hungary's contribution to book
production, especially the illuminated manuscript.

György Haiman was attracted to printing through a kinship with Izidor and Imre Kner.
Imre Kner, who was Haiman's uncle, had a great influence on him. The Kners were
friends of Gyula Kaesz, the director of the Budapest School of Arts and Crafts. Haiman
studied there as a private, non-enrolled guest pupil while still at secondary school. He
then did a two-year apprenticeship, first at the Kner Press in the town of Gyoma, and
later with the Hungaria Press in Budapest. He stayed at this press as a designer under
the direction of another Kner, Albert. He saw active service as a soldier during much of
the war that followed, and then became a Government-appointed director of the Gyoma
Workshops. After 1948, the family purple mantle began to slip as small companies were
nationalised and design work was difficult to come by.

Haiman then worked as a clerk in the state printing co-operatives, but after 1956 (and
the Rising), in a period of relative liberalism, he was allowed by his supervisor to design
books again in his free time (a suspiciously revisionist pre-occupation at that time).
Haiman then found his way to contributing to a revival of quality book production
by promoting the standards which had been set before the war by the Kners.

A keystone in this revival was the setting up, in 1957, of the Helikon Publishing
House. Haiman claims that the planning of this venture was partly carried out in his
bathroom: this was the only available place where a secret conversation could be had
with Helikon's founder, Ferenc Párczer. Haiman worked for Helikon as a freelance
designer. He sent a proposal to the Government suggesting that the Gyoma-Kner
Press be re-equipped. At the same time as this was undertaken, the Government joined

(below left) György Haiman,
Hegel 1977.

(below right) György Haiman,
title spread from *Petőfi Sándor*, 1957.

it together with the bigger Bekescsaba Printing Workshops. This closed a circle as Helikon then commissioned most of their book printing from Kner. In the early 1960's, this partnership of designer, publisher and printer produced sixty volumes of Hungary's finest literature. These substantial, leather bound editions were the first quality books to be published in large numbers in Hungary after the war.

The first books in this series were Monotype hot-metal set, and the final books, which were published in the 1970's, were Monophoto set. They all display a pains-taking regard for typographical detail: visually letter-spaced capitals, careful use of small capitals, a well orchestrated hierarchy of headings, subheadings, running heads, shoulder notes, footnotes and indices. The editions contain proper colophons with full design and production details, and even that usual 'dump bin'– the title verso which houses the copyright and acknowledgement details – was decently attended to. This attention to detail continues to be the hallmark of a Helikon book. They buck the world trend for flashy chapter headings that leave all the remaining bits and pieces to fall where they may.

At 76, Dr Haiman is very active. Teaching takes up one day of his week. He also edits and designs miniature books of printing history that delight his friends (number 17 will shortly appear: a sixteenth-century song, with both words and music about King Mattias, of Corvinus Library fame). He also continues his researches into Kis and the Kners: the exhibition of the bookbindings of Elizabeth Kner in Chicago in 1987 drew largely on his knowledge.

(below left) Tibor Szántó, cover design for *Biblo Neruda*, from the Kner printing house.

(below right) Peter Viragvölgyi, born 1948, Professor at the Academy of Arts and Crafts.

Tibor Szántó, at 78, is of the same generation at Haiman and has been Artistic Director of Helikon Books for 26 years. The term 'Artistic' is significant, for he has contributed more to Helikon than design for book-production. The books he has produced often display his own enthusiasm and encyclopaedic knowledge. He has designed 2,000

books and has recently devoted considerable energy to the fine reproduction of manuscripts. These include an eighteenth-century scroll of *The Book Ester*; the 1516 – 9
Jordánsky Code; and, currently in production, a selection of pages from Hungarian
libraries showing illuminated initials from the fifteenth and sixteenth centuries. The
very best technical resources are focused on these books in order to reproduce the
exact patina of vellum and gold leaf. They sell immediately in very large quantities,
even though they are very expensive and the population of Hungary is both relatively
poor and numbers only ten million people.

Szántó is a leading figure in the typographic world and has held a mirror to international standards with the many editions of his books on the design of letterforms. In
their inspiration, they bow to the work of Tschichold, Mardersteig, Morison and Zapf,
whose works he has done much to introduce to Hungary.

However, his finest achievement may be the judgement which he has shown in
choosing, teaching and encouraging those who follow him at Helikon Kiado.

He could have left Hungary but he says he is both a Hungarian and an adventurer,
so he stayed, and adds '…every ten years a revolution, every ten years a counter-
revolution.' This tag seems to hold true as far back as 1848.

János Kass was born in 1928, trained as a ceramicist and throughout the war was a
boy messenger in the Budapest resistance. In spite of that he was labelled a bourgeois
and suffered all the frustrations that follow narrow political dogma.

However, he did complete an applied arts training at the Budapest Academy and
then two years in Leipzig. Kass is both an illustrator and a typographer but more than
any of the other book designers, he is an artist. He is a prolific fine artist, but he also
brings something that is absolutely entirely of himself; to his book design that super-
sedes the craft traditions within which most book design is constrained. There are not
many *artists* worthy of the label in the world. There are even fewer who have an understanding of books and typography. János Kass is one of those few.

Zoltán Kemény was born in 1941. Another victim of the anti-bourgeois bias, he was
not allowed to enter high school. He became an apprentice printer, then specialised
for ten years as a film and plate operative. A friend of his who escaped from Hungary
in 1956 sent him books by Emil Ruder and Herbert Spencer and copies of *Graphis*
magazine. Kemeny taught himself about typography and started to explore letterforms
with an enthusiasm he describes as 'madness'.

The technical director at the printing office noticed that Kemény could draw so he
was moved into the first Hungarian design office to be set up within a printing works.
He feels that this gave him an advantage over the high school design students who
were deprived of practical printing experience. Ironically, he was later invited to teach
'hands-on' printing at the Academy. Today, Kemény is mainly involved in designing
Hungarian editions of West German magazines.

Book publishing now generally eludes him. He describes the snakes-and-ladders that
have to be negotiated in many publishing houses in order to achieve a decent book. He

says that both authors and designers have little power; the offices are eighty per cent management-staffed. Management decides where print is to be placed and agrees compromises in type, paper, format and processing. This is all part and parcel of most book production in Hungary: management determines standards of quality. The resulting cosy relationship between manager and printer excludes designers as an irrelevance.

Zsuzsa Murányi came straight to Helikon from middle school. She was sent by the Union of Culture to spend three years at Leipzig learning book design in Albert Kapre's School. She returned to Budapest in 1971. Like most other staff designers, she also practises freelance. However, she claims that she could not work without the support of Helikon. Here she can deal directly with printers: 'No one comes between us and there is always time and money for proofs. A bad book is always more of a liability than good one'. The criticism and approval of the design team is important to her.

As we enter the 1990's, there are three kinds of book designer in Hungary. The first category includes the talented and well educated who came through the war. They won through heroically either whilst bucking the system, or by going along with it and holding on to some kind of lesser integrity. Among these are Hungary's best book designers.

What they had to fight against is typified by a 65 year old gentleman, who told me he graduated with a first class degree in Law in the 1940's. Guilty of 'bourgeois intellectualism', he was directed to four years of internal exile working on the land 'digging fields and planting in the wrong seasons'. He then spent three years as a railway clerk, then for 27 years he was a clerk for a printing machinery importer. 'Life hasn't been so bad,' he said, 'I enjoy reading Latin, English and German. I have earned a little money for even less work, I play a little tennis and a lot of chess, go to the opera, and the State looks after my worries. There are more difficult times coming. I am glad I am out of it'.

(below left) Zoltán Kemény cover, blind-blocked and gold-blocked on green 'suede' material. Name day book, *Eva*. 1989.

(below right) Zoltán Kemény. Pages from *Picasso, a drama*.

The second category includes the clever and talented designers, who embarked on their design careers after the war. Up until recently, they knew little of life outside Hungary. Now, with their enthusiasm and energies drained, they feel bitter about 'the forty wasted years'. With some exaggeration, the designer András Nagy said, 'I know what has happened in history, and until the 1950's Austria was the same as us. Look at the difference now!'

The third category includes those in their twenties and thirties with all the benefits of a solid training in the Academy and in Leipzig. Craft traditions have been handed down intact by the old guard who have fought for high standards in book design.

These young designers may now have the freedom to use this as a springboard for the development of new ideas. I also think the Western world can learn from them. Eastern Europe may yet come to the rescue of those in the West who have sacrificed their standards on the altars of marketing and hype.

Since the collapse of the Iron Curtain, there has been a growth of new, small publishers in Hungary – both idealists and opportunists. Unfortunately, there has yet to be a parallel democratisation of design talent and printing resources. The established State publishing houses can generate the convertible currency needed to import higher quality papers from the West and to take control of the best State printing. In the seventeenth century Tótfalusi Kis, in describing Hungarian printing, said, 'it's as though a frog has hopped on paper'. Some of the new publishers are, again, managing to achieve this effect again.

András Nagy.

András Nagy, who is 37, spent five years at the Budapest Academy studying under both Professor Haiman and János Kass. In addition to designing at Helikon, he designs record sleeves and trade marks in his own time.

In this account, one publishing house has been given prominence. But unless a Hungarian publisher can achieve volume sales and turn a large proportion of its earnings into convertible currency, it can not command the best production facilities in Hungary and buy the best raw materials that the free market has to offer. Neither can it expect any loyalty from the best designers.

Helikon has reached a crossroads. The dominant personality over the last two decades has been Tibor Szántó; now he increasingly pursues his personal design interests. Also, a British publishing group have just bought a fifty per cent stake in the imprint. With this higher capital base, it will be interesting to see how much money is spent on good design and production. It will be all the more interesting if the high standards achieved in Hungary find their way into any UK co-editions.

History and culture provide important clues to the understanding of Hungary. The great Hungarian literary epic is *The Tragedy of Man* by Imre Madach,[2] 1860. It is a story of hope brought low by cynicism. In this book, Adam and Lucifer come to London:

Adam: This is the world I have always hungered for. My path lay through a maze until this vision, but now the way lies clear in front of me, I hear the cheerful song of competition.

Lucifer: Like hymns it sounds good from a certain height. All croaks and sighs and moans are sweetly mingled and sound delightful once they reach us here. God hears it this way too, and that is why he thinks his world is such a great success. Down there, however, it sounds rather different. There you can hear the beating of its heart.

Adam: You sceptical mocker, isn't this a finer world than those you've dragged me through? Free competition opens up the road, no pyramids, nor slaves to bear the load.

Well, we shall see.

2 Translation by George Szirtes, 1988

1985 **Peter Behrens as a typographer** Alan Windsor

Peter Behrens (1868 – 1940) is most familiar to us today as an architect and designer, particularly for his Turbine Hall in Moabit, Berlin (1909) for the electrical combine, AEG, often reproduced in general histories of twentieth century architecture. He is also remembered for having had Walter Gropius, Ludwig Mies van der Rohe and Charles-Edouard Jeanneret (Le Corbusier) in his office at various times during the period that he was artistic advisor to the AEG.

Before the First World War, however, he was well known in Germany as a calligrapher and designer of type-faces. He knew, and was well known to, the leading figures in the German movement for reform, and was himself, moreover, recognised at the period as being one of the outstanding artists concerned with letter-forms and with book design.

Behrens studied art in Munich, where, as a painter, he became drawn into the then developing arts and crafts movement. During the time he was there, 1889 – 1899, the celebrated *Münchner Renaissance* of interest in fine printing, typography and book production was in its later years. The influence of the English on this development is well known, and although, for example, Otto Hupp, who designed the whole of his *Münchner Kalender* which appeared from 1885 onwards, anticipated Morris's Kelmscott Press in many ways, his activity made craftsmen in Munich particularly receptive to the example of the English. Rudolf von Seitz and Gabriel Seidl founded a workshop on similar principles to that of Morris's 'Firm', and Behrens's friend Otto Eckmann, a fellow northerner from Hamburg, gave up painting to devote himself to the applied arts, and held a spectacular sale of all his pictures to mark the event. In that year, the first article on Morris's books appeared, in *Pan,* the magazine founded by Otto Julius Bierbaum and Julius Meier-Graefe. Behrens, along with Eckmann, Ludwig von Hofmann, 'Eidus' and E R Weiss, contributed to this magazine as a graphic artist from its inception.

Behrens began to design page headings for *Deutsche Kunst und Dekoration* in 1899, and in that year drew the sailing ship logo for Bierbaum's Insel-Verlag, (left) a device still in use today. It was later the subject of variants by Eric Gill, by Tiemann, Weiss and others. In 1900, Behrens exhibited bookbindings at the *Exposition Universelle* in Paris, where he may have seen the Kelmscott Chaucer and *The History of Godefroy of Boloyne* which were on view while he was in Paris. His participation there was as a member of Darmstadt 'Seven', having been invited to join the artists' colony on the Mathildenhöhe,

(above) Logo designed by Behrens for Bierbaum's Insel-Verlag, 1899.

(facing page) *Behrens-Antiqua,* 1908.

where he was to have his first house built. In Darmstadt, Behrens designed his first
printing type, a kind of *Deutsche Fraktur* known as *BehrensSchrift*. This followed hard
on the heels of *Eckmann-Type*, which had been a sensational success.

Although it was, like Eckmann's, a fusion of roman and gothic lettering (a *Bastard
Schrift* as Renner called it) *BehirensSchrift* differs fundamentally from that of Eckmann
in that its forms were derived from the use of the quill pen not the brush, a point that
Behrens himself stressed very strongly. It marks a turning away from the Art Nouveau.
Through the intercession of Eugen Diederichs, who had recently (1896) established his
Press in Florence, and Peter Jessen, Director of the library of the Berlin Decorative
Arts Museum, Behrens had his type cut by Louis Hoell for publication in 1902 by the
Gebruder Klingspor in Offenbach. *BehrensSchrift* was first used for the Darmstadt
exhibition publication, *Ein Dokument Deutscher Kunst*, this, (1901) and Behrens's own
booklet *Feste Des Lebens und der Kunst* (1900) were considered by Hans Loubier to owe
something to Morris in that, when lying open, both pages visible were considered as a
decorative unity through the design of their borders, something of a novelty in German
book design. *BehrensSchrift* was a popular success, and prestigious books such as Rudolf
Kautsch's *Die Neue Buchkunst* of 1903 were set in it.

Die Tragödie Manfred* by Georg Euchs (1903) was given much more sharply geometri-
cally stylised decorations than '*Ein Dokument*'. However, the Behrens's next type, the

Kursiv, was introduced in 1907 with ornament of an abstract or geometrical character, largely spirals drawn from Greek vase painting, an approach no longer having anything to do with van de Velde, Morris or the English. The *Kursiv* followed soon after Heinrich Wieynk's 'Trianon' of 1905, but was much heavier, and despite its gracious, flowing qualities, it was relatively unpopular.

Behrens's *Antiqua*, which appeared in 1908, was based on uncials of the fifth century, and was the fruit of his continued enthusiasm for calligraphy. Behrens held special courses on calligraphy during the period (1903-7) that he was Director of the *Kunstgewerbeschule* in Dusseldorf. For the first one, in 1906, Behrens invited Edward Johnston to come from England, and in his place Johnston sent Anna Simons, a German pupil. Behrens and Anna Simons together (1909) devised the inscription *Dem Deutschen Volk* for the pediment of the Reichstag, where it is still to be seen, restored, today.

The *Antiqua* was a great success, and was used for a number of distinguished books including Eritz Hoeber's monograph (1913) on Behrens himself, and, above all, on the majestic *Upanishads Des Vega,* published by Eugen Diederichs in 1914. This book was designed by E H Ehmke, who had also been brought to Dusseldorf by Behrens to teach, and by one of their pupils, Ernst Schneidler. They boldly decided to combine two of Behrens's types, the *Antiqua* for the titles, and the *Schrift* for the main text of this impressive book. Loubier used *Antiqua* for his important book, *Die Neue Deutsche Buchkunst* of 1921.

Behrens's *Mediäval* appeared in 1914, an early renaissance *Antiqua* of a kind that had been revived by Tiemann a few years earlier. This was not very much used, perhaps because of the jerky emphasis given to the line by the heavily oblique serifs on the i, n, m and u in the lower case. Lily Behrens also took an interest in book production, and designed papers and cover wrappings for a number of portfolios of etchings.

A valuable analysis of Behrens's typography and graphic design is to be found in the recently published English translation of *Industrie Kultur.* In this collection of essays dealing with Behrens's years with the AEG, Gabriele Heidecker wrote the section *Peter Behrens's Publicity Material for the AEG* and compiled the lavishly illustrated catalogue. The essay deals with the relationship between Behrens's exhibition architecture, his typography, and his graphic design.

Upanishads-Des Vega, 1914.

Vom Schlechten kann man nie zu wenig und das Gute nie zu oft lesen: schlechte Bücher sind intellektuelles Gift, sie verderben den Geist. Um das Gute zu lesen, ist eine Bedingung, daß man das Schlechte nicht lese: denn das Leben ist kurz, Zeit und Kräfte beschränkt. SCHOPEN-HAUER: PARERGA UND PARALIPOMENA: ÜBER LESEN UND BÜCHER.

39. Gebr. Klingspor, Offenbach M.   Behrens-Mediæval, 1914

At the beginning of Behrens's employment, she explains, he used his *Antiqua* (indeed, she maintains that it was designed specifically for the AEG) and specially drawn letters for various tasks, but he soon developed a new, exclusive script for all the firm's printed material – an alphabet for all the AEG brochures, advertisements and posters: a strong, rounded roman face distinguished by a strikingly leftward sloping serif on the A (but not, as a mis-translation of the original German text says, on the G, which is characterised by its high opening). There are emphatically diagonal serifs on the T, echoed in those terminating the exaggeratedly long central stem of the E and the lower stem of the E.

In her text in the original German, the author makes a clear differentiation between the *Behrens-Antiqua* and the new *Antiquaschrift* for the AEG, but in this English version, the abandonment of a number of sub-headings (*Die 'Behrens Antiqua'* and *Die Hist-orischen Quellen* for example) the clear distinction between which one of the scripts is under discussion in different parts of the text is rather blurred. Occasional errors have crept in during the re-casting of the book, such as the mis-titling of Loubier's 1921 work as *Die Neue Deutsche Baubunst* or the misprint on p.178, giving illustration 16 as 15, (quite apart from the fact that illustrations G56 and G57 also referred to on p.178 are of material in rather different typefaces, neither of them the standard *Behrens Antiqua* as stated). Again, exactly the same illustration is used for G55 (a price-list) and P37 (the original design for it). These are minor criticisms, but in an expensive book aiming at great scholarly precision, they give rise to mild confusions in the mind of the trusting student.

The brilliant analysis of Behrens's approach to graphic design (the discussion of the new trademarks by Behrens, still in use today, which replaced those of 1900 by Eckmann, is an example) characterises it as 'simplified drawing within a frame, and the architectonic composition of planes' the treatment of Behrens by the image of the product so that it becomes a 'typical symbol', accompanied by impersonal letter-forms. The affinity between Behrens's graphic and typographical work and his architecture, on the one hand, is convincingly demonstrated by the author, whilst she also firmly establishes his attention to the theories of Alois Riegl concerning the creative process involved in applied decoration. The argument throughout is supported by quotations from Behrens, here in English for the first time. The letterform, he wrote 'gives the most characteristic picture of an age'.

1990 The telephone directory in the Netherlands: a review of the last hundred years Jolijn van de Wouw

Only a few Dutch graphic products actually attract public attention and induce a response, like banknotes, stamps, bus tickets and passports. Even rarer, are those products which cause public disruption by their typographic qualities alone. Typography is not one of the most particularly exciting subjects for the layman. However, the telephone directory in The Netherlands has been able to attract the attention of the general public towards upper and lower case, serif and sans serif and legibility of numbers.

The Dutch Post Museum keeps in its collection, as a small valuable item, a copy of the first Dutch telephone directory from 1884. Even at this date, when Utrecht had more than two hundred and ninety-seven subscribers, the number is first and a change of letter is indicated in bold.

After 1930, there were changes in the typeface, although still in favour of serif faces, bold and roman. At quite an early stage, a sans serif typeface was chosen for the names of cities.

Until 1967, the directories were set in metal type. The setting was kept and formed 'a lead card file system' directory. Even in this metal period, typographic changes in the setting were done because of changing requirements of the PTT. These were mostly: the position of the number, the order of the information and the mentioning, or non-mentioning, of business information.

1571 **Adolph's-brandvrije Documenten**
en **Archiefkasten**, Hoofdvertegenw.
H. B. Goettsch. (9–5 uur).
1517 **Aguilar, Maison Antonio**, Wijnhand.,
Munsterkerkhof 8.
1898 **Aken, J. C. M. v.**, Aannemer, Wester-
kade 15.
685 **Akkermans, J. H.**, Confiseur, Cuisinier,
Oudegr. T.Z. 31.

390 **Andel, Fa. Gebrs. v.**, in Kruidenlersw.,
Voorstr. 66.
1760 **Andel, Fa. H. W. H. v.**, In granen,
Weerdsingel W.Z. 8.
92 **Andrau & Co.**, Wijnkoopertj, Oudegr.
W.Z. 126.
648 **Andreas Gesticht, St.**, Springweg 156.
913 **Andrée, H. M.**, Bakk··. Trans 8.

December 1910. Wide running serif typeface, spacious, number *before* the name-entry, the second line is indented an em quad of the type size, and the number is *not* in bold.

Algem. Brandstoffenh. Utrecht, N.V.
Mariapl. 51 1212
Algem. Bankver. v. d. Middenstand,
v. h. Alg. Credietver., Wittevrouwen-
str. 12 2635
Algem. Intermediair Handelskant.
Krugerstr. 42 3402
Algem. Mij. tot Wederverkoop v. pe-
troleum en bijprod., N.V. Depôt

Antwerpen, P. A. v. fa. P. W. J. v.
Antwerpen, Nieuwegr. 21 635
Apeld. Machinefabr. v.h. Loog-Lan-
daal, Wilhelminap. 23 1969
Apotheek 't Gouden Hert v.h. Ver-
heul & Frackers, Amst.straatw. 44
.... 3158
Apotheek Vredenburg v.h. Verheul
& Frackers, Vredenburg 19 692

July 1922. The number is placed at the end of the line, the line is filled out with dot-leaders, the second line is indented one em and the number is set in bold.

Accountantskant. A. Lammers
Amsterdamschestr.weg 144 F bis 13365
Accountantskant. E. J. v. d.
Maaten Fred. Hendrikstr.27 (na
5½ u. 14113) 12978
Accountantskant., Ned. Onder
leid.v.A.A.H.Bals. Zuilenstr.15 10402
Accountantskant. S. Schouten
Breedstr. 23 14426

Agentuur- en Commissieh.,
Spoorstr. 8 14213
Agterberg, B. Begrafenisondern.
Anthoniedijk 2 12526
Agterberg, C. Beeldhouwer en
Sierkunstenaar, Nobelstr. 12 13220
Agterberg, G. Dienstverrichting.
Geertekerkhof 16 11080
Agterberg, H. Algem. Utr. Be-

January 1927. The number is separated from the column on the right hand-side, contrasting (sans serif) numbers are used.

Boek, Th. H. v. Vert. N.V. Rijwielind. Meppel,
Joh. Vermeerstr. 9 14299
Boek-Slagt, Wed. W. v. Amst.str.w. 84a,
Elmwijk 12406
Boek, H. v. d. Bedr.obaf N.V. Douwe Egberts
tabaksfabr., Poortstr. 36 10832
Boekes, A. M. Beh., stoff., Burg. Reigerstr. 31 12573
Boekes Jr., A. M. Beh., stoff., Oudegr. 316 11775
Boelen, J. J. Exped., transp., Oosterk. 18 12875
Boentwarifabr. Ps. Wed. P. Smits & Zn.,
Hoogelanden O. Z. 3 11824

Berg, J. ten Woonh., W. Barentstr. 53 14708
Berg, C. G. v. d. Beh. en stoff., Obrechtstr. 39 11775
Berg, F. v. d. Wittevr.sing. 83 13471
Verg, F. A. v. d. Vert. v. Ruys' Handelaver.,
F. O. Dondermstr. 64 14707
Berg, H. J. v.h. Vlh. en speksl., Westerk. 34 10850
Berg, H. J. v. d. Donkere Gaard 3 10404
Berg, J. v. d. Schoorst.v., loodg. en metsel.,
Vinkenburgstr. 13 11686
Berg, J. J. v. d. Firm. Osti & Co., Pr. Hendrikl.
15 15116

July 1930. A new, less spacious type face, in a smaller size. Many announcements, such as business information, could go onto one line, names are not in bold, and a decision has been made to use less spacious numbers, also not in bold.

Acorus Reclame Studio Nw. Gracht 79 14646
Accumulatorenfabr. Hollandia v.h. Hutten
& de Vries Le, Nieuwstr. 55 16638
Accumulatorenfabr. Komest Fil. Utrecht, vert.
W. H. Pas, Leidschev. 9 18887
Ashterberg, Fa. K. v. Kol.w., comest., t.
vleeschw., Burg. Reigerstr. 27 12081
Aekal, N.V. Drukk. en Cart.fabr. te Oss Ver-
koopkant, J. Leykenstr. 35 11207
AequoU, D. v. Motor- en rijw.h., P. Nieuw-
landstr. 36 17028

Obrechtstr. 43 17157
Adriani, Dr. J. H. Secr. v. d. Armenraad,
en schadecomm. Nieuwegracht 31 15166
Advertantiebur. Gerbo Adviesbur. v. reclame
en verkoopcontr., Begijnehof 7 16320
Advertantiebur. v.h. D. Y. Alta (Utr. Brk. ad-
vert.bur.), Kr. Nieuwegr. 94 12356
Adviesbur. v. Bedrijfsorgan. (Ir. J.M. Louwerse)
Moreelsepark 3 15440
Aalst, P. v. Bonbons, biscuit en choc., Potter-
str. 6 13251

January 1940. Names in bold again.

19611 Aalberts-v. Asselt, Mevr. Wed. C. Oudegr. 370.
12225 Aalst, W. v. Exped. Utr.—Bodegr.—Alphen—
Leiden, kant. v. Doornik, Nwe kade 78.
Leiden, kant. v. Doornik, Nwe kade 4.
18788 Aannemers- en Bouwvakpatroonsbond, Ned. Chr.
-P. R.C.A.B. Wittevrouwensing. 55.
16039 Aannemers Vers. Mij., N.V. Eerste Onderl. Moreelsel.
39bis.
20594 Aannemings Onderneming Opbouw Boothstr. 8.
28319 Aart, H. C. v. Ref. II d. P.T.T., Waterw. 70a,
de Bilt.

20572 Adviescommissie Vorderingen Bur. Geniez. Utrecht
en schadecomm. II Distr., Nachtegaalstr. 60bis.
13251 Aalst, P. v. Bonbons, biscuit en choc., Potterstr. 6.
14720 Afdeeling Administratiekantoor Waltman & Co.
Oudegracht 92.
20709 Agent.- en Commissieh. Asha Stationstr. 31.
19260 Agerbeek, J. B. Prof. H. de Vriesl. 42.
21110 Agrippina, Vers.groepte Keulen Ao 1844 Alle vers.,
Dir. Lujkt. J. H. L. de Bruin, Kr. Nieuwegr. 21,
21325 Idem,
306 Driebergen Idem dir.

July 1941. The number is again before the line and the successive line is no longer indented.

Two particular graphic designers have initiated the major changes in the production of the directory: Th H Oltheten, director of the State Press, who was interested in the early stages of information technology development, and Wim Crouwel, who became Professor of Industrial Design at the University of Delft.

The graphic industry in The Netherlands during the 1950's was extremely united and full of initiatives! From 1946, Dutch graphics was strongly oriented towards the United States, due to American technology developing throughout the war, while European developments stopped. Many new techniques and business organisation structures

were studied by delegations from Europe. This was reflected in telephone directories in 1958 by the processing of telephone subscribers, using the American Listomatic system. Before this time the directories were set in metal. It is interesting, when compared with current technology, to imagine how many tons of lead the enormous production of more than 1,400 pages required. This needed to be stored in galley frames for the reprint after corrections. The process of correcting and processing the changes must have taken enormous efforts from the typesetters, who had to read the complete text to replace or add lines. At that time, three important pieces of equipment were introduced. These were the teletype, the Intertype setting machine and the Hollorith data-processing equipment which was used to handle the sorting of massive amounts of information.

Although this system was not used in America for the production of telephone directories, Th H Oltheten (who was interested in the development of information technology) recognised its potential for this use in The Netherlands. In America, all the processed subscriber data was printed using a relief rotary press which required large investment. In The Netherlands it was necessary to make large investments in technical developments thereby making the use of the new offset production technique possible. Oltheten recognised the possibility of combining current developments in three different areas of directory production: information processing by the PTT, typesetting system, and production systems at the State Press.

The Listomatic system was implemented in 1958. The printer did not have to use the

(below) An example from the Listomatic directory, a system used from 1958–78.

(facing page) Examples of various texts using the existing *Univers* series.

```
HEIL FLIP Corneillel 2 . . . . . . . . . . . .   3 35 97
HEELSBERGEN  T J v Tandarts spr u 13-
  14 beh do en za wo v 18 30-19.30 Wilh
  park 51 . . . . . . . . . . . . . . . . . .   1 83 68
HEELSUM C G v Br-, Banketb Oudegr 2 .   1 14 07
HEEM N V v d Fabr Abstederdijk 131 . . .   1 65 65
  Pakhuis Lg Rozendaal 17 . . . . . . . . .   2 69 22
HEEMSKERK P A Dickenslaan 56 . . . . .   3 16 27
HEEMSTEDE  OBELTN  V INGENIEURS-
  BUR v Kant Schoutenstr 15 . . . . . . . .   1 88 52
  idem. . . . . . . . . . . . . . . . . . . . . .   2 94 59
  Mag Annastr 27 . . . . . . . . . . . . . . .   1 28 87
  b g g Chef monteur E Reulen J D e d
  Waalsstr 1b . . . . . . . . . . . . . . . . .   2 29 67
  Woonh adm A C Labee Edisonstr 111bis.   2 90 06
HEEMSTRA R Burg v d Voort v Zijpl 28 .   2 70 71
HEEMSTRA Mr J M H BARON v Chef
  Kabinet Burg Nobelstr 3bis . . . . . . . . .   2 60 93
HEEMSTRA S F BARON v Weerdsingel
  O Z 80bis . . . . . . . . . . . . . . . . . . .   2 06 69
HEEP H A Amsterdstrw 449 . . . . . . . . .   1 56 56
HEEMSTRA Mr J M H BARON v Chef
  Kabinet Burg Nobelstr 3bis . . . . . . . . .   2 60 93
HEEMSTRA S F BARON v Weerdsingel
  O Z 80bis . . . . . . . . . . . . . . . . . . .   2 06 69
HEEP H A Amsterdstrw 449 . . . . . . . . .   1 56 56
HEER F de Chef bacteriol lab v d N V De
  Verenigde Blikfabr Chopinstr 52 . . . . . .   3 36 39
HEER J de Pianoh Janskerkhof 5 . . . . . .   1 42 23
HEER Ir J J de Inq N S Lessingl 34 . . . .   3 36 87
HEER B de Weth D M Plompstr 34 . . . . .   2 52 69
```

metal type lines as a lead file system, but changed to a daily updated file of punch cards with the addresses in machine type. From these files, divided into city/place of residence blocks, film cameras produced the different local and regional telephone directories. This did have large advantages. The punch card system could contain three lines of type per card and because of the photographic procedures, both the local and the regional telephone directories could be processed from one system, while the metal type contained two systems. The two units were the Justowriter and the Listomatic camera.

The Listomatic camera handled these cards at a speed of 12,000 per hour. The film had a length of 120 metres which was developed and cut automatically to the right height for the different local and regional telephone directories. The disadvantages were out-weighed by the advantages of speed, accuracy and savings on labour in the typeset-ting and printing departments. The disadvantages were heavily criticised because the typographic possibilities of the system were small. No matter how advanced, the type-writer could not produce a quality image equal to metal type. It was necessary to stick to one variety of type and style, because of the continuous updating of the card system.

The Listomatic directory used from 1958 – 78 consisted of text photographed from cards. For reasons of clarity, a sans serif type was chosen. Names are in uppercase, punctuation marks omitted, the line filled out with dot-leaders, with a freestanding number at the end of this line. Advertisements were not possible at this stage.

The Listomatic system was still in use in 1978, although the information technology

28 23 38	Berg J.v.d, Zomerhofstr. 60 Betonconstr.		Berg J.v.d, Zomerhofstr. 60 Betonconstr.	28 23 38
28 23 24	Idem		Idem	28 23 24
15 78 01	Woonh. Torenln 3		Woonh. Torenln 3	15 78 01
19 32 95	Woonh. J.A.Sluimer, Platostr. 254		Woonh. J.A.Sluimer, Platostr. 254	19 32 95
13 96 02	Berg Ir.J.v.d, Groene Wetering 44		Berg Ir.J.v.d, Groene Wetering 44	13 96 02
23 06 58	Berg Jr.J.v.d, Schippersstr. 49		Berg Jr.J.v.d, Schippersstr. 49	23 06 58
11 50 54	Berg Mej.J.v.d, C.v.Nieveltstr. 12b		Berg Mej.J.v.d, C.v.Nieveltstr. 12b	11 50 54
27 27 60	Berg Mej.J.v.d, C.de Wetstr. 22b		Berg Mej.J.v.d, C.de Wetstr. 22b	27 27 60
17 00 16	Berg Sr.J.v.d, Beyerlandseln 149		Berg Sr.J.v.d, Beyerlandseln 149	17 00 16

28 23 38	Berg J.v.d, Zomerhofstr. 60 Betonconstr.		Berg J.v.d, Zomerhofstr. 60 Betonconstr.	28 23 38
28 23 24	Idem		Idem	28 23 24
15 78 01	Woonh. Torenln 3		Woonh. Torenln 3	15 78 01
19 32 95	Woonh. J.A.Sluimer, Platostr. 254		Woonh. J.A.Sluimer, Platostr. 254	19 32 95
13 96 02	Berg Ir.J.v.d, Groene Wetering 44		Berg Ir.J.v.d, Groene Wetering 44	13 96 02
23 06 58	Berg Jr.J.v.d, Schippersstr. 49		Berg Jr.J.v.d, Schippersstr. 49	23 06 58
11 50 54	Berg Mej.J.v.d, C.v.Nieveltstr. 12b		Berg Mej.J.v.d, C.v.Nieveltstr. 12b	11 50 54
27 27 60	Berg Mej.J.v.d, C. de Wetstr. 22b		Berg Mej.J.v.d, C. de Wetstr. 22b	27 27 60
17 00 16	Berg Sr.J.v.d, Beyerlandseln 149		Berg Sr.J.v.d, Beyerlandseln 149	17 00 16

28 23 38	Berg J.v.d, Zomerhofstr. 60 Betonconstr.		Berg J.v.d, Zomerhofstr. 60 Betonconstr.	28 23 38
28 23 24	idem.		idem.	28 23 24
15 78 01	Woonh. Torenln 3		Woonh. Torenln 3	15 78 01
19 32 95	Woonh. J.A.Sluimer, Platostr. 254		Woonh. J.A.Sluimer, Platostr. 254	19 32 95
13 96 02	Berg Ir.J.v.d, Groene Wetering 44		Berg Ir.J.v.d, Groene Wetering 44	13 96 02
23 06 58	Berg Jr.J.v.d, Schippersstr. 49		Berg Jr.J.v.d, Schippersstr. 49	23 06 58
11 50 54	Berg Mej.J.v.d, C.v.Nieveltstr. 12b		Berg Mej.J.v.d, C.v.Nieveltstr. 12b	11 50 54
27 27 60	Berg Mej.J.v.d, C.de Wetstr. 22b		Berg Mej.J.v.d, C.de Wetstr. 22b	27 27 60
17 00 16	Berg Sr.J.v.d, Beyerlandseln 149		Berg Sr.J.v.d, Beyerlandseln 149	17 00 16

and the electronics were more developed. An electronic typesetting system fed by a network of automated administration was inevitable in the form of the specially developed Integrated Telephone Customers Information System (ITCIS). The whole approach concerned the following main items:

Registration. In 1976, roughly 400,000 new entries, 240,000 changes of address and 200,000 changes of installations.

Telephone financial administration. Once every two months invoicing and debt control of 3.7 million subscribers in 1976.

Directory administration. For use in the production of directories. 3.1 million separate entries, added to 0.7 million sub-entries.

Technical overview of the local networks. 5 million premises with specifications of cable connections, from the premises to the network, 3.7 million connections.

Fault repair service. (Dial 007) 1.9 million questions.

Enquiries. (Dial 008) 37 million enquiries in 1976.

Customer enquiry administration. (Dial 004) 1.6 million enquiries.

The new local and regional directories had four instead of three columns per page. This reduced the amount of paper used by 15%. Columns were separated by vertical lines and capitals were not used, but the names were printed in bold. The overall impression was even, which improves the legibility. It was the aim to search for the right balance between legibility on one side and the reduction of paper on the other.

The STD code, which at the moment is placed next to the place name, was put below the name of the place at the top of the page.

In the current four-column directory in condensed *Univers* without capitals

13 56 39	smit jr, prof dr a d f, groenburgwal 45
37 49 58	smit, r, groenedk 36
16 44 68	smit & co, handelsond handelskd 24J
22 44 66	smit, drs j p. de, helmersstr 1e 77
28 37 49	smit sr, p. de, hendrikkd pr 334
38 48 58	smit, c, hoofdwg 47
35 77 99	smit, drs y, arts huizingaln j 435
76 58 49	smit, g, iepenwg 57
23 46 58	smit en van raalte, vof, jansstr st 5
12 12 67	smit, a, jongkindstr j 14
45 67 89	smit, d g t, kalkoenstr 3
24 37 48	smit, r, kalverstr 6

63 51 03	lefèbre-van rossen, j w, obrechtstr 322
86 36 54	lefèber, a, ln v n oosteinde 83
65 22 53	lefèbre, a, schapenln 52
63 96 28	lefèbre, a j g m c, vlaskamp 262
66 36 52	lefèbre, w, zonneoord 173
63 96 28	lefébure, j a a m g, pr mariestr 33
83 34 83	lefébure, a j g m c, vlaskamp 262
24 97 27	lokkegaard, k, j bildersstr 35
76 09 52	o'breen, j m, watteaustr 17"...
11 48 80	ommeren rotterdam) nv, phs. van, westerln 10 *na kantoortijd*
11 48 94	captain's room ma t/m vr na 18 u za na 12 u
36 04 13	m i v nader te bepalen datum

(presented in 1977), the order is as follows: surname, initials and prefixes, profession, address and number. The number is free standing at the start of the line and name and street names are placed alphabetically. The address follows directly on from the name, because the name and the number in most cases can be placed on the first line. The name of the street increased in importance, therefore abbreviations had to be made: for example 'weg' (road) is abbreviated to 'wg' and 'dijk' (dike) abbreviated to 'dk'.

Everything was targeted at cost reduction. There was also a lot of publicity; several newspapers interviewed Crouwel and real anger developed over some issues inspiring Gerard Unger, who subsequently worked on clarifying the *Univers* numerals, to write a heavily critical review in the graphical trade journal *Compres*.

A discussion developed between the PTT, the State Press (which was privatised in 1988 and now known as Sdu), and Total Design about typography.

Many letters with example pages and proof setting were sent backwards and forwards between those involved in the research.

Meetings and research projects concerning the legibility of type frequently took place until well into the eighties, as there were, within the graphics industry, few scientific facts known about this area. This is apparent from a memo dated 28 September 1987, concerning the legibility of type, which stated nothing that most typographers did not already know, ie. that the choice of typeface and type size are all important, and that no one solution will prove to be 100% satisfactory. It also states, theoretically, that the use of upper case only increased legibility which is untrue.

In 1981, A van Toorn requested that tests be conducted with upper-case text in OCR-B. The optical reading of text for photo-typesetting was by this time advanced.

By using upper-case type, according to van Toorn, the text could be set smaller, with less leading, achieving much saving of space. The State Press argued against this.

(facing page) Examples of texts set using *Univers*, and *Times*.

(below) Example of the 1977 directory. Two (of four) columns shown here.

The public reactions showed that mainly the elderly have problems with the legibility of the directory. But the ladies of 008 (the Dutch enquiry service) also complained about the poor legibility of the new directory.

The Crouwel generation directories are obviously not the best solution. Since the

33 01 64	halma, t, weth bakkerpints 57	33 01 61	kwekerij de witte lelie,
33 04 43	hamers, g, kerkstr 18		kanaalwg 18/b
33 06 37	hart-kuijpers, i, beukenwg 33/3	33 01 16	laan, t, berkenstede 57
33 06 48	hart, t, radboud 77,	33 01 19	laan, a, beukenwg 29
	loodg	33 02 73	laan, pieter, j jongkindstr 91
33 05 88	harteveld, e, wielingenstr 17	33 07 48	laan, w, zwaluwstr 18
33 01 20	hartland, g, vinkebrug 24	33 01 67	laar-nyhoff, mw b s, kalkoenstr 5
33 06 49	hartog, a, den, kerkstr 57	33 02 84	lakeman, g, wielingenstr 181,
33 01 17	hartog bv, radboud 18		drogist
33 03 37	hartsuijker, m, kalfjesln 5	33 02 88	lambert, w t, kerkstr 412
33 02 78	heinia, t, fuutstr 12	33 04 03	lammers, w, kanaalwg 21
33 03 34	heinsen, k, weth bakkerpints 59	33 04 07	lansschot, a, radboud 84
33 03 97	hekhuijsen, f, n beetsstr 18	33 01 27	lanters, g, middenwg 84
33 01 65	helfrich, k, kanaalwg 18/a	33 05 92	lebbing, s, fuutstr 12,

```
731 45 28  ALANDT, F, DA COSTALN 28
831 24 54  ALBARDA, IR H J, PR MARIELN 14,
           DIR ALBARDA BEDRIJFSK BUR BV
711 57 56  ALBERDINGK THIJM, D R M,
           HET GALJOEN 25
802 06 85  ALBERING-WACHTERS, E M J,
           KONINGSWG 17
711 12 47  ALBERS, J W C, TORENLN 16
711 28 63  ALBERT HEIJN NV, EEMNESSERWG 40
731 80 03  ALBERTO DRANKENWINKEL, EEMSTR 2
711 15 50  ALBERTS, C, DE BOTTER 22
831 78 34  ALEM, J M C M. VAN, DOORMANLN 8
711 84 35  ALEXANDER, R TH, BURG PENSTR 61,
           STOFF
711 53 51  BANK NEDERLAND, SPOORSTR 15
731 48 31  BOND VAN AMBTENAREN,
           SCHAEPMANLN 1
831 13 90  FINANCIERINGSMIJ AFM NV,
           R V ROZENBURGLN 7
831 61 41  VERKOOP UNIE BV ALVERU,
           J V LENNEPLN 57
831 71 41  ZIEKENFONDS GOOI EN EEMLAND,
           MOLENWG 2, BIJKANT
711 24 78  ALGERING ELECTRICS, BERKENWG 12
```

(above) A van Toorn's tests with upper-case text in *OCR-B*.

(facing page) Gerard Unger, with Chris Vermass, developed a special corresponding number, known as the 'series 1984' for *Univers*, because the original numbers tended to fill in and were not as legible as the letterforms. From top to bottom: *OCR-B*; design *LM D Smit*; *Futura*; *Univers*; and digital design *Unger/Vermaas*.

introduction of the new directories, the GP s and opticians also frequently received complaints about poor legibility. In-depth research was prepared: an objective research project into legibility; an investigation into public opinion; a qualitative investigation into user problems, and a quantitative investigation by 008 to determine the scale and nature of enquiries.

The Institute of Sense Physiology (TNO) became involved. On 20 March 1979, a weighty report was published by P Padmos and J Bogaard '...the conclusion is that, although legibility is not that relevant for the professional user, the directory, especially for the elderly, is only just legible.' It was discovered that the reduction of the average character width led to a reduction of legibility. Possible successful improvements were: an increase of the white space between the characters of a word, and a change to a typeface with a more open structure of the 6 and the 9.

The report recommended:

1 Three columns per page. Changed code of hyphenation. Printing in bold.

2 Linked with a combined use of two kinds of *Univers*.

3 'The balance between legibility and costs is still difficult.' For example, a non-condensed type is preferred for numbers.

In 1981, A van Toorn advised the board of directors of the PTT 'Without the ascenders and descenders, but with upper-case only, a yearly amount of between 5 and 10 million guilders can be saved, without any investments, in the production costs of telephone directories. The use of larger, clearer and more legible characters, causes an increased line capacity per page of 20% to 30%.'

After this period, Total Design, by this time without Crouwel but with a different designer, Jolijn van der Wouw, got involved in a design process which resulted in a new generation of directories: the 1984 generation. Advertising was impossible during the Listomatic period, but using the new typesetting equipment this was not a problem. New ways of accounting for runs, paper and production costs play a major part. It is now a print order of a very large size, on which two rotary presses work continuously.

0123456789
0123456789
0123456789
0123456789

0123456789

5 5

And again, the directory was set in three columns with the line filled out with dot-leaders.

The discussion finished on 28 December 1983 and the director of the Sdu, C H J Peters mentioned in a press conference, 'The total amount of pages in area directories in 1961 was 5,826, which increased to 18,251 in 1983.'

Previewing the new series of directories, a press release by the PTT states: 'The directory is used in only 21% of the cases nationally to find a required number.'

In 1977, the NIPO (the Dutch Institute for Perception Research) did some research into the use of directories. A personal user looks on average eight times a month in the directory. The same investigation shows how the telephone numbers are known: 33% from memory, 30% out of folders, diaries and so on, 20% from the directory. The remainder from other sources such as advertisements, mailings and so on. Only a *third place* for the directory. Is it worth the effort? There were nearly 10 million directories produced in 1980 at a total cost of nearly 40 million guilders for the PTT.

Translated from the Dutch
by Karel van der Waarde.

1988 **Edward Wright: 1912 – 1988** Joseph Rykwert

That Edward Wright is an under estimated artist is partly his own doing: he chose to
be a man of almost evangelical modesty when the art world was increasingly dominated
by public relations. For all his personal modesty, he set himself the highest standards
and was ruthlessly critical when he saw himself fall short of them, to the point of
destroying a good deal of his work.

Small, slight, informally dressed – but always dapper, feline – he seemed always to
walk on padded toes, even when he danced the tango. That grace marked all Wright's
work. There was a graceful deliberation about the preparing of the canvas, the use of
sizes and glues, the mixing of pigments. He inevitably saw himself much more as a
designer than as an artist in the 'genius' sense. Not that he ever saw his pictures as
undemanding 'industrial design' abstractions. But originality, the development of a
personal manner or style, was of little consequence to him.

His primary concern was the formulation of images, of 'ordinary' images in which
complex and sometimes very ambitious ideas could be expressed, and which would
make a more intense demand on the spectator's attention than the graphic designs.
His work is therefore enormously varied. Sometimes it is on a vast scale – the full
height of the 'Technology and Architecture' pavilion along the South Bank in London
(the building designed by Theo Crosby for the International Union of Architects in
1961) – but it might equally well be a tiny trademark. He never saw such graphics as
a drudge inferior to the painting, but always worked at the two concurrently, moving

from one to the other, integrating the experience learnt through painting into his design, but also trading the other way.

His concentration on communication, and consequently on community, was hopelessly unfashionable when he was first recognised as an artist of some importance, since at that time Existentialism was being taken up by English artists (if not by English philosophers) and the cult of man's solitude had become the obsession of many of them. Wright's passion for the graphic work of the European *avant-garde* – the Dadaists, the Bauhaus, H N Werkman, 'Concrete' poetry; Apollinaire, Van Ostaijen – with their insistence on the interweave of text and figure, also seemed to some of his contemporaries quaint and untimely.

Pop-art, which was the next fashionable movement, was concerned with an omnivorous, uncritical absorption of the opulent man-made environment – and that in Europe, meant the images in American glossies. Wright took the opposite line. In his first important show, in 1948, the drawings of 'Useful and Metaphorical objects' concentrated on the humblest of machine-made objects, one with which an exile like himself had intimate acquaintance: the gas ring, from which he attempted to wrest an epic dignity by giving it a rhythmic, sculptural energy.

He was an exile: in spite of his name, and his native-sounding English. The name came from his ancestor, General Joseph Wright, one of Bolivar's Irish commanders, who had become the first president of Ecuador. His father moved from consular service to the Ecuadorian Legation in London, and Edward was sent to the Jesuit public school, Stonyhurst. Jesuit training marked him as much almost as his origins. His impatience with any form of intellectual pretence was its positive side, the ruthless and often destructive self-criticism the negative. To the Jesuits, perhaps, he owed the tough formulation of his faith – which was both unshakeable and unassertive.

The school was cosmopolitan, yet he felt a foreigner in Britain. After his father's retirement he went back to Ecuador and then to Chile (where his mother's family lived); but there also he did not quite fit – with his English clothes and mannerisms, and the anglophone, if Paris-oriented, way of thinking. He had begun his architectural training in London, in 1930, but his familiarity with other diplomats as well as his own passion for the cinema (particularly German and Russian) brought him into touch with a number of film-makers and actors; he began working on film-titling, which was later

Lettering on exhibition building; International Union of Architects Congress, South Bank, London 1961.

to provide him with a livelihood and open the way to graphic design. However, neither in his home town of Guayaquil, nor later in Valparaiso, was there either the leisure or the money to continue his training. He and his brother both volunteered for the British army, and came to Europe via Buenos Aires. On his return to Europe he was first seriously afflicted by epilepsy, the disease which was to dog him throughout his life and which confirmed to him his status of outsider.

Like many others, he found wartime disorienting. A brief apprenticeship with the designer George Adams (who as Georg Talsoher had been a student at the Bauhaus) directed him to a new vocation. Kitty Stroud, whom he married, provided his first anchor in London, a place to live, and a return to a kind of normality. Opened just after the war in 1945, the convivial if chaotic Anglo-French Art Centre near Lords Cricket Ground provided a different kind of focus for his interests at a crucial time: it acted as a meeting-place with other artists and with visitors from Paris: Fernand Leger taught a class, Andre Lhote and Tristan Tzara lectured. He met Yankel Adler as well as the two Roberts, Colquhoun and MacBryde, who were then considered the most promising British artists; but also younger men who were to become much better known: Francis Bacon, Eduardo Paolozzi, William Turnbull, Richard Hamilton, Lucian Freud and the art-critic David Sylvester.

More crucial to his own development was contact with the typographer/printer, Anthony Froshaug, whose rigorous method and almost unerring eye in the arrangement and matching of type to paper was unrivalled in England. In spite of the enormous differences of approach, Froshaug's inability to deal with figuration, and Wright's much greater fecundity – his equal commitment to painting and typography – they never lost their respect for each other. Towards abstraction Wright had a detached attitude: while he was fascinated by many formal devices and procedures, the idea of an art without reference outside itself was alien to him.

During the Fifties, his studio in Marlborough Hill in St John's Wood became something of a centre: it was not common to meet Freud and Hamilton there at the same time, but it did happen. Wright's transparent personal integrity and his generous interest in the work of other artists, his sharp (but never overbearing) critical attention made him a confidant of much more worldly artists. For him the decade ended with another exhibition at the Mayor Gallery; the admiration of his friends was tempered for him by one violently personal review from a critic which, for a while, checked his commitment to painting and slowed work on his biggest (and probably his best pictures). He had in the meanwhile started teaching: first, in 1952, with Froshaug at the Central School of Arts and Crafts, then at the Royal College of Art, and at the Chelsea School of Art, where he had his own department and where his commitment and enthusiasm created a true 'school'– he truly was a master. He also began working on what may have been another fascinating metier: inscriptions on buildings. The first was the sign of Peter and Alison Smithson's 'House of the Future' at the Ideal Home exhibition of 1958, for which he designed a special typeface. He would design several others – such as that for Crosby's 'Technology and Architecture' exhibition of 1961, mentioned earlier, and where he also designed the panels cladding a tower 80 feet high. He would

Lettering for House of the Future at Olympia, London 1956.

have done marvellous neon or electric signs – but none was commissioned from him.

In 1970, following an invitation to the strange school of architecture at Vina de Mar in Chile, he returned to his roots. There, too, he renewed his friendship with Codofredo Lomi, the Argentine 'poet of happenings', many of whose enthusiasms he shared. He discovered the writings of Ernesto Cardenal, the Nicaraguan priest/poet which was a great inspiration to him. And he began to work on his 'book'.

Edward's book was somewhat in the manner of Mallarme's *Livre*, though it had no pretension to being the central document of a new cult. It was a meditation on the nature of language, as seen through criminals' and beggars' slangs: he took the Buenos Aires *lunfardo* as a central experience, the jargon which pirates ordinary speech, subverts it and builds its own meanings out of anagrams and inversions.

The book was to convey the inexpressible: the intensity he felt in all those individual moments of experiences and in their overlays and combinations: the intensity which made him the great artist he was. But in the end he realised that this can not be condensed into mere text and illustration, however skilfully conjured. It can only be conveyed through the works of art themselves – the paintings and the designs which, in a sense, the book would have replaced; or through a much longer, more episodic and literary commentary on his essential text.

To communicate the incommunicable: Wright had committed himself to that ungrateful task against which Wittgenstein had warned his readers. And yet, when he moved to Cambridge, the green and rain-sodden East Anglian landscape suddenly produced an unexpected flowering. In Latin America in 1970, he had rediscovered water-colours (a medium he had first learnt to use at school); now the brilliant, liquid, transparent colours allowed him to think through a new visual experience in the formal terms he had accumulated through all his travails. These were in some ways unlike any of his earlier work but still recognisably his own, with that particular mixture of grace and impudence no one could emulate.

Perhaps his most impressive single achievement is not one painting, one piece of design, but his notebooks: made of splendid papers, which he bound, and filled with a flood of words and images. The joy and wonder of daily experience is restated: letterforms, impressions, newspaper cuttings, studies for a commission, ideas for teaching. Turning the pages was one of the great pleasures his friendship afforded, to see what that restless mind had turned into yet another surprising metaphor. It was a constant turning of the everyday world into a Wrightian *lunfardo*.

Lettering for rotating sign
for New Scotland Yard 1968.

This index covers people, companies, institutions and key subjects. 'Typefaces' and 'software' are gathered under those headings. Universities and colleges of art, design and printing are gathered under 'education'. *Indicates item is illustrated.

Index of Articles in TypoGraphic: 1971 – 2001
*Indicates article is included in this anthology

TypoGraphic 10 (1977) Editor Brian Grimbly.
Typographic integration at Pentagram
Brian Grimbly.
* A house-style for the seventies *Shona Burns*
Experimental exercises in the teaching of
typography *Brian Brennan.*
Reports of the president, treasurer and chairman.
1977 STD student assessments *Anthony Marshall.*

TypoGraphic 11 (1978) Editor Brian Grimbly.
* Is the quality of typeface design deteriorating?
Günter Lange.
* Extracts from a talk with Derek Birdsall on the
subject of book design *Peter Rea.*

TypoGraphic 12 (1978) Editor Brian Grimbly.
Associate editor Peter Rea.
* The typography of Wolfgang Weingart
Bernd Zürker.
* A process in typography *Dan Friedman.*

TypoGraphic 13 (1979) Editor Brian Grimbly.
(Golden Jubilee, 1928 – 1978, issue)
The STD 1978 student assessment project
Anthony Marshall.
STD debate at the Royal Society for the Arts.
[The theme was 'This house believes that current
phototypesetting techniques are undermining the
basis of typographic design'. Key speakers words
are transcribed from tapes. The speakers included
are FHK Henrion, John Dreyfus, Kenneth Dickson,
Erik Spiekermann and Bernard Moriarty].
'Fit to be a typographer'. STD exhibition, at the
ICA gallery, London. Fully illustrated with a listing
of all included work spaning fifty years.
Books [includes a review by Ruari McLean of
'Fit to be styled a typographer' by James Moran
and Eva Svensson].

TypoGraphic 14 (1980) Editor David J Plumb.
The lettering of Tony Forster *Tony Forster.*
* Creative design and the computer *FHK Henrion.*
The product is the brand is the image
John Slee-Smith and *Bryan Oakes.*
DATEC: the plan *Anthony Marshall.*
The Linoterm photosetter [no author credited].

TypoGraphic 15 (1981) Editor David J Plumb.
Tripping the light fantastic *David J Plumb.*
[the work of Colin Cheesman and Bernard Lodge:
television and film graphics].
The way of which *John Miles*
[design methodology].
Aid from the third world *Hermann Hecht.*
Student assessment *Chris Graggs.*
The EditWriter phototypesetting system
[no author credited].

TypoGraphic 16 (1981) Editor David J Plumb.
Creative incentives in lettering education [issue
given over entirely to the work and teaching
of calligrapher Hella Basu].

TypoGraphic 17 (1981) Editor David J Plumb.
The printing office, Williamsburg *David J Plumb.*
Selected pickings *Ian Pape* [printed ephemera].
The press of the night owl *Dwight Agner*
[American private press].
Words of warning to the itinerant traveller
David J Plumb.
* Typesetting principles that are academic
Fred Thompson.
An evaluation of the Penta [typesetting] System
[no author credited].

TypoGraphic 18 (1982) Editor Jenny Towndrow.
Graphic design at the National Theatre
Jenny Towndrow.
* Who does what and why? *Colin Cohen.*
Letter artist, Werner Bunz [work by Bunz
illustrated with critics' comments].
The Plantin-Moretus Museum *Colin Cohen.*
[Paper] Swatches *Peter Hatch.*

TypoGraphic 19 (1982) Editor Jenny Towndrow.
The STD assessment weekend, April 1982
Jenny Towndrow.
* Students who don't read *Donald Rooum.*
* Are present day design courses really necessary?
Philip Turner.
Marks, handwriting and language
Trilokesh Mukherjee.
Advanced typography *Chris Tunnard* [Peter Rae's
approach to teaching typography at the LCP].
Professionalism *Fred Jessop.*
How to get a job *Liz Lydiate.*
Thoughts on…education: *Michael Wolff,*
teaching: *FHK Henrion,* employing: *Alan Fletcher.*
Berthold at the factory *Eddie Cattel.*

TypoGraphic 20 (1982) Editor Jenny Towndrow.
Chinese types *Edward Burrett.*
* Designing for Prestel – and after
Mervyn Kurlansky.
Olivetti: how to work hand in hand with designers
and serve the public interest *Perry King.*
Is there a perfect type specimen book?
Colin Cohen.
Museé de L'Imprimarie et de la Banque, Lyon
Colin Cohen.
The AM Comp/Set *David J Plumb.*

TypoGraphic 31 (1986) Editor Jenny Towndrow.
* The formative years of Dutch graphic design
Pieter Brattinga.
Alliance Graphique Internationale Congress, 1986.
and a note on Aspen, Colorado *Jenny Towndrow.*
Typographers' bible translated into Japanese
Edward Burrett [Vincent Steer's book; Printing,
Design and Layout].
Frank Pick as a patron for London Transport
Francis Carr.
Apple Macintosh: desktop publishing and beyond
Simon Prais.

TypoGraphic 32 (1986) Editor Jenny Towndrow.
A contribution to the original design of the
new *Independent* newspaper *Stephen Hitchens.*
Front page *Joanna Marcus*
[newspaper headlines].
Art Deco graphics *Penny Sparke.*
Training in taste *Beatrice Warde* [from *The Crystal
Goblet – sixteen essays on typography*, 1955].
When is a WYSIWIG not a WYSIWIG? *Richard Beer.*

TypoGraphic 33 (1987) Editor Jenny Towndrow.
* Maintaining standards with medium to low
resolution digital typefaces *David Saunders.*
Graphic design and the on-screen image in
television *Marc Ortmans.*
* Record sleeve design, the graphic trendsetter
Catherine McDermott.
Notes on laser printing *John Harris.*
The designers' friend *Norman Edwards*
[computers].

TypoGraphic 34 (1987) Editor Jenny Towndrow.
ICOGRADA is good for you *Peter Kneebone.*
Treasure trove of lettering *Mitzi Sims*
[the Central St Martins lettering record archive].
The avant-garde in print *Arthur A Cohen*
[Futurists, Constructivists, De Stijl and their
contemporaries].

TypoGraphic 35 (1987) Editor Jenny Towndrow.
* Rhetoric and design *Hanno Ehses.*
Who needs words anyway *Jenny Towndrow.*
Rhyme and reason *Erik Spiekermann*
[extracts from the book of the same title].
Language as an aspect of teaching typography
Cal Swann.

TypoGraphic 36 (1988) Editor Jenny Towndrow.
The BTG then (1928) and the STD now
Edward Burrett.
Six decades of graphic design
Catherine McDermott.
The way into Parliment House *Garry Emery.*
Japanese culture and graphic design .
Jenny Towndrow [AGI congress in Tokyo].
Australian graphic design '88 *Jenny Towndrow.*
The cultural significance of typography
Haig Beck and *Jackie Cooper.*

TypoGraphic 37 (1988/89) Editor Bridget Wilkins
* Edward Wright 1912 – 1988 *Joseph Rykwert,
Paul Peter Piech, Trilokesh Mukerjee, Dennis
Bailey, Ken Garland, Robin Kinross and
Michael Harrison* [obituaries]
Conversation, handwriting and the poster
Edward Wright
View Pt. Sixty years of the STD
[a selection from the touring exhibition]

TypoGraphic 38/9 (1990) Editor Bridget Wilkins.
[double issue]
British design: new traditions *Bridget Wilkins.*
* British design: image & identity
Frederique Huygen.
The Design Museum, London *Flo Bayley.*
Headline or footnote? *Mark Suggitt*
[the typography of museum exhibitions].
The Netherlands museums *Bridget Wilkins.*
* The new British telephone directory *Colin Banks.*
* One hundred years of the Dutch telephone
directory *Jolijn van de Wouw.*
* Bell Centennial *George Sedak.*
Videotext – the French electronic telephone
directory *Professor Ian McLaren.*

TypoGraphic 40 (1990) Editor Andrew Boag.
Opportunities for teaching type design
Andrew Boag.
Type design at the Gerrit Rietveld Academy
Gerard Unger.
Zeitgeist, a new typeface designed on the
Macintosh *Michael Johnson.*
The Spirit of the letter *Maria Quiroz*
[exhibition review].
Profile and interview: Bruno Maag *Andrew Boag.*
Software review: FontStudio *Andrew Boag.*
* Patriots, philosophers and printers *Colin Banks.*
Information Design Association
[no author credited].

TypoGraphic 41 (1990) Editor Bridget Wilkins.
IKARUS to PostScript *Mike Daines.*
The spirit of the letter *Jeremy Theophilus.*
Gunnlaugur Briem *Bridget Wilkins.*
* The books of Ken Campbell *Ken Garland.*
Micheal Harvey *Bridget Wilkins.*
Hebrew typography: from the sacred to the
mundane *Stephen Lubell.*
Design and technology – Latin and non-Latin
founts: a contrast in typeface sources
David Saunders.
Milner Gray *Bridget Wilkins* [interview].

TypoGraphic 42 (1991) Editor Mike Barden.
[this issue is devoted to Typo90, the international
typographic conference held in Oxford].
Typo90 *Mike Barden.*
Adrian Frutiger *Mike Barden.*
Now's the time to realise that East is not West
Fiona Ross, Ari Davidow [and others].
We're not all flying logo louts! *John Aston*
[current television graphic design].
* Let typography look like typography
Jenny Towndrow [report on a lecture given
by Matthew Carter].
Type à la carte *Mike Barden* [current individual
designers; Octavo, Why Not Associates, Phil
Baines, Zuzana Licko, Neville Brody and others].
* Forget hot metal – it's hot chocolate
Jenny Towndrow [report on a lecture given
by Gerard Unger].
So where do we go from Typo90? *Mike Barden.*

TypoGraphic 43 (1992) Editor Mike Barden.
Pass rates tell only part of the story *Mike Barden*
[1992 student assessment].
A national test with a difference *Mike Barden*
[student assessment proceedures].
STD91 project briefs and results [with examples]
Time to re-assess the assessment? *David Jury,
Brian Iles* and *David Playne* [three articles].
To be clearly read: is this the first consideration
of typography? Peter Rea.
* When will we see what we get? *Andrew Boag.*
La typographie c'est l'art de vivre *Colin Banks*
[describes a meeting of the Rencontres
Internationales de Lure].

TypoGraphic 44 (1992) Editors David Quay
and Freda Sack.
This issue is dedicated to the first STD
International Typographic Awards (1991).
All winning entries illustrated.

TypoGraphic 45 (1993) Editor Mike Daines.
Erik Spiekermann *Mike Daines.*
Changing the face of the Daily Telegraph
Mike Daines.
Corporate A, S and E – a type trilogy for the
corporate culture *Mike Daines.*
* Through the eyes of a child – perception and
type design *Rosemary Sassoon.*
Aldus versus Quark – the typographers
viewpoint *John Clements* and *Mike Baines.*
Letterpress in the education of typography
in the digital era *Jeremy Tankard.*
* Adventure on the Underground *Giovanni Lussu*
[this article was presented as a six-page insert].

TypoGraphic 46 (1993) Editor David Jury.
The Whittington Press *David Jury*
[interview with John Randle].
Private printing at the end of turn of the
millennium *David Chambers.*
* Serving author and reader *Wolfgang Tiessen.*
Bookbinding at Gwasg Gregynog
David Esslemont.
Lion and Unicorn Press *Joy Law* [RCA press].
Paperless publishing *Nick Loat.*

TypoGraphic 47 (1994) Editor Freda Sack.
This issue is dedicated to the second STD
International Typographic Awards (1994).
All winning entries illustrated. Also illustrated:
work from the student assessment.

TypoGraphic 48 (1996) Editor Freda Sack.
This issue is dedicated to the third STD
International Typographic Awards (1996).
All winning entries illustrated.

TypoGraphic 49 (1996) Editor David Jury.
I Just love a blank screen *David Jury*
[interview with Graham Wood at Tomato].
* Typography is too important to be taught
to designers *Cal Swann.*
* Is 50% creativity enough? *Jonathon Doney.*
[assessment criteria for SDT student awards
scheme].
* Due to increased dynamic range… play it loud
Teal Triggs [new technology].
So old it's new *David Jury and Kelvyn Smith*
[use of letterpress technology in education].

TypoGraphic 50 (1997) Editor David Jury.
* Glasgow 1999 – competition to design
a corporate typeface *Patrick Baglee.*
Understanding the undefinable *Gary Breeze*
[stone cutting].
Craft and computer-aided design *Gareth Hague.*
Letters of indulgence *Kelvyn Smith* and
Jeremy Tankard.
* Wim Crouwel – the 1997 remix *Alice Twemlow.*

TypoGraphic 51 (1997) Editor David Jury.
Standing above the crowd *Freda Sack.*
* Never confuse fine words with good deeds
Michael Caine [limited edition 'fine' books].
* Language from the outside *Holgar Jacobs*
[Japanese loan-words].
* What do you consider to be cutting-edge
graphics? *Liz Farrelly* [the rôle of graphic design
within international mine-clearance schemes].
Educating towards a borderless Europe?
Barry Hewson.
Design follies *Ryan Sales*
[designers self-promotion material].
* Johann Cruyff, corporate America and
a shortwave radio *Martin Perrin*
[An Anglophile working in the USA].
* Assisting with enquiries *Clive Chizlett* [previous
attempts at developing a European language].

TypoGraphic 52 (1998) Editor David Jury.
* From now on everything will (continue to)
change *David Jury*
[current state of higher education].
* J H Mason, typography, and the art school ethos
David Jury.
Exercising research *Michèle-Anne Dauppe*
and *Simon Clark.*
The new Bauhaus *Jay Rutherford.*
* A time of change *Justin G Beament.*
[introduction to the Working Party on
Typographic Teaching, WPTT].
* The Working Party on Typographic Teaching,
1968 *Michael Twyman* [interim report].
No excuse *David Taylor* [Committment
to personal standards. Attik Design].
Squaring ideas between triangling and circularity
Teal Triggs [MA typography course, London
College of Printing].
Six honest serving men *Clive Chizlett.*

TypoGraphic 53 (1999) Editor Freda Sack.
This issue is dedicated to the fourth STD
International Typographic Awards (1998).
All winning entries illustrated.

TypoGraphic 54 (1999) Editor David Jury.
Beyond wallpaper *Jan Middendorp* [review
of the work of Dutch design consutancy UNA].
* The languages of design *Jan van Son* [European
language and graphic design].
My pink heaven *Holgar Jacobs*
[social pressures for conformity in Japan].
* Typography versus commercial lettering
Fred Smeijers [the origins of sign-writing].
The token woman *Clive Chizlett*
[the origins of language].
Words and pictures *Elyssa Schmid.*

TypoGraphic 55 (2000) Editor David Jury.
* Designing the real world *Alan Robertson.*
Study and practice of applied design
Reinhard Gassner.
To look good is not enough *Jonathan Doney.*
Going straight *Chris Wilson* [maintaining ideals
in a professional/commercial environment].
Craft before, during and after graphic design
David Jury.
* Real world *Jeremy Tankard* [shock of adapting
to professional practice after leaving college].
Lurking with electrons *Cal Swann* [use of
electronic media in distance learning].
Minimum requirements for typographic training
Peter Burnhill [teaching notes from 1968].
Starting from scratch *Ryan Sales.*

TypoGraphic 56 (2000) Editor David Jury.
Stimulate and sell, titillate and tell *John Galinsky.*
Signs of our times *Anthony Cahalan.*
[recent growth in new typeface designs].
Completely new and very different
[three articles concerning web-site design.
Also includes a transcript of a general discussion
between these three designers about the Web]
* A new medium *Nicky Gibson;*
Typography online *Richard Kwok Wah Ho;*
Limitations of on-screen typography *Mike Reid.*
Wayfinding in complex environments
Colette Miller.
Visual signals – visual thinking
Orna Frommer-Dawson.
Typography: the signs of ideas *Alan Robertson.*
Standing stones *Richard Kindersley.*

TypoGraphic 57 (2001) Editor David Jury.
Hidden recordings: the concept of the (secret) file
Oliver Klimper.
A designer, but not a type designer
Rosemary Sassoon.
Visual Processing *Roger Watt.*
The writing of John Cowper Powis *Chris Gostick.*
Art and type *Alice Twemlow.*
When words are not enough *Mary McGrath.*

TypoGraphic 57 was not available for
selection when the contents for this
book were being compiled.

A complete set of *TypoGraphic*
journals is available at St Bride's
Printing Library, Bride Lane,
off Fleet Street, London EC4Y 8EE.
Telephone: 0207 353 4660

Further information

www.istd.org.uk
(for information concerning ISTD)

www.typographic56.co.uk
(*TypoGraphic* website for general information and
exchange of ideas concerning typography. This site
is managed by DeepEnd, London and illustrated on
pages 220 – 223)

TypoGraphic is distributed by Central Books
Telephone: 0044 (0)20 8986 4854
Email: orders@centralbooks.com

David Jury is the editor of *TypoGraphic* and
Head of graphic design at the Colchester Institute.
Telephone: 0044 (0)1206 518168
Email: david.jury@colch-inst.ac.uk